DATE DUE

04/02/09	
April 23 - 09	
7-1-09	
8/11/09	
7-36	

More Than Black

New World Diasporas

Florida A&M University, Tallahassee
Florida Atlantic University, Boca Raton
Florida Gulf Coast University, Ft. Myers
Florida International University, Miami
Florida State University, Tallahassee
University of Central Florida, Orlando
University of Florida, Gainesville
University of North Florida, Jacksonville
University of South Florida, Tampa
University of West Florida, Pensacola

New World Diasporas Series
Edited by Kevin A. Yelvington

This is the first book in the series, which seeks to stimulate critical perspectives on diaspora processes in the New World. Representations of "race" and ethnicity, the origins and consequences of nationalism, migratory streams, and the advent of transnationalism, the dialectics of "homelands" and diaspora, trade networks, gender relations in immigrant communities, the politics of displacement and exile, and the utilization of the past to serve the present are among the phenomena addressed by original, provocative research in disciplines such as anthropology, history, political science, and sociology.

More Than Black

Afro-Cubans in Tampa

Susan D. Greenbaum

University Press of Florida

Gainesville · Tallahassee · Tampa · Boca Raton

Pensacola · Orlando · Miami · Jacksonville · Ft. Myers

07 06 05 04 03 02   6 5 4 3 2 1

Library of Congress Cataloging-in-Publication Data
Greenbaum, Susan D.
More than Black: Afro-Cubans in Tampa / Susan D. Greenbaum
p. cm. — (New World diaspora series)
Includes bibliographical references (p.) and index.
ISBN 0-8130-2466-8 (alk. paper)
1. Cuban Americans—Florida—Tampa—Social conditions.
2. Cuban Americans—Florida—Tampa—Race identity. 3. Cuban
Americans—Florida—Tampa—Ethnic identity. 4. Blacks—Florida—
Tampa—Social conditions. 5. Tampa (Fla.)—Social cond itions. 6. Tampa
(Fla.)—Race relations. 7. African diaspora. 8. Transnationalism. 9. Cuba—
Relations—Florida—Tampa. 10. Tampa (Fla.)—Relations—Cuba.
I. Title. II. Series.
F319.T2 G69 2002
305.868'7291075965—dc21 2001043726

The University Press of Florida is the scholarly publishing agency
for the State University System of Florida, comprising Florida A&M
University, Florida Atlantic University, Florida Gulf Coast University,
Florida International University, Florida State University, University of
Central Florida, University of Florida, University of North Florida,
University of South Florida, and University of West Florida.

University Press of Florida
15 Northwest 15th Street
Gainesville, FL 32611–2079
http://www.upf.com

For Rosa

Contents

Figures, Maps, and Tables

Foreword

In an influential article titled "Diasporas in Modern Societies: Myths of Homeland and Return" (in *Diaspora* 1:1 [1991]:83–99), William Safran provides general guidelines for identifying a people's experience of diaspora: (1) dispersal from an original "center," (2) the development and maintenance of collective ideas (call them "memories" or "myths") of the "homeland," (3) a belief that they are not fully accepted by or integrated into the host society, (4) a belief that this ancestral homeland is their true home and that they will someday return to it, (5) a commitment to the maintenance and/or restoration of the homeland, and (6) a continued identification and interaction—whether actually or vicariously—with that homeland. In many ways these issues frame or have framed at one time or another all those peoples defined as nonindigenous throughout the Americas. In the present, with the apparent creation and further deepening of forces and relationships that have been described as "globalized," and with the advent of postmodern capitalism, which depends not only on massive transfers of capital but on mobile populations, creating transculturated and transnational groups and individuals in the process who often do not enjoy the benefits of full legal and social citizenship in their new homes, new kinds of diasporas and novel permutations and varieties of "the immigrant experience," the politics of displacement and exile, and identity-formation have come to the fore.

Because of this, the University Press of Florida has decided to launch a series of books entitled New World Diasporas to not only consider recent or contemporary trends and events in the arena of diasporic identity politics, but to place these situations in their proper historical context. This social science– and humanities-based series broadly addresses such areas of inquiry as diaspora processes, representations of "race" and ethnicity, the origins and consequences of nationalism, migratory streams and the advent of transnational communities, the dialectics of homelands and diasporas, trade networks, gender relations in immigrant communities, and the uses of the past to serve the politics of the present, by publishing original, cutting-edge research in disciplines such as anthropology, history, literary studies, political science, and sociology. The series benefits from a multidisciplinary International Editorial Board consisting of scholars whose work on these themes is exemplary. The series as a whole moves beyond conventional ways of examining diaspora to consider the interaction of identity with international flows of capital in the postmodern world. Comparative in nature, the series explicates both the diversity and the commonalities in the New World experience. (The Press welcomes proposals from all potential contributors.)

"Race," ethnicity, nationalism, and transnationalism—with their symbolic, discursive, and structural manifestations and consequences—are perhaps defining phenomena for the societies of the New World, born as they were in the crucible of conquest and colonialism. The ways in which these lines of identity are drawn to include some and exclude others demand analysis. In this book, which is the first volume in the series, anthropologist Susan D. Greenbaum deftly tackles these problems in her ethnohistorical study of the social and cultural adaptations of black Cuban cigarmakers who settled in Tampa, Florida, in the 1880s, and the formation and consolidation of their community and its vicissitudes throughout the twentieth century.

Through archival materials, oral history, and ethnography wrought from more than fifteen years of research and a close association with Tampa's Afro-Cubans, Greenbaum places Afro-Cubans within the immigrant world of Ybor City, a multiethnic, multicultural industrial and commercial enclave. She details their existence as black, working-class immigrants under the U.S. South's Jim Crow laws and their attempts to negotiate this minefield while at the same time being fully involved with the politics of their Cuban homeland. She documents their strategic role in the final Cuban war of independence from Spain (1895–98), and considers in depth the changing relationships of black and white Cubans in the aftermath of the struggle for the independence and the establishment of republican Cuba. She chronicles the foundation—in the face of white Cuban prejudice—and flowering of the Sociedad la Unión Martí-Maceo (named for José Martí, the martyred Cuban nationalist intellectual, and Antonio Maceo, Afro-Cuban general and war hero), a multifaceted mutual aid society and social club that in many ways became the focus of the community. Here she is careful to show how economic ties fostered ties of ethnic solidarity. But Greenbaum also documents the decline of the club's role and membership, and explores the relationships in the second and subsequent generations of Afro-Cubans with African Americans, the assimilating and "racializing" pressures from within and without, and the contemporary status of the Afro-Cuban community in Tampa. That is, she traces the movement from a transnational community—typified by back-and-forth movement of people, goods, finances, and ideas—to one of overlapping diasporas in a more general and imagined sense: Afro-Cubans, Afro-Cuban-Americans, African Americans. But not in a linear progression with an identifiable ultimate end point. Grappling with the advancing age of the club's active members and the formidable menace of urban renewal and gentrification under the guise of "redevelopment," today the club struggles to maintain its presence in Ybor City and its place as a beacon for Afro-Cuban identity. But the fight isn't over yet.

In doing all of this, Greenbaum implicitly challenges not only the theories of Safran and other writers on diaspora, but explicitly seeks to redefine the Cuban-American experience in the United States. These issues converge in this book under the idea of Afro-Cuban-Americans. Hyphenated identities are or have been de rigeur in some North American contexts. And members of some groups have now even argued to take the hyphen out. The idea of Afro-Cuban-Americans is certainly not anticipated or accounted for by Gustavo Pérez Firmat in his *Life on the Hyphen: The Cuban-American Way* (Austin: University of Texas Press, 1994). The hyphen here refers to the white Cuban-American way and the cultural negotiations involved in charting a path between Cubanness and Americanness. In his rendering, whiteness becomes naturalized, assumed, and as a consequence nonwhite Cuban-Americanness becomes erased. This has everything to do with white Cubans being considered the Cubans and being paraded as "model minorities" at a time when their more powerful cohorts have had the ear of conservative U.S. presidents and have shaped U.S. foreign and immigration policy.

But the complete academic, substantive, and political implications cannot be fully drawn out in this brief foreword. Besides, I could not do so better than Susan Greenbaum has done here, which is an admirable beginning to what promises to be an exciting series of books.

Kevin A. Yelvington
Series Editor

Acknowledgments

I owe a debt of gratitude to many people for their assistance in bringing about this book. First, I want to thank Manuel Alfonso, a friend and collaborator throughout this long endeavor. Kevin Yelvington, series editor, offered extremely valuable comments and advice. I am also grateful to Brent Weisman, Mike Angrosino, Alejandro de la Fuente, Kenya Dworkin, Rhoda Halperin, Evelio Grillo, and Cheryl Rodriguez for thoughtful suggestions on earlier drafts.

Institutional and financial support were provided by the Florida Humanities Council, the Wenner Gren Foundation, the University of South Florida Foundation, the University of South Florida Latin American/Caribbean Program, the Tampa Bay History Center, the Ybor City Museum Society, the University of South Florida Department of Special Collections, and Sociedad la Unión Martí-Maceo.

Many students aided this effort. Linda Callejas and Shari Feldman provided important assistance, not only in the research, but also in service to the Martí-Maceo Society. Ginger Baber, Bridget McGovern, Maridelys Detres, Geoff Mohlman, and Carson Riley contributed greatly. Enrique Cordero arranged for the creation of the Martí-Maceo Collection at the University of South Florida Library. Students in my social organization seminar, fall 1998 and fall 1999, made varied and important contributions.

Posthumous appreciation is owed to Francisco Jimenez, Laureano Diaz, Juan Mallea, Sylvia Griñán, Hipólito Arenas, and Juan Garcia, all of whom made special efforts to help me understand.

Finally, I want to thank my husband, Paul, whose statistical advice was critically important, and whose patient and wise counsel in all aspects of the work were of great value to me.

1

Introduction

In Tampa, Florida, in the early 1960s, an Afro-Cuban lawyer, appointed to defend an indigent Mexican farmworker, discovered on arrival in the courtroom that no translator was available for his client. Improvising, he proceeded to serve as both defense attorney and interpreter. Afterwards, the lawyer encountered the presiding judge, who asked him how he had learned to speak Spanish. The lawyer replied: "I always have known how. I was born in Cuba." The judge's retort: "Cuban? I didn't know you were a Cuban. I always thought you were a nigger."

Even in 1960s Florida, the judge's verbal conduct was unseemly, spontaneously offensive. His confusion, as well as his casual racism, captures the rationale for this book. To him, Cubans were not black. Instead, he most likely conjured up the wave of refugees who recently had settled in south Florida. Following the success of Fidel Castro's revolution in 1959, more than 200,000 Cuban exiles arrived in the first three years (Pérez 1992:85), nearly all of whom were white. Cubans were in the news and spread across the pages of magazines, admired for their opposition to communism in their homeland, and for their celebrated enterprise and adaptiveness (e.g., Alexander 1966). How could it be that this obviously black man, this "nigger," was also a Cuban?

In the United States, black Cubans are invisible, to some extent unthinkable. The popular construction of Cuban American identity stands in deliberate opposition to blackness. Media stereotypes have presented Cuban immigrants as a case study in successful striving. They arrived empty-handed and unable to speak the language, but rapidly marshaled their talents and energy in the fresh air of American democracy. Images of their meteoric prosperity were (and still are) juxtaposed deliberately against the stubborn poverty of African Americans, whose position in the economic order of Miami had sunk in tandem with the Cubans' rise (Mohl 1997;

Rose 1989). The hard edges of this contrast leave no space for the possibility of Cubans who are also black.

Related to this rags-to-riches discourse, as well as to tales of a "Cuban economic miracle," is a portrayal of Cubans in the United States as "white," like the majority host society, as opposed to "black," like the African American minority (Croucher 1997:107). The "Cuban American success story," amply inscribed with evidence from various sources, is all about Cubans who are white. This image prevails in spite of the fact that white Cubans are barely a majority in the sending population, and there are now tens of thousands of black Cubans and their descendants living in the United States.

This book is about Afro-Cuban-Americans, the missing faces in the smiling family portrait of Cuban ethnicity in the United States. The context of my examination is another corner of Florida; a different place and time, when an earlier Cuban diaspora, similarly exiled by political upheavals on the island, similarly fired with patriotic zeal, crossed the Florida Strait and set roots in Tampa. This occurred over a century ago, and thousands of the descendants still live there. Included are an identifiable cohort of Afro-Cubans, whose forebears migrated to Tampa along with the rest, came to make cigars and revolution. The trajectory they followed, through disappointed outcomes in Cuba and a hard road in Jim Crow Florida, marks the path of my investigation.

This lost chapter in the Cuban American experience, with its similarities to the better-known saga, also offers striking contrasts, and a suitably long view from which to interrogate the process of ethnic adjustment and the dynamics of race. Over a protracted period of several generations, how have Afro-Cuban immigrants and their descendants defined and negotiated both blackness and Cubanness? What did they encounter along the way, and how did they respond? What in their story helps us understand why, after all this time, they are still invisible?

Invisibility inspired this project. Many years ago, when I first began teaching at the University of South Florida, I designed a course in urban anthropology. I wanted to situate the topic in the familiar social geography of Tampa, to give my students a way of seeing close up how urbanization and urbanity are constituted. In preparation, I gathered information on the early Cuban immigrants, but found virtually nothing about those who were black. A few bare references confirmed their existence, but furnished none of the details of what it meant to be an Afro-Cuban in Tampa, or how Afro-Cubans had fashioned their lives in this place. How unfortunate, I thought—a failed opportunity to examine the interplay between race and ethnicity. How interestingly insulting, I thought, that so little had been recorded about them. One of the students, an African American who had grown up in Tampa, obliged my dilemma by inviting along two older friends, Afro-Cubans he knew, who could help to enlighten us.

That day is vivid in my mind, the opening moment of my own enlightenment. Sitting in the undersized desks of my windowless cinderblock classroom, a man and a woman, a teacher and a lawyer, the same lawyer whose courtroom exchange was just recounted, told it to us then. They both described what it was like to grow up in Jim Crow Florida, black Cubans nested inside of an immigrant enclave,[1] but nonetheless black in a larger society that hated blackness. We learned about the Martí-Maceo Society, a mutual aid organization that served as their primary weapon of avoidance and resistance. In ways that my own lecturing never could have conveyed, our visitors explained the many strange contradictions of their double-hyphenated lives. At the close of the session, I thanked my guests for coming. The teacher then drew me aside, and explained an agenda that had motivated her to come. She still belonged to the Martí-Maceo Society; she had come seeking help on their behalf. They needed to become visible, to cure the very problem that brought her to my class. She was seeking reciprocity of a very direct nature.

Ybor City, Tampa's old cigarmaking enclave, was about to be nominated as a historic district. Documents had been drawn up enumerating the area's cultural resources and mapping the landmarks of its unique heritage. Afro-Cubans were not on the list; Martí-Maceo was not on the map. It was true that their building was not very old, but that was because Urban Renewal had torn down their original structure in 1965.

None of Ybor City's other ethnic clubs (those belonging to white Cubans, Spaniards, and Italians) had been demolished, only theirs. The Martí-Maceo members viewed this prior experience as a deliberate attempt to erase them from the landscape. Back then, they had avoided that outcome by relocating into another structure in what was left of Ybor City. It was not a new building; it was a small warehouse that had been constructed in 1950, not nearly as nice as the one they had lost, but it suited their needs and marked their continued existence. Now twenty years later, as new interest focused on revitalizing Ybor City, they justly worried that they could be dislocated again, this time under the deceptive guise of Historic Preservation. They wanted to preempt that possibility—to marshal evidence of their legitimate place in the history of Ybor City, to assert their right to be preserved. In their estimation, this project required authority and imprimatur. A university professor was needed to help uncover the lost details of their contributions to the cigar industry and their role in the movement for Cuban independence, the twin themes in the rationale for Ybor City's historic status. They needed someone with credentials to anoint their story and strengthen their argument. That someone was me.

There began a collaborative project in applied ethnohistory, in which the politics of the present and the politics of the past entwined to reveal the evolving intricacies of racism. In my initial meeting with the directors of Martí-Maceo, we laid out a strategy that seemed difficult but straightforward. A gap existed; our task was to fill it. With their help, I would gather the information that could be gleaned from their organizational records, other documents, and the memories of those old enough to have lived these experiences we sought to reclaim. Once this material was presented, it would be hard to deny them a place at the table. How naive we were to think that this would be sufficient, but we were correct in believing that it was necessary.

Over the next fifteen years, we learned together. This book reflects the product of a long and intimate relationship that developed in the process, between myself and the people about whom I write. It recounts the history that I learned, and it explores my own observations of events and changes over the extended period of my involvement. It relies heavily on oral history, much of which was collected in the mid- and late 1980s, from elderly people, nearly all of whom have died by now. Their memories of the past and my memories of them meld together in this account, salvaged from the obscurity of death, although inevitably filtered through the lens of the writer. Ethnographic observation and the collection of additional data have continued throughout the years, cumulative lessons and clues that I have attempted to draw together in an analysis of the contemporary meaning of race and ethnicity for Afro-Cubans in Tampa. Observational, oral, and documentary sources have both complemented and contradicted each other, raising questions as well as resolving them. The data that I assembled were diverse and often refractory. Frail memories and the distorted historiography and journalism of the South combined to make this a difficult challenge.

Oral history and records of the Martí-Maceo Society provided the two main sources of information for this book. Beginning in 1985, I tape-recorded interviews with 46 people (21 women and 25 men), most elderly Afro-Cubans, but members of other groups and age cohorts were also included.[2] Multiple interviews were done with seven key informants, and three individuals provided me extensive advice and assistance. Tapes were transcribed and coded for themes and content. Minutes of meetings, beginning in 1900 and continuing with only minor gaps up to the present, offered a running account of events in the community and insight into the conduct of the organization. This was a highly elliptical record, however, that offered few details and omitted many matters of importance. Silence at critical junctures was nearly as informative as what was written on the pages, but it was altogether a spare account. The treasury records provided data on the financial operation, the vital underpinning of the club's material success. These data enabled me to determine how the members were able to make it work, as well as the effects of change in the political and economic environment. Additional facts, data, and background material were gathered from newspapers, city directories, census documents, reports, manuscripts, and relevant secondary sources. The narrative sources were not simply information but also texts that encoded the meaning of race, the landscape of social relations, and the shape of hierarchy.

Authority, the self-deceptive presumption of authors who speak on behalf of other people, raises a critical epistemological problem—not only in assessing the validity of secondary texts, but also in reflecting on my own authorship. A great deal has been written recently about representation and power (Bond and Gilliam 1994; Harrison 1998; Lavenda 1992; Mullings 1994b; Rhea 1997; San Juan 1992). Constructions of the past are themselves part of history. The capacity to define or deny subaltern experience—the omission of Afro-Cubans from officiated heritage—is an extension precisely of the relations in society that explain their subordination. These distortions are not mere oversight, the self-absorbed misattentions of elite historians who write only about themselves, or those they wish to please. Nor are they simply anachronistic, the by-products of a faulty historiography of the past. There was a gap in the official record of Ybor City's heritage, but more was involved in challenging that void than amassing facts to fill it.

The agendas driving historic preservation in Ybor City were, and still are, multilayered. Preserving history is the veneer on top, the enterprise that shapes images and invests them with commercial appeal (Holcomb 1993; Throsby 1997). Cultural landscapes are envisioned as architecture embedded in real estate (Hutter and Rizzo 1997). Unmasked, it is mainly about development and tourism, and Afro-Cuban heritage is not compatible with the marketing strategy. Just as this process is cloaked in its own layering, however, it is also beset with self-contradiction. Written rules and criteria permit challenge and contestation, open channels for presenting alternative histories (Ruffins 1992; Verrey and Henley 1991). Identity politics sometimes places subaltern players and their sympathizers in positions with strength to arbitrate.

Members of the Martí-Maceo Society were determined to intrude themselves into Ybor City's historic space, to use their own knowledge of the past as a weapon and a wedge. My involvement in their efforts offered a unique window on their untold story, as well as an inside understanding of the problems they confronted. I make no pretense of "objectivity," and I recognize the subtler problem of my voice as a proxy for theirs. I vetted drafts of what I wrote with my key collaborators, including this manuscript, but unlike the public documents I wrote on their behalf (e.g., Greenbaum 1986), this one is avowedly told from my perspective.

Along with valuable insights into the nature of the process in which we were engaged, this work also disclosed critical boundaries and interfaces—between black and white Cubans, between black Cubans and black Americans, and between women and men. Mutual aid and the institutional architecture that made it work formed the nexus of community—defined the boundaries of belonging and enumerated those entitled to share. The Martí-Maceo Society was a physical structure within which identity emerged and agency was fashioned. It has continued to serve that function, to concretize their collective existence and aid in transforming determination into action. Goals have shifted over time, but the perceived need to preserve this institution remains.

The final chapter of this book examines our shared experiences with the local preservation establishment. It is but the most current incarnation of Afro-Cuban resistance, the contemporary arena of a very long struggle, in which generations of Afro-Cubans in Tampa have engaged their circumstances and sought to change them. The intervening chapters unfold in generations, lingering longest on the first. My goal is to uncover and analyze the critical formations and relationships that have constituted Afro-Cuban-American identity—whence it came and how it has changed.

Theorizing Identity and Agency

This enterprise is set against current theories about race and ethnicity, about differences between groups in a hierarchical opportunity structure, and about the elusive nexus between that structure and actions undertaken to resist and change it. There is wide agreement that race and ethnicity are social constructs, part of a culturally derived model of society, rather than any kind of natural phenomena (Baker 1998; Banks 1996; Nagel 1994; Smedley 1999). Ideas about race and ethnicity cannot be separated from their political context, in which groups and individuals are differentially endowed with economic power and social and cultural capital (Gregory 1998; Harrison 1995). Differences are denaturalized, and alleged inequalities are revealed as disingenuous metaphors disguising the inequity of privilege. But this insight takes us only to the edge of understanding. It is an abstraction that illuminates but lacks explanatory power. To give substance to the notion of social construction, it is necessary to interrogate the manner in which specific contexts shape the contours of action and the limits of success. I want to move beyond the obvious, although complicated, notion that Afro-Cuban ethnicity in Tampa was constructed and transformed by the context in which it developed. My goal is to disclose the process by which this occurred, and most particularly, the role played by Afro-Cubans in defining their own identity. This project draws on Pierre Bourdieu's evolving theory of practice and his prescriptions regarding the importance of empirical investigation (Bourdieu 1990a, 1990b, 1984). It is both an appreciation of his fruitful inquiries and a challenge to the stubbornly deterministic implications of his conclusions about the relationship between practice and power.

Bourdieu neglects the role of institution building, focusing on individual habits rather than collectivized structures that shape and enable action. Jenkins (1992:89–90) refers to this gap as "a central problem of Bourdieu's general sociology. . . . there is little to be found in the way of a theorised model of institutions, their operation or their relationship to the organisation of social life. They seem to exist as taken for granted, functioning entities with a status similar to individual actors . . . nor does he move beyond a 'black box' model of institutions to understand what might be going on within them." My purpose is to penetrate this conceptual box, to foreground the working out of solutions and alternative constructions of social and economic relations that were effected within an indigenously devised and explicitly cooperative arrangement for mutual aid.

I would argue, as well, that most contemporary conceptions of ethnicity also lack sufficient attention to the institutional underpinnings of group identity. Models emphasizing fluid networks, invisible transactions, and opportunistic shifting among various identities tend to obscure the structure that resides within, and overlook the concrete manner in which collective identities and overt action are organized in time and space. Key corporate structures, such as mutual aid societies, locate ethnicity and serve as vessels for husbanding capital. Ethnogenesis, the unfolding process of group identification, can be better understood by adding a focus on the institutional framework within which this occurs.

Constructing Race and Ethnicity

The story of Afro-Cuban cigar workers in Florida is much involved with the concept of race. Because they descended from Africans and inhabited the Jim Crow South, they were legally "black." That single fact had overriding significance in vital sectors of opportunity, like voting and school. It also determined where they spent leisure time, and whom they were permitted to marry. Race laws enforced a rigid hierarchy and protected the privileges of the lawmaking class. Baker (1998), Harrison (1995), Smedley (1999), and many others have argued that these contingencies are central to an understanding of how the concept of race has been deployed and elaborated. "'Race' is a cultural invention . . . [that] emerged as the dominant form of identity in those societies where it functions to stratify the social system" (Smedley 1998:690).

Afro-Cubans were assigned a place in this hierarchy that was largely, but not entirely, based on their color. That discrepancy, the difference in their condition compared with African Americans, marks the significance of ethnicity. Because they were Cuban, they had access to privileges and resources not available to native-born African Americans. To this extent, ethnicity mitigated Afro-Cubans' racial status, entitled them to a niche that offered relatively more advantages and protection than could be gotten by most African Americans. Moreover, Afro-Cubans shared a strong bond of nationhood with white Cubans, alongside whom they lived and worked in Tampa's cigarmaking enclave. The significance of ethnicity, as opposed simply to race, is inescapable in this example.

Similarly, the importance of ethnic organization and ethnic differences among "black" people has been underappreciated (Bryce-Laporte 1972; Foner 1987; Halter 1992; Sánchez 1997; Stafford 1987). The explanatory prominence of racism obscures group differences in how blackness is perceived in conjunction with language and mannerisms, or how different nationality groups have negotiated this predicament.

The distinction between race and ethnicity is not simply drawn. It is a subject that has been much discussed, but poorly resolved. Most authors insist that there are important differences between the two concepts, race having to do with concocted notions of biology, versus ethnicity as an overt expression of cultural or national identity (Banks 1996; San Juan 1992; Smedley 1999). This divide is heuristic, a convenience that acknowledges the nonbiological character of race, its social constructedness, but which also tends to dissolve the usefulness of the contrast. Discussions often focus on critiquing those writers who have conflated race and ethnicity, or who have failed to acknowledge or examine the uniquely problematic circumstances of blackness in the United States—including comparisons between European immigrants and native-born blacks (e.g., Glazer and Moynihan 1970), and various versions of the "model minority" thesis (e.g., Granovetter 1995; Light 1972; D'Souza 1995; Sowell 1994). In the former, the relatively greater economic mobility of early-twentieth-century white immigrants and their children is contrasted with the enduring poverty of African Americans living in the same cities. The latter emphasizes differences in the contemporary accomplishments of Asians and East Indians and the enduring poverty of African Americans living in the same cities. Such comparisons foreground culture to explain differences that more accurately stem from antiblack racism.

Other commentators argue that equating race with ethnicity diminishes the villainy of racism, making it mere ethnocentrism, and risks racializing all forms of difference (Banks 1996; San Juan 1992). Smedley (1998:700) warns: "What anthropologists must do is to make sure that the ideas of 'ethnicity' and 'ethnic identity' do not become perceived as hereditary, permanent, and unalterable, but remain fluid forms of identity that will make us all 'multicultural.'" The emphasis on fluidity, as an essential quality of ethnicity, mires the comparison. So-called racial identities are similarly negotiated and transgressed. Both are fluid. One of the problems with "social constructs" is that they are inescapably evanescent, and endlessly debatable.

My conception of the difference is that race refers to externally defined ranked attributes based mainly on individual appearance, whereas ethnicity has to do with the organization of individuals and families into groups based on common identity and ancestral origins. Race is a uniform you wear, and ethnicity is a team on which you play. We all have both race and ethnicity, a color-coded phenotypic identity and membership in some historically defined natal community. This is an admitted simplification that acknowledges overlapping ethnic affiliations, indeterminate appearances, and movement among both racial and ethnic categories. Intermarriage guarantees ambiguity, and unequal power relations, which assign great importance to group membership, inevitably destabilize boundaries.

Ethnicity is dynamic and changeable, but it hangs on threads that tie generations together, is infested with familial sentiment and obligation. Conceptions of home and belonging, attachment to place and institutions, ensure continuity and give shape and direction to the process of change. Ethnicity is a contingent process, but its contingencies are knowable. My focus is on the cumulative and residual, on that which has endured, and on the specific process by which transformation occurs.

Tampa offers a site where Afro-Cubans and African Americans coexisted in time and space, confronted similar problems, and pursued distinctive strategies. The concept of ethnicity is highly relevant in comparing their experiences. African Americans, both nationally and within local communities, constitute an ethnic group. They share history, traditions, and institutions, inhabit spatial communities, and meet most other standard criteria for defining an ethnic group. These features stand in contrast with the history, institutions, and traditions of Afro-Cubans. Framing the analysis in terms of ethnicity unburdens the comparison. It eliminates the exceptionality associated with African Americans, the implicit assumption that they have no culture, only race.

African Americans in Tampa have a long history, during which they established churches, businesses, lodges, mutual aid societies, kinship networks, neighborhoods, communal traditions, political leadership, and organized resistance. Although only a minority were born in the city and have roots there, they are all bound together in a shared memory of slavery and the post-Emancipation experience in the South. Moreover, they share deeper memories and similar intervening experiences with Afro-Cubans.

Diasporas

By recasting African Americans in ethnic terms, neither discounting nor ignoring the significance of race, it is easier to view both groups in the context of wider diasporic processes (Gilroy 1987; Harrison 1988; Helmreich 1992; Mintz and Price 1992). Earl Lewis, in a thoughtful essay examining the history profession's treatment of race, posed a question regarding the convergence of diasporic Africans in cities like Tampa:

It is in the nation's cities, after all, where African-descended immigrants encountered American blacks, creating in the encounter what has been called a transgeographical American. Hailing from San

Juan, Havana, Vera Cruz, São Paulo, and Kingston, from impoverished hamlets and towns, from the rural and urban South, these children of the African diaspora became living reminders of the diversity
in black life. Seldom, however, have we asked when and under what
terms they became African American. . . . How do we begin to understand differences within black communities? How do we define and
refine the practice of writing African peoples into a history of overlapping diasporas? (Lewis 1995:786).

Gilroy's discussion of the "Black Atlantic," a reference to broad dispersions
of African people across the entire landscape of European colonialism, has
been influential in calling attention to the need for a wider frame of reference. Afro-Cubans and African Americans in Tampa shared more than a
distant common origin in West Africa. Generations unfolding from the
point of their arrival in Havana Harbor, or some debarkation site north of
the Florida Strait, were cast into parallel histories—scenarios in which captive Africans deployed strategies of resistance and survival against local
circumstances that varied considerably in the details of political existence.
The interplay between African roots and branching cultures in the Americas, what Lewis terms "people-making" (1995:773), frames my analysis.

   Chapter 2 explores the parallel histories of Africans in Cuba and Africans in Florida, situates the ethnicity of both groups, and examines the
different effects of slavery in Cuba and the United States. Chapter 3 brings
them together in Tampa, examining the arrival of Afro-Cubans in 1886
and their involvement in the exiled revolution against Spain. In this context, and in the midst of intensifying racism in Florida, contact and acquaintance between African Americans and Afro-Cubans first established
the boundaries of their separate identities, and the channels of their common difficulty.

Boundaries of Race and Nation

The title of this book, More Than Black, is drawn from a famous statement
by José Martí defining the bounds of cubanidad: "A Cuban is more than
white, more than mulatto, more than black." (Martí 1959:27). This simple
assertion is contained in a probing essay written in 1893 ("Mi Raza"), in
which he condemns racism and pleads for unity, urging whites to forsake
racial pride and blacks to expunge anger. The meaning of "more than
black" ("más que negro") is elusive and multifaceted, however. More than
black, but still black; better than black; not only black; including blacks, as

well as whites, and also the mulattoes—a jumble of divisive nuances that confound the thrust of his argument. Nation may rise above race in the oratory of patriots, but words cannot evade the divisive and inequitable consequences of racism.

Afro-Cubans in Tampa reside within intersecting boundaries of race and ethnicity. Their shifting situational identity—black when with Cubans, and Cuban when with blacks—discloses anomalies and begs questions. How have they negotiated these multiple boundaries? Between color and nationality, which forces pulled the strongest or pressed the hardest, and what meanings do these dynamics illuminate? How have these conditions changed over time?

Barth's landmark essay on ethnicity (1969) argued the importance of interrogating boundaries, of inquiring into conditions that delimit groups and sketch the borderlands between them. Who and what flows across ethnic boundaries, with what consequence for their persistence and change? Concern with boundaries pervades current literature on the social construction of identity (Banks 1996; Nagel 1994)—both the limits that define and enclose, and the porous borders of transgression and resistance.

Boundaries are hard to locate. Individuals may be enmeshed in multiple demarcations, identities of race, class, and culture that may allow manipulation and redefinition of persona and position. Lines of demarcation among groups are inherently fuzzy. Alliances and contests promote interchange and passing. Ambiguities between race and ethnicity add to the dynamic, constituting forces that both press groups into action and, at the same time, encourage individuals to change sides. Historical perspective is needed to trace these fluctuations and their apparent proximal causes, to identify factors and processes at work in the definition and redefinition of racial and ethnic boundaries.

When the Cubans first came to Tampa, they were locked together in a revolutionary nation-building project. The ideology of this struggle emphasized racial solidarity, and white and black Cubans in Tampa were especially unified. In their exiled quest for nationhood, racial boundaries between Cubans were deliberately obscured, although never forgotten. In contrast, ethnic boundaries between black Cubans and black Americans were deliberately sharpened. In addition to language barriers and different political agendas, Afro-Cubans enjoyed distinct economic advantages. Wages in cigarmaking were relatively high, a function of the skills required to do the work and the organized demands of workers. Afro-Cubans shared in this prosperity. Their condition was a stark contrast to African

Americans living in Tampa at the same time. Reconstruction in Florida had just been overturned by Redemption; the slaveholding regime had retaken power. African Americans were disenfranchised. Their labor was subordinated and cheap, yielding incomes that were meager compared with those of the Afro-Cuban cigarmakers. There was little incentive for Afro-Cubans to form affiliations and alliances with African Americans, and every reason to identify as Cuban. As time passed, however, and particularly after the defeat of the Spanish in Cuba, white Cubans in Tampa confronted similar incentives to disaffiliate from their black compatriots. Boundaries between black and white Cubans formally reemerged.

Spain lost hold of her Cuban colony in 1898, but the Cubans lost too. At the end, the United States gained control of the revolution and installed its own neo-colonial regime. Instead of repatriation, many Cuban cigarmaker/revolutionists remained in, or returned to, Tampa, forming an immigrant community. It was at this juncture, two years after the *Plessy v. Ferguson* decision officially launched Jim Crow, that the boundaries between black and white Cubans in Tampa began to crystallize. The all-black Martí-Maceo Society, founded in 1900, was an explicit, although multilayered, reaction to laws and customs forbidding integration.

Jim Crow had pervasive effects on institutional arrangements and greatly raised the stakes on whiteness. One of my Afro-Cuban collaborators related a story about boundary making he heard from his father, who arrived in Tampa in 1910.

> TOMÁS: Let me tell you about how my father came to this country. He had a [white] friend, used to make cigars with him in Havana. . . . He had been to Tampa before. So, he told my father, "Let's go to Tampa where we can make more money." My father didn't want to go, but talking with his friend, he finally said okay. . . . Between Havana and Key West they were friends. So, when they got to Key West, my father said the man stopped talking to him. You know, you got a friend who talks you into coming to a new country, then all of a sudden he stops talking to you. So, he kept asking him, "Hernando, why don't you talk to me?" When they got here to Tampa, he did tell my father, he say, "Well, the Negroes, the black people, you ride in this car on the train, but I'm white and I'll ride in the other car." He didn't talk to him no more. I guess he figured, "Well, if I be friend to him, they gonna think I'm black," and nobody wanted to be black, so I guess he said, "Well, I'll stop talking to him right now."

Hernando's strange behavior, which is all too understandable on one level, signifies both the aversion and the ambivalence that characterized the treatment of black Cubans by former comrades who were white.

The manner in which Cubans negotiated racial identity, in this highly racialized context, discloses cultural themes that are much discussed in the literature on Cuban race relations (Canizares 1990; Carbonell 1993; Casals 1979; Dixon 1982; Fernández 1996; Fernández Robaína 1993; Ferrer 1998; de la Fuente 1998; González 1993; López Valdés 1973; McGarrity and Cardenas 1995; Moore 1986; Serviat 1993). Race in Cuba is an uncomfortable subject to be politely avoided, unlike the rude, confrontational style of the United States during Jim Crow. Nor are Cubans rigidly divided into black and white; rather, there is a spectrum of racial categories, and social success may produce some degree of "whitening." The outcome of racism has been the same in both places, however: it conferred disadvantage on those who were dark. These subtleties had implications for the manner in which African-descended peoples organized and adapted. The hard boundaries in the United States encouraged racial solidarity among blacks, a capacity to mobilize along racial lines. In Cuba, on the other hand, people of color were fragmented, and sanctions against discussions of race disabled efforts to organize against racism. Social familiarity between blacks and whites in Cuba, the enactment of racial cordiality, required renegotiation once inside the United States. Hernando made a rather self-conscious decision to change his behavior in changing his location. Rogelio, my friend's father, was pressed similarly into a mode of behavior appropriate to the rules of this new place. In this transformation, Afro-Cubans also found racial solidarity, first in their relations with each other, and later in alliances with African Americans.

This small tale also betrays another complexity in the formation of Afro-Cuban identity in Tampa. The ease with which these two cigarmakers determined and executed their move, the reference to Hernando's previous trips to Tampa, reveal a pattern of circular migration that had enormous significance. Cigarmaking was an itinerant profession (Cooper 1983, 1987). During the first half of the twentieth century, Tampa was one of several cigar-manufacturing centers in the United States and Cuba, among which thousands of Cuban cigar workers distributed themselves, depending on fluctuations in employment and labor conditions (Cooper 1983; Stubbs 1985; Poyo 1991). Tampa was the largest Cuban colony in the United States during that period, a leading node in the network. In the aftermath of Cuban independence, political exiles transitioned into economic migrants.

Afro-Cubans who were drawn to Tampa's cigar factories were not "immigrants" in the conventional sense of this term; rather, they were "transnationals." Current perspectives on the movement of peoples among nations, particularly the broad migrations of Latin American and Caribbean workers into cities of the United States, have refocused the concerns of earlier research on the "immigrant experience." The concept of "transnationalism [is defined] as the processes by which immigrants forge and sustain multi-stranded social relations that link together their societies of origin and settlement" (Basch, Schiller and Blanc 1994:7). This view challenges Oscar Handlin's (1973) well-known image of "uprootedness," a key assumption about immigrant identity formation and adjustment. The abruptness and agonies of separation from home were interpreted as critical ingredients in the development of communities and the process of assimilation.

Basch et al. and other works (Foner 1987; Kazal 1995; Kearney 1995; Mallon 1994) have linked the rising interest in transnationalism, which emphasizes continuities and movement, to broader forces of globalization. Implicitly, transnationalism is part of the postmodern condition, a world in which flows of capital, power, and people have become "decentered." Cuban cigarmakers, however, represent a historical, more accurately, a "modern" example—early sojourners in the emerging empire of U.S. capital. This long history contributes to a more contextualized understanding of the process of transnational identity formation.

Because the Afro-Cubans arrived in Tampa at approximately the same time as the vast influx of eastern Europeans in other U.S. cities, useful comparisons may be drawn. The white immigrants who also were drawn to the cigar factories of Tampa—Spaniards and Italians, as well as Cubans—enlarge this opportunity. Although Spanish and Italian communities were not completely stable, they were far less migratory than the Cubans. Much has been written about the Ybor City immigrant enclave that connects these workers' experience with those of other immigrants in the industries and cities of the United States (Long 1971a; Mormino 1983b, 1982b; Mormino and Pozzetta 1987; Pacheco 1994; Pérez 1985; Pizzo 1985; Pozzetta 1981). In these analyses, Afro-Cubans tend to be pushed to the periphery, and the migrancy of Cubans is interpreted as a secondary disadvantage, a "peripatetic" pattern that interfered with assimilation and economic success (Mormino and Pozzetta 1987). My approach locates Afro-Cubans at the center of the analysis and reassesses the implications of mobility.

Chapter 4 examines the processes of community formation among all the immigrants in Ybor City, and between Cubans and African Americans. I also attempt to draw the wider context of relations with native-born white elites and their agents of terror against blacks and against labor organizing in the cigar factories. Ongoing interest in Cuban politics, the influx and circulation of migrants, and the establishment of the Martí-Maceo Society, as a nexus in this network of people and information, are also addressed in these two chapters.

Mobility was a significant factor in the strategies of Afro-Cuban cigarmakers. It allowed them to avoid unemployment during strikes and slow periods, and to escape episodic racial problems in U.S. cities, by migrating elsewhere. They were not required to surrender their Cuban identities or to submit fully to the racist regime. The Tampa Afro-Cuban community was in constant flux until the 1930s, when the Depression prompted a large, relatively permanent outmigration. Turnover was never complete, however, and even after the 1930s exodus there was always a significant core of Afro-Cuban families who resided more or less permanently in Tampa.

Mutual Aid

Mobility in the membership also had a curiously felicitous effect on the economics of mutual aid, a finding that I explicate in Chapter 5, which is dedicated to an examination of the Martí-Maceo Society. This organization was an instrumental part of the transnational strategy of Afro-Cuban cigarmakers—a haven for sojourners and a framework for building a community into which they could become incorporated easily.

La Sociedad la Unión Martí y Maceo embodied postindependence realities for black and white Cubans living in Tampa. In 1899, the Cubans began a mutual aid society in Tampa, transforming the patriotic clubs that previously had been used to raise funds for the revolution. Like these earlier groups, the mutual aid society was racially integrated. After only a few months, however, the white majority ejected the black members. The Afro-Cubans began their own club in 1900. The name chosen for this new organization symbolizes its contradictory beginnings. José Martí, apostle of Cuban liberty, dead white hero of a failed quest for social justice; and General Antonio Maceo, the "Bronze Titan" who led the campaign, dead black hero of armed resistance—a pair of icons to remind the white Cubans of their betrayal. The Martí-Maceo Society became the tangible "vessel" of Afro-Cuban ethnicity in Tampa—an institution with formal membership, a charter, a treasury, a place—a material basis for collective action. Within its walls and in the context of group activities it supported, Afro-Cubans elaborated their separateness.

Membership in Martí-Maceo formalized a division between black and white Cubans. It created a sorting mechanism for determining who belonged in which category, similar to the assignment of rail cars from the port into Ybor City. Sorting Cubans was not a straightforward process. Binary distinctions between black and white were not familiar in the racial taxonomies of Cubans, whose categories were more varied and complex. Crossing into the United States, intricate differences in color and personal position, the distinction between *moreno* and *pardo* (black and mulatto), collapsed in a regime less tolerant of status ambiguities. However, frontier conditions also made room for redefinition, for the light-skinned members of black Cuban families to erase their history and assert whiteness instead. The emergent racial identity of Cubans in Tampa was neither normal nor natural, but was socially constructed out of the conditions of emigration and actions of emigrants. Afro-Cubans defined themselves when they joined the Martí-Maceo. Those who were too dark to pass, and those who were disinclined to try, joined in building an institution that was emblematic of who they became.

Afro-Cubans kept themselves apart from African Americans, and the white Cubans did the same thing to them. In consequence, they relied heavily on each other and developed a very solidary community structure of their own. These insular conditions prevailed for more than four decades. The black immigrants enjoyed occupational advantages over native-born blacks, but suffered handicaps in comparison with white immigrant compatriots. The assortment of hierarchy placed them in an intermediate status, gave them ground to protect and hold, resources that attached directly to their ethnic identity.

Institutionalizing Cultural Capital

The Martí-Maceo Society reflected an investment in social and cultural capital formation. In the status advantages that it embodied, and the capacity for provisioning members with valuable material and symbolic resources, this institution represented a shared source of wealth created out of cultural knowledge and social cohesion.

Concepts of nonfinancial capital resources have gained prominence in analyzing the process by which immigrants adjust (Farkas 1996; Light and Rosenstein 1995; Portes 1995, 1996). Knowledge, values, and institutional capacities have been invoked as variables that explain how different groups negotiate conditions of disadvantage. Immigrants who bring along beliefs and traditions that are compatible with the opportunity structure in the United States are considered to be preadapted to succeed. Their cultural capital has currency in the U.S. market. However, this is not a simple process of rapid assimilation. Indeed, for Korean, Japanese, Indian, and several other Asian groups, it is argued that their collective success encourages ethnic loyalty and facilitates nonassimilation (Light 1972). Portes (1987) has developed a similar argument about Cubans in Miami.

This ethnicized dimension of cultural capital, the stock of which depends on maintaining ethnic distinctions rather than eliminating them, hints at a problem with Bourdieu's theory about the exchange properties of cultural capital, at least when applied to the United States. For Bourdieu, cultural capital is denominated within "a *single market* for all cultural capacities" (Bourdieu 1977:187 [emphasis in original]). Cultural capital is convertible to economic capital, but only against a common standard. Subaltern groups are locked out of both, and upwardly aspirant individuals can change their condition only by acquiring the habits and credentials of the dominant system. Bourdieu has used this idea to explicate class hegemony (e.g., 1984, 1977; see also Harker, Mahar, and Wilkes 1990:87–96).

Cultural capital belongs to the powerful, is defined in relation to access to resources such as education and social influence. Class relations are reproduced by monopolizing access to cultural goods, in much the same way that more tangible goods are controlled. The poor have less of both kinds of capital, and the lack of one prevents obtaining the other. This perspective has been criticized for its "static reproductionism," leaving too little room for agency or change (Yelvington 1995:5; see also Jenkins 1992:80–84). Nor can his ideas adequately explain the persistence of cultural differences in spite of economic success that Portes, Light, and others have described.

Bourdieu's conception that knowledge and the strategic deployment of cultural resources are a type of capital formation, is nonetheless useful in thinking about agency. The concept of cultural capital also has been used to describe institutions and social devices invented by the less powerful to marshal the effectiveness of collective action (Stack 1998; Hirabayashi

1993). The poor and the dispossessed can act to redress their circumstances by organizing their ingenuity. Migrant associations and grassroots community-action agencies are two examples of this type of cultural capital. Organizations enable groups to act in concert and invest in each other, creating palpable resources they can use to change their lives.

Under Bourdieu's interpretation of cultural capital, the Martí-Maceo Society both symbolized and effectuated the exclusion of black Cubans, deprived them of advantages and prevented access to opportunities that white Cubans could enjoy. Invoking Stack's use of the concept, however, the Martí-Maceo Society represents the agency of Afro-Cubans in challenging their exclusion, the creation of an alternative institution designed to achieve similar ends. By establishing their own mutual aid society, the Afro-Cubans fashioned a niche for themselves in the institutional environment that the white Cubans and other immigrants developed in Ybor City. It was their share of the larger fund of social and cultural capital formed within the cigarmaking enclave.

My use of the term reflects this alternative perspective, a more dynamic conception of the development and conversion of capital, in which the relationship between cultural and economic capital is less rigidly determined. Bourdieu's discussion of the concept effectively limits it to formal education and elite enculturation (what Jenkins [1992:85] terms "legitimate knowledge"), but "cultural capacities" are arguably more encompassing. Institutional arrangements for the accumulation of cultural knowledge need not be connected to dominant structures. Moreover, the cultural and social formations of ethnic minorities do not necessarily follow the rules of the market. Indeed, defying these rules is often what makes success possible. Mutual aid societies are designed on principles of cooperation and sharing, a kind of generalized redistribution. They are structures for accumulating collective wealth, a capital fund designed to protect the weak and the sick, to shield the members from an exploitative and competitive system (Beito 1993; Cummings 1980; Greenbaum 1991; Soyer 1997; Vélez Ibáñez 1983; Vondracek 1972).

Bourdieu's assumption that these processes do not work for disadvantaged groups, that they cannot alter the equation of power, conforms with the main tenets of rational choice theory. Rational choice theory, an idea that has garnered several Nobel Prizes in economics (Acheson 1994), holds simply that all social behavior is reducible to self-interested actions by individuals (see Coleman and Fararo 1992). Cooperative funds, designed to enable members to share each other's wealth and risks, are considered to be inherently vulnerable to the failings of human nature (Bates 1994; Hechter 1987; Olson 1965). An extension of the so-called tragedy-of-the-commons problem (Hardin 1968), good intentions are thought to be inevitably undermined by the aggregate effects of selfish behavior. Hence the capacity of groups to challenge reigning systems of power by creating collectivized alternatives, such as the Martí-Maceo, or the examples considered by Stack (1998) and Hirabayashi (1993), cannot ultimately succeed (Hardin 1968; Hechter, Opp, and Wippler 1991; Olson 1965; Taylor and Singleton 1993).

The pessimistic assertions of this school of thought have been challenged by anthropologists and others who study the management of shared resources such as fish, timber, grazing land, and other types of common property (Acheson 1994, 1989; Berkes 1989; Bromely 1992; Landa 1994; McCay and Jentoft 1998; Ostrom 1992; Runge 1992). Varied solutions for the so-called tragedy of the commons can be found in long-term operations, across many different settings, solutions that rely successfully on cooperative systems of regulation. McCay and Jentoft argue that rational choice perspectives on collective resources incorrectly identify the cause of "tragedies" to be community failure, when these problems more often reflect market failures.

The economy of mutual aid, as enacted in the Martí-Maceo Society, is addressed in Chapter 5. The financial structure, organizational rules and procedures, and the underlying ideology of leadership and participation are examined in relation to these conflicting ideas about community versus market failures. Hechter (1987:116), a rational choice theorist, asserts that larceny by officers in immigrant mutual benefit societies was an inevitable, and fatal, weakness of these organizations. Further, he argues that mobility of urban immigrant populations inexorably reduced the trust and cohesion needed to make them work. His views exemplify the "community failure" perspective.

It is true that the Afro-Cuban cigar workers were extremely mobile. Moreover, Hechter's certainty about embezzlement is vindicated in this case. A trusted officer in 1915 misappropriated funds to cover gambling debts at precisely the moment the mortgage came due on the building. This was a major crisis in the organization, the ultimate resolution of which revealed added dimensions in alliance formation and the codification of rules of conduct for all future office holders. Although correct about the extent of risk, Hechter underestimates capacity to regroup and survive. His ideas about the effects of mobility proved to be extremely inaccurate.

To gauge the nature of financial redistribution, I examined exchanges within the organization (dues paid and benefits received) over a period of two decades, a literal assessment of the costs and benefits of membership. Were greedy "free riders" and/or larcenous office holders undermining the pool of capital that was supposed to benefit all? In revealing the fluctuating equilibrium between revenues and expenditures, the implicit management and actuarial processes at work, I have attempted to disclose the rules by which they were able to operate this fund. The overall purpose of this analysis was to address the conflicting views of cultural capital outlined earlier. Can human agency by the poor and dispossessed overcome the structures of power, and build social and cultural capital out of the sheer strength of combination? Or does individual greed, and the structures it engenders, always win out in the end? These are larger questions than I can answer definitively, but my findings do help to advance the discussion.

In economic terms, the Martí-Maceo Society was an effective capital generator. In exchange for dues that were manageably low, individual workers obtained benefits that were unusually large. The extent of medical coverage and sick payments matched what was offered by the other immigrant mutual aid societies in Ybor City, and exceeded the benefits provided by mutual aid societies in most other cities of that era (Greenbaum 1991, 1993). As an institution, it also offered a means of developing human capital—in its library and the classes it provided, and in the activities that built leadership skills and useful knowledge. As a vehicle of group representation, the official Afro-Cuban presence, Martí-Maceo was a source of social capital. It was the main organizer of relations among individual Afro-Cubans, and the main site of negotiation with other groups. Their ability to operate the club, to take care of themselves and participate in the cultural life of the immigrant community, earned Afro-Cubans the added currency of respectability. There were, however, nagging contradictions tied to the meanings of Afro-Cuban identity as a source of status and respect.

Dialectics of Gender Relations

The status of Afro-Cubans depended on accentuating the distinctions between themselves and African Americans. In emphasizing their Cubanness, they sought to neutralize their blackness. Afro-Cubans deliberately avoided contact with African Americans, and joined in condemning their perceived cultural values and behavior. Family relations, especially the roles and conduct of women, offered a major site of contrast. Cubans in Tampa disparaged the presumed family values of African Americans as lacking in parental control and responsibility. Males exerted too little authority; females too much. The sexual behavior of children and adolescents was not adequately supervised. It was a familiar argument, the essential conservative explanation of black poverty, drawn sharply against the patriarchal traditions of Cuban families. In the realm of paternal discipline and gender authority, Afro-Cubans could distinguish themselves favorably by embracing traditional Cuban practices. However, Cuban traditions about gender also had much to do with race. They encoded a set of assumptions about Afro-Cuban sexuality not unlike the inferences of Cubans about African Americans. This shadow logic, transferring a stereotype about themselves onto African Americans, was an ironic factor that intensified the significance of gender relations for Afro-Cubans in Ybor City and West Tampa.

Chapter 6 explores the racial complexities of family and community life in the period preceding the Great Depression of the 1930s. This was the time of greatest insularity, when the Martí-Maceo Society grew in size, and the factories provided a steady stream of wages. Ybor City and West Tampa were thriving "Latin" enclaves with vibrant ethnic traditions, radical institutions, and a heavily elaborated culture of work (Mormino and Pozzetta 1987). Afro-Cubans were part of the larger community, but they were also apart from it. Much more than the other groups, they had to struggle to establish and maintain their place. The chapter examines the contours of that battle, with a special emphasis on gender.

Occasional indignities suffered within the Latin community highlight the boundaries that set Afro-Cubans aside and below. They also set the parameters of respectability, rules of conduct that avoided undignified treatment. Winning respect cultivated capital, enhanced their stock as individuals and as a group. Bourdieu's concept of symbolic capital, the creditworthiness of honor (1990a:119–21), and the primary importance of defending it (1977:10–15), which he associated with "virility," can be applied to gender practices of Afro-Cubans in Tampa. The racialized context of sex and gender complicated systems of valuation and rules of performance.

Peter Wilson's (1969, 1973) use of respectability as a symbolic model of color, class, and gender in the Anglophone Caribbean has similarities to Bourdieu's. Respectability is an attribute defined by those in power as part of the ideological "rationale" for their own superior possessions and authority. Conduct by subalterns can be deemed respectable only if it strictly adheres to behavioral expectations of the ruling class, implicitly accepting the principles of cultural dominance. The concept is heavily gendered. The respectability of women defines the status of the family. Men are freer to ignore, or defy, the code of proper conduct. Wilson equates respectability with beliefs and behavior conditioned by colonial hegemony, efforts to emulate qualities valued by those in control. In contrast, *reputation* is presented as a constellation of behaviors that reflect resistance, a validation of indigenous values and an assertion of autonomous control. Sexual virtuousness is at the center of respectability; sexual conquest is the heart of reputation. Wilson's dichotomy points to a dialectic that breaks along lines of gender, but he has been criticized for this simplification (Besson 1993). He tends to glorify *machismo*, neglects possibilities for resistance by women, and overstates the rebelliousness of men. Nonetheless, his work identifies critical tensions in relations among power, color, and gender that were similar to colonial Cuba.

Drawing threads from both Bourdieu and Wilson, respectability can be viewed as a hegemonic device that especially burdens the conduct of women. For individuals within communities, respectability can be viewed as capital, a valued commodity to be pursued and guarded. Respectability is also about sex and marriage, the fundaments of social reproduction. The strategies that groups and individuals adopt in achieving respectability have direct, although not necessarily intended, effects on structures of family and kinship. Contexts in which these strategies are implemented reflect variable contingencies in the outcome, and reveal more nuanced complexities in gender dynamics than are envisioned by either Bourdieu or Wilson.

Within the Latin community of Tampa, and especially in relations with white Cubans, the respectability of Afro-Cubans rested in part on masculine control over women and family. Restricting the behavior of women enabled the Afro-Cuban community as a whole to distance themselves from the negative images of African Americans, to combat tendencies of white Cubans to view Afro-Cubans in a similarly negative frame, and to protect wives and daughters from heightened threats of seduction or rape in the heavily male cigar colony of Tampa.

Afro-Cuban women were stereotypically vulnerable to the sexual advances of white men. *La mulatica*, a diminutive inscribing the forbidden sensuality of race mixing, stood at the center of a viciously constructed paradox (Kutzinski 1993). Afro-Cuban women were at the bottom of a hierarchy of race, power, and gender. But they were also the objects of erotic desire by powerful white men. Attentions paid to women of color offered possible avenues to influence and power, but also bound them in roles as concubines. Cuban literature offers tragic images of women of color caught in this transgression, helpless to avoid the shameful consequences of rape or seduction (Barreda 1979; Dworkin 1998; Kutzinski 1993). The family histories of my Afro-Cuban narrators are similarly replete with illegitimate white grandfathers and tales of their betrayals.

Afro-Cuban men were enfeebled also by this sexual tangle. They were doubly dangerous; injured cuckolds who might rise in anger, and potential rivals who threatened the integrity of white Spanish bloodlines. Subordination enabled control. Race and sex intertwined to make respectability, for both Afro-Cuban men and women, a heavily burdened quest.

The narratives I collected were broadly consistent about the quality of family life and relations between men and women in earlier generations, relations that are well described in literature on gender in prerevolutionary Cuba (Bengelsdorf 1988, 1997; Kutzinski 1993; Stoner 1991). Women were expected to remain subservient to their husbands, to raise children, and to keep a good house. They were expected to suffer in silence while their husbands were free to pursue their pleasures. Women's virtue was jealously guarded, and men validated their masculinity in careless infidelities. Married women were discouraged from having jobs outside of the house. Indeed, relatively fewer black than white Cuban wives worked in the factories, a reversal of what might be expected. Afro-Cuban girls could work in cigar factories, and most quit school at an early age to take these jobs. However, they were chaperoned while walking to and from work, and in all other activities outside of the house until they were safely married. This stereotypic pattern, an extension of Cuban *machismo*, differs little from the larger image of Cuban gender relations. A cultural performance that signified Cubanness and earned respect from other Cubans, built on a scenario in which the roles assigned to black men and women were the essential contradiction of respectability.

In Tampa, Afro-Cubans faced the added complication of another black community, whose degraded status further threatened their own. All the more so, because it also served as a lure. Managing sexuality and marriage was critical to maintaining separation from African Americans, but Cuban customs about gender served poorly in effecting that goal. The oppression of females encouraged rebellion, and the license of males encouraged sexual exploration. Both tendencies favored intermarriage. Close supervision of Afro-Cuban women was particularly aimed at preventing contact

with African American males, the most threatening of all potential se-
ducers. Afro-Cuban males were not similarly restrained. Quite the contrary: their own quests for romance, difficult to indulge within the bounds
of the small Afro-Cuban community, roamed in the direction of African
American women. The stereotype of their steamy sexuality, the "brown
sugar" counterpart of *la mulatica*, found validation among the prostitutes in the nearby red-light district. Presumptuous advances to daughters
of preachers and other respectable working people, however, encountered
indignation that was sometimes confusing, often challenging, and not infrequently eventuated in marriage. Similar liaisons developed between
Afro-Cuban females and African American males, sometimes prompted
by resistance of paternal control and/or yearning for a different way of
life.

These marriage patterns, in part a reaction to the stringency of gender
roles in the Afro-Cuban community, transformed the networks of kinship and family. The generation that married during the 1930s and 1940s,
largely the children of the postindependence immigrants, overwhelmingly
selected African American spouses. Their children were only half-Cuban;
they had cousins, aunts, uncles, and grandparents who were raised in
Tampa's African American community. Many attended African American
churches and easily associated with African Americans at school and in
their neighborhoods. More than any other factor, removal of barriers to
intermarriage helped erase the boundaries between black Cubans and
black Americans.

The separation that Afro-Cubans sought to maintain was challenged
and undermined by the very measures taken to safeguard it. Lies that parents told their children about African Americans were unmasked in experiences at school and other settings where contact occurred. And contact
was inevitable.

Becoming Afro-Cuban-Americans

Bridges between ethnic segments of the black community were paved and
directed by the restrictions of Jim Crow. Segregation placed them together
in school and assigned similar positions in streetcars and other public accommodations. Shared space and a common indignity helped promote relationships. Chapters 7 and 8 describe the coming together of African
Americans and Afro-Cubans—the factors, including intermarriage, that
created strong bonds in the second and third generations. This is a compli-

cated narrative, involving the outmigration of a major segment of the Afro-Cuban community following the collapse of the cigar industry during the 1930s. The Civil Rights movement and the Cuban Revolution, coincident events unfolding in the 1950s and 1960s, had profound effects on Afro-Cubans who remained in Tampa. Urban Renewal destroyed much of Ybor City, including the building that housed the Martí-Maceo Society.

The process by which Afro-Cubans became African Americans, were incorporated into the larger black community of Tampa, cannot be separated from forces at play in the nation as a whole. Intermarriage may have been unwittingly hastened by Cuban gender rules, but it was also spurred by the exodus of Afro-Cubans from Tampa, which reduced the pool of choices. The Cuban Revolution closed the door on contact with the island and established new fractures within the Cuban community of Tampa. The Civil Rights movement had paramount importance in forming positive ties with African Americans, the comradeship of struggle. The destructive effects of Urban Renewal on Afro-Cubans in Tampa, and on African Americans as well, were similar to those experienced by black urban communities throughout the United States (Kusmer 1995; Rhea 1997; Squires 1994). Powerful external forces in this era affected the construction of identity and the practice of community in cities throughout the United States, but the confluence was particularly significant for Afro-Cubans in Tampa.

In the 1970s two other national trends, Sunbelt migration and ethnic revivalism, produced similarly important impacts on this community. Returning New Yorkers bolstered the Martí-Maceo Society, joining with Tampa Afro-Cubans who were rediscovering or reasserting their historic ethnicity. Reverse migration—the influx of retirees who had moved from Tampa as children—rescued the declining organization in a period when preservation, not destruction, had become the reigning metaphor in Ybor City.

Chapter 9, outlined earlier, describes this most recent era, and how applied anthropology came to be included in the stock of Afro-Cuban cultural capital in Tampa. In the current moment, when nearly all of my original informants have died, the future structure of the Afro-Cuban community is impossible to forecast. At this writing, the Martí-Maceo Society still exists. October 2000 marked the centennial of its founding. Pressures of development in the surrounding neighborhood have never been more threatening than they are now, and the energy level of the membership has never been lower—except perhaps in 1965, when Urban

Renewal destroyed the original building; or in 1929, when half the members left town suddenly and virtually all were unemployed. At those junctures and others as well, including the original founding of the club, external challenges and constraints elicited unexpectedly successful responses.

Historic reasons for optimism notwithstanding, the title of the chapter is "Out of Time." This phrase has several meanings, one of which is that the end is near. Another suggests anachronism, that the organization is a fossil relic and a misleading symbol for contemporary meanings of Afro-Cuban identity in Tampa. The last meaning, the one that leans most heavily on optimism, emphasizes endurance and accumulation. The legacies of mutual aid, the heritage of struggle, the affirmation of collective solutions, the efficacy of sharing, and the cumulative wealth reflected in the real estate value of Martí-Maceo, are assets that were handed down—the symbolic, cultural, and economic capital mobilized by long dead Cuban revolutionists.

Stretched across generations, located in a specific cultural and political context, relations of Afro-Cubans with white Cubans, and with African Americans, were both defined and negotiated. Implicated in these transactions was a shifting fund of cultural capital that the Afro-Cubans both created and inherited. In economic terms, the property that they own in common has never been worth more than it is today. The extent to which the members can hold onto this wealth in the heated-up real estate market of Ybor City, whether it can be converted for some contemporary purpose, as opposed to being lost or appropriated, is the final question. At this writing it remains unanswered.

A Note on Nomenclature

The slippery nature of racial and ethnic categories, and the nuanced importance of labeling, become all too obvious in the process of trying to describe these phenomena in words. The terms "black" and "white"—metaphors of unambiguous distinctions—are the most misleading of all. When applied to human groups, the reality of a phenotypic spectrum, shifting criteria for where on the continuum black turns into white, and different rules for how many divisions should be made divorce these words from any semblance of objective clarity. Cuban rules were different from those in the United States, where the line was drawn sharply to exclude anyone with the slightest degree of African ancestry. Operationally, black meant "blackened," tainted by clues of slave parentage. In Cuba, African heritage had the same meaning, but there were more stations on the color hierarchy, a wider array of labels, and less rigidity about movement to higher categories. Personal success could have a whitening effect, and intergenerational mobility could be achieved by producing light-skinned children. *Adelantar la raza*, to advance the race, was the name attached to the latter strategy; a gratuity of concubinage and sardonic legacy of illegitimate fatherhood. That the categories were less labile in the United States does not mean that similar crossing failed to occur. Mulattoes also have a recognized status, were formally enumerated in some early U.S. decennial censuses. Lighter skin has been correlated with greater economic success for African Americans (Russell, Wilson, and Hall 1992:38). Color differences within African American communities have a wide range of social effects and attach to a variety of indigenous labels. Racial categories are not clear, nor clearly dichotomous, in either Cuba or the United States, although there clearly are differences between the two systems. The "Afro-Cubans" about whom I write transgressed this border, transported themselves and their ideas about these things into a new context where meanings changed. The terms I have used to describe them, across a shifting landscape of place and time, are inevitably lacking in precision. Attributions of blackness do not signify color, but rather membership in a group that has been socially defined as black.[3] Meanings of synonyms and variants—Afro-Cubans, African Americans, people of color, mulattoes—are used in a similar fashion and take their specific meaning from the context of the discussion. The real intention is to distinguish the lines of white privilege, to denote those who have been excluded.

Afro-Cuban is a word invented by an anthropologist in 1906, presented in a study that linked crime in Cuba with the presence of Africans and their descendants (Ortiz 1973). The people I worked with did not much like this term, and they rarely used it themselves.[4] They had no effective substitute; they referred to themselves as black Cubans, or colored Cubans, or simply as Cubans. Often, the Martí-Maceo served as a shorthand for group identity in Tampa; the Cubans who belonged to that club were black by virtue of affiliation. Nearly all the obviously black Cubans in Tampa belonged, along with many whose appearances were not obvious at all. In Cuba, blacks and mulattoes belonged to different mutual aid societies, institutional reflections of social distinctions that were not maintained in Tampa. Had the population been large enough to sustain more than one club, perhaps the significance of a third category might have endured. Lack of this division, encouraged by low numbers, was also reinforced by Jim Crow laws that failed to recognize degrees of blackness. Demographically and structurally, Afro-Cuban identity in Tampa equated with the binary distinctions of black versus white, and was revealed in the cleavage between the two Cuban clubs. Although there are problems with the term *Afro-Cuban*, it is the only one in common usage that serves to define what it meant to be both Cuban and black, as opposed to being white and Cuban, or black and something else.

The "something else" that most often connected with blackness in Tampa, referred to native-born "African Americans." This label, although widely accepted, is of recent vintage and was certainly not in use during much of the period I describe. It is the latest in a succession of naming— black, colored, Negro, Afro-American, Black. In recent years, among the more politically radical, "American" has been deleted, emphasizing identity only as "African." The long-running contest over nomenclature, and who gets to decide what black people in the United States are called, is an interesting phenomenon in its own right (with analogies to controversy about *afrocuban*), but it poses practical problems for writing about history, and prospective problems when labels change and texts become marked as out of date. Here, I use the term African American as an ethnic, not racial, label that refers to members of the "native" black community in Tampa, those with roots in the slavery of the South. I have applied it throughout time, although quoted passages from documents of earlier periods often use other terms.

In describing later generations of Afro-Cubans in Tampa, identification becomes more confusing. Many of these descendants self-identify as African Americans, especially the younger ones no longer affiliated with Martí-Maceo.[5] Intermarriage played a large role in the crossover, but so too has identification with the black political agenda in the United States. African American leaders frequently have opposed positions of the Cuban American National Foundation (the most vocal political lobby of Cuban exiles). Well-publicized clashes between African Americans and Cubans in Miami also have served to widen the divide between Cuban ancestry and black consciousness. On a more discursive level, many younger descendants do not speak Spanish, have never been to Cuba, and do not know much about it. They are rarely involved in the activities of the larger Cuban community in Tampa, which is predominantly composed of more recent immigrants, nearly all of whom are white.[6] In the past few decades the meaning of Cuban identity in Tampa has changed, and the reflected meaning of Afro-Cuban identity has narrowed as a consequence.

Contests over naming, transformation of ethnic labels, and distinctions between generations in how individuals define themselves are markers of change in the long history of the African diaspora. Segmentation, alliance formation, factions, and fusions betoken the long struggle for peoplehood on a continent that denied the humanity of people of color. The meaning of terms like black, Afro-Cuban, and African American is inescapably elusive, always on the move, symptomatic and synoptic of the very process of ethnogenesis that this book seeks to disclose.

2

Pathways

Worldwide dusk of dear dark faces
driven by an alien wind;
scattered like seed in far off places,
growing in soil that is strange and thin.

Langston Hughes, *Black Seed*, 1930

Africans forced across the ocean into new lives in the Americas faced a common ordeal with multiple pathways. Those who landed in Cuba entered a slightly different realm of oppression than Africans disembarked in Virginia or South Carolina. From these and other major ports of entry, enslaved Africans of diverse linguistic and tribal identities fanned out into the Americas and were incorporated into virtually all nations emergent on the hemisphere. In colonies controlled by competing imperial powers, within varied local ecologies, and in the context of national liberation struggles of widely different character, uprooted Africans constructed new communities and identities in the grudging soil of slavery.

This chapter is about Africans in Cuba and Florida, two career paths from among the multiple trajectories of the diaspora. These two populations, descendants of contrasting but linked systems of slavery, encountered each other in the late nineteenth century. Tampa's Afro-Cuban community was created from that meeting, forged in the common and distinctive circumstances both groups confronted over the next few generations. Shared roots in slavery and the scorn heaped on its progeny were powerful factors in the equation. It is impossible to understand Afro-Cuban identity in Tampa without taking into account African Americans who also have lived there—their parallel involvements in antislavery and antiracist struggles, the divergent fields whereon they fought and negotiated, and the ideological and institutional formations emergent from these two African American peoples.

A related purpose is to engage questions about the nature of racism, and "myths of racial democracy" (Ferrer 1998; de la Fuente 1999; Helg 1997; Sheriff 2000; Skidmore 1993). In comparing race relations in Latin America to conditions in the United States, the conventional wisdom (implicitly challenged by labeling it a "myth") has favored the former. More fluid racial categories, fewer impediments to miscegenation, and fuller incorporation into wars for national independence, it is claimed, resulted in significantly more harmonious and democratic race relations (Degler 1971; Harris 1964). Brazil, with its infinitely divisible racial spectrum, is the most frequent exemplar, but these same assertions frequently attach to discussions of race in Cuba. Claims that Cuba is/was a "racial democracy" are expressed on both ends of the political spectrum. Recent scholarship on race in Cuban history, however, disputes the validity of such claims. In particular, Helg (1995) argues that racism in Cuba was scarcely less venomous than in the United States, and that pretenses about democracy were a weapon used to smother dissent. Similar arguments have been made about Brazil (Twine 1998; Sheriff 2000; Skidmore 1993).

Categorization vis-à-vis African versus European ancestry, in which a person is given one or more of a number of official and unofficial labels designating degrees of blackness, is regarded as a key variable. According to Skidmore (1993), the United States is considered the classic *biracial* society, where "one drop" of African blood directs assignment in the Negro category, drawing a hard boundary between white and nonwhite. *Multiracial* societies, where mulattoes have a distinct status and multiple gradations of color may be salient, have been presented as inherently more open. They offer what Degler (1971) labeled the "mulatto escape hatch," a way up and out for those with lighter skin. Skidmore (1993) challenges Degler's assumption that the existence of intermediate categories has promoted greater economic mobility among Afro-Brazilians, noting that objective data fail to support this thesis (see also Sheriff 2000; Andrews 1992). Skidmore further argues that the organizational strength mobilized by blacks in the United States, a solidarity engendered by rigid categories, was largely responsible for overturning the Jim Crow regime. In comparison, Afro-Brazilians have been less able to pursue similar strategies because they are divided against themselves in the intricate niches of a color class hierarchy. He concludes that multiracialism, with its multiple distinctions, has ironically disabling effects on the capacity to mobilize resistance. Strong organizations are difficult to achieve, and the lighter, more prosperous African descendants are prone to defection.

Public discourse and political rhetoric in Brazil also conspire against mobilizing racial discontent (Skidmore 1993; Twine 1998; Sheriff 2000). Complaints about racial discrimination are considered offensive, a calumny linking whites in Brazil with those in the United States, and a threat to national harmony. Very similar arguments have been offered about historical patterns in Cuba, where color-blindness has been a patriotic doctrine (de la Fuente 1999; Helg 1997; Ferrer 1998). Silence about race is viewed as a form of social control, a subtle hegemonic deception that enables racial inequality by pretending it does not exist. This is the "mythic" property—meaning fictitious and fraudulent—behind claims of racial democracy in Brazil and Cuba.

Has racism in Cuba been no better, and possibly worse, than that in the United States? Was polarization an unlikely ally in fashioning black resistance in the United States? If the cordiality fabricated in relations between black and white Cubans merely masked discrimination, and did not confer real economic progress, then perhaps African Americans were better off. At least they did not have to steer a maze of hypocrisies and false promises. Segregation of blacks in the United States, it is suggested, instead fostered self-determination. Separatism, which made no distinction for degrees of blackness, structured a broad collective "race" consciousness that made the organization of resistance ultimately more successful.

This is a paradoxical conclusion. A harsher classification system in the United States engendered greater solidarity, which better enabled the oppressed to challenge the oppressor. The frame has shifted to include internal structures of self-help and organized resistance, the habitus from which action was fashioned. Have Afro-Cubans been less able to combat discrimination, because the ideology of *cubanidad* prevents them from organizing along racial lines, or voicing complaints about racial discrimination? In turn, what happened in Florida? Did black and brown people there band together against the extremities of Jim Crow, forming strong associations of mutual assistance and collective agitation? Are the properties attributed to the different systems of rhetoric and categories (multiracial versus biracial) actually evident in the resulting action on the ground?

Africans in Cuba and Florida, from the early arrivals to the modern descendants, exemplify in concrete terms the abstract dualities of race in the Americas. A close inspection of these contrasting systems and their parallels and divergences across time helps focus the inquiry and frame theoretical questions for which there are empirical answers. How did African descendants organize and articulate their respective and varied identities? What kinds of institutions did they develop, and what did they do with them? What is the relevance of historical variables like demography, economy, and politics? Ideological themes that emerged in these respective contexts, authorized patterns of hegemonic control and violent repression, are also of interest. The relationship between silence and violence, alternative weapons for reproducing power, is set against the reciprocal contrast between acquiescence and resistance, alternative modes of subaltern reaction.

Slaves and Free People of Color

Cuba and Florida are separated by ninety miles of water between Havana and Key West. Geography has drawn these two places together through time, but the space in between has had large political importance. For Africans and their descendants in the nineteenth century, the differences were especially striking. Early in that period, when both were still under Spanish rule, and Florida's population was less than 1 percent of Cuba's, the main distinctions were between metropolis and hinterland. Later, after the United States gained possession of Florida, the contrasts were much more profound. The contest over Florida—a multilateral conflict that involved Indians and Africans in various alliances with Britain, Spain, and the United States—set the stage for a highly repressive slave regime in Florida after U.S. possession in the 1820s. This was a change from the previous conditions and different from Cuba in significant ways. Cuba also underwent substantial changes in the early decades of the nineteenth century. The rebellion in Haiti (which ended in 1804) indirectly transformed Cuba from a settler into a plantation society, greatly expanding dependence on sugar and resulting in large increases in the numbers of African slaves.

Looking north from Havana, Florida was a remote untamed territory, a long peninsula with dense palmetto and impenetrable swamps covering much of its southern extension. The principal Spanish settlements, at St. Augustine and Pensacola, were in the far northern part of the territory, deliberately within reach of Britain's colonies in the Carolinas. Thinly populated and poorly defended, these were beleaguered outposts, especially compared with Havana, which was a major port city in the middle of the Caribbean empire. The dramatic difference in scale can be seen in Tables 1 and 2, regarding population data for Cuba and Florida in the several decades prior to emancipation (which occurred in 1865 in Florida and 1886 in Cuba).

Table 1. Florida Population, 1814–1860

	White	Slave	% Slave	Free People of Color	% Free People of Color	Total
1814	1,302	1,651	54	122	4.0	3,075
1830	18,385	15,501	45	844	2.4	34,730
1840	27,943	25,717	47	817	1.5	54,477
1850	47,203	39,310	45	932	1.1	87,445
1860	77,746	61,745	44	932	0.7	140,423

Sources: for 1814, Landers 1995:37; for 1830–1860, Mohlman 1995:49; Garvin 1967:7 (statistics on free people of color).

In 1814, during the final years of Spanish control, Florida enumerated only 3,075 residents, 1,651 of whom (54 percent) were black slaves (Landers 1995:37). In that same period (1817), Cuba's population count was 635,604, of whom 38 percent were black slaves (Martinez-Alier 1974:3). In between enslaved blacks and free whites was another category, designated free blacks; 19 percent of Cuba's population were free people of color, compared with only 4 percent of the population of Florida. This distinction grew wider over the next several decades: in Cuba the percentage of free blacks fluctuated but was never lower than 14 percent, whereas it steadily declined in Florida, from 4 percent in 1814 to 2.4 percent in 1830, and down to less than 0.7 percent by 1860. The overall proportions of African descendants in Cuba and Florida were similar throughout this period, both places teetering on either side of a black majority.

Table 2. Cuban Population, 1817–1877

	White	Slave	% Slave	Free People of Color	% Free People of Color	Total
1817	276,689	239,694	38	119,221	19	635,604
1825	325,000	290,000	41	100,000	14	715,000
1846	757,610	368,417	27	221,417	16	1,347,444
1860	793,484	370,553	27	225,843	16	1,389,880
1869	797,596	363,288	26	238,927	17	1,399,811
1877	1,023,394	199,094	13	272,478	18	1,494,966

Sources: for 1817, 1846, 1877, Martinez-Alier 1974:3; for 1860, Knight 1970:86; for 1825, 1869, Ortiz 1987:38.

The existence of a large cohort of free Afro-Cubans, some descended from the earliest settlers, had major implications for the structure of Cuban society and the embedded meaning of race. Similar, although contradictory, implications can be drawn from the scarcity verging on total absence of free people of color in Florida. Freedom conferred some capacity to earn wealth, gain an education, own property, and openly devise collective strategies to improve existing conditions. Free colored populations, especially in the larger towns and cities of Cuba, had sufficient size to allow the development of complex communities. They were licensed by the Crown to operate mutual aid societies, called *cabildos*, in which they organized religious rituals and festivities that were explicitly African. Separate militias were composed of free Afro-Cubans who carried arms and received military training. Afro-Cubans were able to enter a number of trades and occupations, and a small number were professionals or writers. In 1861, Havana alone had 37,765 free people of color (Rushing 1992:246). Occupations were listed for 6,974 adults; 4,425 (63 percent) were day laborers, but the remainder had skilled trades. Cigarmaking had the largest representation (1,611; 23 percent), more than twice as many as there were carpenters (721), the second most numerous trade.

In Florida, by contrast, fewer than a thousand free blacks were dispersed among several sections of the state, most in the vicinity of older Spanish settlements. In Pensacola, there was a group of "Creoles" (African-French-Spanish descent) predating U.S. ownership of the area. Relatively prosperous and accustomed to privileges attached to an intermediate status that disappeared, many Creoles left the state in a group in 1857 (Garvin 1967:11). For all African descendants who had lived in Florida prior to U.S. occupation, life had changed dramatically. New laws greatly curtailed their rights to move about, carry arms, behave assertively, or gather in groups. Black churches were prohibited; blacks could worship in separate sections of white churches, or itinerant white preachers led them in prayer. Manumission was made extremely difficult, and free people of color were effectively barred from settling in the territory. They had no standing in court proceedings, and if convicted of a felony could be reenslaved. In all respects, they operated under severe political and economic handicaps and were in constant jeopardy of losing their freedom. Most worked as farmers or servants, although artisans of various crafts were included among Florida's free blacks.

The greater degree of latitude granted free Afro-Cubans and their greater degree of incorporation into the mainstream economy are consistent with images of "racial democracy" in Cuba. Antebellum conditions in Florida represented the general lack of freedom attainable by free people of color in the South, the negative standard against which "democracy" is measured. In assessing life's chances, it would seem far preferable to have been black and free in Cuba than black and free in Florida; and statistically, a black person in Cuba was far more likely to have been free. Slaves suffered in both places, especially on plantations, where conditions in Cuba were arguably no better than in Florida (Moreno-Fraginals 1987; Scott 1985; Knight 1970). In Cuba, however, the free black population was far larger, both in proportion and absolute numbers, and their circumstances permitted institution building and the development of leadership cadres to a far greater degree. The foundation upon which subsequent civil relations were constructed in Cuba, the basis of interaction across racial boundaries, would seem to have been wider and deeper, and generative of far less antagonism, than that laid down in Florida. The existence in Cuba of intermediate categories—stepping-stones that allowed those fortunately born with lighter skin to find greater degrees of acceptance, and those with talent to earn status in spite of color—appears to offer a more likely structure for the gradual elimination of racial antagonism. At least, these assumptions have constituted the prevailing logic, until recent challenges issued against the "myth of racial democracy."

In part, the challenge is based on increasingly clear evidence that people of color in Cuba (and Brazil) have not achieved parity, and that racist beliefs have not vanished from the discourse of daily life. Rethinking also reflects critical inquiry into the meanings of race and color, the subtleties with which expanded categories also reproduce power and perpetuate white domination. Multiracial schemes, it is argued, still allocate rewards on the basis of color, idealizing whiteness and despising blackness no less than the dichotomous variety.

Aside from using overarching classifications of *negro, mulato,* and *blanco* (black, mulatto, and white), Cubans make further distinctions that betray a strong bias against physical features considered African-derived in favor of those of European origin. Racial terms heard in everyday conversation include *mulato adelantado* (evolved mulatto), used to describe light-skinned mulattoes with predominantly Caucasian features; *mulato blanconazo* (very white mulatto), a mulatto with so few African-derived physical features as to pass for white; *jaba'o,* a person of light skin color but overtly Negroid features; *trigueno* (wheat colored), a relatively light-skinned mulatto or Hispanic with *pelo bueno* (good hair); *negro azul* (blue black), a Negro so dark that skin appears to have a blue cast; and *indio* (Indian), a mulatto with physical features and/or skin tone that suggests descent from the island's indigenous population. (Moore 1997:14)

Cuban racial nomenclature elaborates rather than diminishes the phenotypic traits of African ancestry, is intricately pejorative rather than generously inclusive. Woe to those with *pelo malo* (bad hair), or other unfortunate features that nurture hatred of self and things African. For Afro-Cubans at the darkest end of the continuum, the fact that Cuban *pardos* were treated better than mulattoes in the United States was of little material consequence. And for those who were lighter, even whose traces of African ancestry were barely discernible, the "stain" of slavery posed lingering disabilities. As well for those who were free during slavery, whose status in society would have been on par with other nonslaves but for the color of their skin, the mark of Africa inscribed limits. Why this obsession with blackness?

Racism, Rebellion, and Social Control

The social distinction between slave and free was mitigated by associations presumed to exist among all who share common blood. People of color never could be fully trusted. What if they sided with the slaves in a general uprising? What if they used their positions and resources to help promote, or even lead, such enterprises? Haiti, the emblem of dread for white slaveholders in the Caribbean and lower South, offered an early demonstration that such fears had substance. The specter of black rule, of ruthless reprisals and inverted power, ever agitated the anxieties of whites (Sheller 1999). In places where blacks outnumbered them, where greed had ballooned the slave population, the plantocracy looked towards Haiti as proof of the need to ensure strong control. And there were examples closer at hand that further emphasized the hazards posed by free blacks.

In 1812, a free Afro-Cuban named Aponte directed a conspiracy to overthrow the colonial government (Paquette 1988: 123–25). Instigated in Havana and referred to as La Conspiración de Aponte, this revolt spread to the eastern end of the island and posed a palpable threat very soon after the Haitian revolution. Again in 1835, free Afro-Cubans in Havana launched an abortive uprising. Nine years later (in 1844), another plot was uncovered, called the Conspiracy of the Ladder (La Escalera). This last uprising sparked massive repression against free Afro-Cubans and slaves; 1844 came to be known as the Year of the Whip (Barreda 1979:25; Paquette 1988).

Each of these incidents invited more restrictions on the lives of free people of color. *Cabildos* were more tightly regulated, and in the aftermath of La Escalera the colored militias were temporarily disbanded. These conspiracies indicated that a great many free Afro-Cubans linked their own interests to ending slavery, which ultimately meant ending Spanish rule. Although the Crown was doubly afraid of such prospects, the extremely large free Afro-Cuban population, most of which predated the expansion of sugar and slavery, limited options to respond. Colonial administrators experimented with combinations of seduction, repression, and ethnic divisiveness based on color, status, and tribal origin. The *cabildos*, which will be discussed at length below, exemplify these efforts at manipulation. They also exemplify the unintended consequences that flowed from this desultory policy.

In Florida, there was far less equivocation. The U.S. incursion into Florida was part of a broad military action, led by Andrew Jackson, intended to vanquish the British, crush the last vestiges of Indian resistance in the southeast, and stanch the flow of runaway slaves across the border. Included among Jackson's enemies in this war were more than a thousand black maroons living in Florida and allied with the Seminole Indians (Mulroy 1993; Porter 1996). Not counted by the census of 1814, these were truly free people of color who fled across the frontier into Spanish territory, often in direct association with Seminoles, who were also escaping south from Georgia and Alabama. Africans among the Seminoles were treated as a tributary group, following familiar patterns of incorporation in the Creek Confederacy, of which the Seminoles had been a part. Known as "Black Seminoles," the Africans lived in separate villages under their own leadership, but with ties of "vassalage" to particular Seminole town chiefs (*miccos*) (Mulroy 1993:18). These arrangements were mutually advantageous, both economically and militarily.

When Jackson invaded Florida in 1818, the combined Seminole forces proved to be his most intractable foe. The British were routed, and the Spanish were forced to surrender their colony, but the blacks and Indians fought on in the most costly and prolonged war the United States had ever waged. Black involvement was not limited to the Seminole maroons. Slaves on plantations in north and central Florida were known to have aided the rebels, hardly surprising in view of their deteriorating rights under the U.S. occupation. They too could, and did, run away and join the Black Seminole colonies (Garvin 1967). Patterns of dissemblance emerged, in which trusted house servants and respectable free people of color feigned allegiance to the whites, while using their positions to aid African and Indian foes. At least two black scouts employed by the United States were accused, apparently with reason, of betraying the troops. One incident of presumed double agency resulted in the massacre of 105 U.S. soldiers, one of the worst losses of the war (Porter 1943). The eventual pacification of Florida established lines of antagonism against blacks, both free and enslaved, that corresponded to their status as vanquished enemies.

The vast majority of Black Seminoles were deported at the end of the war, although some who had switched sides and fought with the United States were permitted to remain. For the most part, however, the legacy of this period resides in its subsequent repressive impact. Black Seminoles were to Florida what Aponte and La Escalera were to Cuba. Unlike the regime in Cuba, where the large size of the free Afro-Cuban population required a more negotiated solution to the dangers of future insurrection, the regime in Florida ruthlessly eradicated all vestiges of power held by free blacks. This was easily done because there were so few remaining free blacks to contend with, and the laws of the territory left them little room to maneuver. In Cuba, on the other hand, free Afro-Cubans were integrated into the society and economy to a far greater extent. Ties of patron-clientage, affection, and even kinship complicated the situation. Although free Afro-Cubans had been involved in slave revolts, there was no automatic presumption that all were disloyal to the Crown. And in any case, the Crown had other enemies among the people of Cuba. Shared propensities for insurrection nurtured alliances with white creoles who were hatching schemes of independence.

During the 1850s, a lull in both places, diametrically opposite tendencies were at work in relations between blacks and whites in Cuba and Florida. As the white people of Florida consolidated their affinity with the slave states to the north and prepared to join in secession, white creoles in Cuba were incubating their own plans to secede from Spain. In these gathering national contests, black and white Cubans were lining up together, while black and white Floridians were on opposing sides. The belligerence associated with race relations in Florida, and other parts of the U.S. South, was nurtured by mutual perceptions as enemies. Similar perceptions in colonial Cuba were greatly mitigated, although scarcely eliminated, by the pragmatic need for cordiality between black and white allies in the independence movement. These divergent tendencies arose out of intercolonial intrigues and warfare, structures of domination aimed at upholding slavery, and restive stirrings for independence and self-rule. Conditions for Africans in Cuba and Florida were shaped by these larger interconnected dramas, in intelligibly different ways, but in response to the same underlying contingencies and tensions.

Slavery that excuses itself in the name of racial superiority births contradictions that cannot be tamed or swallowed. The very properties that make human chattel so valuable, intelligence and the capacity for coordinated effort, are the same traits that make this commodity inherently unmanageable. More slaves meant more wealth, but also greater dangers. The calculus of color and demography, in which collective fears were vitiated by individual greed, produced societies with perilously large numbers of captive humans. The end of slavery in Cuba and Florida was hastened by the active engagement of slaves acting out of a concerted desire to gain their freedom. Because the defense of slavery rested on beliefs about African ancestry, free people of color also had a stake in its abolition. Their collective aspirations found opportune alliances with other disaffected groups in these respective arenas—Seminoles in Florida and independence-minded white creoles in Cuba. State and colonial administrators were challenged in devising ways to prevent such aggregations. Repression, the solution of choice in Florida, was less practical as an overall strategy in Cuba. There, the more complex problem of managing a large free black population with links to both black slaves and poor whites was reflected in a version of indirect rule.

Institutionalizing Resistance

In colonial Cuba, Africans of various "tribal" origins (e.g., Yoruba, Congo, Carabali) were grouped together in a series of formal organizations known as *cabildos de nacciones* (Howard 1998; Rushing 1992). These were a type of mutual aid society, with origins in European guilds, brotherhoods, and friendly societies. King Alfonso X institutionalized a system of *cofradías* in Spain as part of the *reconquista*. "[*Cabildos*] apparently originated in efforts of the municipal authorities in Sevilla . . . to organize (and thereby control) the large numbers of mendicant blacks and mulattoes swarming their cities since the late 15th century, and quickly diffused to . . . Havana around the turn of the 17th century [where] large numbers of '*negros horros'* and highly mobile slaves had similarly become an administrative problem" (Palmie 1993:341).

Among Africans in Cuba, however, this structure converged with familiar patterns of West African secret societies (Ortiz 1921). Spain's solution to her perceived "administrative problem" provided people of color in Cuba, both slave and free, with an administrative structure of their own that they, in turn, were able to mobilize against Spain.

Cabildos were explicitly intended as an instrument of social control. Leaders of the *cabildos*, called captains, were legally responsible for their members' behavior, inducing the Afro-Cuban leadership to police the masses. The *cabildos* also were viewed as a recreational safety valve for a very large subordinated caste, offering distractions in social rituals and entertainment to absorb restless energy. In reinforcing distinctions of language and ethnicity, they sought to fragment and divide the larger African population. Organizations for African Cubans, to which white Cubans did not belong, also provided for orderly social separation between Hispano-Cubans and their colored compatriots. Counterpoising these strategic benefits, however, were the organizational and fund-raising capacities thereby conferred on Afro-Cubans, which they could and did use as the basis of insurrections.

Aponte's uprising of 1812 resulted from a multilateral conspiracy involving a network of *cabildos*, representing all the major tribal groups, spread across the length of the island. Aponte was the captain of the Cabildo Shango Tedum in Havana, which was Yoruba. In the course of planning his uprising, he managed to effect an alliance that included *cabildos* that were Mandinga, Carabali, Ashanti, Bakongo, and Mina. As well, he had forged ties with former insurgents from Haiti and free blacks and abolitionists in the United States (Howard 1998:76). The 1835 plot similarly originated in a *cabildo*. One of its leaders, Juan Nepomuceno Prieto, was captain of the Cabildo Lucumi Ello u Oyo, also a Yoruba association (Rushing 1992:274–77). Although the role of the *cabildos* in the later Conspiracy of the Ladder is less clearly established, some of the principal instigators were members of these organizations, and *cabildos* were temporarily disbanded in its aftermath (Paquette 1988:109).

The establishment of *cabildos* offered unintended opportunities for displaced Africans and their creole offspring to marshal the power of collective organization. Included, perhaps paramount, among the weapons of resistance, was religion. As in many other settings where the imposition of colonial religion gave birth to creative syncretism, Afro-Cuban *cabildos* offered a framework for implanting and reinvigorating African sources of mystical power. Among those arrested after La Escalera was one described as a "slave sorcerer . . . convicted of selling *brujerías* (magic charms) to make one invincible" (Hall 1971:58). Others implicated in the plot were accused of using witchcraft and fetishes as part of their strategy. Although Spanish officials dismissed these efforts as "ignorant," belief in the super-natural powers of African magic was prevalent among the whites of Cuba, whose European belief system also included "witches who sucked the blood of children and flew on broomsticks to celebrate their Sabbath" (Ortiz 1993:27). Predisposed to view African religion as "black magic," white Cubans feared its power and thus bolstered its inherent strength.

That Spanish authorities and the Catholic clergy permitted slaves to practice traditional forms of worship is somewhat paradoxical, especially in view of the foregoing concern about sorcery and the backdrop of the Spanish Inquisition. Brandon's (1997:71) thesis is that "Through this guided syncretism the priests hoped that the Africans would be swept up into the mainstream of Cuban Christianity, in time forsaking African cus-toms. In the meantime, the church allowed *cabildo* members to inject an African flavor into the European Christian rites." Hall (1971) has argued that this development was less a result of guidance than an inability to exercise oversight. Plantation owners neglected religious education and efforts at conversion as too expensive and impractical. Urban *cabildos* and the religious practices of slaves in the countryside were thus free to de-velop along the lines of familiar belief systems only thinly veiled as folk Catholicism.

Santería, an Afro-Cuban religion still practiced widely in both contem-porary Cuba and the United States, had its origins in this process. Yoruba deities were renamed as Catholic saints, and Catholic ritual observances were adopted and adapted. Canizares (1993) regards this transformation as "dissimulation" rather than syncretism. However the Catholic veneer on Santería may be interpreted, the context within which it emerged enabled a consolidation of influence that drew heavily on African sources. Divina-tion and healing, the capacity to effect magical outcomes, lent power to the practice of Santería and attracted followers broadly throughout Cuban so-ciety (Bascom 1950; Brandon 1991; Duany 1982). On a more secular level, *cabildos* offered concrete settings and institutional resources within which, and by means of which, they could define and carry out collective actions of various sorts, including conspiracies against their oppressors.

In the United States during this same period, free blacks also developed institutions based on religion and mutual aid. As in Cuba, religion became a central organizing principle in African American social structure. There are some similarities, but many differences in the manner in which this was configured. Most basic were the contrasts in denominational affiliation; Cuba was predominantly Catholic, and the United States was mainly Protestant. Klein (1966), in an early discussion of differences between slavery in Cuba and the United States, suggested that the value systems associated with these different forms of Christianity had produced distinct modes of treatment of slaves, with Catholics the more benign. This analysis has met considerable challenge as simplistic and overly idealist (Góveia 1966; Scott 1985a:14). A different approach to such a comparison, however, involves the structural implications of these different systems, the manner in which church institutions were organized and controlled. Also important are relationships between church and state, and between church leaders and slavery. How did the religious infrastructure of these two colonial systems influence the options and responses of Africans who were incorporated into the national societies that emerged in Cuba and the United States?

In Cuba Catholicism was a state religion, rigidly hierarchical and firmly connected to colonial domination. The colonies that gathered into the United States were established explicitly to separate church from state, and were fractiously divided into autonomous Protestant sects. Religion was pervasive in early U.S. politics, but it was not centralized, and Africans were incorporated into religious organizations in a far less systematic way.

Quakers opposed slavery on theological grounds, and the Great Awakenings (1720–40 and 1790–1815), which swelled the ranks of Baptists and Methodists, reflected mystical themes of liberation and personal relationships with God that inescapably conflicted with human bondage. The strength of these contradictions contributed to the eventual abolition of slavery (although not an end to racism) in northern states, drawing the sharp geographic divide from the slaveholding South.

Baptist and Methodist missionaries in the South learned to accommodate and embrace the notion that African bondage was ordained by God, a compromise that enabled the establishment of churches in that field. A split in Methodism over slavery led to the creation of the Methodist Episcopal Church South in 1844 (Simpson 1978:225). Baptists also contended over these issues, and the national Baptist church also split between north and south in 1845 (Lincoln and Mamiya 1990:25). For the Southern churches, the problem remained of how to bring religion to slaves without encouraging rebellion.

Religious instruction was designed to reinforce control, to persuade the slaves that their condition was a sacred duty, that rewards for piety awaited them in the afterlife. However contorted the presentation of scripture, Old Testament tales of delivery from bondage in Egypt and New Testament gospels of redemption nevertheless offered mobilizing themes for slave rebellions. Gabriel Prosser, Denmark Vesey, and Nat Turner, the best-known plotters of slave revolts in the South, were all biblically inspired exhorters. After three serious rebellions in thirty years (between 1800 and 1831), severe restrictions were placed on slave religion; unsupervised congregation was illegal, black preachers were banned, and it was against the law to teach slaves to read and write. Until after the Civil War, the practice of religion by slaves in the South was formally confined to attendance at white churches or revivals conducted by white evangelists, the pattern that existed in antebellum Florida.

Northern churches, where black members were free, and where many white Christians explicitly opposed slavery, followed a different course. In most places, African Americans developed separate congregations and several specifically black denominations. These separations arose in response to racist treatment by leaders and members of white churches, who denied them a voice in church affairs and physically segregated them during worship—a curious distinction having been drawn between theological abstractions and everyday life in a racial hierarchy. The earliest all-black denomination was the African Methodist Episcopal (AME), formally established in Philadelphia in 1815. Richard Allen, the founder, had been a Methodist preacher who withdrew from the church in 1787, following an incident when his friend, Absalom Jones, was pulled from his knees while praying and forcibly shoved into the "black" section of the church. Several months prior to this rupture, Allen and Jones had been leaders in a mutual aid society, called the Free Africa Society, composed of forty black Methodists who all attended the same white Methodist church. This organization provided the initial framework for the new church. A similar progression occurred in other northern states—Maryland, Delaware, Pennsylvania, and New Jersey—where early mutual aid societies gave birth to churches (Woodson 1929).

From the beginning, the AME Church was dedicated to ending slavery in the United States. AME churches served as stations in the Underground

Railroad, helping slaves who escaped from the South. During the Civil War, as escaped and confiscated slaves were gathered into Union army camps, AME missionaries followed the troops and began converting and instructing new members (Simpson 1978; Hildebrand 1995). Membership in the AME Church swelled from these efforts, and hundreds of new AME churches were formed in the South during and after the war. The AME Zion Church, another breakaway black denomination formed in 1801 in New York City, under circumstances very similar to those confronting Allen and Jones, also developed missionary activities towards the end of the war (Lincoln and Mamiya 1990:56).

Black Baptists in the North remained affiliated with the white denomination, but in segregated congregations. Baptist organization involves considerable autonomy in local churches, and the black congregations became strongly aligned with abolition and the Underground Railroad. Black Baptists also undertook missionary work in the South after the end of the war, stimulating the explosive growth of independent black Baptist churches in the South.

The AME Church, which had the greatest autonomy and grew very large in the period leading up to the Civil War, spearheaded black efforts to end slavery. In its aftermath, the leaders of this denomination mobilized a new army of preachers and teachers who fanned out across the South attempting to organize freed slaves and help mitigate their suffering. These evangelists, especially the preachers, would play a very significant role in Reconstruction politics in Florida and elsewhere in the defeated Confederacy. Black Baptists were also on the scene, playing similar roles in religion, education, and politics. In all these realms, and especially the latter, Baptists and Methodists were highly competitive with each other, a factor that weighed heavily against success in the perilous environment of Florida politics in the late 1860s.

The ascendancy of black churches in the U.S. South paralleled a period of decline in the Cuban *cabildos*. During the 1860s, the growing threat of insurgency encouraged a new wave of repression by Spain, including a law enacted in 1864 aimed at preventing Cuban-born children from joining their parents' *cabildos* (Howard 1998:111). They hoped to rid the nation of *cabildos* through attrition, that is, with the eventual passing of the present generation of members. New taxes and more rigorous official oversight were also imposed. Although the government was ultimately not successful in doing away with the *cabildos*, the increased repression impeded their operation and gave impetus to the formation of new kinds of organizations. Many younger Afro-Cubans disdained the tribal aspects of their parents' organizations and eagerly sought acculturation and acceptance within the larger Cuban society. Motives of the members of a *cabildo* who sought to reorganize as an instructional society were explained as follows: "As they lived in a society of culture and progress, they wanted to learn the most elementary notions of human knowledge in order to deserve the consideration of the more educated social classes and not to remain in the state of ignorance and backwardness in which they were born under the sun of the African coast" (quoted in Helg 1995:30). This proffered explanation, in which members of a beleaguered organization were seeking sanction to continue to exist, is open to several interpretations. They may have been dissembling to fool the authorities, or they genuinely may have believed that their African legacies needed to be expunged, or maybe both of these tendencies were at play.

The *sociedades mutuo socorro y recreo* (mutual aid and recreational societies) were directly patterned on the mutual benefit societies established by Spanish immigrants and workers in particular Cuban industries, especially cigar workers (Howard 1998; MacGaffey 1961; Stubbs 1985). These organizations, nineteenth-century descendants of the early Spanish *cofradías*, returned to Cuba with a massive influx of poor Spaniards recruited by the Crown for the explicit purpose of increasing the relative size of Cuba's white population (a policy known as "whitening"). They provided economic benefits to members, including medical care and education, and sponsored social activities. Afro-Cubans were quite familiar with how this was done, based on prior experience in *cabildos* and readily developed similar organizations of their own. Whereas the *cabildos* betokened separation, the mutual aid societies urged incorporation. "Pan-Afro-Cuban societies were concerned primarily with providing their members with the means to gain social justice and equality, while the *cabildos* were established to maintain and promote their members' African customs" (Howard 1998:241).

The mutual aid societies emphasized education and acceptance of Spanish culture as the means of attaining equality. Membership criteria eschewed tribalism, and members were drawn from among those Afro-Cubans who resided in the same locality, or who shared the same occupations, or who had other kinds of common interests. They also established schools, libraries, and newspapers, and in the latter part of the nineteenth century became heavily involved in civil rights activities on behalf of Cubans of color. This new type of voluntary association spread rapidly throughout Cuba, and ultimately gave rise to more than one hundred Afro-Cuban newspapers (Deschamps Chapeaux 1963). These publications became organs of acculturation as well as race consciousness, exhorting the readers to improve their morals and hygiene and to assert their rights as citizens of the nation (Orum 1975:25). Juan Gualberto Gómez, born in 1854, emerged as the central figure in this movement. As the new system of *sociedades* was developing, he and other Afro-Cuban leaders sought to coordinate the power of these institutions not only for self-help, but also for revolution against Spain.

The institutions that Africans fashioned in Cuba and the United States, institutions aimed at resolving the social, economic, political, and spiritual dilemmas of their racial status in society, followed distinctive pathways forged out of divergent circumstances. Mutual aid of an increasingly secular variety characterized the Cuban path. Religion had two faces: the dour dominance of Catholicism and the subterranean resistance of Santería and other African beliefs. Catholic domination was linked to colonial control, easing the disloyalty of Afro-Cubans who fought against both. In the United States, by contrast, Africans created religious institutions in uneasy collaboration with Protestant sects directly connected to the ruling interests. Plurality in those interests, both sectarian and regional, aligned with divisions enacted in the African churches. These schisms and cross-connections were more fractious in their political consequences for African Americans than was tribal divisiveness among the Afro-Cuban *cabildos*. The *cabildos* were constituted on ideological charters of African provenance, whereas the AME and other U.S. black denominations were held by reins of Christian doctrine. The later Afro-Cuban mutual aid societies repudiated, at least overtly, the African traditions of the precursor *cabildos*, but they did not embrace Catholicism in the process.

Not all African American institutions were religious. The churches began in mutual aid societies, and these economic organizations proliferated in both the North and South after the Civil War (Greenbaum 1991; Harris 1936; Woodson 1929), stimulating the growth of banking, insurance, and self-help. Black leadership also represented business and education, and included secular activists like Frederick Douglass and Sojourner Truth, who met in periodic national "conventions" to discuss political strategies and organize action (Meier 1963:4–10). These conventions were both similar to, and a model for, the network of mutual aid societies that Juan Gualberto Gómez and his colleagues developed in Cuba. Nonetheless, the overarching influence of religious leaders and organizations in the United

States, and especially in the South, was a principal contrast between the institutional systems of Africans in Cuba and Florida during the nineteenth century.

1868–1878: War and Reconstruction

A crucial decade for Afro-Cubans and African Americans in Florida, the period between 1868 and 1878 bracketed in both places an unparalleled ascendance of black political aspirations, punctuated by defeat and betrayal. In the United States, the Civil War ended in 1865 with the emancipation of all slaves. The process of "Reconstruction," a massive challenge with much of the South lying in ruins, placed heavy demands on the organizational infrastructure that had developed among free blacks in northern states, but also ushered in extraordinary new opportunities for political involvement in the vanquished southern states. In Cuba during the same period, unresolved grievances against Spanish economic and political control were boiling into open rebellion. The issue of slavery, perhaps made more insistent by abolition in the United States, was a central factor in the emergent insurrection. By the end of 1869, about twelve thousand Afro-Cubans, both free and bound, had joined the war, not only bolstering the forces on the ground but also bringing to the fore important military and civilian leaders like Juan Gualberto Gómez and the incomparable Antonio Maceo. Maceo, in particular, became a lightning rod for racist contradictions among the rebel forces (Howard 1998:109).

Afro-Cuban organizations, both *cabildos* and the mutual aid societies, played an important role in the insurrection. Fearing that the black organizations might become involved, the Spanish began clamping down on their activities. El Liceo Artistico, a black mutual aid society in Sancti Spíritus, was closed by the authorities in 1870. Immediately in response, the members took up arms and joined the insurrection (Howard 1998: 109). The Abakua society also supported the insurgents and its members took part in the revolt. Known also as *nañigos*, members of Abakua were part of a secret underworld, feared as witches and gangsters, wielding powers that were hard to tame or control (Ortiz 1921; Palmie 1994; Rodríguez Sosa 1982).

Constituting more than a third of the population of Cuba, and a far greater proportion of the non-Spanish-born Cubans, Afro-Cubans held the key to success in winning independence from Spain. Their interests in the struggle could not be ignored. For these reasons, black participation in the 1868 rebellion signaled the ultimate end of slavery in Cuba and helped to intrude demands for social justice and racial equality into the political platform of the independence forces. Independence, however, would not come for another thirty years, and the abolition of slavery took nearly as long.

Cuba's Ten Years' War was directly responsible for the first colony of exiled Cubans in Florida, in Key West, founded by cigar manufacturers and their workers in 1869 (Poyo 1989). Tobacco was Cuba's second most important crop. The industry in Cuba was complex and vertically integrated, combining small holding reminiscent of the settler era and preindustrial relations quite different from those involved in sugar production (Stubbs 1985). Fernando Ortiz, Cuba's most celebrated ethnologist, devoted an entire treatise to the contrast between sugar and tobacco (Ortiz 1947), a transcendental analysis of the symbolic significance of these products in forging Cuban identity. From Ortiz's perspective, tobacco was the protagonist in this metaphorical contest over the soul of *cubanidad*. Dark and pungent or light and sweet, color forms a heavy subtext and is intertwined with themes of rebellion. Cigarmakers were among the vanguard of Cuban insurgency, and cigarmaking was a vocation heavily populated with Afro-Cubans.

Cuban cigars were (and still are) premium in the world market. Climate and soil in the province of Pinar del Río yield tobacco plants of extraordinarily fine quality. Converting raw material into finished cigars required finely honed skills, an artistry in hand production that bestowed cigarmakers with a reputation for independence and pugnacious pride. Literacy, political awareness, and organizing in pursuit of common goals were prominent matters of concern among nineteenth-century cigar workers in Cuba. In the late 1850s, cigarmakers in Havana instituted a custom known as *la lectura*. The workers pooled funds to hire a reader to entertain and educate them while they sat at their benches making cigars.

"The cigar maker is a worker, who, through his tradition of struggle, his discussion on the shop floor, the daily readings of his press and literary works . . . has a cultural veneer which makes him feel superior in this respect to other workers. . . . The cigar maker is a sworn polemicist. He loves discussions and this can be explained in terms of the way he works and his wide knowledge. There are daily debates in and out of work and there are times when they gain such impetus that the whole gallery takes part" (quoted in Stubbs 1985:88). Workplace traditions of the cigar workers aroused their political sensibilities and shaped their revolutionary aspirations. Within this context of labor militancy and patriotic activism Afro-Cuban cigarmakers developed beliefs and intentions that they brought with them in exile, first to Key West and later to Tampa—during the long interlude between 1868 and 1898 in which they helped plan and execute the war against Spain. As Cubans of color, their motives in effecting revolution also included beliefs and experiences that arose from slavery, and from the restless ghosts of martyred leaders in La Escalera.

At the time of their arrival, Key West was also a major stronghold of Republican activism in Florida. Afro-Cubans and African Americans were briefly involved with each other in this setting, in common pursuit of electoral and labor politics (Poyo 1983:230–36), but it was a short alliance in a losing struggle.

Florida's population in the 1860s was 47 percent black. Many white residents had been disenfranchised for their participation in the Civil War, whereas freed slaves had won the right to vote. Black votes were the key to Republican control of Florida politics. Black men (only men could vote) who were poised to take advantage of this circumstance, who sought to use this opportunity to recast power and ease terrible conditions, faced a formidable challenge. Too formidable.

At the state's first Republican convention in 1867, fifty of eighty-two delegates were black (Klingman 1982). A sizable number of black elected officials gained and held office in Florida during the late 1860s and '70s; 111 African Americans were elected to the state legislature between 1868 and 1889, and one, Josiah Walls, served in the U.S. Congress (Brown 1998). Although their numbers were large, divisions between them weakened their position, and very few of their white allies were willing to support their interests to any great extent. Race was an ever present source of tension among the Republican forces in Florida. More conservative elements, including the head of the Florida Freedmen's Bureau, Thomas Osborne, deliberately courted once-powerful planters and other ex-Confederates, and cynically manipulated black leaders through demagoguery and patronage. Most of the Baptist leaders were allied with Osborne in an organization he formed called the Lincoln Brotherhood. The AME leaders were allied with the radicals; they formed a group known as the Mule Team. True radicals among the white Republicans in Florida, dedicated abolitionists and incipient populists, were few in number (Klingman 1982). The Mule Team struggled to find reliable allies among the loyalists and carpetbaggers, and they struggled with the Lincoln Brotherhood, and they occasionally did battle with each other. The cadre of black leaders who emerged in post–Civil War Florida, both Baptist and AME, were forced to negotiate alliances with former slaveholders and whites who strongly believed in black inferiority.

The unofficial, but decisive, players in the scenario, the forces with which there could be no negotiation, were the night riders of the Ku Klux Klan. Black electoral strength depended on black voters casting their ballots. Terror was an effective weapon in this contest for white power. In rural areas throughout the state, especially in the central counties where blacks were a numerical majority, political violence was largely unchecked, even after imposition of Military Reconstruction in 1867. Measures to police this behavior, introduced by black legislators in the capital at Tallahassee, were easily defeated by coalitions of white lawmakers who tacitly approved of the effects.

The statewide network of churches played an important part in the unfolding struggle to win black rights. Greatest gains were made after the 1872 election of Ossian B. Hart, a loyalist Republican lawyer who practiced for a time in Tampa (Brown 1997b). Hart's election was due in large measure to black support, especially from the AME leaders. Hart died suddenly in 1874, however, and his successor was drawn from the opposing faction of the party, including black Baptist leaders, but more importantly, the stridently antiblack conservatives. These latter Republicans later formed what was known as the "Lily White" Republicans, a move that hastened the death of the party in Florida. Democrats regained control in 1876, and Reconstruction also died. Similar scenarios unfolded in all parts of the South following the election of Rutherford B. Hayes and the removal of the armed occupation forces. A new era, labeled "Redemption," was beginning, a period of extreme violence and repression that would endure for nearly a century.

In Cuba the fortunes of the rebels were also turning sour. Unstable alliances between blacks and whites were a significant problem in that arena as well. The Spanish effectively exploited widespread fears of *el peligro negro*. Some sectors of the rebel leadership were openly racist and had initially favored purging Cuba of its African population and their insidious influences on Cuban culture and society. Others, especially the slaveholders, were highly susceptible to fears that the large number of blacks in the rebellion threatened to turn it into a black-controlled government, as in Haiti (Duharte Jimenez 1993). Although they recognized the need to court black demands, they also struggled to maintain control of the Afro-Cuban forces and wrestled internally with divisiveness over the race issue. In the

end, the dissentions within the rebel leadership hobbled their military effectiveness and so weakened their resolve that they were forced to surrender (Ferrer 1999). Belligerence was terminated by the Pact of Zanjón on
February 10, 1878. Antonio Maceo refused to sign the pact, and in the
following year attempted to resuscitate the rebellion in a short-lived
struggle known as La Guerra Chiquita (the Little War) (Ferrer 1991). The
failure of this effort drove Maceo and several other Afro-Cuban leaders
into exile.

The exiled cigar workers in Key West hunkered down to prepare for the
next uprising. Black and white workers labored together in the factories
and in the revolutionary clubs and newspapers that they formed. The political environment of Florida was becoming increasingly less hospitable to
such arrangements, although the remote location of the key helped ame-
liorate the effects. By 1878, the Democrats were in firm control of the legislature, courts, and the governor's office. The number of black elected officials plummeted, although some managed to retain office through the
next decade. Any collective power they might have held had been ruthlessly vanquished. Churches were burned, leaders assassinated, and prospective voters intimidated. Religious leaders, AME as well as Baptist,
withdrew from politics and embraced new roles of moral tutelage and
spiritual salvation (Rivers and Brown 2001).

In the aftermath of these struggles in Cuba and Florida, both of which
involved black-white alliances fraught with tension, the defeated Cubans
rededicated themselves to healing the breach. In Florida, victorious whites
pursued extreme measures to widen the distance between themselves and
black adversaries.

Cubans were not finished with their project, just temporarily at peace.
They all recognized that maintaining a combined force of black and white
was critical if they hoped to win. Ferrer (1999:112–38) offers a lucid analysis of Cuban nationalist rhetoric in the period following the Ten Years'
War, in which she argues that discussions of race were carefully refash-
ioned to assuage white fears. Accounts of the rebellion deliberately emphasized the sacrifice and bravery of black rebels, the comradeship of war, and
the gratitude and loyalty of freed slaves. These messages, although calculated to promote acceptance of black participation, were nuanced. "Equality
was cast as a gift of the white leadership, and the black slave, knowing it
was a gift, enjoyed it respectfully and obediently. The transgression of
boundaries that allowed him to challenge colonialism and slavery was, in
these writings, less a transgression than an extension of his subservience

to a white insurgent master. And his heroism was one grounded in gratitude and unrelated to black political desire" (Ferrer 1999:121).

The sexual, as well as political, threat of black involvement was also
neutralized in these renderings. Patriotism was a masculine affair, a bond
between black and white men forged in shared death on the battlefield, but
not in the mingling of blood in miscegenation. This emphasis had two implications. "First, the vision of a transracial Cuba essentially left intact racial categories like white and black, even as it argued for their transcen-
dence. And second, the making of a transracial nation in war—and not in
sex—excluded women from the symbolic birth of the nation" (Ferrer
1999:126–27). Gendered images of nationhood upheld the boundaries between black and white, as well as those between men and women, contradictions that will be explored more fully later on.

In Florida, and elsewhere in the South, writers and editorialists were
also engaged in the production of rhetoric, in defining black and white
roles in the recently concluded era of Reconstruction. The messages of this
tradition, which began appearing in 1878 with a published account titled
The Prostrate State (James S. Pike, cited in Lewis 1992:vii), demonized
white Republicans and reserved special vitriol for their black allies. The
extremity of this portrait, the implications it held for the position of blacks
in the post-Reconstruction South, are epitomized in Thomas Dixon's later
book *The Clansman*, published in 1905 and serving as inspiration for the
film *Birth of a Nation*. In this drama: "The Negro was a brute, and Reconstruction a tragedy beyond all bearing. The Negro was not a citizen and an
equal, not even a child as yet unprepared. He was a semisavage descendant
of an old and degenerate animal race. 'For a thick-lipped, flat-nosed,
spindle-shanked negro, exuding his nauseating animal odour, to shout in
derision over the hearths and homes of white men and women is an atroc-
ity too monstrous for belief'" (cited in Chalmers 1965:25).

Whereas the Cuban writers of nationhood were manipulating nuances to devise a comfortable charter for black-white cooperation, white
southerners were crafting an uncompromising polemic of absolute separation based in biology. The latter images were also gendered. Sex between
the races was viewed as an unnatural act, and sex between black men and
white women was an abomination justifying the most heinous acts of violence.

The institutions of black people in Cuba and Florida were much affected
by changes in the 1880s. *Cabildos* continued to suffer repression, although
many simply went underground. Slavery in Cuba ended in 1886, a gradual

process in which the newer Afro-Cuban *sociedades* had an important role to play. Although Spanish authorities were wary about black organizations' prior involvement in the Ten Years' War, the huge task of transitioning former slaves into free laborers encouraged reliance on the social and educational programs of those organizations. In 1885, leaders of the Afro-Cuban societies formed an umbrella organization called the El Directorio Central de la Raza de Color; by 1892 it included members from sixty-five Afro-Cuban mutual aid societies throughout the island (Helg 1995:39). Juan Gualberto Gómez, who returned from exile in 1890 and assumed leadership of El Directorio Central, coordinated and encouraged the development of schools, libraries, and newspapers. In his widely circulated publications (*La Igualidad* and *La Fraternidad*), he also spoke out against divisions into *pardo* and *moreno* societies, arguing that all were part of *la raza de color*, "children of the same trunk, made brothers by common affronts and common disgraces" (quoted in Helg 1995:39). He was not advocating racial separatism, but merely pointing out that both blacks and mulattoes were excluded from the white societies. Cubans of color were forced to develop social organizations of their own, a contradiction of racial democracy that passed largely without comment. Silence about race included failure to mention a significant example of racial segregation, as if social separation were somehow "natural." In this oversight, the strength and importance of these institutions in combating the shadowy circumstances of racism have been overlooked as well.

In Florida, the networks of black churches continued to function as local and statewide leadership structures. Although primary targets in the early stages of redemption, white authorities were more interested in taming than in destroying the churches of freed slaves. Pastors of these churches made a strategic retreat from political engagement; those who persisted in such activities were forced from the field.

There was a brief attempt in the 1880s to develop alliances with the Knights of Labor, a multiracial labor movement that was then sweeping the South (Brown 1997c; Brown 1998; McLaurin 1978). The Knights in the South were easily vanquished by powerful external resistance and debilitating internal problems. The organization's radical platform, and especially its biracial composition, attracted fierce opposition from employers and conservative white politicians. Inside the organization as well, black and white members had difficulty cooperating and were divided into segregated assemblies. Florida's organization, whose main strength was in Jacksonville, was notoriously fractious (McLaurin 1978:178).

The Knights collapsed, nationally and in Florida, by the 1890s. The demise of this movement left black church leaders in Florida with very few white allies, and with little choice but to turn their attention inward. Roles of black pastors shifted away from civil rights activism and onto the moral education of the former slaves. In this work, their posture towards white authority was inevitably accommodationist. Defiance invited harm to themselves and their congregates. Denominational divisions, which continued to proliferate in addition to AME and Baptist, and legacies of competition during Reconstruction, made coordination of efforts and resources more difficult.

Although segregation in Florida resulted in all-black organizations, and self-determination existed by default, these conditions did not encourage solidarity, nor did they produce power. In the larger connections these institutions had to their national conventions and the broader range of activities that took place in northern states, there was access to power and political determination that in the long run would produce real change. When the Cuban cigarmakers arrived in Tampa in 1886, however, the local African American community was cowed and divided. Its leaders and organizations must have appeared very feeble in comparison with the strong voice of El Directorio, or the military might of Maceo and the other black Cuban generals.

3

José Martí and Jim Crow

The powerful antiracist messages of José Martí, the "apostle" of Cuban liberty, stood in ironic contrast to the extreme racism visited on black people in Florida at the close of the nineteenth century—the tightening noose of Jim Crow. Within the exile Cuban community in Tampa, particularly for Afro-Cubans, these contradictory circumstances reinforced a sense of Cuban nationhood based explicitly on racial inclusion. This notion of inclusiveness was not unproblematic, a theme explored in Chapter 2. However, in the flush of the coming battle for independence, among exiled patriots in a strange and dangerous land, solidarity between black and white Cubans reached its apogee. At this same time, relations between African Americans and their white neighbors, former allies and adversaries alike, were rapidly polarizing in formal structures of exclusion and racial belligerence.

This chapter describes the arrival of Afro-Cubans in Tampa and the development of an exile enclave that was almost totally absorbed with the liberation of Cuba. The period bracketed begins in 1886 and concludes in 1898, a brief but crucial twelve years that included not only the run-up to Cuban independence, but also the *Plessy v. Ferguson* decision by the U.S. Supreme Court that legally anointed the doctrine of "separate but equal" in the United States.

More than a century after his death, José Martí's image still inspires patriotic fervor in Cubans on both sides of the Florida Strait. Ownership of Martí's legacy remains one of the most bitterly contested stakes in the ongoing conflict between Miami and Havana (Kirk 1985; Ripoll 1994). For Afro-Cubans in early Ybor City, however, Martí was more than a disembodied icon of contradictory dreams. He was flesh and blood; a friend and guardian to the black and white cigarmakers of Tampa, who helped him plan the revolution against Spain. His words to them came straight from his lips. The men and women who later founded the Martí-Maceo Society included individuals who had known him well, who could still visualize him, and who had inspected his persona fully in the round. José Martí's beliefs and ideas profoundly shaped the exile community of Cuban cigarmakers. For the black cigarmakers, especially, his message of racial justice resonated with yearnings that were centuries old.

Cubans in Florida

Florida's cigarmaker communities originated in Cuba's Ten Years' War (1868–78). Shortly after the outbreak of hostilities, part of the cigar industry moved north across the strait. War was the major push factor, but U.S. trade policies exerted considerable pull. United States tariffs discouraged importation of cigars, but not tobacco. Cigars made in Florida, with imported Cuban tobacco and labor, eluded the expensive tariff on cigars made in Cuba. Key West, officially U.S. soil, was only ninety miles from Cuba's shoreline. Cigar manufacturers who supported independence from Spain reasoned that by exiling their operations to Florida, they could avoid persecution, aid the revolution, and greatly increase their profits. Over the next few decades, major cigarmaking centers were established in Key West and Tampa, and smaller operations were built in Jacksonville, St. Augustine, Gainesville, and Ocala (Poyo 1989; 1986a).

Although intended to strengthen the manufacturers' position, the move set the stage for penetration and ultimate control of the Cuban cigar industry by the voracious U.S. Tobacco Trust. As early as the 1850s, U.S. companies had used tariffs to gain a foothold in the "clear Havana" tobacco trade (Stubbs 1985:19). Responding to the low tariffs on raw tobacco, warehouses in Havana exported large quantities of leaf to New York, where cigars were produced cheaply in factories and through outwork. Domestic products made with Cuban tobacco outcompeted the more expensive imports, weakening both labor and capital in Cuba. Spanish authorities failed to intervene, refusing manufacturers' demands for export restrictions on tobacco. This costly inattention motivated most Cuban cigar manufacturers to support independence from Spain, and many longed for annexation by the United States. Seeking alliances with their competitors to the north was hazardous, however, and U.S. interests eventually did come to dominate the industry, both in Florida and Cuba (Stubbs 1985).

The gradual expropriation of the Cuban tobacco industry by the United States reflected the same forces that also transformed the Cuban independence movement into the "Spanish-American War." In their efforts to oust Spain, the Cubans faced two very difficult, and ultimately insurmountable, challenges. They needed to maintain harmony among their own forces and autonomous control of the revolutionary process. Racial conflict was a significant threat to harmony among Cubans, whose military capacity greatly depended on black involvement, but whose civilian leadership was nearly all white. In relations with the United States, racism was also a threat to the position of Cubans in an alliance. Self-serving beliefs about the natural superiority of Anglo-Americans authorized domineering, rapacious conduct in U.S. foreign affairs. An intricately contrived racial hierarchy consigned Cubans of any color to a relatively low position, and those who were black were particularly close to the bottom.

The first Cuban settlement in Florida was at Key West. A Spanish émigré cigar manufacturer named Vincente Martínez Ybor established the first new factory there in 1869. He was soon joined in the move by several other factory owners. Cuban cigarmakers began pouring into Key West. Production there climbed from 8.5 million cigars in 1869 to 25 million in 1875. Cessation of hostilities in Cuba three years later did little to discourage the growth of this new Florida industry. By 1880, Key West's factories had increased from 4 to 44, and by 1885 there were 90 factories employing 2,811 mostly Cuban cigarmakers (Poyo 1983:207). With this growth, Key West emerged as an extremely important center of Cuban insurrectionist activities. Although a Spaniard by birth, Ybor actively supported independence for Cuba. Many other factory owners shared his grievances against the colonial regime.

Cigarmakers, as well as manufacturers, had been involved in the early stages of the independence movement, and this interest continued in exile. Worker-led revolutionary organizations had sprung up in Key West almost immediately, and the cigarmakers began to vie with the more elite New York–based leadership over ideological control of Cuban independence (Poyo 1983). Conflicting interests of capitalists and aristocrats versus workers and abolitionists were no less salient in exile than they had been in Cuba. Separatist cigar manufacturers were joined in an uneasy alliance with their independence-minded workers. This somewhat unnatural state of affairs restrained labor activism, but did not eliminate discontent over wages and working conditions.

The end of the Ten Years' War brought a hiatus in the patriotic partnership between workers and owners, which gave birth to a new tobacco workers union in Key West and a strike in 1879. Although workers were initially successful, the manufacturers rallied in 1881, refusing to recognize their union. In that same year, a labor organizer was murdered in Key West, presumably at the behest of one of the factory owners (Poyo 1983:221).

Resumption of rebel conspiracies brought Antonio Maceo and Máximo Gómez (also a general in the Cuban revolutionary army) to Key West in 1885, where the cigar manufacturers pledged strong support for the next insurrection. Unmoved by their employers' patriotic generosity, cigar workers struck in August of that year. The strike posed a dilemma for the revolution. Manufacturers staunchly held out, and when the strike fund was depleted, strikers got offers of support from the Spanish, eager as always to capitalize on dissension among the rebel factions. Revolutionary leaders in New York intervened in the negotiations between strikers and owners, and an agreement was reached. However, the workers remained skeptical about the patrician motives of the revolutionary command, and the manufacturers took steps to preempt future labor unrest. One measure taken was a large-scale relocation of cigar factories up the west coast of Florida to the small port town of Tampa (Poyo 1983:213).

Ybor, who had started the first factory in Key West, also pioneered in the move to Tampa. A few months after the Key West strike in 1885, Ybor and a group of Cuban and Spanish cigar manufacturers from New York made a deal with the Tampa Board of Trade. In exchange for pledges to build a cigar industry in Tampa, the local business group agreed to subsidize purchase of land. Importantly, they also offered assurances of labor peace (Westfall 1985:10–11). Although he initially planned to build only a small factory in Tampa, a massive fire in Key West destroyed Ybor's operations there in 1886, prompting him to abandon that city and concentrate all his holdings in Tampa. Other manufacturers also established factories in this new site.

Within the decade of the 1880s Tampa's population ballooned—from 720 to nearly 6,000. The cigar industry was not the only factor responsible for this explosive growth, but it was a major contributor. Nearly a third of the newcomers were Cuban (1,313) and Spanish (233) cigarmakers and their families. About 15 percent of the Cubans were black. There was a small influx of West Indians, some of whom were involved with cigars, and the others working on the docks. Recent arrivals also included a small group of Italians who initially had been lured into Central Florida to cut sugarcane (Mormino and Pozzetta 1987), and a small number of Romanian Jews who came to Tampa with the factories, or to open businesses (Apte 1998; Brown 1999). Not all of the new arrivals were immigrants. Tampa's booming growth of the 1880s more than tripled the size of the native-born white population, and the African American population (not counting new black immigrants) increased by 534 percent (Mohlman 1995:77). Cuban exiles in Tampa did not enter an established host community, but rather arrived in the midst of a vast economic and demographic transformation that affected all of the groups involved.

Ybor City

The immigrant cigar workers settled onto a ninety-acre tract situated to the east of Tampa's small commercial center. This subdivision was owned by the Ybor City Land and Improvement Company, of which V. M. Ybor was president. Ybor City, as it was named, was annexed into the city limits in 1887, in spite of strong resistance from the recently formed company that owned it (Westfall 1985). Lying between Ybor City and the commercial center of Tampa was the African American settlement known as the Scrub, which increased greatly in size and density during the 1880s.

Well buffered from the heart of the host community, Ybor City developed into a relatively insular geographic enclave. Separatism was enhanced by the fact that the factory owners, as well as the workers, were foreigners. There were few pressures or incentives to "Americanize." Doctors, shopkeepers, and virtually everyone who had contact with each other in Ybor City spoke Spanish. Rarely was it necessary to go outside of the neighborhood. Ybor City during the 1890s was much more a satellite of Cuba than a suburb of Tampa. The largest Cuban settlement in the United States at that time, surpassing Key West, it was also the most mobilized in support of Cuban independence.

Sympathetic factory owners, like Ybor, were instrumental in establishing these conditions, but it was the workers who dominated revolutionary efforts in Tampa. They established organizations to raise funds and newspapers to raise consciousness. Tampa's cigarmakers contributed thousands of dollars to the cause, the largest single source of monetary support for the rebellion. Among the whole of Cuban independence forces, cigarmakers in Tampa and Key West were in the vanguard of fund-raising, speech making, pamphleteering, filibustering, and, ultimately, raising troops to fight against Spain. Workers' visions of a free Cuba, where social justice and economic progress would go hand in hand, differed sharply from those of the wealthy manufacturers, who favored an independent laissez-faire economy similar to the United States (Poyo 1986a; 1986b; 1985a; 1985b).

In spite of their shared goal of defeating Spain, these conflicts were never far from the surface.

Vincente Martínez Ybor was an iron hand in a velvet glove. A refined Spanish gentleman who espoused the ideals of Cuban independence, he was also a serious-minded businessman unsympathetic to the anarcho-syndicalist rhetoric of many of his compatriot workers. He attempted to co-opt the militancy of his new workforce by building a well-planned community. Ybor's settlement provided sound, reasonably priced housing, along with recreational and commercial amenities, including a doctor to see to the workers' medical needs (Westfall 1985). As architect and lord of this new community, Ybor took a paternalistic approach to controlling his restive laborers. He often served as godfather to children born in the new settlement, provided emergency loans to individuals, and sometimes helped to pay funeral expenses. He also sponsored periodic picnics for the workers and at Christmas "dispatched wagons laden with gifts of suckling pigs and pastries for his employees and their families" (Pérez 1985:24).

In the background of Ybor's seigneurial generosity lurked the menacing forces of Tampa's home guard vigilantes, well practiced in the use of extra-legal terror against the Knights of Labor. When cigarmakers in Tampa's new factories struck in 1887, the Board of Trade made good on its commitment to help out with labor problems. An ad hoc "Committee of Fifteen," which included some of Tampa's leading citizens, was appointed to identify the instigators of this trouble and run them out of town (Ingalls 1985:120). This was the first of many such collaborations between Tampa's native business elite and their counterparts among the newly arrived cigar manufacturers.

Politics in late-nineteenth-century Tampa involved complex crosscurrents, which produced both accommodation and conflict between the cigar industry and its host community. The factory owners and the Board of Trade shared a conservative antilabor position that forged strong common interests. In addition, Tampa's white business elite generally embraced the expansionist aims of the United States towards Cuba, which encouraged them to support the independence activities of the manufacturers. Cultural conflicts, however, produced stresses in this relationship. Although wealthy Spaniards and their families gained a degree of acceptance in Tampa's exclusive social circle, their swarthy Cuban workforce was not similarly welcomed. Ybor and his colleagues' struggle to maintain control over their enclave included defending the right to violate local blue laws against liquor and gambling, and to engage in other activities that offended the prudish southern values of native Tampans (Steffy 1975:18–19).

The manufacturers sought to protect their workers against these kinds of encroachments. Partly they were motivated by the belief that such harmless pleasures siphoned off potential discontent and prevented cigar-makers from accumulating savings that could underwrite strikes (Steffy 1975:19). However, support for their workers' rights to cultural self-deter-mination also reflected patriotic sensitivities, and a privately shared view that the Tampa Crackers' air of cultural superiority was both offensive and delusional. To cosmopolitan immigrants from Havana, on the whole far better educated than their hosts, Tampa's backwoods aristocracy and their scruffy little settlement—which was unpaved, unpainted, and infested with mosquitoes, snakes, alligators, and palmetto scrub—were decidedly unimpressive.

Racial etiquette was a particular point of contention. White Tampa re-garded the treatment of Afro-Cuban cigarmakers, who lived and worked side by side with their white compatriots, as distressingly permissive. In Cuba, about one-quarter of cigarmakers were Afro-Cubans (Rushing 1992: 246). This proportion was slightly lower among the Tampa cigarmakers (15 percent, as ascertained from U.S. Census microfilm reels for 1900), but black faces were highly visible among the growing mass of Cuban immi-grant workers. Afro-Cubans were also prominent in revolutionary activi-ties and many joined the ranks of the early labor activists.

The rigid patterns of segregation taking shape in the other parts of Tampa were not replicated in Ybor City. Ybor's master plan for housing included no provision for a Negro section, and cigarmakers' wages de-pended on skill rather than color. As in Cuba, racial discrimination in Ybor City was subtle, consisting of behaviors and attitudes that likely would have escaped the notice of white southerners in Tampa.

With the growth of the cigarmaker communities in Florida, problems related to both class and race loomed ever larger. The Florida colonies were more populous than the Cuban settlement in New York, and the cigarmak-ers were highly dedicated to the cause. Their monetary contributions were crucial to the financial needs of the revolution. In addition, counted among their ranks were several of the most ardent and articulate theorists of the revolution.

Financial well-being in the Florida cigar industry proved an enormous advantage to the revolutionaries, but the money was drawn far more from

wages than profits. Revolutionary clubs became the main vehicle for raising these funds. All the Florida settlements hosted these workers' clubs;
forty-six were formed in Tampa alone (Muñiz 1976:88). The revolutionary
organizations comprised a loose network of patriotic cells, whose fund-
raising potential was enormous. Members pledged to make regular contributions from their wages and staged frequent special events, like bazaars
and fiestas, aimed at securing added donations. Clubs competed with each
other in ostentatious displays of patriotic generosity. Clubs in Ocala and
Key West began what was called the "*día de la patria*," donating one day's
pay per month to the cause. In response, the clubs in Tampa upped the ante
by donating one day's pay per week. In addition, some cigarmakers began
working on Sundays, donating the proceeds to the cause. Spontaneous
matches erupted in which one worker would plunk down a sum of money
on a table and invite the others to follow suit, quickly producing a mound
of cash (Steffy 1975:71–73).

Cigarworkers' generosity earned them a stake in steering the course of
the revolution and gave meaning to their dissent over political and economic issues underlying the movement. They were not all of the same
mind about these issues. Some of the revolutionary clubs heavily emphasized anarchism, socialism, and/or the demands of labor. Others deliberately opposed labor activism in favor of independence (Poyo 1985b). The
revolutionary leadership in New York lacked the moral force to control
these various factions, and their social conservatism jeopardized access to
the much-needed funds that could be raised at the grass roots in Florida.

José Martí

In the early 1890s, José Martí emerged as a leader capable of healing these
divisions. Born in Cuba in 1853, the son of poor Spanish immigrants, his
natural abilities were recognized at an early age by the well-known Cuban
poet María de Mendive. With her assistance, he managed to acquire an
education. Martí was only fourteen when the Ten Years' War erupted. Pro-
independence activities while he was still in high school led to his impris-
onment by the Spanish authorities. Incarceration seriously damaged his
health, and he was debilitated for the remainder of his life. His imprison-
ment was ultimately commuted to exile in Spain, whence he later traveled to Mexico, Guatemala, Venezuela, and, finally, New York (Abel 1986;
Belnap and Fernández 1998; Foner 1989; Manach 1950).

His odyssey through the Americas brought him into conflict with one despotic government after another, while he drew widening acclaim in intellectual circles for his literary and political writing. With maturity came a clear and compelling vision of self-determination and human freedom. Although Martí admired the United States, and the figures involved in its independence, he did not share the slavish attachment of many other Latin American intellectuals for the U.S. model of politics and economics. He was unmoved by the positivistic arguments of the laissez-faire theorists, and especially rejected the view that the strong had a natural right to dominate the weak. Nor was he enamored with the socialist writings of his era. Martí's ideas were infused with a kind of mystical humanism, a belief in the nobility of the spirit and the uncompromising right of all people to freedom of thought, speech, and action. When he arrived in New York in 1881, his influence as a scholar and advocate of Latin American interests earned him a central role in planning the liberation of Cuba.

Slender and bookish, he seemed an improbable revolutionary hero. He was little known to the cigarmakers in Florida prior to his first visit in 1891. What they knew, they did not especially like. In the mid-1880s, Máximo Gómez and Antonio Maceo had attempted an unsuccessful military expedition, launched out of Key West. Martí had opposed Gómez in this effort and openly expressed concern over his possible dictatorial aims. The conflict was interpreted by many as evidence of Martí's timidity (Poyo 1989:67–68). Regarding him as a dreamer and a poet, the bellicose cigarmakers were initially unimpressed with Martí's revolutionary credentials. Nevertheless, in 1891 the Tampa leadership issued him an invitation to speak at a planned celebration on November 27, the anniversary of the deaths of Cuban students murdered by the Spanish in the early stages of the Ten Years' War. Martí's acceptance marked his first visit to Tampa; it also became a watershed in mobilizing the rebellion.

Martí's train pulled into the Ybor City station at midnight on November 25. About fifty cigarmakers waited in the rain for his arrival. He was first taken to the meeting hall of the local revolutionists, the Liceo Cubano. Although weary from his journey, he spent about an hour with the group who had assembled there. The next morning there was much excitement in Ybor City, as Cubans draped their houses with flags and turned out in large numbers to view the visiting dignitary. Martí's itinerary included the major cigar factories, where the cigarmakers pounded their knives (*chavetas*) on the tables in polite welcome, but their eyes reflected skepticism

(Manach 1950:271). Martí quickly assessed the challenge. "These Cuban workers were too familiar with the glow of vain words, the incandescence of fund-raising visitors . . . and no results. He would not be one more to defraud them" (Manach 1950:271).

That evening, he spoke before a large crowd assembled at the Liceo Cubano. In his first speech to the Tampa patriots, Martí made a plea for unity and sacrifice and a promise of justice for all. Beginning with the words, "For Cuba who suffers" and closing with the famous phrase "with all and for the good of all" ("*con todos y para todos*"), his message was carefully measured and artfully delivered. "Either the Republic has as its foundation the basic character of every one of her sons, his habit of working with his hands and thinking for himself and respecting, as if it were a matter of family honor, the unrestricted freedom of others—in short, the passion for man's essential worth—or else the Republic is not worth a single one of the tears of our women nor a solitary drop of a brave man's blood" (quoted in Manach 1950:273).

Tears of women mingled with the blood of men—an evocative metaphor of the gender division discussed by Ferrer (1998). Continuing, Martí specifically addressed the issue of racism and the role of Afro-Cubans in the task of national liberation. "What then do we have to fear? . . . Shall we be afraid of the Negro, or the Negro brother who, because of the Cubans who died for him, has pardoned forever the Cubans who mistreated him? . . . To all Cubans; whether they come from the continent where the sun scorches the skin, or from countries where the light is gentler, this will be the revolution in which all Cubans, regardless of color, have participated" (quoted in Steffy 1975:48).

Dismissing the differences between black and white Cubans as mere effects of climate on coloration, Martí refused to sanction the idea that Africans were a different sort of humanity and, most importantly, argued against the dangers of black reprisals. Black Cubans had demonstrated their loyalty in battle, and had forgiven their white Cuban compatriots who died in those same battles. This line of reasoning, which indemnified white Cubans' mistreatment of Africans by virtue of the efforts of some to end slavery, and which discounted the depth of black grievances and the residual racism of many white Cubans, formed a critical element in emergent doctrines of race and nation. It was an ideological seed from which grew the myth of Cuban racial equality, the silencing of discourse for the sake of patriotic unity (de la Fuente 1999; Ferrer 1998). But framed in the moment of their delivery, his words were like magic balm.

At the conclusion of Martí's speech, those in attendance stood on their chairs waving and shouting acclamations and then pressed around him hoping to shake his hand and get a closer look at this electrifying new celebrity. The following day was spent in meetings with local leaders, who initiated him into their organization, La Liga Patriotica Cubana. That evening he again spoke before a bulging crowd at the Liceo Cubano, delivering one of his most famous orations—"Los Nuevos Pinos." The Cuban revolutionaries, Martí proclaimed, were "new pines," like the verdant young shoots that emerge in the sunlight on the floor of a forest blackened by fire.

On the anniversary of the murder of young Cuban patriots, he chose to emphasize rebirth. It was a fitting metaphor. Martí, himself, felt reborn. Recurring illness, personal losses, and political disappointments had plunged him into despair in the period before he visited Tampa. Buoyed by the adulation of the cigarmakers, he recentered his goals. It was here, among *"los pobres de la tierra"* (the poor of the earth), that he gained the clarity and confidence to proceed with the final liberation of his homeland (Manach 1950).

Martí's visit to Tampa marked a turning point in the war for Cuban independence. A month later, he traveled to Key West, where he again succeeded in assuaging doubts. The unruly cigarmakers of South Florida were galvanized. Martí's strategy and his unfolding social agenda caused some consternation among the elite group in New York, but he was unwilling to offer concessions to these patrician misgivings. He had found his true constituency. It was in Tampa that he chose to launch the Cuban Revolutionary Party (PRC), based on a set of democratic principles drawn up in consultation with the cigar workers.

In the period between 1891 and 1898, Tampa cigarmakers were singularly obsessed with winning Cuban independence. Despite the financial problems plaguing other cities in the United States during the early 1890s, Tampa's cigar industry prospered. In 1892, a second cigarmaking center was established in Tampa, called West Tampa. Located about two miles from Ybor City, this area was developed by a Scottish immigrant entrepreneur named Hugh MacFarlane (Mendez 1994). Modeling West Tampa on Ybor City, MacFarlane offered cigar manufacturers free land for their factories in exchange for the prospect of selling houses to the workers. He calculated well, as building boomed and the price of lots soared with demand. Within a few years, West Tampa had grown to a city with nearly three thousand residents and sixteen cigar factories. Expansion of the cigar industry and the accompanying growth in construction fueled a period of dramatic prosperity. By 1894, the annual wages of cigarmakers in West Tampa and Ybor City amounted to almost $2 million (Steffy 1975:54).

By some accounts, worker donations from Tampa constituted the largest single source of financial support for independence (Day 1898:347). The funds came from regular pledges secured by the clubs from their members, bolstered by periodic fund-raisers called *veladas. Veladas* were often staged to meet some specific need. On one occasion, for example, workers were called on to pledge enough to buy ten thousand rifles and ten million cartridges (Steffy 1975:71). Organizers were also given access to the cigar factories, in which they circulated among the benches soliciting donations. These contributions were in addition to the *día de la patria*, mentioned previously. Women were very active in fund-raising; women's clubs organized bazaars, parades, and fiestas. The wife of one of the revolutionary leaders donated her silverware and tea set for sale at a bazaar in 1895. One concert organized by the women garnered $500 for the cause (Steffy 1975:148).

Funds gathered from these various activities were turned over to the local treasurer and subagent of the PRC, Fernando Figueredo, who sent the money to New York. His monthly remittances each amounted to several thousand dollars; in February 1897, for example, he sent $3,235. To gauge the magnitude of these contributions, the total party treasury when the war started in 1895 was no more than $100,000 (Steffy 1975:73).

Afro-Cuban Patriots

Both black and white Cubans took part in this effort. Black participation is acknowledged in accounts from the period and in contemporary renditions of Tampa's role in Cuban history as well as Cuba's role in Tampa history. In these depictions Afro-Cubans play shadowy and supporting roles, are portrayed as simple and unlettered. Many who contradicted this stereotype were either not mentioned at all, or their identities as Afro-Cubans are not indicated.[1]

Tampa's best-known Afro-Cuban patriot was a woman, Paulina Pedroso. Of the many historic markers that have been erected in Ybor City, the only one that alludes to Afro-Cuban involvement in the war is a plaque that bears her likeness.[2] Locally, she is the symbol of Afro-Cuban patriotism. Her persona is plain and humble, self-sacrificing and dedicated—an embodiment of the unquestioning loyalty that Martí ascribed to Afro-

Cubans in the movement. She was an undeniably important figure, and she had a particularly close relationship with Martí, but the focus on Paulina Pedroso has tended to distort the larger picture of Afro-Cuban involvement. Her gender is anomalous. Many more Afro-Cuban men than women were activists, and white Cuban women were far more numerous in the revolutionary clubs than were black Cuban women. This gendered image, which neglects the presence of men, especially men of letters and ideas, subordinates and diminishes the significance of race in this local movement. In what might appear to be a gesture of racial and gender inclusion, the stereotyped danger of black males is tamed by exclusion. The actual number of Afro-Cubans involved in these events is reduced to a handful and symbolized in a single nonthreatening figure. Paulina's husband, Ruperto, is also portrayed as a simple man with dogged loyalty to Martí and the cause.

Two other Afro-Cuban men who are recorded in early accounts, but rarely in those that are contemporary, were Bruno Roig and Cornelio Brito. Roig had a grocery store in Ybor City; the nature of Brito's establishment, which was also in Ybor City, is unknown. Brito was a director in El Club Revolucionario, and was among the select welcoming party for José Martí when he first visited Tampa in 1891 (Muñiz 1976:58). Roig was also centrally involved in arranging Martí's visit. As treasurer of Ignacio Agramonte, it was his job to gather funds and pay the travel expenses. Muñiz described his role. "Bruno Roig pointed out that no one had taken notice, as if it were of secondary importance, that there would be expenses involved . . . with the trip of Martí. Everything was left in mid air until the next meeting when Roig was to present a budget covering the proposed expenses" (Muñiz 1976:46).

There were many others, however, including a large group of journalists and labor activists. Several Afro-Cubans were involved with local revolutionist publications—Joaquín Granados, Emilio Planas, Julian González, Primitivo Plumas, Francisco Segura, and Teofilo Domínguez. Planas, Domínguez, and González also contributed work to well-known Cuban publications, including *La Fraternidad,* Juan Gualberto Gómez's magazine, and *Minerva,* an early publication dedicated to items of interest to Afro-Cubans (Montejo Arrecha 1998; Domínguez 1899). Domínguez's future wife, María de Jesús Viernes, was also an active supporter of Cuban independence and reportedly sewed the flag that was carried into battle when the war began in 1895.[3] In addition, there were Afro-Cubans associated with organizing revolutionary clubs, especially those that espoused labor activism and political radicalism. They included Manuel Granados, who was Joaquín's brother, and Guillermo Sorondo, who had been involved with the Reconstruction Republican Party in Key West during the early 1870s. Sorondo had also been the founder of at least two Afro-Cuban mutual aid societies in that city (Poyo 1985a:227, 233).

Two sources that profile Afro-Cubans involved in writing and publishing—Deschamps Chapeaux's *El Negro en el Periodismo Cubano en el Siglo XIX* (1963) and Domínguez's *Ensayos Biograficos* (1899)—were written precisely because so little credit had been accorded to these individuals and their intellectual accomplishments. Teofilo Domínguez, author of the latter, was himself editor of a revolutionary weekly in Tampa and a close associate of Juan Gualberto Gómez (Deschamps Chapeaux 1963:104). He was also friends with Gustavo Urrutia, an Afro-Cuban writer who is only now gaining recognition for his role in shaping Cuban political thought (Fernández Robaina 1998:123).[4] Domínguez remains an undeservedly obscure figure in the history of Cuban revolutionary journalism. Between 1897 and 1899, he published a weekly literary and political magazine in Ybor City called *El Sport.* Listed among the founders of this publication is Generoso Campos Marquetti, an Afro-Cuban general in the liberation army who served in the Cuban legislature after independence (Deschamps Chapeaux 1963:104).

In addition to his magazine, only fragments of which survive, Domínguez wrote a short volume profiling some of his even lesser known colleagues. Originally published as a series of biographical sketches in a Key West magazine in July 1898 (at the height of the final battle for Cuban independence), these pieces were reprinted by Domínguez as a book in 1899, after the war was over, along with several essays he had written about the importance of education in effecting Martí's vision for Cuba.

This publication includes information on Julian González, Emilio Planas, and Joaquín Granados. There are common themes in their stories, around difficult struggles to achieve an education and early connections to independence politics and each other. Julian González, born in Havana in 1871, was a cigarmaker who attended night classes sponsored by the Bella Unión Habanera.[5] González edited a magazine named *La Pelota (The Ball Game)*, which was dedicated to coverage of literature and sports and served as the official newspaper of the Cuban Baseball League of Tampa. Although not explicitly political, all proceeds from the sale of the paper were contributed to the PRC.

Emilio Planas, born in 1868, spent his early childhood in Key West, where he attended classes at the San Carlos Club, the principal mutual aid organization among cigarmakers in that city. Planas completed his education in Jacksonville, however, at the Goodman and Free Men Institution, a school for African Americans begun during Reconstruction. He graduated in 1888 and settled in Tampa in 1890. Planas was one of the founders of Domínguez's *El Sport* and contributed essays under the pen name Jonatas. He also started his own weekly, called *El Patriota* (see also Muñiz 1976:35).

Joaquín Granados, the best known of this group, was born a slave in 1854. At an early age he began to write and publish political essays and became a protegé of Martín Morúa Delgado. Granados had collaborated with Morúa Delgado in establishing a mutual aid society in Matanzas, Cuba, in 1879 (Domínguez 1899; Deschamps Chapeaux 1974b). Named La Armonía (Harmony), its purpose was to ease the problems that followed the end of the Ten Years' War and the gradual abolition of Cuban slavery, begun in 1870 (Howard 1998:168). Granados and his brother, Manuel, were born in Havana. Their parents were slaves but managed to purchase their sons' freedom at an early age. Joaquín learned cigarmaking and Manuel became a barber. A self-taught scholar who won certification as a schoolteacher, Joaquín began to write poems and political essays that were published in a variety of progressive papers and magazines. He was heavily involved with Juan Gualberto Gómez and Martín Morúa Delgado, two leading Afro-Cuban intellectuals who were rivals of each other (Serviat 1993). Morúa Delgado favored complete assimilation and repudiated race consciousness. Gómez pursued a similar goal of racial equality, but based on attacking racism and organizing collective self-help (Helg 1995:121; Ferrer 1998:237). Joaquín Granados collaborated with both, serving as vice-president of Gómez's Directorio Central de la Raza de Color. He worked with Morúa Delgado in Matanzas (Morúa Delgado was also a founder of La Armonía) and later in exile in Key West, contributing to *El Pueblo* and *La Revista Popular*, revolutionary magazines edited by Morúa Delgado (Poyo 1983; Domínguez 1899).

Both Manuel and Joaquín Granados moved to Tampa in the late 1880s. Manuel had a barber shop in the Liceo Cubano, where Martí got his hair cut when he was in town (Muñiz 1976). Both became members of the most influential revolutionary clubs—Vanguardia de Flor Crombet and Ignacio Agramonte—the former named for an Afro-Cuban general, the latter for a white Cuban patriot of the Ten Years' War. The Crombet club was later converted into La Liga Patriotica Cubana, a highly secret organization, in which Manuel Granados was treasurer. Joaquín was also elected secretary of the Tampa delegation to the PRC in 1892 (Muñiz 1976).

Guillermo Sorondo was also among the leaders of the PRC. He had been a central figure in political activities in Key West, where he was associated with most of the individuals previously listed. Sociedad El Progreso, an Afro-Cuban mutual aid society he founded there, included Emilio Planas, Joaquín and Manuel Granados, Martín Morúa Delgado, and Francisco Segura (Poyo 1983:227). Sorondo moved from Key West to Tampa in 1888, but left temporarily in 1892 to help form a Cuban colony in Ocala, a small settlement in Central Florida. This Cuban enclave was known as Martí City (Westfall 1995). It collapsed in 1897, and Sorondo and his colleagues moved to Port Tampa, a small cluster of residences in the area surrounding the port section of the town. Sorondo was head of the PRC delegation from Martí City and also headed the Port Tampa delegation when its founders returned to Tampa (Muñiz 1976). Sorondo was allied with Carlos Baliño, a white anarchist who later was one of the founders of the Cuban Communist Party (Liss 1987). In Tampa, Baliño edited a paper called *La Tribuno del Pueblo,* to which several of the Afro-Cuban writers contributed.

Francisco Segura, another Afro-Cuban writer in Tampa during this period, had been a director with Sorondo in Sociedad El Progreso in Key West. He also relocated from Key West to Tampa, in the early 1890s. Segura was an associate of Ramon Rivero, a white leader of Tampa's PRC. Segura was on the editorial staff of Rivero's magazine, *La Revista de Florida* (Poyo 1983:338). Rivero also edited the official organ of the PRC, *Cuba,* which published writing by Segura and the other Afro-Cubans previously described (Poyo 1983:345; Domínguez 1899).

La Liga de Instrucción

José Martí deliberately cultivated relationships with black Cubans in the Tampa leadership. He was acquainted with several through ties to Juan Gualberto Gómez, and he recognized their importance as individuals. Martí was also interested in the symbolism of his association with Afro-Cubans, and in mobilizing their collective support for the movement. Although Juan Gualberto Gómez was an important ally in the revolution, Martí was concerned about the race-conscious orientation of his activism (Helg 1995:46). In countering what he regarded as Gómez's separatist tendencies, he also cultivated the more moderate and assimilationist views of Morúa Delgado and his associates. The Afro-Cubans in Tampa were similarly intent on maintaining relations with both camps, as exemplified in their many cross-cutting affiliations with Morúa Delgado and Gómez.

Rafael Serra, a New York–based Afro-Cuban journalist, supplied a common connection. In Cuba he had been involved with Joaquín Granados and Morúa Delgado in the La Armonía mutual aid society. Serra also had been in Key West, where he belonged to Sociedad El Progreso, along with Sorondo, Morúa Delgado, Planas, and the Granados brothers (Domínguez 1899:17). He settled in New York in 1887 and began a career as an activist writer and teacher. His most noteworthy project was a night school he founded in 1890, called La Liga de Instrucción (Helg 1995:42). Pupils were mainly Afro-Cuban and Afro–Puerto Rican adults; the goal was to teach them to read and write, and to think and act politically. José Martí regarded La Liga as a highly worthy endeavor, and he spent Thursday nights teaching classes there. According to Manach (1950:264), his interactions with the pupils in these classes personalized and reinforced his dedication to the "humble." It was they who first began calling him El Maestro, the schoolmaster.

On his first visit to Tampa in 1891, Martí organized a chapter of La Liga among the Afro-Cubans he met there. La Liga in Ybor City, which brought together most of the men who have been named thus far, has received a great deal of attention by historians (Hewitt 1995; James 1998; Manach 1950; Mirabal 1995; Mormino and Pozzetta 1987; Muñiz 1976). It is regarded as emblematic of Martí's dedication to racial inclusiveness and his belief that education would be the surest path leading to equality. There were two ironies in its establishment, however. First, by all accounts it was a racially segregated organization and a duplication of the integrated night classes that were already available at the Liceo Cubano. Second, the Afro-Cuban cigarmakers had relatively high rates of literacy, approximately the same as the white Cubans.[6]

La Liga of Tampa was organized in the home of Cornelio Brito, the most prosperous Afro-Cuban in Tampa. The most complete account of the founding of La Liga de Instrucción de Tampa is as follows: "He [Martí] had noted in Tampa that, probably because of the influence of the Yankee example, there was a certain condescension in the attitude of the white Cubans towards their Negro compatriots. That had to be checked. With great finesse Martí told Cornelio Brito, who because of his intelligence and wealth was outstanding among his race, what La Liga was doing in New York, the spirit of fraternity and justice cultivated there. That same afternoon [November 26, 1891] in Brito's house the Tampa League for Instruction was founded, with thirty members. Another link in the chain" (Manach 1950:276).

Many of the other members, although not mentioned by Manach, can be identified. Bruno Roig is cited as one of the "most enthusiastic sustainers" (Deulofeu 1904:36). Joaquín and Manuel Granados were involved (Deschamps Chapeaux 1974a:28), as were Emilio Planas, Julian González, and Teofilo Domínguez (Domínguez 1899). The account is misleading in suggesting that Tampa's Afro-Cubans needed to be told about La Liga. Many were already well acquainted with Rafael Serra and had worked with him on similar projects in Cuba and Key West. Moreover, the emphasis on this organization in most texts dealing with Afro-Cubans in Tampa's independence movement conveys the impression that they were illiterate and in need of leadership to establish such an institution.

According to Deulofeu (1904:150), La Liga de Instrucción de Tampa's membership grew to two hundred, although this figure seems improbably large, since it exceeds the estimated total Afro-Cuban population in the 1890s. Deschamps Chapeaux (1974a:64) states that, like the one in New York, it offered classes through the week in varied subjects—writing, Castilian grammar, basic and business math, English, history, and world geography. He lists the teachers as Emilio Planas, Julian González, Luis Otero, and Joaquín Granados. Deschamps Chapeaux also indicates that it dissolved shortly after Martí's death in 1895 and was replaced by another all-black organization known as La Verdad, whose directors included Emilio Planas, Primitivo Plumas, and Hilario Zayas. La Verdad was a mutual aid society affiliated with Juan Gualberto Gómez's Directorio Central in Havana (Deschamps Chapeaux 1974a:66).

Paulina's House

The Pedrosos, discussed earlier, were not involved in founding La Liga de Instrucción. At the time of Martí's first visit to Tampa, Ruperto and Paulina were still living in Key West. The Pedrosos originated in the tobacco-growing region of Pinar del Río, in a village named Concepción del Sur (Rodríguez de Cuesta 1952). During the Ten Years' War, they traveled first to Havana and then to Key West. Ruperto was a cigarmaker and Paulina was a tobacco stripper (a low-paid job, mostly done by women, that involved removing the central stems from the leaves).

Martí first met the Pedrosos in Key West in December 1891. The Pedrosos were cigar workers, but they also owned a "saloon." When Martí made his first visit to Key West, he was accompanied by some of his friends from Tampa, including Cornelio Brito. Brito had persuaded his friend Ruperto to host a luncheon in honor of Martí, but Paulina was reluctant. "She was an old-line patriot, a fanatical follower of Gómez and Maceo, men of action. And, moreover, there was no meat at this time at the Key. . . . Ruperto suggested that her grandmother's prize kid might be sacrificed. . . . Martí found it tender and delicious, but he understood the dramatic antecedents of that capital dish, and Paulina's resentment. When the party was over, he kissed her on the forehead and said to her: 'Paulina, you are going to help me a great deal here for Cuba'" (Manach 1950:282).

From this first encounter, Ruperto and Paulina became fervent supporters of Martí. Shortly after, in early 1892, the Pedrosos moved to Ybor City, where they also operated a boardinghouse. A large contingent of Ruperto's relatives also moved to Tampa around the same time. His brother José had a restaurant and boardinghouse down the block (at 1117 Eighth Avenue), where fifteen other members of their extended family also resided (José's wife, Juana; his brother Vincente, sisters Sinensia and Ignacia; mother, María; brother-in-law, Manuel Herrera; and nine nieces and nephews).[7]

Paulina and Ruperto are not listed on the 1900 census, and their literacy status is thus unknown. However, it is noteworthy and perhaps indicative that only one younger sister, Sinensia, among all his adult relatives who were also living in Tampa, could either read or write. Their illiteracy makes them unusual in contrast with most of the other Afro-Cuban families in Tampa at that time, and particularly distinguishes them from the other Afro-Cuban independence figures previously discussed.

The large Pedroso family left many descendants, some of whom are still involved in the Martí-Maceo Society (the founding of which is described later on). Their two boardinghouses, and a number of other Afro-Cuban residences and businesses located in the same vicinity, became the geographic center of early Afro-Cuban community life in Ybor City (see Map 1). Manuel Granados's barbershop was a block away at 1223 Seventh Avenue. Brito lived down the street from the Pedrosos on Eighth Avenue, and he owned property at Thirteenth Street and Seventh Avenue (which may have been his store). Bruno Roig's store was two blocks to the west, on Eleventh Street and Seventh Avenue. Pedro Miró operated a small warehouse at 1016 Eighth Avenue. Many, although by no means all, of the residences in this general area were inhabited by Afro-Cubans.[8]

This concentration, in the shadow of Ybor's factory and the Liceo Cubano (then located at Thireenth Street and Seventh Avenue), was in the

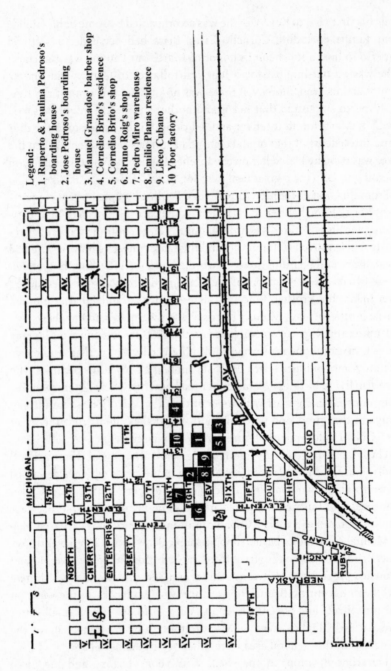

Legend:
1. Ruperto & Paulina Pedroso's boarding house
2. Jose Pedroso's boarding house
3. Manuel Granados' barber shop
4. Cornelio Brito's residence
5. Cornelio Brito's shop
6. Bruno Roig's shop
7. Pedro Miro warehouse
8. Emilio Planas residence
9. Liceo Cubano
10 Ybor factory

Map 1. Afro-Cuban Sites in Ybor City, late 1890s

heart of the original Ybor City development, the historic center of independence activities. In later years, Pizzo (1985) and Muñiz (1976:28) described this area as the "colored" section of Ybor City, mainly due to this association with so many early Afro-Cuban families. However, in the 1890s and for many years to come, Afro-Cuban families were scattered throughout most sections of Ybor City and West Tampa, and others were living in Port Tampa and other neighborhoods. The identification of this location with Afro-Cubans is based more on the symbolic association between Martí and the Pedrosos than on the actual spatial distribution of the black Cuban population at that time. The site of the boardinghouse is now a park, dedicated to José Martí, but with the previously mentioned plaque bearing Paulina's likeness fixed to the wall behind El Maestro's statue.

On his visits to Tampa, Martí always stayed in the Pedrosos' boardinghouse. These were very humble quarters for such an important luminary. He chose this location ostensibly for safety, but also for symbolic effect. After an attempted assassination of Martí by Spanish spies, Paulina had insisted that he be moved into their house, where she felt he could be properly looked after. While Martí was in residence, Ruperto stood guard outside his door to prevent any harm from being done to him. Martí's practice of strolling along Seventh Avenue with Paulina on his arm has been mentioned frequently, interpreted as a deliberate gesture of solidarity with Afro-Cubans, a sign of respect and intimacy that he hoped the other Cubans would emulate. Paulina at that time would have been in her late forties, a large woman who was described by those who had seen her as quite homely. Her relationship with Martí was never construed to be sexual, but rather as that of a "second mother" (Deulofeu 1904:263).

The feverish activity of fund-raising and organizing that went on in Tampa in the early 1890s bore fruit in January 1895. Martí and the exile leaders in New York drew up a document directing the generals in western Cuba to commence the uprising. This document, addressed to Juan Gualberto Gómez, was transmitted to Cuba via Tampa, where it was rolled into a cigar and smuggled through Spanish customs in the shirt pocket of Gonzalvo Quesada, who was posing as a Tampa cigarmaker (Muñiz 1976:93). The planned uprising was nearly aborted after a large shipload of arms was intercepted off the eastern coast of Florida. An urgent call went out to the Florida colonies for additional funds to replace the captured cargo. Martí wrote to the Pedrosos on January 30, 1895, asking them to sell their house and give the proceeds to Cuba (Muñiz 1976:93; Deulofeu 1904:174).

This request is a critical element in the folklore surrounding the Pedrosos. Although their willingness to make such a sacrifice is indubitable, sources that indicate that they did so (Muñiz 1976; Hewitt 1990b; Mirabal 1998) are incorrect (see also James 1998:342, who notes this error). An examination of property records from the period reveals that by 1895, the Pedrosos no longer owned the house in which they lived, hence they were in no position to sell it. Also omitted from most accounts was their connection to Cornelio Brito and the large sacrifices that he made in support of the war effort. Land records from the 1890s detail a series of property acquisitions by Brito, his wife, Delfina, and the Pedrosos—transactions that are clearly linked and that, within a few years, resulted in both families having liquidated nearly all of their holdings, presumably to provide funds for Martí. All of this, however, was concluded by July 1894, six months before Martí wrote his letter to Paulina.

The Pedrosos purchased their boardinghouse in May 1891, while they were still living in Key West. They moved to Tampa in early 1892. In May 1892, they purchased a piece of property from Brito at Seventh Avenue and Thirteenth Street, and they bought another piece of property at Sixth Avenue and Eleventh Street, very close to the site that would later hold the Martí-Maceo Society building. Although they are frequently characterized as poor people, their real estate holdings at that time were relatively substantial.

This condition was temporary, and by the time Martí wrote his letter in 1895, the boardinghouse no longer belonged to them. In early 1893, they began selling these parcels in fairly rapid succession. On January 12, they sold the lot on Sixth Avenue to Cornelio Brito, and the next day they sold the property on Seventh Avenue. Two weeks later, on February 3, Brito bought their boardinghouse. It is likely that the $4,750 the Pedrosos realized from the sale of their property in 1893 was dedicated in part to the revolution, although what they did with the money cannot be confirmed.

It was during this exact same period that Paulina delivered a celebrated extemporaneous speech while accompanying Martí on a fund-raising visit to the factories. At the steps of the factory, they reportedly heard someone inside comment that the "bandit" was on his way, apparently in reference to Martí's gathering of donations. Once inside, Paulina is reported to have climbed onto a table, grabbed hold of her skirt, and exhorted the men in the audience: "Gentlemen, if any of you is afraid to give him money or go to the savannahs to fight, let him give me his pants, and I'll give him my petticoat" (Manach 1950). Her defiance on this occasion may reflect resentment based on her own generosity in donations to Martí. It is also noteworthy that Paulina wrapped the shame of her opprobrium in symbols of femininity.

It is certain that Brito, who by that time had purchased most of the Pedrosos' real estate, made very large donations to the cause. In April and July of 1894, he sold the Pedroso house and another lot he owned on Eighth Avenue to a real estate company in Tampa for $2,100. By his own account Brito gave all of his personal wealth to Martí in 1895 (Guerra 1947:22). Deschamps Chapeaux retrieved the following testimonial written by Brito himself: "I am the Afro-Cuban Cornelio Brito who was a comrade of Sr. Maestro José Martí, the only Cuban capitalist who believed in José Martí. I put all my capital in the hand of Martí, and he that day sent 11,000 pesos to Gen. Máximo Gómez" (Deschamps Chapeaux 1974a:63).

It was Brito, not the Pedrosos, who converted this real estate into munitions when the war broke out. The Pedrosos continued to live in their boardinghouse, even after Brito sold it, and several years later (in 1897) Ruperto and Paulina purchased it again and continued to live there after the end of the war.[9]

The Deaths of José Martí and Antonio Maceo

Greatly fortified by the generosity of cigar workers and individuals like Brito, the war commenced in earnest. Early reports from the field were encouraging, and Martí decided to join the fight. He departed for Cuba, and on April 11, 1895, he set foot on Cuban soil for the first time in many years. Within six weeks he was dead, killed by an anonymous Spanish soldier in an obscure place known as Dos Ríos. Ignoring all pleas to stay out of danger and return to the United States to raise more funds, Martí plunged into battle and fell almost immediately, a vainglorious end to a most significant life.

Martí's death was a tremendous blow. When the news first reached the cigarmakers in Tampa, it was taken for Spanish-inspired disinformation aimed at demoralizing their efforts. But when confirmation arrived from their own leadership in late June, all the Cuban houses, factories, and public buildings in Ybor City and West Tampa were draped in mourning. When Cornelio Brito learned that Martí had died, he packed a few belongings, bid farewell to his friends, and left to join the fight in Cuba (Deschamps Chapeaux 1974b:110). Although Martí's martyrdom did not dampen revolutionary resolve, it could be argued that in that fateful moment at Dos Ríos the cause was lost.

Martí's replacement as head of the PRC was Tomás Estrada Palma, a very different sort of Cuban patriot. He was a strong admirer of the United States, to the extent of becoming a naturalized citizen. Restructuring the PRC, he converted the organization from one of grassroots cells into a series of local "embassies," the main goal of which was to gain diplomatic recognition and political support for the insurgency. "After April 1896, Estrada Palma no longer reported directly to the local councils of the party, which were, in effect, displaced as relevant policy makers in the insurgent process" (Poyo 1989:119).

Emphasis shifted away from organizing exile communities to lobbying the State Department and attempting to orchestrate a campaign in the U.S. press to win sympathy for the Cuban cause. Estrada Palma and his associates were pinning all their hopes on U.S. intervention. They were also subtly demobilizing the local exile organizations, especially those in Tampa and Key West.

In the ten years prior to his death, Martí had become increasingly disenchanted with the United States as a model for Cuban democracy (Ferrer 1998; Foner 1989). Estrada Palma's moves in the direction of alliance with the United States ran exactly counter to the course that Martí had attempted to chart. Military figures in Cuba, especially Antonio Maceo and Máximo Gómez, also evinced skepticism and concern about potential usurpation by U.S. forces, should they enter the war.

Antonio Maceo was killed in battle at Punta Brava in December 1896. His death further weakened the military power of the insurgents and the progressive social ideals of the independence movement. The demise of Cuba's most influential Afro-Cuban general deprived the revolution of what would have been an effective spokesman for the interests of black officers and troops in the aftermath of the war.

The same year that Maceo was killed also marked the official onset of legally sanctioned racial segregation in the United States. On May 18, 1896, the U.S. Supreme Court delivered its decision in the *Plessy v. Ferguson* case, upholding the right of states to impose separate accommodations on the basis of color (the "separate but equal" doctrine). This decision drew relatively little notice at the time (Lofgren 1987), especially among the Cubans in Tampa, who were highly distracted with the liberation of Cuba. The major effects of this new repressive era of Jim Crow would not be felt until after the war ended, but the limits it imposed on Cuban solidarity had already begun to intrude. In 1895, the Florida legislature had enacted a law against integrated schools, punishable by fines of up to $100 (Jackson 1960:106). Fernando Figueredo, local leader of the PRC, was appointed superintendent of schools in West Tampa on September 14, 1895—two weeks after this law took effect. When he attempted to secure public funds for the integrated school the Cubans had established in the Céspedes Hall, he discovered that it had become an illegal enterprise (Mendez 1994:79). The Cubans in West Tampa neither protested nor acquiesced. They simply withdrew the request and presumably continued the previous arrangement, in private violation of laws that they did not respect. Heavily preoccupied with the war that was raging in Cuba, confident in their ultimate repatriation, both black and white Cubans could ignore for the moment the growing assault on the rights of black people in the United States. They were scarcely oblivious to its effects, however, and they were surely aware of the growing climate of violence in Tampa that was directed against immigrants as well as native-born blacks. Afro-Cubans were doubly vulnerable, and the forces of white domination inescapably intruded into their lives.

As the Cubans increased their reliance on U.S. political support to win the war, they also wooed influential native-born Tampans in local efforts to raise funds and win sympathy. These gestures had a cost. At a rally held in the courthouse square on October 29, 1895, Afro-Cuban speakers were ejected from the bandstand by a city official who explained that the forum was "for white men, not niggers."[10] Strange alliances were sought. At another celebration in October 1897, a street parade of floats by various revolutionary clubs and local groups included one representing the Daughters of the Confederacy.[11]

Cuban women had formed a number of revolutionary clubs, one of whose primary functions was to organize hospitality for American dignitaries and influential groups (Hewitt 1995, 1991a, 1990a; Steffy 1975). Unlike the men's revolutionary clubs, which were integrated, the women's clubs were virtually all white. In spite of her luminous reputation within Ybor City, Paulina Pedroso did not belong to any of these clubs (Hewitt 1990b). Nor did the future wife of Teofilo Domínguez, María de Jesús Viernes, even though she too had played an active role in independence activities. Also missing were the wives of most other high-profile Afro-Cuban leaders. Women's revolutionary clubs in Cuba were racially integrated (Stoner 1991:24–25), but not so in Tampa.

A likely explanation for the absence of black women in the clubs in Tampa is that their presence at fund-raising social events for white Americans would have offended the guests whom they hoped to solicit. A strategic exclusion perhaps, but further indication of the effects of Tampa's racism on the social relations of black and white Cubans.

Relations with African Americans

In the same period that Afro-Cubans were being shunted to the background of white Cuban activities, they were increasingly involved with African Americans. These contacts had begun earlier. Indeed, early residence patterns of Afro-Cubans reflected more spatial integration with African Americans than was true in later years. In 1893, the Tampa city directory identified nineteen Afro-Cuban households, seven of which lived in or near the Scrub, well beyond the limits of Ybor City. One of these residents was José Valdés, who operated a restaurant at 1100 Central Avenue, squarely in the midst of African American businesses and residences. Up above the store he had a small boardinghouse, where he lived. Among his tenants was Luis Garban, Afro-Cuban owner of a small cigar factory (a "buckeye") in the back of the restaurant. Valdés's other tenants included a black cigarmaker and two black laborers, all with English surnames. Any or all could have been West Indians, although it is equally possible that they were African Americans.

Customers in Valdés's restaurant undoubtedly included African Americans. This was the only restaurant on Central at that time. We don't know if José Valdés spoke English, but it is reasonable to assume that he did. Nor do we know what he heard and learned from his neighbors and customers, although it would have been difficult to avoid knowledge of the growing problems that they faced. This period was filled with episodes of antiblack violence and increasing pressures to exclude blacks from white spaces.

During the late 1890s, the number of black businesses on Central Avenue increased steadily as newcomers arrived and existing black business owners were forced out of the downtown area. Valdés and Garban operated inside a growing and tightening black enclave, which formed the basis of an emergent leadership structure of mostly African American business owners, pastors, journalists, and teachers. Afro-Cubans did not belong to the many clubs, lodges, and organizations that were formed in this period by African Americans, but they did join them in efforts to reverse their political misfortunes by supporting the Republican party. José Valdés was one of 20 Afro-Cubans who registered to vote in June 1898. Others included Bruno Roig, Emilio Planas, and several individuals who later would be involved in organizing the post-independence Martí-Maceo Society. There were only about 80 African Americans who registered, but these names included several who played significant roles in the community.[12]

Baseball was another arena in which segregation promoted contact between black Americans and black Cubans. Afro-Cubans in Ybor City organized a team called the Tampa Baseball Nine. Although black and white Cubans were initially part of the same league in Tampa, by the middle of the 1890s Afro-Cuban ball players had been reassigned to the growing circuit of black teams in Florida. In May 1894, they played in Tampa against an African American team from Gainesville (about 120 miles to the north). It was a major event of the season, and four hundred black fans from Gainesville came by train to watch the game. Local African Americans also turned out in large numbers, and the "Tampa Colored Band" played music for the crowd that had assembled.[13]

More intimate relationships with African Americans were reflected in numerous marriages between Afro-Cuban males and African American women. It is perhaps noteworthy that there were no examples of Afro-Cuban females marrying African American men. Census schedules for 1900 list 16 Afro-Cuban–African American unions, more than 10 percent of all the two-parent households enumerated that year (156). Of these 16 marriages, 15 included children over the age of four, indicating that the couples were already married in 1896, when *Plessy* was decided. Mixed marriages brought contact not only with American spouses, but also included American in-laws and a logical connection to networks of other friends and neighbors who were black Americans.

English-speaking West Indians from Nassau and elsewhere in the Bahamas were also part of the complex linkages that drew Afro-Cubans into the larger black population of Tampa. The St. James Episcopal Church, a mostly Caribbean congregation (Jamaicans and Bahamians) that also included some Cubans, was founded in 1891 on Constant Street, just off Central Avenue. Members had come from Key West, where they previously belonged to another, earlier black Episcopal church.[14] The first pastor, Mathew McDuffie, was a prominent church and civic leader in the African American community, and a strong supporter of Booker T. Washington. In 1900, fourteen Afro-Cuban men in Tampa had West Indian wives; five of these families also lived in the Scrub. Cuban members of St. James primarily consisted of these in-married spouses.

Nearly one in five Afro-Cuban families included an English-speaking wife, a factor that would have diminished the language barrier to interactions with black Americans. Kinship and neighborly relations began to develop, and school ties were also forming during this period. There were three schools in the Scrub area. The Harlem Academy, built in 1889, was a public school organized and established by members of the African American community. St. James Episcopal began a parochial school in 1892. In 1894, St. Peter Claver Catholic Church was founded in Tampa, as a mission church and school for black Catholics. St. James school included Cubans and Americans, as well as West Indians. Some Afro-Cuban families sent their children to the Harlem Academy, out of disaffection with Catholicism and/or an inability to pay the fees at St. Peter Claver. Several African American families, especially those who were prosperous, sent their children to St. Peter Claver, which they felt provided a superior education

St. Peter Claver was originally sited near downtown Tampa, but ten days after it opened the structure was burned to the ground by white vigilantes who opposed black education and did not like Catholics. Harlem Academy's first building had met the same fate, only days after it was constructed in 1889. Although a public school, no public funds had been provided to build it. That task was accomplished by donations of cash and labor from the African American community. One can imagine the pride they felt in getting it built, and the sickening discouragement of watching it burn. But engendering defeatism and discouragement was one of the reasons to burn it down, along with preventing black people from learning how to read contracts and such. Similar motives prompted the destruction of St. Peter Claver, in 1894, reasons that were made very clear in a newspaper editorial published shortly thereafter: "The citizens do not propose to submit to a negro school in the midst of a white and residential section of the city and warn that in case another institution of the same character is operated in this vicinity, it too will certainly cause destruction of the convent and your other churches. Remember this."[15]

The warning, delivered by the editor of Tampa's leading newspaper explicitly condoning arson against the church, was duly heeded. The archdiocese built a new school and church but located them in the Scrub.

The 1890s brought major changes. Tampa's black population, which had been flooded by newcomers in the late 1880s, grew by an additional 172 percent in the next decade, from 1,607 in 1890 to 4,382 in 1900 (Mohlman 1995:77). Many were poor people from nearby rural areas drawn by opportunities in the city—in construction, on the docks, on the railroad, and as servants. Increased violence against rural blacks contributed further to the flow of migrants into Tampa. Others who moved in were educated professionals, skilled workers, and/or entrepreneurs, attracted by the growing importance of the city and its reputation for cosmopolitan tolerance. The number of black-owned businesses increased from 4 in 1886, to 21 in 1893, to 74 in 1899 (Mohlman 1995:79). Most were small stores and shops that catered to black customers, or services like undertaking that were rigidly segregated. Bars and wine shops, and the unlisted bawdy houses in upstairs rooms, also did a thriving business. The base of local black leadership broadened with this influx of business owners, to which was also added a new group of pastors and an increasing number of teachers. These individuals and their businesses, churches, and schools were largely concentrated in the Scrub, on Central Avenue, in an area that adjoined Ybor City to the south and west (see Map 2).

Tampa's economy remained strong during the 1890s, sheltered by the prosperity of tobacco from the depression that engulfed much of the nation by mid-decade. Growth in the black community paralleled a sharp increase in the white population in the same period (from 3,900 to 11,425). Racial proportions remained essentially unchanged: blacks were 29 percent in 1890 and 28 percent in 1900. In the space of a decade the city contained thousands of newcomers, of both races and at all levels in the class hierarchy—an avalanche of strangers, whose presence recast and destabilized customs and relationships. In addition to the large cluster of recently arrived immigrants, there was a large group of native-born white newcomers, mainly from other parts of Florida and the lower South. Their arrival ratcheted tensions and increased the dangers to black residents.

Respectability and Resistance

Respectability is a concept well treated in literature on black culture in both the Caribbean (Besson 1993; Fox 1973; Momsen 1993; Sutton 1974; Wilson 1969) and the United States (Baker 1998; Gatewood 1990; Harris 1981; Kelley 1993; Mullings 1994a; Trotter 1995; Williams 1989; Wolcott 1996). Wilson (1969, 1973) presents this concept as tinged with cultural compromise and a delusional quest for approval from the holders of power. It is a strategy of capitulation, in which the oppressed emulate their oppressors and are thereby manipulated to serve them. These discussions, however, disclose both a paradox and a dilemma. According to Gatewood (1990), respectability required adherence to values of thrift, hard work, self-restraint, refined behavior and dress—qualities that might earn the esteem of white middle and upper classes, whose belief system validated such traits. That same belief system, however, also despised blackness, the

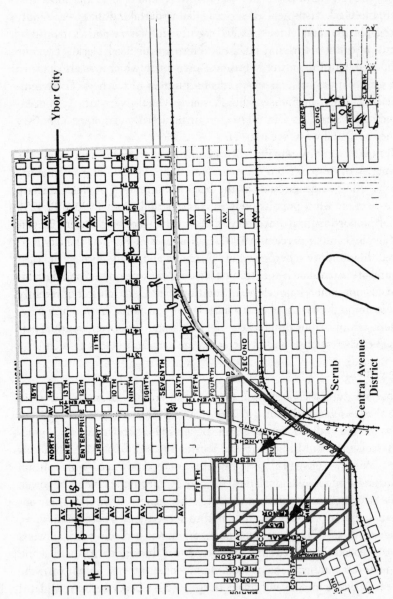

Map 2. Ybor City, Scrub and Central Avenue, circa 1900

one trait that could not be significantly altered. It was only through self-segregation in the black community that a full measure of respectability could be achieved.

Black intellectuals of this era struggled with these contradictions, with the elusive but critical need to find dignity and self-respect (Meier 1963). Within their own world, respectability also entailed courage, the ability to find somehow the narrow space between practical accommodation and unavoidable resistance. This perilous negotiation was wrought in the institutions of black self-help, organized alternatives to the social benefits from which they were excluded by Jim Crow, and in the specialized enterprises designed to challenge these restrictions (Butler 1991; Carson 1993; Goings and Mohl 1995; Greenbaum 1991; Harris 1936; Harris 1979; Kilson 1976; Rabinowitz 1994).

The African American community in Tampa was organized around goals that differed little in substance from those of the Afro-Cubans. In form, however, the contrasts were greater. The African American strategy relied on separate development, on the elusive quest for a "group economy" (Du Bois 1907), from which to develop power and skills. No white person of comparable stature to José Martí spoke on their behalf. The social equality and integration espoused by the Cuban leader was a radical heresy compared with the Social Darwinist views of Tampa's elite. The powerful white families with whom African Americans sought alliances were the same individuals who organized posses to burn churches, attack labor organizers, and enforce the distinctions that denied blacks access to resources (Ingalls 1988).

As individuals, blacks were encouraged to regard each other as a threat. Those who were unskilled, unpropertied, and uncouth were considered to be as dangerous to the interests of black progress as the white night riders and demagogues. In seeking to establish themselves as "respectable," African Americans distanced themselves from, and in effect validated the unworthiness of, the masses. These divisive circumstances were not fundamentally dissimilar from those that ensnared Afro-Cubans in Cuba, where color status further complicated the spectrum of class relations. In Tampa, however, there was far greater class homogeneity among Afro-Cubans, and the ideology of patriotic solidarity tended to dampen these tendencies both within and across color lines.

The social organization of the African American community was more complex and fragmented along class lines. By the 1890s there were six black churches and several chapters of the Masons and Odd Fellows. Membership in these institutions, especially the lodges, was exclusionary and tended to divide the community into defended circles, although there was some degree of connection between these social groupings. The truly poor and transient masses mostly did not belong to lodges, and often not to churches either (Howard and Howard 1994b). There were some organizations explicitly designed to promote the interests and well-being of all. The Watchman's Club, begun in 1894, was aimed at "watching over and protecting the welfare of the colored race." However broad in purpose, its members were drawn from the small group of professionals and entrepreneurs, the "talented tenth" of Du Boisian ideology.

This project inevitably joined the interests of black elites with those of laborers, domestic servants, and the restless unemployed. The ever present threat of violence, episodes of thuggery, and outbursts of indiscriminate racial hatred placed all black people in a vulnerable condition. Respectability was not a sufficient protection, nor was self-restraint unfailing in the face of insults and provocation. Threats surfaced in unpredictable situations that sometimes led to violence.

In the three years that the Cubans in Tampa were actively making war against Spain, between 1895 and 1898, a different sort of war was going on just beyond the bounds of Ybor City. African Americans were caught in combat with the rising effects of Jim Crow, played out in a city beset by the turbulence of growth and change (Adler 1995). Traces of these events can only be found in the white daily newspapers, the *Tampa Tribune* and the *Tampa Daily Times*, sources that are clearly wanting. The renditions do, however, provide details of much interest and insight into the ideological weapons of the Jim Crow regime. These public narratives of racial encounter were heavily encoded. Stories were replete with messages of intimidation against blacks who defied white authority, and themes of encouragement for whites who resorted to violence in enforcing it. "Big black brute" was a favorite term of reference. Rape and rumors of black uprising are pervasive themes. Numerous stories appeared about lynchings in other places, laced with lurid detail and editorial approval. Such approval was often qualified, decried as a necessary evil avoidable if only the blacks would forswear all right to resist. Attached to a report about the capture of five blacks accused of planning a "race war" in a nearby rural community, the *Tribune* writer offered the following advice: "The negroes ought to know that a race war, whether of small or great proportions, can only end one way—in the destruction of the blacks engaged in it. A few whites may be killed, but there can be no doubt as to the fate of the negroes. Our advice to the colored people is to cultivate friendly relations with the whites, live honestly, and be industrious and economical and the results will be satisfactory. A race war means annihilation for the negroes engaged in it."[16]

In the spring of 1895, a few months before the preceding item was written, Booker T. Washington delivered his famous speech in Atlanta, outlining a plan for a peaceful racial coexistence based on self-help, segregation, and surrender of political power. This comforting prescription was echoed approvingly in the *Tribune*'s foregoing editorial. A contingent of Tampa's race leaders traveled to the exposition to represent their community and listen to the speech.[17] The delegation was headed by the Reverend Mathew McDuffie, pastor of the St. James Episcopal Church. Not long after his return from Atlanta, two other Tampa blacks by the name of McDuffie—apparently not related to the pastor—became central actors in a drama that disclosed the limits of Washington's strategy.

On June 10, 1895, Jim McDuffie, a former employee of Spitler's Stable, confronted his white boss over wages he was still owed. An altercation ensued, which drew in a white employee of a nearby business and Jim's brother, John. In the scuffle, the white intervener was stabbed, either by Jim's knife or John's razor. The McDuffies managed to escape the scene, reportedly with the aid of other black people in the vicinity.[18] The fugitives instantly became the objects of an intense manhunt. The sheriff appointed a dozen deputies, who scoured the countryside for the next three days. Accounts of their progress received daily front-page coverage. In the frenzy to find the perpetrators, all black men were at risk of misidentification. Two men thought to be the McDuffies were arrested in Plant City (about fifteen miles away), and a lynch mob rapidly formed at the train station in Tampa to await their arrival. However, "the lynching party were [sic] sorely disappointed. The sheriff [who had gone there to identify them] reported that the negroes captured at Plant City were not the ones wanted."[19] On that same day in another location, another posse had stumbled onto a black woodchopper who broke into a run when he saw them. When apprehended, he managed to convince them that he was not one of the McDuffies. He escaped unharmed but badly frightened. The news item describes him whimsically as "the worst scared man in seven states."[20]

They finally did capture Jim McDuffie, although John made good his escape. Jim had hidden for two days in the dense undergrowth east of the Scrub, a jungle refuge well known to blacks who lived along its edge. He was caught when he attempted to reach his hometown in Central Florida.

Like the other men who had been arrested by mistake in Plant City, McDuffie's capture failed to result in a lynching, but only because the mob was deceived about his route of entry. "At the jail the gate [to the cell] was unlocked and McDuffie pushed it open himself so anxious was he to seek its friendly protection against supposed mob violence."[21] The news story about his capture was careful to note that Jim McDuffie was not the brother who had attacked a white man with a knife, even though earlier reports suggested that he had. The later disclaimer was likely inserted to defuse plans to lynch him.

It is significant perhaps that no lynchings or other murders actually were committed during this manhunt. Whereas acts of unspeakable ferocity occurred often in the rural reaches of the surrounding counties, Tampa was comparatively urbane and cosmopolitan, and far more civil in dispensing law and justice. Beyond city limits there was a reign of terror, within it was merely a reign of intimidation punctuated at intervals with murders of varying legality.

Harry Singleton, the most illustrious resister of white authority in this time and place, died by legal execution. His hanging was an event of extraordinary theater, a public festival that drew a huge crowd of both black and white Tampans. The crime occurred on September 26, 1895, at Salter's Bar in the Scrub. In the previous month, Tampa's mayor had declared "war on bawdy houses" and the "mongrel denizens of Ybor City and the Scrub" who operated and patronized these establishments.[22] On this particular evening, a pair of policemen, one black and one white, were attempting to arrest Ella Felter. Harry, who lived with Ella, intervened and shot the white officer dead on the spot. He immediately escaped into the Scrub. Ella also fled but was later captured hiding under a pile of laundry. Although this happened late at night, word of the murder of a white man by a black man, still at large, rapidly produced a large posse of volunteers. By the time they arrived at the scene of the crime, Harry was long gone. Singleton, who was twenty-nine years old, was a well-known gambler and sport. He was no ordinary outlaw, but rather educated, intelligent, and likable, a member in good standing in the Masonic and Odd Fellows lodges. In the subterranean social world of African Americans, the boundary between respectable and racy was less clearly drawn than it was in public. Saloons were prosperous businesses, and gambling offered an independent livelihood that avoided the need to labor. Singleton was admired for his dignity and courage, and the news coverage hints at prior confrontations between him and law enforcement over the treatment of black women. A black guard at the jail was arrested because he was friendly with Singleton and had been involved earlier when Singleton objected to the dead policeman's sexual harassment of black women.

"Several prominent negroes" beseeched the sheriff "not to terrify the Scrub with his subordinates." The Tampa Rifles, the local militia, and about fifty volunteers attempted to find Singleton, but he had retreated deep into the adjoining area. A deputy reported on their lack of success. "I have no doubt that Singleton is in that marsh, that scrub, or whatever it is called; but it is too big to be surrounded and too boggy to go over thoroughly. You can't ride a horse through it, and only a desperate man could manage to stay in there."[23] Days passed with no sign of the fugitive, only shadowy reports of aid by local blacks who sent food and clothing into his jungle hideout. Another sighting was in Ybor City. The *Tribune* inferred that "he is being fed and cared for by his colored friends. There is no doubt that he has the sympathy of his people to a great extent and that his prominence in the Odd Fellows and Masons has given him a big pull where it will do him the most good."[24]

The reward climbed from $200 to $300 and finally $400, at which level it yielded betrayal. A tip led the police to the room of a black woman who lived on Central Avenue. Inside a large trunk, they discovered Harry. Events unfolded slowly in a trial, retrial, and ultimately execution. Captured in early October 1895, he was hanged on January 8, 1898.

As Harry was led from his cell to the place of execution, loud wails sang forth from the black women in the crowd. On the gallows, Harry addressed the crowd for nearly an hour before the trap was sprung. Accompanied by the pastor of the AME Church, former symbol of black political assertion, Harry proclaimed his conversion to Christianity. "I stand here as one of the luckiest men in the crowd for I can say that Jesus has forgiven me and saved me." He also used his brief time on stage to voice his defiance. "You are not hanging me because I was convicted by the court. You are hanging me because I am a negro and killed a white man." A black man in the crowd stepped forward to ask if he was guilty. "My answer is yes." A short drop through the opening beneath his feet, a legend became a corpse. His body was taken to the church he had so recently joined, and a large solemn funeral marked his final passing.

There was no apparent injustice in this act. The accused was guilty; he was fairly tried. The propriety and solemnity of the proceedings only underscored the power of the state and the limits of subaltern resistance. An outpouring of sympathy from the black community, however, the closing of ranks around a courageous desperado, also signaled resolve to find meaning in struggle and dignity in loss. Respectability was not just about pious acceptance and careful decorum, it was also about standing up and fighting back.

A few months after Singleton's execution, a battalion of black warriors arrived in town, Buffalo Soldiers who were conscripted into the war against Spain. If Harry's example of upright resistance was worrisome to Tampa's white populace, the actions of these men surely struck terror.

A Spanish-American War

As developments rapidly moved forward in Cuba, the U.S. State Department showed growing interest. The "Pearl of the Antilles" seemed at last to be within their grasp. By late 1897, U.S. ships were sailing around the waters off Tampa Bay and reconnoitering the shoreline in search of good locations for deploying troops. A few months later, the *Maine* exploded in Havana Harbor, and the stage was set. The destruction of the *Maine*, blamed on the Spanish, offered a pretext for intervention.

In what has become a legendary example of journalistic propaganda, the press launched a campaign aimed at demonizing the Spanish and gaining sympathy for the Cuban patriots. Estrada Palma was likened to the forefathers of U.S. independence, a courtly and educated man who was quite comfortable in the drawing rooms of the rich and influential. Behind the facade of moral suasion, however, was a cynical strategy by the State Department to co-opt the Cuban independence movement and launch an era of unprecedented expansionism by the United States. For their part, however, the Cuban exile leadership welcomed this new attention after so many frustrating years of seeking aid. Estrada Palma became convinced that victory could be achieved only through alliance with the powerful North Americans (Pérez 1983).

Back in Ybor City, growing U.S. support for their belligerence drew a mixed reaction among Cuban patriots. On the one hand, there was jubilation that victory seemed at last to be near. On the other, there was concern that the principles of José Martí were being bartered away in the process. In the year after Martí's death, Rafael Serra had begun publication in New York of a periodical entitled *La Doctrina de Martí*, aimed at maintaining Martí's ideological perspective. He correctly perceived that, with the departure of El Maestro, the elitist faction would regain control of exile politics (Poyo 1989:128). His fears were shared among a significant contingent of the cigarmaker patriots. In February 1897, a meeting was called in Manuel Granados's barbershop, chaired by Guillermo Sorondo and attended by both Afro-Cubans and radical white labor activists. The purpose was to raise funds to support Serra's publication, which was threatened with insolvency (Poyo 1985a:94). Their efforts helped rescue Serra's magazine, but at that point no one could halt the juggernaut of U.S. imperialism.

Tampa was chosen as the point of debarkation for the troops that were being assembled rapidly to liberate the island. By late May the city swelled with the arrival of thirty thousand soldiers and war correspondents— more than twice the number who were permanent residents. Among the first U.S. troops to be dispatched to Tampa were four black regiments of the regular army. These regiments, commanded by white officers, had been deployed from the West, battle-hardened in fights with Indians. Altogether, some four thousand black soldiers served a brief but unpleasant tour of duty in Tampa (Gatewood 1972; Mohlman 1999).

The arrival of such a large contingent of black troops in Tampa was met with alarm. They were heavily armed and prone to swagger, and their presence offended white Tampans, leading to a series of ugly incidents. The *Tampa Tribune* described them as "black ruffians in uniform," and noted with incredulity that they "insist on being treated as white men are treated."[25] Indeed, they had been out of the South for a very long time and were conditioned to respond aggressively when assaulted. On one occasion they "shot up" a barbershop where the proprietor had yelled obscenities and refused service. They also managed to close down several saloons and cafes that had refused to serve black soldiers.

The worst incident occurred just prior to departure for Cuba. On June 6, 1898, a group of intoxicated white troops from Ohio "decided to have some fun" with a two-year-old black child. Snatched from the arms of his mother, the child was used as a target for several soldiers to demonstrate their marksmanship. The winner was the soldier who sent a bullet through the sleeve of the boy's shirt (Gatewood 1970:8; 1972; Mohlman 1999:54–55). Although the child was ultimately returned unharmed to his mother, word of this episode quickly reached the black troops of the 24th and 25th Infantry Regiments. A spontaneous riot erupted. "They stormed into the streets firing their pistols indiscriminately, wrecking cafes and saloons which had refused to serve them, and forcing their way into white brothels" (Gatewood 1970:8).

The rampage was finally quelled when white troops from the 2nd Georgia Volunteer Infantry were called in to restore order. Acting with gusto, the Georgians waded in. The next morning twenty-seven black troops and "several" white Georgia volunteers were transferred to a hospital in Atlanta suffering from serious wounds. The death toll was not published, but one likely exaggerated account indicated that "the streets of Tampa ran red with Negro blood" (Gatewood 1970:9).

Within the week, U.S. troops were off to Cuba, sailing into battle on ships that were rigidly segregated—black troops on the starboard side, white troops on the port side (Gatewood 1970). When the war was first declared, many (although not all) black Americans welcomed the opportunity to prove themselves in combat and help in the liberation of the oppressed colored people in Cuba (Gatewood 1972). Their experiences in Tampa, at the hands of soldiers and civilians alike, erased all such illusions. The experiences of their Afro-Cuban brothers were similar.

Cuban cigarmakers also mobilized for the final campaign. During the years between 1895 and 1898, large numbers had already departed to fight in Cuba; at least twenty-seven filibustering expeditions were launched from Tampa in that period (Steffy 1975:100). Cubans in uniform drilled in public and then departed in secret. When war finally was declared by the United States, hundreds from Tampa went to join Gómez. Although it was their war, and their country, they were largely ignored by U.S. military officers. War correspondents in Tampa regarded the Cubans with a mixture of amusement and contempt. And it was at this juncture that the reporters began to discover a fact conveniently left out of the press reports leading up to the war: more than half of the Cuban liberation army was black (Ferrer 1999:3; Helg 1995:86).

U.S. officers refused to recognize the Cuban military organization that had been established, negotiating separately with each field commander and relegating the Cubans to a secondary support role (Pérez 1983). Their leaders were not consulted about tactical decisions, and the troops were assigned menial tasks. Resistance to these assignments was interpreted as lassitude by a racially inferior and ungrateful ally. Reports back from the campaign described the Cubans in varied derogatory terms: "a wretched mongrel lot"; "treacherous, lying, cowardly, thieving, worthless half-breed mongrel"; "mango-bellied degenerates" (quoted in Pérez 1983:206).

When victory came on August 12, a scant two months after the U.S. troops set down on Cuban soil, Teddy Roosevelt issued the following assessment of the role of the Cubans: "We should have been better off if there had not been a single Cuban with the army. They accomplished literally nothing, while they were a source of trouble and embarrassment" (quoted in Pérez 1983:201). In one short pronouncement by a future president of the United States, the cumulative struggle that had been waged since 1868, the vast financial sacrifices of the cigarmakers and the thousands of lives that were lost, were all accounted as worth "literally nothing." Spain was out of Cuba, but Cuba was not free.

The exile government in New York waited helplessly as the propaganda campaign turned viciously against them. Such a beggarly and cowardly nation had no business governing itself. In what became known as the "Spanish-American War," the Americans were the only victors. In conventional fashion, the term "American" was restricted to the United States. In December 1898, the PRC dutifully disbanded, and Estrada Palma issued a directive that the local revolutionary organizations should be dissolved.

These declarations only formalized a reality that already existed. Revolutionary organizations in Tampa had virtually ceased to function with the departure of the volunteers. With the United States in the conflict, there was less urgency in raising funds. Expatriate Cubans, clinging to the belief that victory had been won, returned to the island in droves following the Spanish surrender. Ramon Rivero was among the first to leave, taking along all of the equipment in his print shop (Muñiz 1976:126). He and his newspaper, *Cuba*, were going home.

4

Exiles

A lot of the Cubans, not all but a great many of them, went back
to Cuba [after 1898]. They left their jobs, thinking to go back to Cuba.
When they got there, they found that they could not live.

Tomás

When the war ended, the Cuban colony in Tampa entered a new phase, less
focused on national politics and more on creating a community in exile.
Initially, there was a large exodus back to Cuba of celebrants who would
soon confront disappointing realities.[1] The Cuban economy was in ruins,
and Cubans were not in control of its rehabilitation.

> TOMÁS: So they had to come back and start all over again. Getting a
> job and everything. So they, what they did was try to go to Cuba
> every year, because they had a great love for the island. They were
> very patriotic. They [factories] used to have a big layoff around
> Christmas, and as soon as the holiday was over they would rehire
> everybody. They would go for Christmas. They loved their country.
> Everything is Cuba. . . . My father used to go a lot. My mama told me
> he used to save money. Then when it came he would leave and come
> back broke. This happened every year. Every year he'd go to Cuba and
> spend all his money and come back and say, "Can't marry you till
> next year." That wasn't only my father. There were others.

Cigarmakers left en masse for Cuba at Christmas, and many came and
went as individuals throughout the year. Slowdowns in particular factories, disagreements on the job or in the neighborhood, word that they were
hiring in factories in Havana, family emergencies back home—countless
reasons took them back, sometimes permanently. Not all paths led to
Cuba. There were colonies of Cuban cigarmakers in Key West, Jacksonville, Philadelphia, and New York. Tampa was a stop along a broad circuit,
and movement followed the contours of activity throughout the industry.

Modern scholars of immigration increasingly have discovered that old categories do not fit new circumstances, that many who leave home to settle in the United States keep one foot on the soil of their birth, join a broader field of experience, assume a *transnational* identity (Basch, Schiller and Blanc 1994; Kearney 1995). In the case of the early Cuban immigrants in Tampa, new categories also fit old circumstances. Cigarmakers moved freely between Cuba and Florida and never lost touch with home. They viewed themselves more as expatriates, always holding in their minds the possibility that victory would be theirs one day, and they could finally go home to stay. This does not mean that they did not form a permanent community in Tampa. They were not just migrants, or guest workers, who did not invest and did not feel obliged to reckon the conditions of their new political environment. Quite the contrary. Sojourning required careful construction of a safe route, welcoming institutions and predictable modes of interaction with a host community that, for Afro-Cubans in particular, was anything but hospitable.

Black immigrants in a Jim Crow city faced challenges that differed greatly from those of Europeans who settled in industrial cities of the North, and they optioned advantages not shared by those who had put an ocean between themselves and the homeland they left. Afro-Cubans in Tampa did not simply constitute another chapter in the immigrant experience of that era, nor were they simply another chapter in the black experience. But they were in some measure both of those things.

A number of studies have examined the differences between white immigrants and black natives—the paradoxical advantages that foreign whites exacted from the racism of their host communities, and the processes of enclave development that contrasted sharply with the punishing ghettoization of African Americans in the cities where they lived (Bodnar, Weber and Simon 1988; Appel 1966; Glazer and Moynihan 1970). But what about black immigrants arriving in the same period? Were they doubly disadvantaged, or did they too derive paradoxical privileges from the fact that they were foreigners? And what about this business of transnationalism? How did the facts that the Cubans were not so far from home that they could not return, or that cigar work was inherently mobile— what Cooper (1983) labels the "traveling fraternity"—play into the adjustment of Afro-Cuban immigrants in early-twentieth-century Florida? And what about the multilateral ties of race and ethnicity in this setting— between black and white Cubans, or Afro-Cubans and African Americans, or Afro-Cubans and the other immigrants who lived in Tampa, or Afro-

Table 3. Ethnic Composition of Hillsborough County, 1890–1910[a]

	1890	1900	1910
White Cubans	1,116	2,993	5,227
Black Cubans	197[b]	540	900
Spaniards	233	963	3,746
Italians	56	1,315	3,919
Native-born of Foreign Parents	na	4,207	10,950
Native Whites	9,721	15,853	33,954
Native Blacks	2,917	8,445	16,445
Hillsborough Population	14,941	36,013	78,374

a. This table should be read with care. The geographic units pose problems in deriving clear proportions of immigrant groups in the urban population. The municipal boundaries of Tampa changed among the periods, and West Tampa was enumerated separately until 1930. The distributions of Cubans, Spaniards, and Italians are represented for the county as a whole, as are the other main ethnic categories. The children of these immigrants are mostly, although not entirely, of the category "native born of foreign parents." There were small numbers of immigrants (both black and white) who were not from Cuba, Spain, or Italy. In 1900, for example, there were 719 born in other parts of Europe (mainly England, Germany, and Ireland), and there were 440 from the Anglophone West Indies (12th U.S. Census, Population Reports, part I, vol. I, p. 742).
b. There are no separate figures available for black Cubans in 1890; this figure is an estimate based on 15 percent of total Cubans (1,313).
Sources: 11th, 12th, and 13th U.S. Censuses for Hillsborough County, Florida.

Cubans and native-born whites? This chapter takes up these interrelated questions.

The enclave that developed in Tampa in the early part of the twentieth century was unique in various dimensions. The immigrants did not simply arrive in a city where they found work, they created the city out of the work they did. And there were so many of them that their numbers alone transformed a sleepy town into a booming urban center. Table 3 illustrates the rapid growth in Tampa's population between 1890 and 1910. In 1908, it was estimated that 65 percent of the population consisted of immigrant families, and the wages paid to immigrant cigar workers accounted for 75 percent of Tampa's total household income.[2] Well organized and relatively well paid, the immigrants constructed a city within a city, where radical alternative institutions and ideas proliferated. The main groups were Cuban, Spanish, and Italian. Cubans were in the majority through the entire period, but Italians and Spaniards also grew into sizable groups. Counted separately, black Cubans constituted about 7 percent of the immigrants and 15 percent of Cubans. Within the larger population, African Americans accounted for about one-fifth of the native born. White Anglo Tampans were actually a minority group, although they controlled most of the wealth and formal sources of power. However, the well-being of the entire local economy depended on the cigar industry. The workers' skill and their conscious efforts to protect the value of their labor formed a significant factor in the sociopolitical equation.

Industrial immigrants in a southern city forged a proletarian community where Old World socialism and Latin American independence joined in an ongoing struggle against the imperialism, Social Darwinism, and voracious capitalism that were the signature of the era. Cuban revolutionaries with a strong commitment to labor activism found allies in the Italian and Spanish peasants who also settled in Tampa. They had left rural villages in northwest Spain and southwest Sicily that were similarly wracked with poverty and political upheaval, where many had been romanced by ideas of socialism and anarchism. In a small frontier city on the west coast of Florida, they practiced these ideas in the construction of an insular settlement whose ideological foundations contrasted starkly with the post-Confederate southern belief system that characterized the host community.

A Latin Enclave

The immigrant cigar workers who lived in Ybor City shared a common border between themselves and the native-born population. Together they constituted a group known locally—both self-defined and externally designated—as "Latin." The connotation included Latin America and both Spain and Italy. They were regarded as Latin "races," people who shared Catholicism, languages that were similarly derived from Latin, and a certain swarthiness. They were differentiated in contrast with the whiter, English-speaking, northern-European-derived Protestants, who constituted the dominant, native-born elite. More fundamentally, the immigrants shared geographic isolation, common attachment to the cigar industry, and a common set of beliefs and values about labor and politics. Many factors knitted them together into a community. Beneath this umbrella of Latin sameness, however, rested an intricate internal hierarchy based on nationality and color.

Afro-Cubans were Latins, but their very existence jeopardized the meaning of the term—expanded the color spectrum of Latin identity and implicitly confirmed the likelihood of "impure" bloodlines. This tension reflected North American concepts about race and blood, coupled with similar notions about *limpieza de sangre* (purity of blood) imported from Europe and Cuba. Latin identity, as defined by the immigrants themselves, reflected legal and customary effects of Moorish occupation centuries earlier. Spaniards, a few of whom moved freely in the upper circles of Tampa society, were particularly averse to being labeled together with Cubans of African descent. Sicily's long occupation by the Saracens insinuated potential African ancestry into their national identity, and they also tried to avoid being too closely associated with Afro-Cubans. White Cubans, for whom such association was most likely and most natural, were thus most in need of demarcation. The white Cubans, as distinct from the Spaniards, were considered to be darker and more mixed in their backgrounds, a less pure variety of white people. This was a stereotype they protested, and against which they struggled. External and internal prejudices about African "blood" mirrored and reinforced a class hierarchy embedded in the organization of the cigar industry and the economic opportunity structure of early Ybor City.

In terms of class, Spaniards were at the top, but this group was also the most diverse in economic circumstances. The wealthiest immigrants were the Spanish factory owners, the aristocrats of the community. Many who occupied the slender middle class in Ybor City were Spaniards. Shopkeepers, boardinghouse owners, foremen in factories, bookkeepers and accountants, workers who performed the prized tasks of sorting and packing finished cigars, all tended to be Spaniards rather than Cubans. Most Spaniards in Tampa, however, were far less affluent. A large cohort were regular cigarmakers, often less skilled and not as well paid as their Cuban counterparts. They were relatively recent immigrants from impoverished rural regions of Spain, lured first to Cuba by an official policy aimed at "whitening" the population. Many of these immigrants brought their discontents against the Church and Crown along with them to Cuba, even as they served as pawns in the scheme to dilute the dangers of a darkening and restive creole population on the island. In Ybor City, many of these Spaniards had switched sides and supported independence, and afterwards they played significant roles in labor organizations. Although internally differentiated, Spaniards as a whole had the greatest access to privilege.

Sicilians arrived in Tampa under circumstances different from the rest. Initially, they were not part of the cigar industry. They came as refugees from a vicious system of labor in other parts of Florida and Louisiana, and from an incident in 1891 in New Orleans when eleven Sicilian immigrants were lynched for alleged association with the Mafia. This eruptive violence resulted in an exodus of Sicilian families from that city into Tampa, where they joined a handful of families who were already there. Others who arrived during this period had been working as laborers in sugar and phosphate (Mormino & Pozzetta 1987:81). These two industries in Florida were organized around a system of forced labor and debt bondage. Most of the workers were African Americans, but labor contractors also conscripted new immigrants in the North with false promises that were easily broken in the remote swamps and forests of Florida. Many Sicilian immigrants who managed to extract themselves from these disadvantageous arrangements settled in Tampa, where they found a kind of oasis in Ybor City. They still confronted problems and were not initially welcome in the cigar factories, but the climate of life was considerably freer there. Over time the Sicilians experienced unusual success in this setting, to some extent gained at the expense of Cubans.

A Special Racism

Internal differentiation and external solidarity produced unusual race relations within the bounds of the Latin community. These conditions have been interpreted in various ways, most of which emphasize the contrast with black-white relations in the rest of Tampa. Harmonious relations among Latins are set against the harsh inequities of Anglo Tampa. Mormino and Pozzetta (1987) assign considerable weight to the effects of shared ideologies of class struggle.

> Ybor City radicals operated in a community that precluded any facile acceptance of Jim Crow practices or beliefs. The facts of everyday life gave the lie to the most negative racist assertions about black inferiority and undesirability. The intermixture of substantial numbers of Afro-Cubans in the neighborhoods, workrooms, and union halls accustomed residents not only to the presence of black faces but also to interacting and working with these people on a day-to-day basis. . . . To be sure Ybor City residents, including radicals, accommodated southern racial practices in some respects. The founding of the all-black Martí-Maceo Club [sic] represented such a compromise, at least in part. To flaunt more vigorously the racial mores of Anglo Tampa was to risk even greater manifestations of vigilantism, an ever present danger. Radicals preferred to work in ways that promised less overt danger—that is, by accepting dark-skinned people as comrades,

by working next to them at cigar factory benches, by building strong labor unions with them, and by living near them in the streets and alleyways of the community. (Mormino & Pozzetta 1987:153)

The story that is told about Ybor City—and it is not just the rendering of these authors—paints an ennobling contrast with the wretched treatment of African Americans who lived not very far away in an enclave of their own, which was called the Scrub. Other chroniclers of this dual example of race relations in Tampa, both immigrants and natives, repeat and confirm this story of racial harmony among Latins (Anthony 1989; Brady 1997; Howard and Howard 1994b; Kennedy 1989; Long 1965b, 1971b; Muñiz 1962, 1963; Pacheco 1994; Pizzo 1985).

As a text, it bears analysis. For white Cubans, it supports the myth of racial equality, fidelity to the ideals of José Martí. Other white immigrants who tell it validate their moral superiority in comparison with native thugs and pious churchgoing racists. White natives who tell this tale use it to make invidious comparisons between Afro-Cubans and African Americans. Black Cubans were regarded as superior, were assumed to possess larger quanta of white "blood," and to have cultural attributes that distinguished them favorably from native-born blacks. The degradation of African Americans could be thus attributed to their own innate characteristics, a naturalized explanation for their subordinated status. African Americans had their own reasons for believing in the "racial paradise" of Ybor City. For them, it provided an example of how things should be between blacks and whites, proof that harmonious relations were theoretically possible. The relatively better treatment accorded to Afro-Cubans also provided a rhetorical weapon in the litany of unfairness about which African Americans rightly complained. Perceptions that Afro-Cubans enjoyed material advantages and escaped the indignities of racism sharpened envy and bitterness towards them by African Americans. Finally, the version told by Afro-Cubans themselves was both nuanced and multifaceted. There was a contradictory inside story that focused on betrayal and hypocrisy, and a conciliatory outside story that reflected comity, pride, and gratitude. For the most part, however, there was silence—an unwillingness to speak about race, and a studied discomfort about voicing complaints when white Cubans and their other white immigrant neighbors "accommodated southern racial practices" by excluding or insulting them.

In the absence of objection by the Afro-Cubans, white Cubans and their Spanish and Italian comrades could maintain the fiction of racial solidarity, with the most obvious departures (such as the existence of a segregated all-black mutual aid society) blamed on the harsh laws and vicious customs of the host. My own interpretation of the special conditions of race relations in Ybor City, crafted in connivance with memories of elderly Afro-Cubans, challenges this comfortable convenience. The goal is to turn the myth of racial equality inside out, to examine the Afro-Cubans' private understanding of the process by which patriotic solidarity among Cubans in Tampa fell away under the weight of Jim Crow Tampa. It begins with an origin myth, framing the frequently cited, inescapable fact of racially segregated Cuban organizations.

Ethnogenesis

Ethnic distinctions within the Latin community were institutionalized in a series of mutual aid societies formed in rapid succession prior to and after the turn of the century. The earliest was Centro Español, begun in 1891 at the height of tensions between Cubans and Spaniards. Founders of the society included wealthy Spanish factory owners who sought to offer protections for their compatriots and themselves against the threat of Cuban belligerence. The Sicilians began theirs a few years later, in 1894, also motivated by perceived threats to their collective security—not from Cubans but from Anglo Tampa. The formation of L'Unione Italiana was, in a somewhat literal sense, the defining moment of group identity. A highly publicized murder in Ybor City just before the club was founded was attributed to the Mafia. Memories of New Orleans, and awareness that Tampa also nurtured vigilantes, motivated a public display of denial. Mormino and Pozzetta reproduced a portion of the statement published by a group of Sicilian business leaders and former sugar cutters.

> Reference having been made by newspapers to the effect that the atrocious crime was . . . the act and deed of the dreaded Mafia, and knowing that it is liable to injure the reputation, business standing and character of the Italian residents in the city of Tampa, therefore we repudiate and deny having any such organization, and we hereby pledge ourselves to help and give the authorities our support in ferreting out the criminals of such act. (Mormino and Pozzetta 1987:86)

In describing themselves as Italian rather than Sicilian, they redefined themselves. In repudiating the secret society, they also took steps to form an open, respectable organization, a mutual benefit society. Mormino and

Pozzetta (p. 87) speculated that "by using 'Italian' in its incorporated name, the club may have been trying to deflect some of the negative connotations surrounding 'Sicilian' that existed in Tampa."

Cubans during the 1890s channeled their organizational energies into the revolutionary clubs in Ybor City and West Tampa. When Estrada Palma issued a directive in 1898 to dissolve the clubs, they followed the discipline of the party and duly disbanded (Steffy 1975:130). The Liceo Cubano had not been a revolutionary club exactly. Although organized by revolutionists, it was much broader in function. It served as a social hall, educational facility, and as a mutual aid society, more along the lines of the *sociedades* in Cuba. They determined that Estrada Palma's order did not affect the status of the Liceo. There was no reason to disband it, and many reasons to keep it in operation. The Cubans decided that they also needed a mutual aid society (Muñiz 1976:128).

Liceo Cubano was transformed into El Club Nacional Cubano, Octubre 10 (October 10 was the day on which the Cuban revolution was first launched in 1868, *el grito de Yara*). Its formation was announced in a brief notice in the *Tampa Tribune* on December 2, 1899. A well-known Afro-Cuban, Guillermo Sorondo, was the first secretary, one of four directors. In the words of a white Cuban contemporary who arrived in Tampa shortly after the war, it "was composed of white and black members—a sort of rice with black beans."[3]

The new organization was simply Cuban. Membership by both white and black Cubans, especially given their recent comradeship in the struggle against Spain, was perhaps unremarkable. In the beginning, at least, it would have been awkward to suggest they be constituted otherwise. To raise the issue of race in determining who should belong to the Cuban national organization surely would have been problematic. But then something happened to shatter the silence and force the issue. As an integrated organization, the October 10 Club lasted not quite a year. A new Cuban organization was begun on October 26, 1900. Named Los Libres Pensadores de Martí y Maceo (Free Thinkers of Martí and Maceo), its twenty-four founding members were Afro-Cubans who previously had belonged to the October 10 Club.

This was the official opening moment of the schism that occurred between black and white Cubans in Tampa. It was decisive and precise, and directly resulted in a material restructuring of Cuban ethnicity in that setting that lasted from that time forward. The scenario was enacted in two meetings. The first was of the October 10 Club, at which a decision was made that black and white Cubans could not belong to the same organization. It is not clear when this meeting took place, probably sometime in October of 1900, possibly having some connection to planned celebrations of Grito de Yara on the 10th. What is clear, however, is that henceforth the black Cubans could no longer belong or attend. They proceeded to form their own club, and the white Cubans retained occupancy of the old Ybor factory building that had once housed the Liceo Cubano.

The split was described by José Rivero Muñiz, a Cuban author who lived in Tampa during that period and may have been present.

> It was necessary to overcome difficulties that were based more on custom than on law. This was the racial attitude existing in the southern states where the white majority considered it inconceivable that individuals of different races in the community could belong to the same organization. Fortunately, there had never existed racial prejudice among the black and white Cubans. There had been always the most cordial relations between them. But in this part of the United States it was necessary to face the reality of the facts. . . . They began to look for a solution, in spite of the fact that there was opposition among those who believed in equality for all. The idea was to organize two different organizations. One was to be made up of white members and the other of blacks. Both had the same desire of trying to be useful to the Cuban colony. (Muñiz 1976:128–29)

Muñiz's disingenuous assertion that there had been no "racial prejudice" among Cubans, that they simply sought a shared solution to the "reality of the facts," is the same interpretation offered by Mormino and Pozzetta (1987). He does note that this decision was not forced by the reality of "law," only that of "custom." Indeed, there was no formal law against interracial organizations yet; most of the Jim Crow ordinances that gave better cover were not passed until several years later. The force of custom should not be underestimated, and Muñiz does not explicitly identify which or whose custom he was referring to, a matter I will elaborate shortly. A local custom of white Anglos in Tampa was a belief that association determined social identity. Had the white Cubans continued to share social space with their black compatriots, the result would have been to define all Cubans as "niggers," something that the more bigoted Anglos routinely did anyway. Muñiz also alludes to opposition to the split, efforts to resist compromise for the sake of racists, by "those who believed in equality for all." A curious modifier, as if to suggest that the others, the apparent majority, no longer believed in equality, had quietly abandoned the vision of "*con todos y para todos*" ("with all and for all").

The identities of the dissenters are not given, and the discourse that preceded the action is unfortunately lost. Muñiz's account is the only written record of what took place. We do not know which of the Afro-Cuban independence activists were involved in this conflict, although we do know the identities of those who formed the Martí-Maceo Society. Guillermo Sorondo left Tampa at about the time it happened, as did Manuel and Joaquín Granados, and most of the other journalists. Ruperto Pedroso's family stayed, along with Teofilo Domínguez and Bruno Roig. All three were among the founding members of the Martí-Maceo Society.

The meeting at which it occurred was held in the front parlor of Ruperto and Paulina Pedroso's boardinghouse. It was a small group, but in a crowded space. The opening meeting lasted four hours, from 8:30 P.M. to 12:30 A.M. The recorded minutes of this initial meeting are only two pages long. These pages contain no information about the previous organization and only the barest of explanations for why this one was formed, simply to allow them to meet "outside the house, in a manner acceptable to men of dignity."[4] A telegraphic reference to possible indignities that motivated this action is all that the record provides. The opening paragraph lists the names of twenty-three men, some of whom are recognizable as having been involved in independence activities. In addition to those previously mentioned was José I. Ramos, an associate of Domínguez, who was elected president. Others included Antonio Palacios, who had been an officer in one of the revolutionary clubs during the war, and Alejandro Acosta, who became a long-standing symbol within the club of the independence legacy.[5]

Domínguez took the floor to explain the purpose of the new organization. It would be modeled on a club in Cienfuegos, to which several of those present had belonged—Libres Pensadores Antonio Maceo de Sta. Clara (Freethinkers Antonio Maceo of Santa Clara). Echoing the goals of La Liga, Domínguez stated that the main purpose of forming an organization in Tampa was to complete their education. Discussion then arose over the relationship between the Tampa club and the one in Cienfuegos. It was decided that there would be no formal connection, only a similarity in charters. (They never joined El Directorio Central.) The group decided that Bruno Roig should be present, based on his knowledge of the club in Cienfuegos, and presumably his former stature as an officer in local independence organizations. Roig had not originally attended the meeting owing to illness, but they adjourned for half an hour and went and got him. They continued to debate the form and purpose of the new organization, and shortly after midnight a committee was appointed to draft the by-laws and procedures.

They also adopted a name—Sociedad de Libre Pensadores de Tampa "Martí y Maceo." The reasons for choosing the name are not disclosed. It is tempting to speculate on the significance of including both Martí and Maceo, when the counterpart from which the name was lifted honored only Maceo. This modification appears to reinforce the biracial images of Cuban independence, to symbolize the ideals of Martí, and possibly served to remind the white Cubans who so easily seemed to forget. I found no evidence, either oral or documentary, that the name carried any accusatory symbolism. There is, however, confirmation that the founders of Martí-Maceo were bitter towards their white compatriots, and that relations between the two clubs were frequently tense.

The story of the split was related by several of the people I interviewed, one of whom was seven years old when it happened. Too young to remember it directly, he had spoken about it with those who were involved, had heard it discussed at intervals afterwards when the subject of conversation turned to the white Cuban club.

> LUIS: The one [who] used to tell me a lot about what used to happen was Alejandro Acosta. They resented the way some of the white Cubans, back when they moved from the first club, that they separated themselves. And some of the blacks resented it, you know, very hard. [But] many people would come and go. All of 'em didn't know what happened, you know, didn't care much. Some resented it, must have, they used to discuss it in those meetings, what happened, you know.

Within the walls of Martí-Maceo, stories were told that differed from the account given by Muñiz. The reference to people who "would come and go," to the mobile character of the community, offers some insight into how the schism was ameliorated. The individuals who were actually involved were few in comparison to the numbers of subsequent arrivals, and many of the principals involved in the split did not remain in Tampa. It became a fuzzy collective memory. As the story was handed down, the burden of blame fell increasingly on Jim Crow, more in line with Muñiz's apologia, although without exonerating the white Cubans. Another informant, whose grandfather was part of the founding group, explained it this way:

TOMÁS: What I heard from my parents was that when the black and white Cubans migrated to Tampa, they used to be together and they had the same club. They all went to the same club. And there came a time when they had to go one way, and the others had to go the other. First because of the law, the state demanded that they had to be separate. There was no such thing as Cuban integration. And then the [white] Cubans, being that they were in a country where they had discrimination, they started discriminating against the black. So there was enough Cubans, black Cubans, here to start their own club.

Mormino and Pozzetta maintain that there was no discrimination within Ybor City, only nominal compliance with laws and regulations. Accounts by Afro-Cubans, however, present a less charitable view. They indicate that white immigrants did practice active discrimination—that they often reflected subtle racist attitudes in their interactions, and gained certain obvious advantages from the exclusion of blacks—because the setting both encouraged and permitted them to do so. It was part of learning to be an American, a prerogative attached to their white skin. In my narratives, these observations were almost always offered in a qualified and somewhat sympathetic manner, affirming that white immigrants treated blacks far better than Anglo Tampans, and comprehending their desire to avoid problems for themselves and their families. Those individuals who had been part of the independence movement in Tampa, whose former comrades had expelled them to protect their own social comfort, were reportedly less forgiving of ideological concessions made by white Cubans to the problematic circumstances of Jim Crow Florida, although they too could understand the "reality of the facts" (as Muñiz so carefully put it).

Text and Context

The split between the two Cuban clubs has been a recurrent feature in published accounts of Latin race relations in Tampa, interpreted in various ways, and nearly always viewed through a lens of "presentism" and/or self-serving distortion. This episode is a knot in the fabric of the tale, a stubborn anomaly that begs explanation. In virtually no time at all, racial segregation drove an effective wedge between Cubans in Tampa, unlocked their patriotic embrace, and repudiated one of Martí's central tenets. How do these facts square with portraits of Latin Tampa as radical, politically energized practitioners of working-class solidarity? Rationalizing such apparent contradictions has entailed a type of double dissembling; first to avert the realities of racism in Cuba (as in Muñiz's contention that such never existed), and then to explain somehow why the white Cubans surrendered their principles, without making them appear cowardly. In the process, actions of the past have tended to be filtered through explanatory frameworks of the present, judged against contemporary values about race and courage.

It is important to ground this process in a clearer understanding of the political context in which it occurred and the customary arrangements to which it pertained. *Sociedades* in Cuba had always been segregated by color. Even in the independence period, Afro-Cubans in Tampa had formed a separate mutual aid society, La Verdad, which had been affiliated with Juan Gualberto Gómez's Directorio Central. La Liga de Instrucción, Martí's own creation, had been racially separate. There were certainly precedents for divided organizations in the aftermath of independence, and in Cuba only Morúa Delgado forcefully argued for disbanding the *sociedades de la raza de color*.

The integrated character of the October 10 Club in Tampa was therefore a departure from Cuban custom, unusual in itself. Given the intensity of Martí's influence in that place and time, it is not surprising that this custom might have been set aside in Tampa; but, given also the sharpening intensity of racism and segregation in Tampa during that period, it is equally unsurprising that this arrangement would have failed.

The climate in which these events unfolded was not simply hostile; it was menacing. A two-pronged campaign of terror against African Americans and labor activists was becoming part of the quotidian backdrop of life in Tampa. In the months that preceded the formation of the October 10 Club, there was a spate of violent episodes that surely urged caution for many white Cubans. In June, M. J. Christopher, an African American newspaper editor, was murdered in a restaurant to which he had been lured by the police. This episode culminated a protracted effort by leaders in the black community to protest the violent behavior of police towards a "respectable" black woman. The editor had dared to print a vituperative story about this treatment and was subsequently killed for this affront. The principal city newspaper, the *Tampa Tribune*, which was read in translation to cigarmakers in the factories, covered the story in extended detail (Orrick and Crumpacker 1998:64–65), and its pages were also filled with stories about lynchings and race riots in other places. Also in June 1899, the same time that protest in Tampa was building, the paper reported on an armed rebellion of five hundred blacks in Dunellon, a small phosphate-mining

town about seventy miles to the north. Trainloads of whites, likely including some from Tampa, were reported to be on their way to put down the
unrest. Details of the conflict, which began in response to two lynchings,
were sketchy but frightening, suggesting that more lynchings had occurred after the arrival of white reinforcements. Then, nothing more was
reported, a news blackout noted by the *Tribune*. "There seemed to be a sort
of rigid censorship in vogue which strictly prohibited any communication
of facts to the outside world."[6] The story of what apparently was a massacre never has been told, but order was restored in the phosphate camps. In
another highly publicized incident, in August 1899, W. C. Crum, a white
Republican editor and postmaster in Hillsborough County was "white-
capped," a reference to hooded vigilantes (Hawes 1987). Crum's "flamboy-
ant" political writing and his appointment of a black deputy postmaster
provoked a visit from night riders, who horsewhipped him and poured car-
bolic acid on the wounds.

The attack on Crum revealed the consequences of violating local customs about race, whereas the murder of Christopher signaled the limited
space for black defiance. Dunellon, the bloodiest event, combined race and
labor agitation. In the precise moment this was occurring, black and white
workers in Tampa's cigar factories had begun to reassert themselves. The
détente with factory owners who supported Cuban independence was over.
In May 1899, the workers called a strike against Eduardo Manrara, who
was Ybor's surviving partner. The editor of the *Tribune*, whose board included three cigar manufacturers, published a warning that vigilante action might be needed to get the workers back to their benches (Ingalls
1988:60). The *Tribune*'s dire warnings failed to materialize, at least this
time, and the workers actually won this action.

> Manrara, in an efficiency move that smacked more of Yankee busi-
> ness sense than of Latin custom, put scales in his factory to weigh out
> the filler tobacco. Cigar rollers were outraged at this affront to their
> honesty and their traditional way of work, and they promptly walked
> out. The large manufacturers banded together and locked out their
> remaining workers on July 10, putting almost 4000 men and women
> out of work. But by mid-August, the manufacturers capitulated. The
> cigar workers had won their first and only strike. They would soon
> organize a union they called La Resistencia, and the cigar factories
> would soon become part of the national tobacco trust. (Orrick and
> Crumpacker 1998:64)

In this first major strike, the cigarmakers had been able to withstand the loss of income and maintain solidarity. Many workers simply had left town during the lockout, taking temporary refuge in Key West and Havana (Ingalls 1988:58). The strikers discovered, if only briefly, the strength they could muster in resistance.

Indeed, their union was named La Resistencia. Both black and white cigarmakers belonged. The leaders embraced very radical beliefs, attacking the Cigar Makers International Union (CMIU) and other American Federation of Labor unions for their undemocratic procedures and narrowly economistic goals. La Resistencia was envisioned as more than a union; it was aimed at social and political revolution (Ingalls 1985; Long 1965b; Mormino 1982a; Pérez 1975; Poyo 1984; Pozzetta 1981; del Río 1950; Yglesias 1985). The October 10 Club was formed a few months later, in this heady but volatile period that immediately followed victory in the "weight strike." Buoyed by their own success, it must have seemed like they were making their own history in a new place and a new century. Marx's observation that "men make their own history, but they do not make it just as they please; they do not make it under circumstances chosen by themselves,"[7] applies in this case. The unraveling racial solidarity of Tampa's Cubans, in spite of clear efforts to hold it together, illustrates agency colliding against limits.

The violence that raged around them, the power and ruthlessness of their opponents, could scarcely be ignored. Nor were their own activities being ignored. Oral accounts by descendants suggest the Ku Klux Klan had paid the white Cuban founders a visit, that terrorism did play a direct role in dividing the October 10 Club.[8] Various forms of intimidation were used more openly against La Resistencia not long after the split occurred. The fate of La Resistencia, which is much better documented, also illustrates the intrusion of northern capital and U.S. labor organizations in shaping cigar culture in Tampa.

Cigars

The business of Tampa was making and selling cigars. Early gains by workers in the "weight strike" of 1899 provoked the manufacturers to form their own combination, called the Cigar Trust (Mormino and Pozzetta 1987:116). This local cartel of owners in turn attracted the interest of the American Cigar Company of J. B. Duke, architect of the real trust, who began taking over factories in Tampa in 1901.

There was complicity between outside robber barons and the local business interests. But there was also competition. The cigar manufacturers' initial failure to control La Resistencia opened a space into which Duke's trust could easily move. Northern penetration occurred in other segments of Tampa's economy in this same period. A Boston firm gained control of the Tampa Electric Company in 1900. A New York company waged "two years of competitive warfare" and finally gained control of the Tampa Street Railway in 1894 (Long 1971a:338). Outside penetration also occurred in union activities. The CMIU had been attempting to organize the Tampa cigar workers even before La Resistencia was formed. When La Resistencia called another strike in 1901, CMIU organizers cooperated with the manufacturers to help break the strike and the rival union. This strange alliance bore bitter fruit in 1910, when the factory owners visited even greater brutality against the CMIU than had been used on La Resistencia.

The 1901 strike was over the issue of a closed shop, a far more contentious demand than in the "weight strike." The tobacco trust joined with local Board of Trade members in coordinating lockouts with evictions, foreclosures and other economic pressure, and squads of hooligans who waged terror. The two city newspapers printed stories condemning the strikers, encouraging repression against them, and warning that black strikebreakers would be used. Vigilantes kidnapped fifteen union leaders at gunpoint in the middle of the night and transported them to Honduras, including the treasurer, whose absence froze the union bank account (Ingalls 1988:74). Thugs broke into the office of the union newspaper and smashed the printing presses (Barcia 1957).

Luis Barcia, editor of the paper and one of those kidnapped, wrote about the incident in his memoirs. He recorded the following exchange with a fellow journalist.

[D. B.] McKay, the owner and editor of the [Tampa] Daily Times, and who appeared to be one of the principal organizers and directors of the clandestine outlaws who had kidnapped us, spoke to one of the workers, who was sitting next to me and asked him to tell the Leader of the Federation [the union newspaper] (that was me) that now I could go back to Africa to educate my parents. I did not answer a word. Probably McKay was thinking this was a big offense. Poor man! He did not know that men are equally valuable whether they are from Africa, or Europe, or America, or Asia and whether they are white, red, or black and that, besides I was never in Africa, nor did any of my relatives, and that I could not go anywhere to educate my parents, because they were deceased. (Barcia 1957:43)

The foregoing passage reflects many things. The fact that D. B. McKay himself was among the vigilantes, and was apparently the leader, confirms an intimate connection between the Anglo elite and the strategy of violent repression (Ingalls 1988). McKay was an heir of Tampa's most prominent pioneer family, and he was married to the daughter of a wealthy Spanish cigar manufacturer. He was also a hooded outlaw. His crude attempt to insult Mr. Barcia elicited a mini-lecture in Barcia's memoir outlining his personal theory of racial differences, or lack thereof. Barcia's musings confirm that the philosophy guiding La Resistencia was antiracist. However, not all the white cigar workers shared Barcia's sublimely informed view of race, especially when confronted by news stories in the *Times* that black cigarmakers were planning to break the strike.[9] Barcia's counterparts and would-be successors in the CMIU actively condoned racial discrimination (Cooper 1987:25).

The consolidation of the CMIU, after La Resistencia was broken in 1901, deepened and intensified racial divisions among the cigar workers. Former members of La Resistencia continued to oppose the CMIU, especially the Afro-Cubans.

> LUIS: They didn't want the international. Wherever the international union was they segregate the colored guys. They don't publicize that. You live it and you see it. La Resistencia, my father was part of that. I was six or seven years old. Then they [CMIU] try to push in, and they done it with the Citizens Committee. The Citizens Committee was the Ku Klu [Ku Klux Klan]. And the colored cigarmakers didn't want the international union because after you was in it, when you leave Tampa, you couldn't work with your book to none of the locals, factories that was organized with the international.

Tampa's local CMIU retained a degree of racial integration, although it was rigidly separated by craft, unlike La Resistencia. Afro-Cuban cigarmakers could belong, and some continued to be active in labor issues. But segregated shops in other places meant that their membership, their "book," had no value when they traveled. Because traveling was an integral part of the job, that was a serious impediment. And race continued to be a divisive issue in the union at Tampa, surfacing during the strike in 1910, when the threat of black strikebreakers was again used as a lever by the manufacturers (Long 1971b; Pozzetta 1980).

The manufacturers' utter resolve to avoid unionization in the factories, along with workers' lackluster support for the CMIU, presented serious challenges for maintaining, much less improving, the privileged circumstances of the cigarmakers. Handmade "clear" Havana cigars were the pinnacle of the tobacco market, expensive elite products targeted at wealthy gentlemen. Rollers with skill and talent, but little formal education, earned unusually high wages in the Tampa factories (Jacobstein 1907:149). The relative affluence of cigar workers, compared with other skilled laborers in the city, afforded the creation of institutions like the mutual aid societies and *la lectura* (reading in the factories), which nurtured their material, social, and intellectual well-being. The community they forged on the basis of this industry has been lyricized as an example working-class solidarity (Mormino and Pozzetta 1987; Pacheco 1994; Pizzo 1985). Race, class, and nationality—in addition to the bitter contest waged by the owners—inexorably eroded the foundation of this communal structure.

Workforce conditions in Tampa's factories in the early years of the century reflected a host of divisions, captured in considerable detail in a report filed by the U.S. Immigration Commission in 1911. Part of a nationwide study inspired by muckraking accounts of immigrants in meatpacking, a separate section was devoted to cigar workers in Tampa. The text of the report reflects Darwinian influences on emerging social science, with frequent references to "racial" characteristics of the workers. These discussions are not about color, but rather nationality, which was biologized and ranked.

> The tradition that skill is a question of race remains the fundamental idea of the Cuban cigar maker. As the dominant race in Cuba, the Spaniards seem to have relegated the Cubans to such positions as they were pleased to consider inferior. (p. 187)

> While the Cuban may possibly have the advantage in point of skill, they lack stability and power to adapt themselves to innovations. As competition grows keener, the manufacturer exercises greater care in his methods and demands a stricter economy in the use of material. ... The Cuban ... does not seem to understand that in the new era he must submit to the restrictions that govern his fellow-workmen or yield his place to such that will. (p. 203)

Apparent displacement by Italians is noted: "The Italians are gaining ground in the cigar industry at the expense of the Cubans and bid fair to

Table 4. Nationality Differences among Tampa Cigar Workers, 1910

	Cuban	Spanish	Italian
Percent of Tampa Cigar Workers	40.5	22.9	18.6
Average Annual Earnings	$780	$947	$747
Average Daily Earnings (males)	$2.34	$2.56	$2.00
Average Daily Earnings (females)	$1.20	$1.52	$1.30
Percent with Working Wives	11.9	8.1	23.3
Percent with Working Children	23.3	24.3	25.6
Percent Previously Farm Laborers	7.0	28.4	39.2

Source: 1911 U.S. Immigration Commission Report.

drive them completely from the field" (p. 192). This prediction failed to materialize. The Italian workers also proved unwilling to "submit to the restrictions," and in any case they regarded the cigar industry as a stepping-stone, not a destination.

The report contains no comparisons of black and white Cubans, only a single notation of 45 foreign-born Negroes (p. 195), a figure that is more than ten times smaller than the number of black Cuban cigarmakers—504—listed in the 1910 census. The author does take note of the existence of Martí-Maceo and Círculo Cubano (the name given to the all-white Cuban club after the split in 1900), and curiously paints the former in a very positive light (p. 228). The many tables that compare Cubans with Spaniards and Italians either have omitted black Cubans or included both without making distinctions of color. Given the overall tone of the report, it is surprising that the authors did not address the issue of racial divisions among the Cubans (also disappointing from the standpoint of my own research). There is, however, a plethora of data about nationality differences.

Spaniards were the best paid (averaging $947 annually), but the Cubans were only slightly better off than the Italians ($780 versus $747).[10] The small discrepancy between them is surprising in view of the fact that Cubans were far more experienced in the trade, and that a disproportionate share of the Italian workers were women, whose average daily earnings were lower. Figures on average daily (as opposed to annual) earnings, in which the Cubans are closer to Spaniards and considerably higher than Italians, suggest an explanation based on constancy of employment. Cubans earned more per day, but worked fewer days, partly because they spent more time away from Tampa.

More than half of the Cubans (54 percent) had traveled outside the United States, compared with only 24 percent of Spaniards and 10 percent of Italians.[11] Mormino and Pozzetta suggest that the stability of Italians, compared with Cubans, was a major factor in the steady acquisition of property that eventually provided wealth. Much of this real estate was in small farmsteads on the outskirts of Ybor City, which supplied meat (including poultry) and produce for sale to cigar workers. A large fraction of the Italian workers (39 percent) had been farm laborers prior to emigration, compared with only 7 percent of the Cubans. The Spaniards also reflected an Old World peasant background, 28 percent having been farm laborers in Spain.[12] Spaniards and Italians in Ybor City more closely fit the generalized image of immigrants of this era—uprooted and dispossessed peasants fleeing an exhausted and strife-torn homeland, finding refuge in the New World. Cubans, on the other hand, were subaltern colonials from the continent below, "black birds" who came and went.

The demography of Cubans in Tampa reflected their sojourning. Many who were listed in the census and the Immigration Commission reports as single had wives and children in Cuba. Their remittances helped relieve economic problems back home, and the proximity of the island allowed frequent visits. Affinity for Cuba, and the common purpose of returning someday for good, impeded acquisition of property in Florida. In this period, few Cubans purchased homes or started businesses. The factories were everything, even as their once-commanding positions in these workplaces steadily eroded after the collapse of La Resistencia. The status connected to their struggle for Cuba also eroded, as the image of Cuban nationals was converted from freedom fighters to subordinate subjects of U.S. imperialism. The Immigration Commission suggested that the Cubans were scorned for their failed revolution. In reference to their loss of control in the factories, the report observed: "The events of the years 1896–97 [should have been 1895–98], however, brought about a change in their fortunes which resulted in a complete loss of prestige."[13]

Average wages in the industry mask large variations in rates paid for different levels of skill. The different types of cigars ranged widely in quality. Workers who produced the most-valued types, invincibles, earned almost seven times as much per thousand as those who made the lowly cheroots. This disparity was reflected in average weekly earnings that varied between $7 and $35.[14] These differences were not only arrayed by skill levels, but also reflected differences in ethnic access to the more highly paid work. Only 6 percent of Cubans and 2 percent of Italians earned more than $3.50 per day, compared with 16 percent of Spaniards who earned that much or more. Strippers and stemmers, nearly all of whom were women, earned far less, between $4 and $12 per week.[15]

About 20 percent of the adult workers were women; 44 percent were Italian, 30 percent were Cuban, and 7 percent were Spaniards.[16] Cuban women earned the least of all three categories; only 16 percent earned more than $2 per day, compared with 28 percent of Italian and Spanish women.[17] Many of the women workers were single, but others were married. The report indicates that about one-quarter (23 percent) of Italian families had wives employed in the factories, compared with only 12 percent of the Cuban families, and 8 percent of Spanish.[18] Afro-Cubans are not distinguished in the report, but the 1910 census lists the occupations of wives in Afro-Cuban households, indicating that only 8 percent were employed in the cigar factories. This pattern is a departure, placing Afro-Cubans at the same rate as the Spaniards, although the different data sources make interpretation difficult. The relatively low rate of female employment by Afro-Cubans may reflect discrimination in the factories, but it was also consistent with a preference, discussed in Chapter 6, for Afro-Cuban men to prevent their wives from working outside the home. The relatively high rate of female employment by Italians is consistent with Mormino and Pozzetta's thesis that multiple earners and the wages of Italian wives were a central element in their economic strategy.

Finally, there was a large number of children between the ages of 14 and 18 (actually many were younger than the lower legal limit of 14), about 8 percent of the total workforce. Their earnings were lower than those paid to women, slightly more than $1.50 per day for boys and about $1.25 per day for girls. Child employees were distributed fairly evenly among the three ethnic categories, although there were no Spanish girls who worked in the factories.[19]

Wide discrepancies in pay among individual workers and economic divisions by nationality, gender, and age tended to undermine solidarity and contributed to downward pressures on all wages. The report offers a sanguine prediction of further growth and prosperity in the Tampa cigar industry. It fails to note, however, that wages in the industry had declined severely ever since the loss of the strike in 1901. Long (1971b:554–55) estimated that wages in the first five years afterwards decreased by 25 percent, while the profits of the manufacturers increased in the same period by as much as 300 percent. Use of child labor, women workers, and excessive numbers of apprentices, along with a lack of uniform wage rates in the various factories, enabled these growing discrepancies to occur.

Even as the report was being compiled, the CMIU was organizing for a renewed effort to reverse these conditions. A strike and lockout began in the summer of 1909 and lasted seven months, with disastrous results. There were several violent incidents, the most serious of which resulted in the death of two Italian immigrants. They were found handcuffed and hanging in a tree in a prominent location in West Tampa. The lynching was explicitly connected to the strike, although the victims were apparently selected arbitrarily on the basis of their alleged Mafia connections (Ingalls 1988:96; Long 1971b). This and other acts of violent repression broke the strike and crippled the union. The CMIU continued efforts to organize the Tampa cigar workers, but conditions and wages continued to decline through the teens.

There is little information from the Immigration Commission report on the specific nature of working conditions for Afro-Cubans. The general folklore is that they were treated equally, discriminated against only on the basis of skill. My interview narratives consistently report, however, that Afro-Cuban males were the ones most likely to be laid off in favor of Italian women and other cheaper workers, and that they experienced other more or less subtle forms of disadvantage. One of the largest tobacco trust factories, Havatampa, did not employ any black workers, although managers at this factory attempted to avoid immigrant workers of any color to the extent possible (Long 1968, 1971b). Despite strong support by most of the Afro-Cuban workers for the principles of organized labor, inhospitable treatment by the CMIU alienated the black Cubans and isolated them from the marginal benefits of belonging. At every turn, they confronted the legal limits of Jim Crow and the more subtle impediments of customs and structure inside the Latin community.

Ethnogenesis II: Legal Segregation

In 1901, white primaries were declared legal in Florida, sealing the absolute power of white Democrats in the state (Price 1957). In the years that followed, a series of laws were passed that increasingly restricted access of blacks to facilities and services, regulated their conduct, and denied them protection. During the first decade of the twentieth century new laws were enacted tightening the definition of miscegenation (already illegal under the 1885 constitution), and effecting formal segregation in rail and streetcars, waiting rooms, public accommodations, prisons, hospitals, and text-books (schools were already segregated). The Florida legislature passed a resolution in 1913 refusing to accept federal appointments of black officials at any level in the state (Bates 1928; Jackson 1960). Within Ybor City, in the workplace and in housing, some of these problems could be avoided. But coffeehouses, restaurants, schools, parks, churches, and a host of other settings, including the mutual aid societies, were racially segregated. It was required by law that blacks be excluded, and for the most part white immigrant proprietors complied without objection.

The division of Cubans into two organizations, and the growing distance between black and white immigrants, deepened the disadvantages confronting black Cubans and greatly intensified the significance of color. This same process also intensified the importance of the new Afro-Cuban organization. Its members especially needed the benefits of mutual aid to offset problems of segregated facilities and nonexistent medical care for blacks. And if they did not establish a categorical presence as Afro-Cuban, they risked being labeled simply as "colored," along with the other black people living in Tampa.

Martí-Maceo became a formal arbiter of color classification within the Latin community. In choosing to join, or in being told it was their only choice, Afro-Cuban cigarmakers who settled in Tampa collectivized their identity in contrast to those who belonged to Círculo Cubano, the white Cubans. Defining who was an Afro-Cuban in Tampa's immigrant community, however, was not straightforward. Identification rested on an unstable combination of color determination (both by other immigrants and Anglo Tampans), family reputation, and self-identification. Crossing into Florida could result in reclassification. In some cases, early choices about whom to associate with, or whether to enter the Jim Crow car in the train from Port Tampa, might have significant consequences that could not easily be undone. One of my narrators mused that his father, who was very light-skinned, could have passed for white if he had made the right moves.

TOMÁS: My daddy made a mistake when the boat got to Port Tampa. You used to come from Port Tampa to Ybor City by train. So, they had a car right next to the engine for black, and the rest of 'em for white. So when he got in the train, he went in the one behind the engine, so that automatically made him black.

Light-skinned males who arrived alone might shift categories upon the later arrival of a wife and children who were darker. Color was an ambiguous marker, made all the more confusing by the incommensurate systems that existed in Cuba and Florida, and the insistent problems that confronted dark-skinned people in southern cities like Tampa.

There were some too dark to join Círculo Cubano, but who also declined to attach themselves to the stigma of the Martí-Maceo. Those who were trying unsuccessfully to pass, who shunned identification with the Afro-Cubans, lived in the shadows without benefit of mutual aid. They lost the advantages of membership and the protections it would have offered. This practice also reduced the overall size of Martí-Maceo's membership compared with the potential pool, meaning less revenue from dues payments. Afro-Cubans in the club resented this as both a snub and a financial handicap to their organization, added reasons to be contemptuous of passers. In contrast, there were others who might have passed, but who deliberately chose to be assigned membership in the black category. They confronted problems as well.

WANTED TO WED A NEGRO

Judge Torres called at the office of Deputy Judge F. M. Robles, July 23 and obtained a marriage license for Miguel Díaz and Tate Belle Cooke for whom he expected to tie the connubial knot a few hours later. He had only met the Cuban [Díaz], and was utterly astounded when a jet black female negro walked out to be made the wife of a man of comparatively light complexion. "Are you a negro, Miguel?" queried the indignant judge. "Yes, I am part negro," replied Díaz nervously, as he realized that his chances for wedding the lovely ebonite were gradually vanishing. Despite his claims, Judge Torres refused to perform the ceremony, and yesterday returned the license to Judge Robles.[20]

This incident was unusual, but not unique. A similar occurrence in 1904 led to a different outcome. According to the *Tampa Tribune*, "The case against Louis Maz and Ynez Sanchez on the charge of violating the law preventing intermarriage of whites and negroes was before Justice Evans today and Louis Maz proved that he was also a negro."[21] In this later case the bride was lighter than Miguel Díaz's intended, and the judge was an Anglo. The couple was already married, but they had been charged with miscegenation. The husband, who appeared to be white, was required to file an affidavit attesting that he was a Negro. The document was witnessed by his brother-in-law, who explained to the judge that this was a "runaway match" (an elopement), a pretext frequently used in Cuba to circumvent laws against miscegenation (Martínez-Alier 1974:117–19). Charges against

the couple were dismissed, with the notation that "there was but little difference in the complexion of the two."

The 1900 census for Tampa discloses a handful of immigrant households (7 out of 156 Afro-Cuban families) in which husbands are listed as
white and wives and children are black or mulatto. It is noteworthy that in
none of the mixed marriages reported in the census, nor in the two cases
discussed above, was the wife white and husband black. Laws in Cuba
sometimes tolerated marriages of white men to black women, but never
the reverse (Martínez-Alier 1974). The interracial unions among Florida
Cubans were mainly formed prior to emigration.

Díaz's failed effort to marry in Florida reflects the intricacies of racial
identification on several levels. Both judges mentioned in his case were
Spaniards, part of the small group who had entered the ranks of the elite
power structure in Tampa. Robles's descent traced to Florida's Spanish colonial period. Strictly speaking, Díaz should have been regarded as a "Negro"; Florida law at that time included anyone of measurable African
ancestry regardless of appearance. Díaz was, in fact, a member of the
Martí-Maceo Society at the time of his attempted marriage.[22] An American judge might have conceded his claim and permitted the marriage to
occur, as was done in the later case. Judge Torres, however, may have been
more sensitive to the implications of sanctioning such a blatant contrast in
color between the pair. Allowing them to marry would only confirm beliefs, widely held among the white Americans, that all the Spanish-speaking immigrants were of mixed race and/or that they did not condemn miscegenation. Whatever the reason, Díaz did not remain long in Tampa; he
dropped out of the club shortly afterwards and did not return.

Racial problems in Tampa added to the mobility of the Afro-Cuban
cigarmakers. Would-be passers, in both directions, were encouraged by the
institutional and legal circumstances to move on. Those who were too dark
or too light to fit their notions of themselves into the racial paradigm in
Florida found it difficult to remain.

Within this setting, Afro-Cuban ethnogenesis was founded on resid-
uality and constant change, sifted and shaped by forces of racial categorization. The Martí-Maceo Society served as a nexus in an extremely
fluid network of Cuban cigarmakers who sojourned in Tampa for varying
lengths of time. A conflation of voluntary and involuntary factors diverted
some of them into the Martí-Maceo during their stay, which sometimes
turned out to be permanent. The club was constituted of a core group of
leaders and their families, along with a constant stream of newcomers,

usually single men or women who sometimes joined relatives in Tampa, or brought family members over in time. Although many of the prominent Afro-Cuban independence figures left Tampa soon after the war, several remained or returned periodically. In spite of the swirl of mobility and change during the early decades of the century, there was continuity with soldiers and projects of *Cuba libre*. However, there also was an increasingly embodied consciousness about what it meant to be black in Florida, where blackness was less ambiguous and equated more squarely with subordination.

African Americans

Afflictions associated with being black in Florida are best illustrated in, and were situationally defined by, the experiences of Tampa's African American community. In the earliest years of Afro-Cuban settlement there had been considerable interaction with African Americans, but with the increase in racial violence and legalized discrimination, this pattern shifted to avoidance.

Between 1900 and 1910, the African American community nearly doubled in size (from 8,445 to 16,445), an increase roughly comparable to the overall growth of Tampa's population.[23] Although black settlement remained scattered in different sections of the city, the greatest increase was in the Scrub, the principal entrepôt for newly arrived rural migrants. As this emergent ghetto expanded its borders, it brushed against the bounds of Ybor City. The Central Avenue district, the commercial corridor that ran along the western edge of the Scrub, was less than ten blocks south of the Pedroso boardinghouse and the Martí-Maceo Hall on Eighth Avenue. Another concentration of African American jooks and saloons, called Old Fort Brooke, was located just below the Italian club in the northeast section of the Scrub. Many African Americans lived within Ybor City (600 in 1900, compared to 577 Afro-Cubans).[24]

Reconstruction politicians, early black pioneers who still owned land, newly arrived business leaders, pastors, and teachers formed a leadership who responded to the opportunities occasioned by the population growth, and to the steadily worsening racial climate in the opening years of the twentieth century. Unlike the Afro-Cubans, who were together in a single organization and heavily concentrated in a single industry, the African American community was much more heterogeneous in class, geographic origins, religious affiliation, club membership, and occupation. Many were migrants from Georgia and Alabama, or from other parts of Florida; most came from rural areas (Howard & Howard 1994b:2). The railroad, the docks, and a boom in building construction offered work for unskilled laborers—low-paid menial work, but an improvement over debt slavery in cotton or sugar fields, turpentine camps, and phosphate mines, which were the primary alternatives. Growth in the white middle class provided work for black domestics. Commerce in the dollars earned by these workers fueled the growth of black-owned businesses.

Black population growth also multiplied the number of black churches. In 1893, there were 6, which grew to 9 in 1901, and by 1903, there were 11 different black churches—4 Baptist, 4 Methodist, 1 Presbyterian, 1 Episcopal, and 1 Catholic (Howard and Howard 1994b:5). There was a similar proliferation of lodges and clubs. Masons, Odd Fellows, and Knights of Pythias all had chapters in Tampa. The Odd Fellows built a lodge hall on Scott Street in the Scrub, quarters that served for meetings of all the men's lodges and their ladies' auxiliary societies. The most prestigious clubs were the Afro-American Civic League and the Paul Lawrence Dunbar Literary Society, where most of the members were business owners and letter carriers. The latter club, which was begun in 1910, aimed to "be a perpetual impetus to the aesthetic life of our people."[25] Members organized literary programs, offered prizes for students, and held fund-raisers to buy books for the Harlem School. Influential whites—such as D. B. McKay, former kidnapper and then mayor of Tampa—were invited to address the group. The primary purpose of both the Dunbar Society and the Civic League was uplift, and the members waged an ardent campaign against vice. E. J. Moore, who served as president of both clubs in 1915, wrote articles decrying the "red light" districts in the Scrub and Fort Brooke.[26]

Women were also active in these efforts, both in concert with the Dunbar Society and the Afro-American Civic League, and in organizations of their own. The City Federation of Colored Women's Clubs was formed in 1915 to coordinate their charitable work and social activities (Anthony 1989:6). Women were especially active in church organizations.

Several churches had mutual benefit or burial societies. Mount Sinai AME Zion Church, founded in 1863, started a mutual aid society in 1886, and the Beulah Baptist, begun in 1866, established "The People's Investment Company" in 1890 (Brady 1997; Brown 1997a). The pastor of the Mount Moriah Primitive Baptist Church formed a local chapter of the Grand Pallbearers Union of Florida, a statewide organization started in 1898. In addition to sick benefits of 50 cents a week, the organization provided wooden caskets constructed by members for the burial of those who died, thus avoiding the final indignity of interment in a burlap bag. An elderly school teacher who had belonged during the teens explained that "you were really somebody if you were buried in a wooden casket."[27] She added that burial benefits were needed in part to cope with the problems of early unexpected death: "Back then, there were so many lynchings of black folks." Statistically, such deaths were a small fraction of causes during that period, but her perceptions of the dangers of the times were not distorted.

Stresses associated with the large influx of newcomers exacerbated racial tensions in Tampa. Many of the white newcomers were also from rural sections of Alabama, Georgia, and other parts of Florida. Implicitly in competition with unskilled black labor and experienced in the use of terror to enforce their advantage in this regard, this sector was especially dangerous. White elites, both those born in Tampa and prosperous business owners who had come more recently, relied on this threat of violence to contain the wages and activism of black workers. There was a difficult balance to be maintained between practical encouragement of white hooliganism, and a desire to prevent bloody excesses from staining Tampa's reputation and hurting business (Ingalls 1988).

White politicians and economic elites also implicitly relied on the "respectable colored" to help ensure calm and compliance inside the black community. The impoverished black masses, who lived in the Scrub and earned subminimum wages, those most victimized by the racial conditions of that time, were cast instead as the cause of many problems. Degrees of exclusivity in the churches, and especially the lodges, helped the more affluent blacks—the small number who achieved some measure of success or property[28] distance themselves from the problematic and newly arrived poor, whose sometimes unruly or hapless behavior was viewed as a threat to all black people living in Tampa.

James Weldon Johnson, writing about Florida during this same period, characterized communities of this sort as divided among three classes, the first being the most dangerous. "There are those constituting what might be called the desperate class—the men who work in the lumber and turpentine camps, the ex-convicts, the barroom loafers are all in this class. These men conform to the requirements of civilization much as a trained lion with low muttered growls goes through his stunts under the crack of the trainer's whip. They cherish a sullen hatred for all white men, and they value life as cheap" (Johnson 1965:434).

This image was the one that induced terror in the minds of white em-

ployers and landowners, and fueled their conviction that violence was necessary, providing the rationale that unleashed the tormentors who lynched
and rousted—a cycle of hatred from which there seemed to be no escape,
and which, in Johnson's opinion, could ensure neither order nor safety.
"Decreasing their number by shooting and burning them off will not be
successful; for these men are truly desperate, and thoughts of death, however terrible, have little effect in deterring them from acts the result of
hatred or degeneracy" (Johnson 1965:435). Johnson reflects remarkably
little sympathy for these desperate brethren, although his suggestion that
genocide will not eliminate them must be regarded as sardonic. (Indeed,
this passage comes from his *Autobiography of an Ex-Colored Man*, the
whole premise of which is sardonic.)

His proposed remedy for their depraved state was a program of uplift
orchestrated by the "better class"—"the independent workmen and trades-
men . . . [and] the well-to-do and educated colored people" (p. 436). Johnson as narrator belongs to this class. He mused over the unfortunate irony
that this group of black people, who most closely adhered to middle-class
values and whose manners were impeccable, were the least visible to the
larger white community. "They are as far removed from the whites as the
first [desperate] class I mentioned. These people live in a little world of
their own" (p. 436). Their own sense of dignity and respectability could
only be secured by withdrawal; there was no option to assimilate, but they
could distance themselves from the unlettered and dangerous black folks.
The clubs and institutions they created aided in this separation, but as
Johnson recommended, they also attempted to use their organizations to
develop self-help and charity for the less well off in their midst.

The third class, the solid workers—maids, hackmen, laborers—literally
domesticated to their service in the white-dominated economy, was the
group that had the most contact with whites. They raised white children
and cooked their food, were trusted around the premises as gardeners
and delivery men. Their arms and backs built the buildings and unloaded
the ships. Personal relationships between black employees and white employers, however vacuous and qualified, sometimes put trusted and loyal
individuals into the category that the whites reserved for "respectable
coloreds."

The white definition of this respectable class, emphasizing loyalty over
achievement, differed from Johnson's more indigenous category of local
black leaders. Whites tended to regard educated blacks with suspicion and
scorn for their pretenses. This class disjunction, noted by Johnson as a

misperception based in self-isolation, put them at a comparable risk for violence, especially in cases where educated blacks spoke out in protest. As Johnson knew well, conditions in Tampa exemplified these dangers.

M. J. Christopher, the black editor murdered in 1899, had been a partner with Johnson in a daily black newspaper they briefly operated in Jackson-ville (Suggs 1983:102–3). Christopher's associates in Tampa included most of the founders of the Dunbar Society and Afro-American Civic League, men who had encouraged his protest at the time. Indeed, all were outraged that the woman he defended, who had been brutally treated by police, was also a member of the better class. Christopher's fatal attempt to speak out in this case was a sobering lesson for his surviving comrades. In the follow-ing years, there were several added examples to intimidate dissenters among the better class and terrify potential miscreants among the masses. Two grisly events in 1903 offered especially strong warnings and a depar-ture from prior efforts to avoid high-profile violence within the city. In late July, a black man named George Houston was observed embracing a white woman (apparently with her consent). He was seized by vigilantes and castrated, although not killed. His fate was highly publicized, giving rise to a new expression—"Houstonizing." The next victim, Lewis Jackson, who was lynched in December 1903 for a similarly ambiguous sexual offense, was "Houstonized" before he was murdered. His castrated and lifeless body was discovered late in the evening of December 4, hanging from a tree on Fifth Avenue between the Scrub and Ybor City, where it remained until ten o'clock the next morning. The authorities delayed removing his corpse to ensure that all could view it. "Large crowds made the pilgrimage to the spot near Fifth Avenue where the lifeless body of Lewis Jackson hung rigid from the stately oak which served as gibbet for his execution. Every walk of life was represented in these visitors, and it is estimated that practically the entire colored population went to the place during the morning and saw the silent reminder of the power and effectiveness of the mob."[29]

The location of this display was only two blocks south of the main drag of Ybor City, suggesting that many of the cigar workers also viewed it. Black cigar workers observing this gruesome testament to the "power and effectiveness of the mob" would have identified more quickly with the victim, would have absorbed the message more directly. Such experiences only underscored the importance of their differences with black Ameri-cans, even in the common risks that both shared. Afro-Cubans could take some comfort from their isolation inside the immigrant community, and in the knowledge that they could always go home if things got too bad in Tampa. However, there were tensions and growing difficulties in both of these options.

Fracturing Cuban Solidarity

In spite of racial divisions, black and white Cubans were inescapably joined in their ongoing concern for events back home. There was much to engage them. In the brief period between independence and the establishment of the Cuban Republic (in 1902), the *mambises*, especially those who were black, lost ground under U.S. domination. Disgruntlement by veterans, unable to find work or proper respect for their sacrifices, produced unrest and jockeying for power by emergent opposition parties. Cubans in Tampa maintained an intense interest in these developments, and the two clubs in Ybor City served as points of articulation.

The Cuban consul in Tampa, Rafael Ybor, who was the son of Vincente Martínez Ybor, was among the founders of the October 10 Club. He maintained cordial relations with both clubs after the split and used them as forums for mobilizing support for the shaky new government. The delicate issue of representation by Tampa Cubans surfaced at the time the republic was formed. The independence veterans were invited to attend the celebration held in May 1902 in Havana, but the composition of the delegation posed a dilemma. Officers of Círculo Cubano (which was then still named Club Nacional Cubano) had written to the board of the Martí-Maceo, seeking their participation in some type of joint commission. Minutes from a meeting on May 18, 1902, indicate that the Martí-Maceo members hotly debated their involvement. Some favored joining the white Cubans in a mixed delegation; others objected, citing their complaints against the members of the white club as reason to be represented separately. After a lengthy discussion, in which it was argued that the cause for celebration preceded the split in the clubs, and that this matter transcended their grievances about they way they were treated, they voted unanimously to join in a mixed delegation.

In the years that followed there were periodic references to failed efforts at collaboration between black and white Cubans and notations that reflected hostilities. In 1906, the two clubs discussed plans to make a common plea to the Cuban government for financial aid for their projects. The members of Martí-Maceo elected not to join this plea, on the pretext that the nature of their needs (for funds to start a school) differed too much from those of the white Cubans (who were raising funds for a building).[30] This was, however, a particularly inopportune moment in Cuban politics, as we will see. There were likely other unstated reasons they declined involvement.

In 1908, the Cuban consul requested donations from the two Cuban clubs for victims of a fire that had destroyed large sections of Ybor City. The discussions surrounding this request reflect bitterness and ambivalence.[31] Many Martí-Maceo members favored making the donation, but only to avoid being ridiculed for not giving. One member offered the opinion that it would not matter, that no one would help them if they needed it. Nonetheless, they voted to make a contribution, as a gesture that would preserve their dignity. In that same year, Martí-Maceo was attempting to raise funds to erect a new clubhouse. The reference to low expectations about reciprocity may indicate refusals by the other clubs to help them with the fund-raising and/or that funds were sorely needed for their own project.

As Martí-Maceo's new building neared completion in the spring of 1909, they deliberated about whether to invite Círculo Cubano to the inaugural opening and decided not to do so. In an uncharacteristically churlish notation the secretary explained that "given the attitude Círculo Cubano has assumed towards us, we should do the same to them." This decision was reaffirmed in the June meeting.[32] The white Cubans did not attend, although they sent a letter of congratulation, as did the other Latin clubs in Ybor City. A few months later, in planning the annual October 10 celebration, the members again aired their problems with the white Cuban club. "Mr. Palomino proposed that the orators who are to take part in the evening party, and any others who are present, should completely abstain from mentioning El Círculo Cubano, for good or ill, since they acted in such a terrible way towards us. This was seconded by Mr. Domínguez Gerardo and it was accepted."[33]

Hostilities were still evident in January 1910 when the Cuban consul visited Martí-Maceo to discuss an upcoming public celebration of the opening of the Panama Canal. The consul explained that he wanted both clubs to be represented at the ceremony, but he was concerned that the animosities between them might result in public embarrassment in front of the visiting dignitaries. The members agreed with his concern, referring to this as a "delicate issue" and expressing a desire to avoid ridicule.

Whenever Cubans were required to share public space, or ceremonially represent their common national identity, the arrangements elicited ambivalence and conflict, and a need to explicitly negotiate the conditions. Awkward contradictions surfaced and old grievances were ignited. The prevalence of such notations in the minutes of the Martí-Maceo Society was much greater during the first decade of the club's existence than in the years and decades that followed. This changing trend may reflect a gradual adjustment, but it also coincides with an extremely turbulent period in Cuban politics into which Tampa Cubans were unavoidably drawn.

La Guerrita de 1912

Afro-Cubans, who had abundant grievances about racist conditions and discriminatory practices during the U.S. occupation, had been led implicitly to believe that once the republic was formed they would finally obtain their "rightful share" of the spoils of independence (Helg 1995). White Cubans, who were themselves scrambling after slivers of the political economy not controlled by North Americans or Spaniards, were not prepared to make good on that promise.

Veterans of the Liberation Army, a group heavily composed of Afro-Cubans, organized demands for unpaid wages and access to more patronage. Some concessions were won. Fearing a resumption of armed rebellion, the new government did make payments to veterans. However, by then many Afro-Cubans already had sold their claims to such benefits for a fraction of their value to speculators. The Afro-Cuban general Quintín Banderas, a leading figure in the veterans organization, had been a victim of this scheme (Helg 1995:120). Discontented veterans in all ranks (and disproportionately black) formed armed bands—some engaged in banditry, others operating as military contingents in opposition politics, and some doing both (Orum 1975:115; Schwartz 1989). The election of 1906, which the Liberals justly claimed was stolen by the Moderates (Estrada Palma's party), provoked an armed uprising (the August Revolution) that foreshadowed a wider and much bloodier rebellion in 1912 (La Guerrita de 1912).

In the ten years between the installation of the republic and what came to be described as the "Little War" of 1912, Cuban governments of both the Moderate and Liberal parties demonstrated a willingness to use lethal violence to suppress black demands. Quintín Banderas was assassinated at the outset of revolt in 1906, and that uprising was swiftly put down with the aid of U.S. intervention, with the U.S. reoccupying the island for the next three years. Thousands were massacred in 1912, most noncombatants who

were lynched arbitrarily because they were black. The United States refrained from intervening in 1912; the zealous actions of the Cuban government obviated the need to interfere.

During that same ten-year period, new North American–style segregation and old-fashioned Hispanicized racism proceeded unchecked. Unlike
African Americans in Florida, Afro-Cubans retained the franchise. That
measure of political power did constitute an important difference, but
Afro-Cuban beneficiaries were most often the educated elite (de la Fuente
1997). For the black masses, and periodically for the black elite as well, life
in Cuba had gotten worse instead of better.

Afro-Cubans in Tampa were well acquainted with what was going on in
Cuba. Itinerant cigarmakers carried a constant flow of news. The Martí-
Maceo library subscribed to Cuban newspapers. *Lectores* read newspapers
in the factories. Major events were reported in the *Tampa Tribune*.

The uprising of 1906 began on August 16, with coordinated outbreaks
in Havana, Pinar del Río, and Santa Clara Provinces. The *Tampa Tribune*
first picked up the story on August 21, with a feature about Quintín Banderas leading a growing force of rebels near Havana. Three days later, on
August 24, the *Tribune* announced Banderas's death along with news about
the widening conflict and a promise of U.S. intervention. The August 24
story also contained the following: "It is reported on reliable information
that a Cuban secret society consisting of 60 members, a large portion
negroes, held an important meeting on 13th Avenue yesterday for consid-
ering ways and means for aiding the Cuban revolutionists. It was decided,
so it was reported to take passage to Cuba at an early opportunity to assist
in person."[34]

There is no independent verification that such a meeting occurred. No
mention of it is found in the minutes of Martí-Maceo, although silence on
this matter is hardly conclusive. The location cited, Thirteenth Avenue,
offers little clue, and may have been an error. The Pedroso boardinghouse
was on the corner of Thirteenth Street and Eighth Avenue.[35] On August
25, 1906, the *Tribune* offered the following: "Tampa people are taking a
lively interest in the Cuban insurrection, believing that it is sure to affect
the cigar industry here to some extent. There are a number of people here
in Tampa who are personally acquainted with the leaders. . . . Some citizens
are of the opinion that the trouble is purely a racial one between negroes
and Caucasians, while others are of the belief that the gist of the excitement is caused by disappointed politicians. Those who are of the opinion
that the trouble is . . . racial . . . have spent some time in Cuba and are

qualified to speak."[36] The headline on this section was "Racial Trouble Said to Be Principal Cause for Present Uprising in Cuba."

This portrayal cast suspicion on the Afro-Cubans in Tampa, linked them to dangerous goings-on in Cuba. The previous day's coverage of the "secret society" asserted there were insurrectionists among the local Afro-Cubans. Such reporting would have attracted dangerous attention to the activities of Afro-Cubans. This uprising, and the one in 1912, were virtually the sole occasions when the *Tribune* reported on the existence of a "colored Cuban" society in town.

The *Tribune* was surely correct about the existence of ties between leaders of the revolt and Cubans in Tampa. Military leaders included some of the most revered heroes from the war for independence, and civilians in the Liberal Party included former colleagues in Tampa factories. Given the positioning of Tampa's Cubans in the preindependence political structure, there should have been widespread support for the rebels in 1906. The Afro-Cubans were especially likely to have shared their grievances. Helg reports that preceding the uprising Rafael Serra and Ricardo Batrell, another Afro-Cuban activist, visited black organizations in the United States to solicit support for the black veterans (1995:142). Minutes of the Martí-Maceo contain no record of such a visit, although it is difficult to imagine that Tampa would have been omitted from the itinerary. If there was a secret organization, this might explain why this contact went unmentioned, or perhaps it simply never occurred.

Officially, the Martí-Maceo Society opposed the rebellion and supported the government of Estrada Palma. Their public opinions, however, were constrained by Anglo fears of black rebellion and dependence on Cuban authorities for protection and assistance. They could not afford to offend the consul, nor was it wise to call forth the attention of the Ku Klux Klan. The 1906 unrest not only signified the failed promise of Cuban independence, it also coerced complicity in defeat. The Martí-Maceo Society had no choice about its public position, an expedient gesture that need not reflect the real opinions of most. But this constraint also impeded them from using the organization to mobilize aid for the rebels. Tampa's potential value as an exile base was considerably reduced in comparison with the independence period. Covertly, individuals could, and surely did, support the rebels, but they could not rally or openly raise funds. There is very little family lore about 1906 among Tampa's Afro-Cubans that would confirm or deny these activities.

This was a time just beyond the memory of oral history; my oldest informant was thirteen in 1906. The written evidence is scant. Minutes of the Martí-Maceo Society record these events very sparingly. No mention is made of any secret meeting on August 23 of supporters of the revolt. A meeting of Martí-Maceo did occur on August 22, 1906. Formal minutes, however, reflect only deliberations of the request by Círculo Cubano to join the petition for funds from the Cuban government. No mention is made of events in Cuba.

Another meeting, held a few days later on August 26, did concern the revolt. The Cuban consul in Tampa and a committee from Círculo Cubano had asked the president of Martí-Maceo to cosign a telegram to Estrada Palma. It was to be a communication of "deep concern and sorrow on the part of the Cuban emigrants for the bloody revolution." Members agreed to the request.

The *Tampa Tribune* also reported on the telegram, which was sent on August 28. Citing only sponsorship by the Cuban Club (i.e., Círculo Cubano), the *Tribune* confirms the language of "sorrow [over] the spilling of blood," but goes on to explain that: "700 men have signed a pledge . . . to fight for the Republic if President Palma so desires. A prominent Cuban stated that the sympathy of the Cubans of this city is almost wholly with the government and only a few favor the revolutionists."[37]

The essentially neutral language in the minutes of Martí-Maceo was transformed into belligerent support for Estrada Palma. Perhaps the minutes omitted the parts that were unpalatable, about bowing to pressure to swear loyalty to an unpopular government. Or they may have been tricked into affirming a statement that contained other language, or the *Tribune* was embellishing. Public postures about this affair most likely masked private views that were very different, on the part of both black and white Cubans.

The defeat of the rebellion and the occupation of Cuba by U.S. forces in November 1906 signaled more problems for Afro-Cubans in Cuba and Tampa. And it did not end the agitation. Despite the occupation, armed bands of black Cubans continued to operate in the countryside (Orum 1975:120–21). Santa Clara Province was a major locus of unrest. In August 1907, the Antonio Maceo Association in Cienfuegos held a "closed meeting of a political nature" attended by Afro-Cuban dissidents (Orum 1975:143). This was most likely the same organization after which the Martí-Maceo Society was patterned in 1900, only a few years earlier. Several of the founding members had belonged to the Antonio Maceo Society—Bruno Roig, friend of José Martí; Juan Franco, a West Tampa independence veteran who was a *santero;* Diego Caballero, who would serve as president during the turbulence of 1912; and there were likely others.

This part of Cuba became the object of intense recruiting by the Independent Party of Color (IPC), an organization begun in 1908 by dissatisfied Afro-Cubans. Formation of the party, explicitly aimed at redressing racial grievances, provoked strong opposition from U.S. officials and many sectors of white Cuban politics. Organizers were accused of inflaming racial fears and showing disloyalty to the *patria* and legacies of José Martí. Tactics of black unity surfaced old fears of *el peligro negro.*

The IPC was not intended as a revolutionary organization. Its leaders were primarily seeking access to jobs and relief from discrimination. They favored integration and assimilation and disparaged African culture (Helg 1995:148). Nonetheless, most Cuban politicians refused to acknowledge the demands or the legitimacy of this party. The Morúa Law, passed in 1910 under the sponsorship of Morúa Delgado, who was then the only black member of the Cuban Senate, prohibited political parties based on race. The law made the dissidents into outlaws, more by definition than from their own acts. However, conditions reeled out of control over the next eighteen months. On May 20, 1912, the tenth anniversary of the republic, after another thwarted attempt to repeal the Morúa Law, the IPC called a nationwide armed protest. The Liberal government, led by Miguel Gómez, declared open warfare and, in less than a month, ruthlessly crushed the movement. Its leaders were killed, as were thousands of other Afro-Cubans.

More than the uprising of 1906, this event had palpable consequences for Afro-Cubans in Tampa. The records of the Martí-Maceo Society again portray a public show of support for the Cuban government and a remarkable absence of comment about the disturbances. They met on May 28, 1912, a week into the uprising, but no mention is made of the conflict. The *Tribune* published an earlier story on May 23 stating that: "Diego Caballero, president of the Martí-Maceo Club (negro) requested [the Cuban consul] to cable the Cuban government in the name of the society that the negro colony . . . was against any uprising of negro people in Cuba."[38]

A few days later, the *Tribune* reported that: "While loyal members of the Cuban colony in Tampa have declared . . . [support for the government], information brought here yesterday is that the negroes of Cuba are endeavoring to organize themselves . . . [to] get reins of power . . . [to] put white men out of office."[39] The story declares that racial domination is the goal of the rebels, but carefully exempts Tampa's "loyal" Afro-Cubans. The following day (May 28) the *Tribune* wrote that Martí-Maceo had joined in a second cable of support via the consul—a story also reported on that date on the front page of *La Lucha,* a newspaper in Havana.

A third cable was sent in early June 1912, at which time the full ferocity of the government repression was well known. This communication reportedly expressed sympathy with the methods being used to quell the uprising. Minutes of a Martí-Maceo meeting on June 12, 1912, confirm this posture, although they hint at some division.[40] Two proposals were offered; one to hold a public demonstration opposing the revolt, the other to publish a manifesto supporting the government. After lengthy discussion, the majority vote supported a manifesto, the wording of which was not included. Oral history is consistent with this apparent lack of support for the rebels. An elderly informant, who was nineteen at the time of this incident, explained it this way:

> LUIS: In Tampa, they [black cigarmakers] were not illiterate, you know . . . they knew that the Negroes in Cuba [were being killed], and they knew what it was all about. He was not even Cuban [Ivonnet, one of the leaders]. He was from Haiti, and the other guy was from Santo Domingo [Estevez, the other leader]. . . . They was half ignorant. They thought because they fought like the devil in the war . . . they thought they were gonna be somebody. And José Miguel Gómez [president of Cuba in 1912] was the one that coaxed 'em to go out there to crush 'em in order for him to be the big man . . . that he crush the revolution. That's what he had in mind. . . . They kill 'em. They got 'em all. But José Miguel Gómez didn't get what he wanted. Average colored Cuban didn't like him, because they all knew what he did was use those two guys . . . and he stole everything. He used to be corrupt. He lost the election.

His explanation, which was offered by others with whom I spoke, was that the insurgents foolishly had been entrapped in a power play by President Gómez. The uprising was led by irresponsible outsiders who brought death and destruction. If his rendition fails to indicate support for the rebels, it also belies the public posture of the Martí-Maceo's support for the Gómez regime. There are also indications that members at the time were more involved in the uprising than their minutes or cables to the government would suggest.

Membership records for this period reflect unusual volatility. In January 1912, there were 236 members; by May it had dropped to 164, and at the end of June there were only 148. Between the inception and close of hostilities in Cuba more than one-third of the members (37 percent) had left Tampa. At the end of the conflict, there was a corresponding rise. By August there were 157, and membership rose to 216 in September (a 48 percent increase over the number in June). Departures at the front end may have included members who left to join the fight, or quit the organization in disagreement with its stance. The large number of new members afterwards could reflect Afro-Cubans returning, or new arrivals seeking refuge from the violence.

I queried my elderly informant about these movements. He claimed not to recall. A close reading of the transcripts of my interviews with him on this subject reveals a pattern of avoidance, of changing the subject whenever I raised the issue of the race war. Memories of valor and success logically outlive those of defeat and disappointment. These events also contained painful contradictions. Veterans of the glory of independence were forced to adopt a public face that repudiated its ideals. Questions about the race war probed the intersection of several uncomfortable topics—repression, betrayal, and renegade religious beliefs.

Santería, driven underground in Cuba during U.S. occupation, was a potent and perilous dimension of the struggle. Intertwined with grievances about discrimination were fears of persecution and even lynching of Afro-Cubans suspected of practicing African magic. In 1904 a spate of accusations of witchcraft involving allegedly sacrificial murders of white children produced hysterical reactions and a campaign of repression. It was this atmosphere that led Fernando Ortiz to undertake his initial studies of Afro-Cuban *cabildos,* but his motive at the time he began this work was to eradicate these "centers of infection" (Helg 1995:113).

Even the IPC overtly denounced African culture and *brujería* (witchcraft). However, several party leaders were members of *cabildos.* The IPC's official symbol was a rearing horse—associated with Changó, Yoruba god of fire (Helg 1995:150). *Cabildos* had played an important role in the network of secret mobilization against Spain and remained involved in postindependence political conspiracies. Subterranean loyalties and ambivalent attachments, epitomized in the secret religions of Africa, remain part of the unwritten story of this terrifying period.

On February 13, 1912, a letter was received by the president of Martí-Maceo that affirms connections to a *cabildo* in Cienfuegos, the same city where the Antonio Maceo Society was located. The writer of the letter was president of Sociedad de Instrucción y Recreo, Nuestra Sra. de las

Mercedes, Nación Lucumi y Hijos. This organization, officially chartered in November 1906, was one of many *cabildos* that maintained a precarious existence under the watchful eye of the government. Its origin doubtless preceded 1906, but it was in that year that the officers were first required to submit annual reports to the provincial government in Santa Clara. Provincial Archives in Cienfuegos contain copies of these reports between 1906 and 1912, with a brief note written in 1935, indicating that the organization had ceased to exist only a few months after the officers wrote the letter to Martí-Maceo.

The purpose of the letter was to inform the president that he had been elected "honorary president" of the *cabildo*. Martí-Maceo is described as a "sister association." The letter was sent in the same month that the IPC delivered an ultimatum to the Cuban government threatening to use force if the Morúa Law was not repealed, an act that marked a turning point in the escalating conflict (Helg 1995:190). The ultimatum was delivered in Sagua la Grande, a city in Santa Clara Province not far from Cienfuegos. This region of Cuba was a center of IPC activity and the site of some of the worst violence in the coming summer. Although the contents of the letter are seemingly innocuous, the time, place, and identity of the sender suggest otherwise. The minutes of Martí-Maceo for the meeting that followed receipt of the letter contain no mention of its arrival, in spite of the fact that correspondence of this nature—invitations, felicitations, and so forth—were routinely recorded. My informant who was a member at the time claimed not to know anything about it, and it is quite possible that he did not. Relations with a *cabildo* would have been a delicate topic and might not have been discussed openly.

Diego Caballero, president of Martí-Maceo, was not known to have been a *santero*, although he may have been an adherent. There was at least one *santero* among the founders of Martí-Maceo, Juan Franco. Both Caballero and Franco had been members of the Cienfuegos Antonio Maceo Society. This organization, whose members had been active in the 1906 uprising, could have had ties to the Nación Lucumi y Hijos, but no evidence confirms such a link. The Provincial Archives in Cienfuegos contain no information about the former. Wisps and clues, but nothing solid, connect the officers of Martí-Maceo with heart of rebellions over race and religion that were enacted in Santa Clara Province during this period. Their public face, however, strongly repudiated any such connections. The leaders of the club sought instead to achieve an image of respectable citizens and patriotic supporters of the new republic.

Both Círculo Cubano and Martí-Maceo were officially nonsupportive of rebellions by their former comrades. Unlike the independence period, when white Tampa supported their cause, the Cuban uprisings in the early years of the century were viewed as a threat to U.S. interests. The racial dimension of these conflicts held particular jeopardy for the Afro-Cubans. In the aftermath of 1912, the Martí-Maceo Society enforced a complete ban on formal discussion of political matters in the club. This posture was a necessary adjustment, a way to avoid divisiveness within the membership, potential conflicts with Círculo Cubano or the Cuban consul, and unwelcome notice by the Citizens Committee.

Martí-Maceo came to symbolize rectitude rather than rebellion. An explicit goal of the officers was to establish a reputation of collective respectability for Afro-Cubans. Distance from home and the hopelessness of struggle counseled a compliant strategy. As conditions in both Cuba and Tampa worsened, and Afro-Cubans reconciled the elusiveness of their revolutionary goals, they sought invisibility and the protection of their mutual aid society.

1. Early-twentieth-century Afro-Cuban family, ca. 1910; daughter standing to the right is Caridad Lavin, grandmother of Francisco Rodríguez Jr. Martí-Maceo Photo Collection, Special Collections, by permission of University of South Florida Library.

2. Paulina Pedroso, circa 1890. Tony Pizzo Collection, Special Collections, by permission of University of South Florida Library

Souvenir from a literary and musical performance held at Martí-Maceo, August 29, 1909 celebrating the official opening of the new building. Courtesy Francisco Rodríguez.

La Unión Martí-Maceo

RECUERDO
de la
Velada Literaria Musical
efectuada por esta Institución en celebración
de la
Apertura Oficial de su Nuevo Edificio

Original building of La Unión Martí-Maceo, erected 1909.

3. Original social hall for the Martí-Maceo Society, erected in 1909 at Sixth Street and Eleventh Avenue in Ybor City; demolished in 1965 by Urban Renewal. Martí-Maceo Photo Collection, Special Collections, by permission of University of South Florida Library.

4. Founders of Sociedad la Unión Martí y Maceo, 1904. Seated man with gray hair and Panama hat on his knee is Bruno Roig. Martí-Maceo Photo Collection, Special Collections, by permission of University of South Florida Library.

5. Hipólito Arenas, circa 1930. Martí-Maceo Photo Collection, Special Collections, by permission of University of South Florida Library.

6. Bando Roja/Bando Azul Queen Sinesia Menendez and her court, 1930. Martí-Maceo Photo Collection, Special Collections, by permission of University of South Florida Library.

7. Sexteto Floridano, circa 1940. (Left to right): Bilingué Garcia (bongos); El Cojo (guitar); Nilo Oxamendi (bass violin); Ramon Padron (tres guitar/bandleader); Chichito Garcia (maracas), Gerardo Beriel (guitar); Currito (trumpet). Martí-Maceo Photo Collection, Special Collections, by permission of University of South Florida Library.

1805- 7- 9²-11- 13th St

8. Pedroso boardinghouse in 1950s, viewed from Thirteenth Street looking north; top story of the Ybor factory can be seen in upper left. Tony Pizzo Collection, Special Collections, by permission of University of South Florida Library.

9. Afro-Cuban and African American teenage members of Pan American Club (founded by José and Sylvia Griñán) perform skit on dance floor of Martí-Maceo patio, circa 1950. Martí-Maceo Photo Collection, Special Collections, by permission of University of South Florida Library.

10. Rumba contestants Manuel Alfonso and Sinesia Menendez, ca.1938. Martí-Maceo Photo Collection, Special Collections, by permission of University of South Florida Library.

5

Sociedad la Unión Martí-Maceo

The Martí-Maceo Society was the focal institution around which, and inside of which, Afro-Cuban identity emerged in Tampa. The turbulent events of the first decades of the twentieth century, in both Florida and Cuba, were collectively experienced, assessed, and acted upon within this context. As an institution, it provided an economic safety net of immense importance, and it established formal membership, a legitimacy of belonging, within the larger enclave of immigrant cigar workers. This chapter examines the growth and establishment of this crucial institution.

The ethnic mutual aid societies in Ybor City fostered an elaborate system of group medical care, fashioned along the same lines as the *sociedades* in Cuba. The actuarial principle underlying this system was relatively simple. Dues paid by large numbers of members, most of whom were young and healthy, provided pools of capital that enabled the provision of encompassing care for those who fell ill. Each paid 60 cents a week, in exchange for which they were entitled to whatever medical attention they needed—operations, examinations, and pharmaceuticals. In addition, members who were too ill to work were paid stipends of $1.50 per day. This was an extremely generous benefit payment. Many workers in Tampa, including a fairly large proportion who worked in the cigar factories, earned this much or less per day from their regular labors. This system offered protection against the terrifying specter of family ruin caused by prolonged illness of the principal earner. It developed in a context where publicly funded health care was simply not available, and private services in Tampa were primitive and costly. At the time this system was established, there were no hospital facilities for black people in Tampa. In 1908, an African American nurse named Clara Frye converted part of her house into a makeshift hospital. It had only a few beds and, except for nurse Frye, no permanent staff (Brady 1997; Jones and McCarthy 1993; Mays and Raper 1927). Clara Frye's sacrifices and lifelong hard work in trying to bring health care to the black community are recognized as a legacy of black history in Tampa, but the facilities were woefully inadequate.

The medical benefits provided to members of the Martí-Maceo Society offered important advantages to Afro-Cubans. They avoided reliance on the Clara Frye Hospital by covering the costs of operations in Cuban hospitals, along with expenses involved in making the trip home. The sick benefits available to members of Martí-Maceo were more than twenty times as generous as those paid to members of the Grand Pallbearers Union ($10.50 per week compared with 50 cents per week). The social hall erected by the Martí-Maceo Society in 1908 was the largest secular meeting facility available to blacks in Tampa, bigger and better than the lodge hall built by the Odd Fellows on Central Avenue. The Afro-Cubans were a small minority within the black population, but they were unified in a single organization instead of being divided among many small churches and lodges. They were able to mass their resources and hence optimize the benefits.

It is also true, however, that the wages earned by Afro-Cuban cigarmakers were considerably higher than those paid to most African Americans, and this greater measure of prosperity facilitated the success of their institution.[1] The tangible presence of the Martí-Maceo Society and the valuable benefits it provided served to underscore the status discrepancy between Afro-Cubans and African Americans. It provided a major source of social, cultural, symbolic, and economic capital that directly attached to identification as Afro-Cuban.

For all the immigrants, the accomplishments of the mutual aid societies were a source of pride and the basis for belief in their own organizational superiority compared with the native born of Tampa. The immigrants in Ybor City pioneered in the establishment of health maintenance organizations—contract medicine aimed at prevention. By setting the sick benefits so high, they encouraged sick members to rest and recover, rather than working with minor illnesses that could worsen into debilitating ones. The ideology that drove this development in Tampa was explicitly socialist. Surpluses that accumulated from the difference between dues revenues and benefit payments were not profits to be allocated as dividends, but rather underwrote the expansion of benefits for members and the construction of elaborate and commodious social halls. Much of the labor required to operate these organizations was unpaid and voluntary, reducing overhead costs to enhance the size of the common fund. In each of the organizations, dues paid for sick benefits and the health care system provided an economic foundation for organizing a major share of group activities. These included dances, picnics, plays and musical performances, and meetings for all kinds of purposes. The social halls that each constructed were collecting points of community life, and they channeled these collectivities along lines that were distinctively ethnic. Although separated by nationality and race, the individual organizations in Ybor City were highly coordinated in their arrangements with doctors and pharmacists, and the scale effected by their large combined memberships attracted a sufficient number of both. It was a system of socialized medicine that was remarkably successful and enduring.

In all parts of the United States, immigrants of many different nationalities created similar formulas for providing health care and burial insurance in cities where such services were otherwise unavailable to them (Beito 1993; Bodnar 1981; Chyz and Lewis 1949; Cummings 1980; Greenbaum 1991; Soyer 1997; Vondracek 1972). Italians, Poles, Croats, Swedes, Irish, Germans, Jews, and many other immigrant groups created organizations to meet their respective needs. Local societies established national networks (like the Croatian National Union and the Polish National Alliance) that facilitated intercity migration and offered benefits such as loans and scholarships that were made possible by the broad scale of operation. African Americans in the earliest years of the republic, and especially in the period after the Civil War, also established a large number of mutual aid and burial societies, similar to the Grand Pallbearers Union. In some cities, especially Atlanta and Richmond, Virginia, these organizations grew large and branched into banking and commercial insurance (Browning 1937; Butler 1991; Carson 1993; Du Bois 1907; Ergood 1971; Greenbaum 1991; Harris 1936; Harris 1979; Kuyk 1983; Pollard 1980; Williams and Williams 1992; Woodson 1929).

The history and significance of these ethnic organizations, alternative institutions that greatly mediated the risks and hardships facing their members, have been little studied or appreciated (Cummings 1980). The organizations in Ybor City were scarcely unique, nor were they the most ambitious or successful operations of this type. There was, however, a distinctively collaborative dimension to the development of mutual aid in Ybor City. The success of the overall system rested on the capacity of the different groups to cooperate across national and, to a large extent, racial lines. Class solidarity among the cigar workers, and their abiding faith in socialist remedies for the problems they faced, bridged divisions and rose above narrow nationalist preoccupations.

Cooperative endeavors of this type stand in contrast to the individualistic strategies that epitomize capitalist avenues to success. Disadvantages were negotiated collectively, risks were minimized by sharing, and participants availed the power of their numerical strength through corporate institutions. In Ybor City and in cities throughout the United States disadvantaged ethnic groups established communitarian financial institutions in the midst of, at the very height of, robber baron capitalism. This apparently anomalous, but extremely ubiquitous, economic development has gone largely unnoticed and unanalyzed. "The fact that immigrant groups created explicitly economic institutions for purposes of influencing the distribution of income and wealth and expanding employment opportunities has largely escaped the attention of most economists" (Cummings 1980:8).

One reason for this gap, what Cummings has described as a "uniquely politicized oversight," rests on the assumption that these organizations were not really successful and could not compete with private market solutions, like commercial insurance. These assumptions, in turn, are grounded in a conviction that altruistic institutions are ultimately incompatible with the "rational choices" that guide human economic behavior (Bates 1994; Hardin 1968; Hechter 1987; Knoke 1990; Olson 1965). It is believed that schemes for sharing resources, however well intentioned, invite abuse by "free riders" who will seek to benefit more than they contribute. Because it is rational for an individual to behave in this way, and most humans are rational, it is virtually certain that such abuses will occur. This paradox has been labeled "the tragedy of the commons" (Hardin 1968). Michael Hechter (1987) has invoked this concept in specific reference to immigrant mutual aid societies. He argues that these institutions were doomed by the urban environments in which they operated—a breakdown in cohesion resulting from mobility and modernization—and by the inherent limitations of those entrusted with managing the funds—an inability to calculate risks accurately and the great likelihood of attracting dishonest leadership. "*State enforcement of laws against embezzlement and outright theft* is, therefore, virtually a precondition for the long-run survival of insurance groups" (Hechter 1987:116; emphasis in the original).

Interrogating the Commons

The mutual aid societies of Ybor City were financial institutions where the currency of the shared resource was fluid and easily misappropriated. Maintaining solvency depended on a complex combination of actuarial knowledge, bookkeeping skills, and diligent oversight. The social matrix in which these institutions arose in Ybor City placed a strong ideological premium on honesty and compassion. However, they were set within a rapidly expanding urban area with multiple communities, transient membership, and sometimes conflicting loyalties—a location that would seem structurally conducive to selfishness and the ease of escape into anonymity.

The treasury records of the Martí-Maceo, in combination with oral histories of elderly former officers, provided the basis for examining the operations and problems that existed within this particular organization. These records, and the interpretive knowledge of some of the men who created them, made it possible to reconstruct a profile of costs and benefits associated with individual membership. The purpose was to determine the stability of the fund over time, and to look for rational choice factors in the distribution of costs and benefits that could have gradually undermined the equilibrium between member contributions and demands on the benefit system. Were the officers, who donated their labor and assumed burdensome responsibilities of managing the common fund, differentially rewarded in unseen ways for their apparent sacrifices? Or did the highly mobile members, who benefited from the existence of the Martí-Maceo but rarely contributed anything beyond payment of their dues (i.e., "free riders"), perhaps unduly benefit from the system?

Answers to these questions could be gleaned by reconstructing individual cost/benefit ratios and then analyzing these measures for the effects of different status positions (Greenbaum 1993). This analysis and the qualitative information provided by former officers produced results that were surprising. With one fairly spectacular exception, officers were shown to derive *less favorable* cost/benefit ratios than regular members. The exceptional case, embezzlement by a highly trusted treasurer, occurred early and precipitated a crisis over controls that resulted in much more effective internal oversight. It did not, as Hechter insists, produce state interference. The problem was resolved with the help of an ally inside the Ybor City community and was accomplished discreetly without involvement of police or other authorities.

The other hypothesized problem, mobility and attenuated commitment by the large number of members who traveled, disclosed instead a significant financial advantage to the organization. The cost/benefit ratios of this class of members were the most unfavorable; the highly mobile members rarely collected any benefits at all. Their dues payments were almost pure profit to the organization, and their existence effectively underwrote the viability of the fund. In this case, and one might suspect in others as well, the mobility of urban industrial life actually enhanced the operation of the mutual benefit system. These findings and the data on which they are based are described at some length in this chapter. Before turning to this analysis, however, it is useful to examine the overall context of mutual aid and ethnic organizations in early Ybor City.

Mutual Aid Societies in Ybor City

The five major ethnic societies in Ybor City were all founded within a short interval, between 1891 and 1902. Centro Español was the first, begun in 1891 by Spanish factory owners, but drawing the bulk of its membership from Spanish cigarmakers. The members included both Galician and Asturian Spaniards, who temporarily set aside regional differences in a common front against the belligerence of Cuban patriots in the cigar factories. L'Unione Italiana was established in 1894. El Club Nacional Cubano (originally called the October 10 Club), which briefly included both black and white Cuban cigarmakers, was founded in 1899. A year later, the Marti-Maceo Society came into existence. The circumstances surrounding this split already have been described. The white Cubans renamed their club El Círculo Cubano in 1902 when they erected their first building. El Centro Asturiano, the last and also the largest, was begun in 1902 by dissident members of Centro Español who were predominantly from the province of Asturias. It was a formally chartered branch of El Centro Asturiano in Havana, headquarters of an umbrella organization of Asturian mutual benefit societies in Cuba.

Spanish immigrants in late-nineteenth-century Cuba had established dozens of regionally based mutual benefit societies. The approximately ten thousand Asturians had, by 1900, developed a highly coordinated system of group medical care, as well as the usual burial insurance and social benefits. The central building in Havana was a magnificent edifice, with a Mexican onyx staircase and polished marble floors. Its library, which occupied several floors, contained five thousand volumes (MacGaffey 1961: 104–5). Centro Asturiano in Ybor City was one of many satellites of this powerful metropolitan institution (Long 1965a:418). Within Cuba, Centro Asturiano influenced the growth of many Cuban (as opposed to Spanish) mutual aid societies, and white Cubans were increasingly accepted as members in the Spanish organizations. Similarly, Centro Asturiano in

Ybor City also quickly relaxed membership requirements to permit other Spaniards, Italians, and white Cubans to belong (Mormino and Pozzetta 1987:182).

Traditions of mutual aid in Ybor City were, in effect, secondary transplants. For the Spanish, they originated with Spanish nationals who had gone first to Cuba and then to the United States. Creole Cubans copied the structure in organizations of their own, in Cuba and later in Key West and Tampa (MacGaffey 1961:105). Afro-Cubans drew on a long history of institutionalized mutual aid, in the colonial *cabildos* and in later secular societies patterned on those formed by the Spanish. In Ybor City, Centro Asturiano pioneered the development of comprehensive medical care, but the concepts of "contract medicine" and mutual benefit arrangements had been imported from Cuba along with the first cigarmakers who arrived in Ybor City.

The earliest organization, La Igual (The Equal), was actually an entrepreneurial operation begun by a Spanish doctor from Cuba in 1887. He instituted a plan whereby subscribers could obtain medical treatment when needed in exchange for weekly payments of 50 cents. A year later, a group of factory owners imitated and expanded this system in an organization called El Porvenir (The Future). This was also a strictly capitalist institution. The organizers were motivated by the twin desires of profiting from the premiums and reducing absenteeism in the factories (Long 1965a:424). By hiring a doctor on salary to provide routine treatment for factory workers who paid $1.25 per month, El Porvenir was able to cut the rates charged by La Igual by $1.00 a month and still show a profit. Two other private competing medical organizations were formed: La America and La Fe. A pharmacy, jointly operated by La America, La Fe, and El Porvenir, was opened in 1902, adding pharmaceuticals to the package of benefits (Long 1965a:424). Hospitalization was not included in these plans, and they had no explicit connection with the early ethnic societies, except that most of the members of these organizations were also subscribers to one of the medical programs.

Shortly before the turn of the century, a debate arose in Centro Español over the management of group medicine. The Asturians especially argued in favor of direct provision of medical care and the establishment of a hospital. The leaders of Centro Español, which included factory owners involved in El Porvenir, resisted these suggestions. This disagreement led to the secession of more than two hundred Asturians and other like-minded Spaniards, who formed Centro Asturiano in 1902. They hired their own doctor, who operated out of a clinic in Ybor City. A small "sanatorium" was established in a building purchased by Centro Asturiano, and a fund was started to build a new modern hospital. By 1903, membership in the society had ballooned to more than a thousand and, within the next year, Centro Asturiano in Havana granted approval to begin construction on a hospital in Tampa.

In response to the drain of members, Centro Español established its own medical plan. In 1905, the year that Centro Asturiano Hospital was completed, Centro Español also began building a hospital. These two facilities not only rivaled each other, but were among the best-equipped hospitals in the South at that time (Long 1965a).

Members of Centro Español and Centro Asturiano had unlimited access to hospital care, as well as routine and preventive treatment, dental care, and pharmaceuticals as needed. Benefits of membership also included generous stipends to supplement wages lost to illness, burial insurance, travel costs for specialized medical treatment, and use of recreational facilities in the elaborate social halls that each had constructed in Ybor City. Dues were $1.50 per month, only 25 cents more than the limited health care offered by El Porvenir. Unlike El Porvenir, there was no profit in this operation. Indeed, dues alone were insufficient to pay the costs. Added funds were raised by bar sales, and admission charged at special cultural and social events. In capturing these consumer revenues, the organizations reinforced social ties among the members as well as bolstering their treasuries. It is often assumed that commercial and for-profit insurance arose in response to the shortcomings of socialized varieties of mutual aid. In this case, however, the socialistic versions followed entrepreneurial ventures that could not compete with the profitless calculus of the ethnic societies.

The other ethnic societies—Círculo Cubano, L'Unione Italiana, and Martí-Maceo—developed similar medical and social programs, but without hospitals. Black Cubans established their benefit system in 1904, when the earlier Martí-Maceo Society merged with the recently established La Unión. It is noteworthy that the official founding date listed in documents and press releases by the society is always given as 1904, rather than the earlier date of 1900, when the first organization was formed. This emphasis reflects the importance attached to these benefits, at the expense of the greater prestige of an earlier founding date. White Cubans at Círculo Cubano did not institute medical benefits until 1908, after the election of a reformist president.[2]

Members of Círculo Cubano and the L'Unione Italiana were able to arrange for hospitalization through contracts with Centro Asturiano and Centro Español, but black Cubans could not be treated in these hospitals. As was mentioned already, when Afro-Cubans required hospitalization, their passage to Cuba was paid along with the costs of care in a Cuban hospital. This added expense, a kind of tax on their color, was a further burden on the financial requirements of mutual aid for Afro-Cubans, but worth the cost in view of the limited alternatives in Tampa.

Institutionalizing Cultural Capital

The original members of Martí-Maceo included some noteworthy local Afro-Cuban leaders in the struggle for independence—Ruperto Pedroso, Bruno Roig, and Teofilo Domínguez, all of whom had been among the founders of La Liga. The early leaders were strongly identified with the legacy of their organization's namesakes. Although Martí-Maceo was started in Pedroso's house, Ruperto was active in the organization for only the first few years and never served as an officer. His brothers, Juan and Justo, did remain active and still have descendants among the current members. Ruperto and Paulina returned permanently to Cuba in 1910, during a long strike in the cigar factories. Domínguez and Roig were very active in forming the organization, but Domínguez died of tuberculosis in 1902. Roig's involvement gave rise to the first major crisis confronting the Martí-Maceo Society, an episode that will be described shortly.

The first meetings of Martí-Maceo were convened in the parlor of the Pedrosos' boardinghouse. By 1902, they were able to secure a two-story rented house on Eighth Avenue a few doors down from Pedroso, which they converted into a social hall. Initially, it was constituted as a recreational and instructional organization. The first committee was for "Bass Ball," and the first activity was formation of a team, later named the Cuban Giants (Los Gigantes Cubanos). Teofilo Domínguez argued forcefully for the immediate establishment of night classes. It was his position that the major purpose of the organization was "the social and intellectual improvement of the most needy classes."[3] Domínguez also advocated developing a newsletter to articulate the purposes of the organization and serve as an organ to recruit new members. In April of 1901 they raised $88.00 to stock a library, but the classes were delayed for years and the newsletter never materialized, probably due to the untimely death of Domínguez. His death was an unfortunate loss, stilling a contentious voice in favor of continuing the social and political purposes of the patriots.

Many of the voices in the meetings were contentious. A pattern of debate that was always vigorous, and often rancorous, is evident in the earliest minutes. To some extent, this ambience of agitated discussion leading often to ultimate consensus, was stylistic. Through the decades that followed, heated exchanges remained commonplace in the accounts of meetings, frequently over matters that would seem to have been trivial. However, the beginnings of Martí-Maceo reflect seriously divided opinions about what the organization was designed to accomplish, how inclusive its membership would be, and how to apportion the work of running it.

Some, like Domínguez, viewed it as an extension of the revolution and a vehicle to secure social purposes. Others were interested in the issue of representation, to achieve a more dignified status and a forum for ensuring that Afro-Cuban contributions would not be forgotten or discounted. And there were many who simply wanted a place where they could socialize and organize enjoyable activities denied them on the outside by the growing restrictions of Jim Crow. The early activities included picnics and dances, and members (all of whom were males) met there daily to play dominoes. Membership grew slowly, and leadership was difficult to retain. Resignations and votes of confidence were frequent.

In 1904, a rival organization, La Unión, was begun by Juan Franco (the *santero* mentioned briefly in the last chapter). He had been a Martí-Maceo member from West Tampa who was narrowly defeated for election as treasurer in 1903. His new organization, which offered medical as well as recreational benefits, threatened to siphon off members from Martí-Maceo, a problem that was averted through consolidation. The merger resulted in La Unión Martí-Maceo, and the growth in both members and revenues greatly enhanced the organization's treasury. Shortly before the merger, Martí-Maceo showed a balance of $41.24; by the end of 1905, the total had climbed to $1,851.90, and by the end of the next year it was up to $3,035.20. Part of this increase was due to the doubling of fees, from 25 cents to 50 (and soon after to 60) cents a week, and the other part stemmed from increased membership, from about forty to just under one hundred. More members and a larger base treasury permitted the development of more fund-raising activities, like dances and picnics, which further enhanced the revenues going into the treasury.

Even with the added expenses of sick benefits, doctors' fees, pharmacy and funeral costs, La Unión Martí-Maceo had become a money-making operation. By the middle of 1907, the directors felt sufficiently secure that they purchased a lot in Ybor City at Eleventh Street and Sixth Avenue, a few blocks south and west of their previous location. This particular site had once belonged to Cornelio Brito, part of the real estate holdings he liquidated to support the war effort. Hilario Zayas, another member of La Liga and former director of its successor, La Verdad, owned the property next door. Numerous members lived within a few blocks of the new building. Alejandro Acosta, for example, lived less than a block away.

The land cost them $518.60, which made only a slight dent in the balance, by then in excess of $3,600. Additional fund-raising in 1908 made it possible to contract for construction of a building. In August 1908, they formally incorporated under Florida law; and in November, they paid $2,500 to initiate construction. Once the building was under way, the members focused much of their energy on fund-raising and increasing the size of the membership. At the time of incorporation, there were 98 members; by the time the construction contract was let, they had grown to 123, and when the building was finally opened (at the end of August 1909), there were 175.

They now had a fine two-story brick building, with an iron grille balcony that circled the second floor. It boasted a cantina, a library, game rooms, meeting rooms, and ballrooms on both floors. The new building was an effective marketing device, and the growth in dues revenue, in combination with personal donations and the proceeds from a large benefit dance, had enabled them to come up with the final payment of $2,000 to complete the construction. In all, however, the building cost $18,000, leaving an outstanding debt of just under $13,000, repayment of which would take more than twenty years. It should not have taken them that long, but a financial crisis in 1915 posed a serious setback that not only threatened their ownership of the building, but also rocked the moral foundation of the enterprise that they had labored so hard to construct.

The Bruno Roig Affair

Bruno Roig, who is mentioned frequently in accounts of Tampa's involvement with José Martí, played a central role in organizing and leading the Martí-Maceo Society. He served as treasurer continuously from 1904, when the economic benefits were started, until 1915, when he was abruptly forced to resign.

Roig was an obvious choice for stewardship of the treasury. He had been treasurer of Ignacio Agramonte, the leading revolutionary club in Ybor City. This club had organized Martí's first visit. As treasurer, Roig had collected the funds for Martí's expenses, made the arrangements, and paid the bills. He is credited as the only one among the organizers who had the presence of mind to worry about the costs of the visit (Muñiz 1976). Roig was older than most of the others (fifty in 1904), and he had lived in Ybor City since 1887. His reputation was impeccable. As the owner of a grocery store and several parcels of real estate in Ybor City, he was one of the few Afro-Cubans with the requisite skills and experience to manage the growing common fund.

The high level of trust that was vested in him, however, enabled him to get away with using institutional funds to cover his debts. Behind his sober exterior, Roig was a compulsive gambler. Sometime in the early months of 1915, he incurred large losses that he paid from the Martí-Maceo treasury. This act coincided with the due date for the mortgage, an amount that the remaining funds were insufficient to cover. Faced with foreclosure and other bills they could not pay, it seemed like the short history of Martí-Maceo was about to come to an end.

Adam Katz, a Jewish merchant in Ybor City, rescued the situation. He paid off their existing mortgage and extended them a new one. Katz also managed to persuade Bruno to turn over the deeds for two rental houses in Ybor City to the Martí-Maceo Society as restitution, and as an added source of revenue.

I first learned of Bruno's crime and Katz's intervention from a very elderly informant. He described Bruno's lapse as a momentary act of weakness, not a pattern of scurrilous behavior. The real villain was an unnamed white Cuban gambler who had finagled control of the Martí-Maceo from poor Bruno. Katz, who learned of their plight, intervened to defeat the vicious intentions of the white Cuban, in a refracted identification with the persecution of Jews he had experienced in his native Romania. Chastened and forgiven, but with his reputation ruined, Bruno was assisted by the members of Martí-Maceo to leave Ybor City and return to Cuba.

Based on this narrative account, I began to search for corroborating information and a clearer understanding of this remarkable episode. A cache of mortgage papers that was discovered in a storage area of the current Martí-Maceo building supplied a wealth of detail about what had transpired, and minutes from meetings of the period in question provided added information. In outline, the story they revealed was essentially the same as the one told by my informant, but many of the details proved to be contradictory. The discrepancies between his remembered version, compared with what I could glean from the documentary sources, disclose subtle processes of demonizing and heroicizing events and personalities from the past that have particular symbolic value. The narrator was twenty-two years old when this episode occurred. Both he and his father were members, but neither was on the board of directors or personally involved in the dispute. His account reflects a combination of what he had been told, what he had managed to remember across such a broad span of time, and what he may have wished had been true. My informant's version, in his words, is as follows:

LUIS: Now this Bruno, he was the treasurer of the club. He went into gambling and lost everything . . . we was broke. And they came and were going to foreclose everything. A Jew guy that had a big store on Seventh Avenue, Adam Katz, found out what was happening to us and he came and said don't worry. He go to the place, he paid everything, two or three thousand dollars, and he took us out of the mortgage this guy [the shadowy Cuban gambler] had put us in. And [Katz] took the houses that the guy [Bruno] had. He said, You give me them three houses or you going to jail. And [Katz] gave the three houses to Martí-Maceo. He said now this money you owe me, you pay it without interest. Don't care if you pay it now, tomorrow, or if you don't pay it. They tried to take advantage of y'all and I ain't going to permit it.

SG: Why would he have done this for them?

LUIS: He done it because he felt that he was a Jew and that the Jews had been kicked around enough and now they was trying to kick us around because we wasn't white, and he wasn't going to permit it. That was Adam Katz.

SG: What had happened to Bruno? How was he able to get the club's money and what happened when it was discovered?

LUIS: He had access to the money. He was the money man. He's a nice guy. Nobody didn't believe he would do such a thing as that, but when you're gambling. . . . It was hard luck. He took the money figuring he's gonna win it back. Now when he didn't have nothing . . . he lost everything. We give him money to go back to Cuba. Oh yeh, we wouldn't let him down.

My informant's story was inspiring, affirming a shared sense of victimization, triumph of good over evil, and redemptive forgiveness. These themes validated the political ideals of my informant, a die-hard socialist who had never forgiven the betrayal of black by white Cubans. In his scenario, Jews and blacks formed an interethnic alliance to fight injustice. The Martí-Maceo Society was saved by the altruistic gesture of a similarly marginalized friend. And poor Bruno, as much the victim of callous exploitation as the perpetrator of a crime, was let off easy. Unlike white Cubans, who had too easily dismissed the patriotic contributions of Afro-Cubans, members of Martí-Maceo would not forget what Bruno had done in Martí's time, in spite of the wrongs he later committed.

Documents tell a less romantic version of this tale. Bruno's tenure as treasurer of the organization evidenced a fairly long-term pattern of irregularities. He did not succumb to momentary temptation in what was perhaps a rigged game of chance. Rather, he apparently had been availing himself of opportunities to make unauthorized loans from the fund for quite some time before he was discovered. After he was found out, he was extremely slow to accept responsibility for his acts, and he made restitution only under duress.

Financial ledgers and brief minutes of meetings reveal much about how this happened and the effects it may have had. The accounting system that was set up in 1904 did include controls on the activities of the treasurer, a double-check ledger on which the accountant entered weekly income on one page, and the treasurer recorded deposits to the treasury on a separate page. Monthly balances were reconciled with a bank statement. What was lacking, however, was a strong external auditing system that could monitor these ledgers and ensure the accuracy of the receipts and deposits. For the first few years, there were no apparent problems. Entries in both are in near-perfect agreement with minor discrepancies traceable to math errors. By 1910, however, the discrepancies became more frequent and sizable, with year-end differences amounting to several hundred dollars. There is no indication of how these problems were detected, or what might have been done in response, but in 1913 the two ledgers were again temporarily brought into agreement. However, between June 1914 and April 1915, no double-check ledger was kept.

Only the general ledger, controlled entirely by the treasurer, recorded receipts and deposits. It appears likely that this absence of oversight, however it may have been arranged, generally corresponded to an increase in Bruno's embezzlement activities. First indications are a few months earlier. He withdrew $96 in sick payments during the month of December 1913, reflecting sixty-four installments in one month, an amount that could not have been legitimate given the fact that these were daily payments of $1.50 (maximum possible was thirty-one). Moreover, in December of 1913 the club had 184 members, whose dues revenue for that month should have totaled $588.60. The treasury balance for that same month showed dues credit of only $384.95, a difference of more than $200.

The actual details of Bruno's misdeeds cannot be fully reconstructed, but there are scattered clues like the ones above, and the inescapable fact that minutes from a series of meetings in July and August 1915 indicate that he was forced to resign his position. These minutes also testify to Bruno's recalcitrance.

On July 3, 1915, a mortgage the club had taken out in 1912 in the amount of $2,300 came due. The note, held by a C. C. Whitaker, carried interest of 10 percent. Apparently, Martí-Maceo had managed to make the interest payments over the three years, but the principal was still outstanding. It is quite likely that this day of reckoning was the event that precipitated awareness of the state of Bruno's treasury.

The first meeting by the board of directors to address the problem was on July 21, 1915; Bruno was not in attendance. At that meeting he was "suspended due to irregularities in his department." He reportedly had agreed to meet with the board on the following day (July 22), but minutes of that meeting indicate he was "indisposed" and hence unable to attend. He promised to come the next day (July 23), but was again indisposed, promising to come the next day. On the twenty-fourth the meeting again convened without him, but a special commission had gone to the bank and to Bruno's house to obtain all the documents needed to assess the extent of their problem. Bruno had told the commission that he had avoided the meetings for fear of unpleasantness ("*un malo rato*"). He also conveyed his desire to make restitution by selling one of his houses, indicating he would do so as soon as possible.

In the meantime, on July 28, the directors executed a new arrangement with the Ybor City Bank to cancel the Whitaker mortgage and establish a new one (for $2,350), at 8 percent interest, but payable in only one year. Presumably, this could be paid with money from the sale of Bruno's houses. At the next membership meeting (July 29), which Bruno finally attended, it was revealed that these properties were mortgaged already. He claimed this was not really a problem, that he could secure another mortgage. Members present expressed relief and a willingness to forgive. It was first proposed that the club not charge interest on the repayment of Bruno's debt, but after a lengthy discussion they decided that it would probably be necessary to do so, because they would need the money to pay off the bank.

The next meeting (on August 11, 1915) reflects a less generous mood on the part of the members. The extent of Bruno's indebtedness and inability to make restitution had come to light. They voted to censure him and fire him as treasurer. They were still willing to allow him to continue as a member, provided he made good on his debt. The minutes state that he had improperly taken $846.54. Discrepancies in treasury balances generally accord with this level of misappropriation, although net losses were considerably larger. In December 1914 the overall balance had been $1,324.17; by July 1915 it was down to $169.89.

Adam Katz owned a dry goods store at 1330 Seventh Avenue in Ybor City. He was part of a small group of Jews in Tampa who had fled pogroms and discriminatory laws in Romania around the turn of the century. Like Katz, many were merchants in Ybor City who spoke Spanish (an easy transition from the Ladino spoken by Sephardic Jews) and found a comfortable niche in the immigrant enclave. It is not known how Katz became associated with Martí-Maceo, but in 1901 he had his store at 1330 Seventh Avenue. In that same period the Martí-Maceo social hall was located at 1321 Eighth Avenue. The two buildings were almost directly across the alley from each other; they were very close neighbors.

The first evidence of Katz's involvement in the club comes in August 1916, apparently inspired by the club's inability to pay off the bank loan they had secured the previous year. Katz paid the Ybor City Bank loan and related charges, which totaled just under $2,600. A separate mortgage was executed between him and the Martí-Maceo Society for $2,600, payable within six years. Interest on the note was 8 percent, and they were expected to make monthly payments of $46.94 (a total of $3,380).

This was not a grant, nor was it an informal agreement. It was a very businesslike transaction carrying a standard rate of interest and penalties for failure to observe the terms. These facts do not diminish the value of Katz's assistance, and it is evident that he expended considerable effort in making the arrangements, which also involved an auditor and at least two different attorneys. Although he stood to profit from the loan, it is likely that other potential creditors would not have undertaken the risks. Nevertheless, my informant's characterization of Katz's actions and motives is considerably exaggerated.

The loan in August 1916 did not resolve the club's financial problems, and Bruno's promise to make restitution remained unfulfilled. It was only in February 1917 that Roig finally turned over deeds to two (not three) houses, in another complex transaction orchestrated by Katz. On February 9, 1917, a warranty deed was executed that reassigned ownership of these two houses to the Martí-Maceo Society. On that same day, Katz extended a second mortgage to the Martí-Maceo Society in the amount of $2,400, payable in three years at 8 percent interest. This loan was secured by Bruno's properties. On February 19, 1917, an "indenture" was drawn up between Bruno and the Martí-Maceo Society wherein Bruno assigned ownership of his properties to them in exchange for $1 and a formal release from his indebtedness and "certain other agreements" dating to July 1915. The document was witnessed by Adam Katz.

The new loan paid off all the mortgages and other costs of Bruno's properties, amounting to just under $2,000. In addition, the new mortgage to Katz provided that $100 would be paid to Bruno's wife, Enriqueta. It seems likely that this payment was the "assistance" that my informant said had been paid to Bruno to enable him and his family to return to Cuba. It is noteworthy that the payment was made to his wife. She was more than twenty years his junior and the mother of a young child, an innocent victim of her husband's bad habit. By the time this gesture was offered, there was apparently little remaining good feeling towards Bruno himself.

Although the documentation on these transactions is very complete, it is terse regarding the emotions of the transactants. The only evidence of the effects of this disgraceful experience on the once-mighty Bruno Roig can be seen in the faltering signatures he affixed to these documents. Handwriting that had been bold and confident in earlier documents was there reduced to a childlike scrawl. Bruno returned to Cuba, broke and humiliated, sixty-two years old. Nothing further is known about him.

Katz continued to serve as friend and occasional benefactor for Martí-Maceo until his death in 1924. The treasury regained equilibrium, and the income from the houses was about equal to the payments on their second loan to Katz. He made other loans when they needed money. In 1918, they borrowed $500 to meet unexpected costs and revenue losses from the influenza epidemic.[4] In 1922, when the 1916 loan came due, they secured a new mortgage from him, this time in the amount of $2,900. In 1923, he loaned them $345.34 to pay the fines of several members who had been arrested for gambling in the club. This incident, which was considered to be harassment in view of the ubiquity of gambling in all the clubs, initially carried a fine of $575—a huge amount of money in that period. Katz's lawyers filed a petition to the court that resulted in a reduction, and he then loaned them money to pay the smaller fine.

Katz died on November 19, 1924. The Martí-Maceo Society still owed him $2,460. The mortgage papers for this period include a copy of Katz's will (written a year before he died). In this document, no mention is made of Martí-Maceo, although he did leave $1,000 to each of two charities (an orphanage and an "old people's" association, neither of which appear to have been Jewish). The balance of his estate was left to his wife, children, siblings, and their children.

Martí-Maceo continued to make payments to his estate, finally discharging their debt in February 1929, in full and on time. At last, they owned the building free and clear. The long-delayed prosperity would, however, last only a few months. At the precise moment that the Martí-Maceo Society achieved solvency, banks in Tampa and all over the nation were on the verge of collapse.

Bruno's embezzlement was a costly but valuable lesson for members of the Martí-Maceo Society. The original amount that he misappropriated was small in comparison to the added fees and interest charges that they ultimately were forced to pay. These debts proved to be very burdensome for a treasury that had deficits in nearly as many months as it showed a positive balance. Year-end balances through the teens and early twenties never again climbed above $1,000. However, their experiences with this incident prompted drastic reforms in how they managed their finances. A new rigid standard was adopted, with biannual reviews by the Glosa Comisión, an internal auditing process conducted by an independent committee of members. Mechanisms of oversight were less significant than the ideological resolve engendered by the experience. This high-profile betrayal strongly reinforced the rule that no individual should profit from the organization. Henceforth, officers were not only expected to be honest, but office holding carried an implicit obligation to make personal sacrifices when needed and possible. Oral histories cite several examples of officers who did not collect benefits owed to them, because they knew the club could not afford the payments. For the next eighty years there was no recurrence of fraud or theft. The only other charges of irregularities were leveled in the 1930s, when two collectors had given some unemployed destitute cigarmakers receipts to allow them medical benefits when they could not afford to pay their dues. This was a case of misplaced charity, rather than personal gain, but it drew extreme opprobrium from the members. They too had to struggle and sacrifice to maintain dues payments, and they demanded that the offending collectors be fired and ousted. In the late 1990s, another instance of embezzlement nearly destroyed the club. This will be described in a subsequent chapter.

Katz's intervention was indeed the salvation of the club during this critical period. The fact that aid came from a Jew, and that white Cubans did not help them, widened the chasm between black and white Cubans and helped underscore the significance of shared discrimination in the construction of Afro-Cuban identity. My informant's story emphasizes these themes by distorting Katz's benevolence and fictionalizing a white Cuban antagonist. Bruno's losses may have been to a white Cuban gambler, but this man did not gain control of the mortgage to the building. The note was held by an Anglo (Whittaker) who had negotiated it many years earlier in a transcaction to which Roig was not even a party. In casting this scenario as one of color discrimination, when the actual perpetrator was one of their own, the story redirects the blame. Katz's sympathy for their plight was not a simple matter of protecting them from the predations of their white compatriots, although the problems they faced as people of color may well have played in his motivations to help them. And he did so as a businessman, not as an altruistic benefactor.

The importance of what Katz did overshadows the fact that he charged them interest and insisted on collateral. He was the only one who provided them this kind of assistance, and he had little to gain in championing their cause. Were it not for his involvement, the organization could not have survived. In summarizing Katz's contributions, my informant said the following: "Adam Katz, he was the father of Martí-Maceo. Anything we need, we go to poppa." This language of paternalism signifies the dependency that they inescapably confronted. In isolation, they were not self-sufficient. Their small size and disadvantaged position in relation to the other clubs created a constant state of uncertainty in the flow of funds that demanded credit in order to withstand periodic crises. For nonwhites, credit was extremely difficult to obtain, and Katz performed that critical function.

The role of the officers and members in negotiating and fulfilling the terms of Katz's loans also should not be underestimated. Although they were dependent, they were also dependable. They were able to convince Katz to trust them enough to grant the loan, and they were extremely diligent in abiding by the terms and making repayments. The subsequent loans were equally important, and they finally managed to pay them all.

Within the complex and partly socialist economy of Ybor City, they found a capitalist with a heart.

Hechter's prediction that corruption is inevitable in common funds was borne out by what Bruno did. However, his assumption that this problem should prove fatal, which would have been the certain outcome had they turned this matter over to the hostile court and police system of Tampa, did not take into account the nature of local circumstances or human resource-fulness in coping with the crisis. Moreover, and more importantly, Hechter's pessimism also fails to take into account unobtrusive factors in the economic calculus of costs and benefits that underpinned the system. In particular, his implicit assumption that mobility would undermine cohesion and jeopardize the operation of immigrant mutual aid proves to be very wide of the mark in this case.

Cost/Benefit Analysis

The data I gathered on the relationship between dues paid and benefits received shed light on how it was possible for the club to survive. The small pool of capital that Martí-Maceo was able to assemble was vulnerable not only to the disaster of Bruno's theft, but also to periodic problems like the strike of 1910, when dues revenues plummeted, or the influenza epidemic of 1918, when demand on the sick benefits spiked. The more gradual, but inexorable, effects of an aging membership also represented a potential problem for maintaining solvency.

My analysis of the treasury was inspired by a nagging question that arose early in the research about how amateur bookkeeping, unpaid management, precariously small numbers, and the inevitable disadvantages confronting people of color during this period could have been negotiated successfully over the course of decades of continual operation. The methods and results of this investigation have been reported elsewhere (Greenbaum 1993). I will not revisit the details of this study, but rather summarize the main findings in relationship to the themes of individual rationality versus socialist constructions of common welfare, and the effects of mobility (i.e., the transnational character of Afro-Cuban ethnicity) on the operation of the mutual aid society.

The data for this analysis were gleaned from treasury pages that listed individual sick benefit payments (called *dietas*) and the membership rosters that indicated the extent of weekly dues payments made by individual members.[5] For each individual member, a ratio was calculated representing benefits received divided by dues paid (actually a benefit/cost ratio) over the period between 1904 (when benefits began) and 1927 (a cutoff date made necessary by gaps in the record after that year).[6] I then coded each individual according to the duration of membership, number of interruptions in membership, and whether or not the individual had served as an officer. I wanted to determine whether officers could be shown to have more favorable ratios, an indication of unseen rewards for their participation. I also wanted to ascertain whether the highly mobile members, especially those who joined only once and did not stay long, had ratios that might indicate that they were getting more than the stable members who made various contributions of labor. My informants confirmed that this class of transient members ("birds of passage") rarely involved themselves in the club or interested themselves in its problems. Records confirm that none in this group (defined as those who stayed for less than a year and did not rejoin in the future) ever served as an officer. This group was regarded as the potential "free riders," who benefited from the existence of the organization but did not contribute anything beyond obligatory dues payments.

Neither of my hypotheses, derived from rational choice theory, was sustained in the analysis. To the contrary, officers as a group earned significantly lower ratios of benefits to costs, got relatively less in return for their extra effort, than those who did not serve (.162 versus .227). The lowest ratios of all, however, were earned by the one-time, short-term members (.085). This cohort, which accounted for nearly half of all the people who ever joined the club (514 out of a total of 1,038), realized almost no direct return on their dues investments, although they were equally eligible to collect, and there is no indication that their claims received discriminatory treatment. The itinerant cigarmakers were younger on average than those who traveled less, although age alone was not a significant variable. More stable members in the same age group collected relatively more benefits. The explanation likely resides in the fact that illness is a probabilistic occurrence; the shorter the tenure, the lower the probability of getting sick during the period of eligibility.

The actuarial condition of Martí-Maceo was positively affected by the transience of so many members. Mobile members paid a small cost for their sojourning, and that relative discrepancy was helpful in balancing the treasury. They enjoyed all the general benefits made possible by the existence of Martí-Maceo. For newcomers, it offered an easy point of entry in a city that could be dangerous. They could attend recreational activities, get to know people, and find out about various opportunities (including information about jobs elsewhere that might take them to another place). They also had the security of knowing that if they did fall ill, their incomes would not be threatened. However, they were less likely to make use of these potential benefits, and that margin of difference accrued to the relative advantage of those members who did not travel as much. Indeed, the most stable members, those long-term members who never traveled ($n =$ 64), had the highest benefit/cost ratios of all (.406). When I recalculated the hypothetical amount of benefits that would have been paid if all members had been stable, the total that would have been required nearly doubled in size (from $22,686 that was actually paid to a predicted $40,624).[7] Stability might have had some marginal advantages in regard to enforcing norms of honesty and participation among the members, but the much larger benefit costs required in operating under such conditions either would have depleted the treasury or required drastically adverse changes in the structure of dues and benefits.

The economic advantages of having a mobile membership were largely unknown to the officers who managed the fund. The four former officers I asked about it were both surprised and bemused with what I had found. They certainly knew of the existence of this large group of transient members, and they were generally aware that Martí-Maceo was helpful to all who traveled periodically (which included them as well), but they never suspected that the aggregate effect of these conditions contributed to the solvency of the fund. In an unusal application of the "invisible hand," contingencies and demands of the larger system produced results that could be neither understood nor controlled.

The former officers I questioned were not at all surprised at my other finding concerning the lower ratios earned by officers. One of my informants, who had served as treasurer from the early 1920s to the late 1960s, proudly explained that in all that time he had never once collected a sick benefit, in spite of the fact that he had been too ill to work on several brief occasions. Others told me similar stories about officers who not only donated their labor to keep the club in operation, but also refrained from collecting benefits that they were legitimately owed. Their intimate acquaintance with the occasionally precarious state of the treasury encouraged them to forgo their own claims when possible to help keep the books in balance.

This other component in the equation that made the financial system workable—lower returns paid to officers—reflects agency over structure.

To maintain the system in the face of adverse conditions, selected individuals were willing to abstain from consuming their share of the resource. More important sacrifices of officers involved the time they devoted to managing the club. The directors, especially the treasurer and president, spent ten to twelve hours a week in the conduct of their offices. This was time that could have been spent in other pursuits that would have profited them individually, or simply in leisure at the end of a long workday. Only a few were willing to do this, but a few was all that they needed. There was too much to lose if it should fail.

> LEONARDO: My father got sick and he belongs to Martí-Maceo, and he was sick for about five or six weeks with his leg, and he took no [sick] benefits, only benefits he took was the doctor. They did that because they knew that's the only place to go. Do away with that and we lose contact with each other.

The narrator's father was a *vocale* (a collector), and the unofficial leader of the West Tampa group. He made use of the doctor's services, a fixed cost to the organization, because he needed to be healed. But he was willing to refrain from collecting the individual benefits, because he could afford to do so. The fear of possibly losing the Martí-Maceo overshadowed his own immediate needs. The perception that this organization was all that they had was a recurrent theme in the narratives.

> TOMÁS: If you lose that, you feel like you lose your home. That was home for us, so we had to keep it up.

> JOSÉ: The main reason we worked so hard [was] because we were black. Over here in the United States this was the only thing you had.

Images of sacrifice by officers were deliberately cultivated and disseminated, part of the lore intended to provide examples to the other members. Admiration and respect were the rewards that these gestures earned. These intangible benefits were apparently sufficient to encourage enough members to undertake the effort.

Public displays of generosity validated a shared ideology of mutual aid, principles that were directly connected to the love of *patria*. The Martí-Maceo Society represented a little piece of Cuba, defilement of which was a traitorous act. The former treasurer who was just mentioned had been living in Cuba at the time of Bruno's ouster. He had heard the story there, but the version he was told included another twist—a mistress whose de-

mands for clothes and jewelry had prodded Bruno's treacherous and fool-hardy behavior. This added element in the tale may have been true, or it may have been an embellishment. The suggestion that a woman might have been partly responsible also hints at gender issues in Afro-Cuban identity that will be explored at length in the next chapter. The lesson of Bruno was a negative example, the antithesis of the expected persona that leadership in Martí-Maceo embodied. His crime had tarnished their repu-tation, subjected them to public ridicule, and forced them into dependent relations with outsiders. A personal friend of José Martí, a leader in Tampa's revolutionary movement, his disgraceful behavior diminished the patriotic capital of all of the members, as well as threatening the very exist-ence of the Martí-Maceo Society.

Comunidad

The status hierarchy of Ybor City was reflected in the structures that each of the ethnic societies built. The Martí-Maceo social hall may have been at the pinnacle of the black community, but it was the bottom tier of immi-grant architecture in Ybor City. The other clubs, whose memberships were each more than five times as large as Martí-Maceo, were able to erect mag-nificent structures. Taller, larger, and more elegantly appointed, these buildings gave testament to the greater power their members commanded. Nonetheless, the fact that the Afro-Cubans had one at all established a niche and allowed them to participate in the institutional system that was created. The relative ease with which they were able to coordinate its con-struction was belied by the extreme difficulties they endured in trying to keep it. This accomplishment earned respect and added to the perceived need to work hard on behalf of the organization. Within its walls they orchestrated a strategy to avoid the problems of Jim Crow and fashion a satisfying community life. Martí-Maceo embodied the social and cultural capital held by Afro-Cubans in Tampa, functions that were highly inter-twined with the economic capital that it represented.

Without the medical coverage, it is unlikely that officers would have expended such a large degree of effort, or that members would have been as diligent in paying their dues, but Martí-Maceo was much more than an insurance plan. It was an all-encompassing institution—a refuge from dis-crimination and the material foundation for devising solutions to the problems they shared with other immigrants, and those that were unique to their status as people of color. The leaders in the organization were men, but the whole family was involved in its activities. Classes and programs for youth, a "ladies committee" in charge of organizing dances and cooking for banquets and picnics, cultural events like plays and musical performances, and countless other shared activities brought men, women, and children of all ages into contact with each other, reinforcing ties of kinship and camaraderie among Afro-Cubans living in Tampa.

The men who belonged to Martí-Maceo came there daily after work and, in the process, got to know each other extremely well. Even those who did not stay long in Tampa would be encountered again in Key West, New York, or other stops along the circuit followed by the Cuban cigarmakers. Transience did not confer anonymity. The network may have been far-flung, but the individual members of this "traveling fraternity" recurrently bumped into each at various points. In Tampa, Martí-Maceo was a primary collecting point. Afro-Cuban families, who were more stable than the single migrants, also got to know each other at the dances, picnics, and other organized activities of Martí-Maceo. Except for a small section of West Tampa that was predominantly inhabited by Afro-Cubans, residential patterns in the enclave neighborhoods were racially and ethnically mixed. Few families owned the houses they lived in, and movement within and across neighborhoods was frequent. The Martí-Maceo Society provided a stable center in the formation of friendship ties among the Afro-Cubans in Tampa.

The library envisioned by Teofilo Domínguez was finally established, as were the classes he hoped would bolster their intellectual development. Adults were tutored in English to aid their survival as immigrants, but children were drilled in Spanish to ensure that they could read and write and properly speak the language of Cuba. Cuban history and literature were also important subjects, material their children would not learn in the public or parochial schools they attended in Tampa. They subscribed to a variety of Cuban newspapers and magazines, and purchased copies of books and pamphlets that the *lectores* read in the factories. Both youth and adults participated in plays that were performed in the theater that occupied much of the first floor. Admission fees charged those who attended these productions brought added revenue, but the main purpose of the events was to showcase talent and provide entertainment. Aspirant musicians found a venue in the hall, as well as a place to practice and cultivate technique and reputation. Professional Afro-Cuban musicians and entertainers who traveled from Cuba to the United States gave performances at Martí-Maceo and became acquainted with the local talent, sometimes recruiting them into professional careers. The building and its facilities offered opportunities to develop human resources, organize recreation, and raise funds. Needy families and ambitious individuals sometimes created shows that they performed in the club, splitting the proceeds from admissions with the treasury.

In time, the Afro-Cubans also would open up their building for use by African American entertainers. This added function enlarged their capacity to earn revenue and brought them into closer contact with their African American neighbors. But in the beginning there was resistance to any type of involvement. Separation was deliberate, part of the distinction that allowed them to claim a special status. In January 1910, the board of directors received an invitation to a party hosted by African Americans.[8] This invitation posed a dilemma. They did not want to appear rude in refusing it, but they were also reluctant to accept. George Middleton, the individual who signed the letter inviting them, was a highly respected man within the African American community. He became a well-known civic leader and entrepreneur; a black high school in Tampa was later named for him. At the time he issued the invitation, he had a federal appointment as a clerk in the post office and was involved in many organizations in the black community (Brady 1997). The directors of Martí-Maceo called on the Cuban consul in Tampa to translate the letter and help them decide an appropriate response to the invitation. His advice was to accept, but to make clear that they were doing so as "Cubans." He counseled them to enunciate their differences, to indicate that joining with black Americans in a social event did not signal an interest in becoming part of their group.

Nor were African Americans permitted to join the Martí-Maceo Society. The original by-laws stated that membership was limited to individuals who were born in Cuba or whose parents were Cuban. Exceptions were made only for the Casellas brothers, Afro–Puerto Ricans who operated two small cigar factories and a broom factory in Ybor City, but a special vote of the members was required to allow them full membership. The club's exclusionary provision violated a state law passed in 1909 that prohibited clubs and fraternal associations from discriminating against American citizens.[9]

Martí-Maceo's rules and practices escaped official notice until 1915, when they received a directive from the state to amend the nativity provision in their bylaws that conflicted with state regulations.[10] Although there is no indication of what exactly prompted this intrusion, this was a period of growing pressures on immigrants in the United States. A few months earlier, in January 1915, a law that would have forbade entry of black immigrants into the United States was under debate in the U.S. Congress.

The Cuban consul, Rafael Ybor, lodged a formal protest against this portion of the immigration bill. He argued that the "Cuban colored people are orderly and hard-working citizens, beneficial to the community" and that their "industrial ability and behavior have won them the respect of Tampans."[11] He also made the point that they were not really immigrants, that "the movement back and forth of these people makes it a migration, rather than immigration, in most cases." Ybor met with the Afro-Cuban cigarmakers in a gathering at Martí-Maceo to reassure them and offer his support. He also solicited and won the support of two powerful local figures—the mayor (D. B. McKay, kidnapper of the leaders of La Resistencia) and the president of the Tampa Board of Trade. The consul's willingness to intervene on their behalf, a gesture endorsed by such high-status Anglos, discloses much about the status of Afro-Cubans.

The error in the above quotation, designating them "citizens," when the controversy was actually about incoming aliens, is an interesting act of inclusion. It was well known that Afro-Cubans generally avoided becoming naturalized citizens, that they came and went like "blackbirds."[12] Their migratory behavior was in fact part of Ybor's argument that they deserved special treatment. This fluidity in the tobacco workforce was advantageous to the factory owners, and they objected to any impediments in the free flow of migrant workers. Indeed, the economic interest of owners was explicitly mentioned: "he also indicates the injury it [the law] will do the cigar industry here."[13]

The Afro-Cuban community served a useful purpose, and they did not cause trouble or pose a threat that would warrant their exclusion. It is not clear whether Ybor's willingness to help them was based on their economic value to the industry, or if he framed his appeal to the powerful in those terms in order to win needed support. Afro-Cubans were a negligible portion of the workforce. The potential loss of a few black workers was probably not a real threat to production. It seems more likely that Ybor exaggerated the economic impact as a way to help his friends in the Martí-Maceo Society. Whichever is true, Afro-Cubans were accorded a reputation and a status that included protections and benefits not ordinarily extended to African Americans. The threatening political climate for immigrants, especially for those who were nonwhite, heightened the importance of protection. The added threats against native-born blacks, the escalating violence and deepening racism of the teens and early twenties, were conditions that greatly encouraged Afro-Cubans to avoid involvement with African Americans.

This was also a period in which the African American community was again asserting rights and becoming more vocal about their grievances. In 1913, the installation of the Wilson regime in Washington resulted in the firing of all remaining black federal appointees in Tampa. George Middleton was dismissed in this action, as was J. N. Clinton, one of the leaders of the protest that resulted in the death of M. J. Christopher in 1899. The black postal workers were the group most affected by the changing climate of the new Democratic administration. They were part of the black elite in Tampa, founders of the Paul Lawrence Dunbar Literary Society begun in 1910 to provide a forum for discussions of literature and culture.[14] Members of the Dunbar Society were shaken by this new assault on their livelihood, and the worsening conditions of Democratic rule in both Washington and Tallahassee prodded new stirrings of protest and resistance.

In 1915, another black weekly newspaper, the *Tampa Bulletin,* was begun. Its editor, the Reverend Marcellus Potter, joined in that same year with a black letter carrier named Herbert Lester, president of the Dunbar Society, in an inquiry to the NAACP about establishing a branch in Tampa.[15] This charter was granted in 1917, although the organizers wisely decided to headquarter the organization in West Tampa, which was still a separate municipality under control of more progressive elected officials (Howard & Howard 1994a).

Increasingly high-profile activities of African Americans, escalating threats by nativists and eugenicists, renewed activities of the Ku Klux Klan—all contributed to a general disinclination of Afro-Cubans in Tampa to admit African Americans into their organization. However, when they received the letter demanding that they alter their bylaws in conformity with Florida statutes, they had little choice but to comply. The minutes of the meeting at which this action was taken contain no explanation of the debate that ensued, except that it was apparently long and rancorous. When the vote was finally taken, the proposed amendment of the nativity clause was formally accepted. The reported vote was 24 in favor and only 4 opposed. However, it was noted that 32 other members (a majority of those present) abstained from voting at all. Moreover, they all agreed that the article in their bylaws that specified the use of Spanish in all official proceedings would remain. They argued that this clause was not intended to exclude anyone, but rather to facilitate the work of the organization. Use of Spanish was, however, an effective barrier to participation by Americans, and it was this feature of their regulations that they sought to maintain.

Respectability

These events of the period just preceding the First World War underscored the importance of maintaining boundaries around the official identity of Afro-Cubans in Tampa. The Martí-Maceo Society played a crucial role in effecting these distinctions. It offered the means to avoid social involvement outside of their own community, and it provided a tangible symbol of their separateness. It also was an organized mechanism for enforcing behavioral standards, for helping to ensure that reckless actions of individuals would not jeopardize the safety of the rest. The bylaws explicitly stated that to be eligible for membership, one had to be of good moral character, and lapses were cause for expulsion. Images of respectability were deliberately cultivated and reinforced in rules of conduct and appearance.

> JORGÉ: You did not go into our hall without a jacket. Nobody came in here without it. They all had on a shirt, tie, and a jacket. In other words, they were showing respectability. They gave themselves respectability to the community. The [black] Cuban people, they presented a different respectability.

When the immigration status of Afro-Cubans was threatened, the Cuban consul could vouch for their worthiness without fear of contradiction. The mayor and the head of the Board of Trade (the nexus of white economic and political power in the city) were both willing to attest to their collective reputation as "orderly and hard working citizens, beneficial to the community." Martí-Maceo's medical and sick benefits were also viewed as protection against unseemly images of destitution, a way of ensuring that indigent Afro-Cubans would not cause embarrassment to the rest. One of the former officers explained:

> CASIMIRO: During that time they wouldn't let one of their brothers, someone of their color, be on the corners or trying to ask for a dollar or two. They would take care of those things, so we wouldn't look bad [for] being an immigrant, you know.

The Afro-Cubans' quest for dignity was constrained, however, by implicit expectations of deference and subservience that defined the safe zone for all people of color. Respectability meant knowing one's place and staying within it.

TOMÁS: We always stayed in our place in the community. We never had no scandals or nothing like that.

The privileges inherent in status distinctions between themselves and African Americans were purchased at the cost of the rebellious resistance in which the organization and community were born. Images of fierce *mambises,* followers of Maceo, were traded for a much milder reputation as "respectable colored."

This did not mean that the Afro-Cubans actually repudiated rebellion, or that they had forgiven the U.S. government for subverting the revolution in Cuba. Efforts to achieve respectability did not signify acceptance of the racist practices in Florida. Rather, the cultivation of respectability was part of a narrowly confined strategy to convert their Cuban ethnicity into tangible cultural capital. Respectability was a resource, a means of access to credit and assistance, and a shield against the dangers inflicted on people of color.

The Martí-Maceo Society was an indispensable part of this strategy. It was a palpable symbol of their existence as a separate group, and a central mechanism for collecting and disbursing a shared pool of wealth. The club also supplied a social setting that helped to channel the activities of children away from forming associations with African American schoolmates, and it offered a modest outlet for the cloistered discontent of wives and young single women. Afro-Cuban ethnicity in Tampa was produced and reproduced within its framework.

6

Divided Lives

SG: What about single women who belonged to Martí-Maceo?

JOSÉ: Women members used to pay thirty-five cents, but
the only time they get benefit [was] when they die. They got
medicines and they got doctors, but no *dietas*.

SG: Even if they worked in the factory and got sick and couldn't work?

JOSÉ: No. It was just for the men.

The most important financial benefits that the club provided—the stipends that subsidized unemployment during illness—were monopolized
by men. Management was also monopolized by males, who set the rules in
accord with tradition and in line with the implicit assumption that women
should not be independent. The reduction in the dues the women owed
was not commensurate with the reduction in the benefits to which they
were entitled. They had no less need for the stipends; arguably they needed
them more. Single working women accounted for 14 percent of Tampa's
Afro-Cuban adult population; two-thirds of them worked in the cigar factories. In 1910, there were 54 women in this category, many of whom lived
alone in boardinghouses or in small rental quarters with their children.[1]
Their earnings in the factories were generally much lower than men's. In
addition to financial disadvantages, women did not take part in the daily
social activities at the club, and they were not eligible to participate in the
decision-making. Why should these members, who were also compatriot
workers sharing exile in Tampa, have been excluded from the primary advantages of Martí-Maceo? What was the impact of this and other gender
inequities in the early Afro-Cuban community? This chapter addresses
these questions and explores the more general implications of gender in
the construction, maintenance, and permeability of the boundaries that
separated Afro-Cubans from African Americans. Also examined are the

effects of both race and gender on the boundaries that separated Afro-Cubans from their white immigrant neighbors.

Cuban conventions about gender intertwine with the social dynamics of color. The frigid "purity" of Spanish women counterpoises the lustful sensuality of African women. The assertive masculinity of Spanish men is drawn in contrast with the servile dependency of African men, who must be subordinated because they are potentially very dangerous. The parameters of power and demography in colonial Cuba accentuated the attractions of Spanish males towards women of African descent, while intensifying the perceived need to cloister Spanish women from possible contact with African men. Competitive tensions played onto the hierarchy of control. In Tampa, where color assumed new layers of meaning, gender relations were also affected.

The tenuous position of Afro-Cubans in the Ybor City community heightened the importance they attached to dignity and respectability. This aura of respectability, and its implication of moral superiority to African Americans, secured the distinctions that were made in favor of Afro-Cubans and entitled them to special treatment. Respectability was an important element in the cultural capital of Afro-Cubans in Tampa. Practicing traditional gender relations, which meant enforcing the proper conduct of Afro-Cuban women, was necessary for upholding status and avoiding scandal and ridicule.

The added burden placed on women, as standard-bearers of family respectability, had several implications. Married women, most of whom did not engage in paid labor because working outside the home was not deemed respectable, were less able to make financial contributions to the family income. According to Mormino (1983b), wages earned by Italian wives formed a key element in consolidating economic success in the first generation in Ybor City. Afro-Cuban family practices reduced the likelihood of pursuing this kind of strategy. Lesser opportunities to become educated, because girls beyond a certain age were usually not permitted to attend school, reduced investments in human capital and limited aspirations. More significantly, oppressive conditions confronting girls growing up in Afro-Cuban families bred dissatisfactions that encouraged marriage with African Americans. Intermarriage posed the most profound threat to boundary maintenance, and the effects of gender subordination gnawed from within.

Gender and Respectability

Respectability is a familiar theme in African diasporic literature, one that connects to issues of both race and gender. Peter Wilson's (1969, 1973) exploration of the normative complex of respectability among Anglophone black Caribbeans is seminal to this discussion. He argued that the perceived need to achieve respectability in the eyes of white colonials, to conform to their values and engage in appropriate conduct, served as an element of hegemonic control. Female sexual morality is represented as a central factor in achieving respectability in this context. Wilson also advanced a counterpoint, in the notion of "reputation," the complex of male rivalry that encouraged acts of rebellion and challenge. His dichotomy between respectability and reputation aligned with gender; women sought respectability and men pursued reputation. These gender differences also disclosed what he considered to be a dialectical relationship between external systems of control and internal modes of resistance. This conception has been criticized for oversimplifying the distinctions between reputation and respectability, and for ignoring inconsistencies in how these two notions map onto gender categories (Besson 1993; Sutton 1974). Yelvington (1995:174) argues that both reputation and respectability are implicated in the system that controls not only women, but also subaltern men.

The dynamics of status, color, and gender in Ybor City played out in scenarios that are highly compatible with Yelvington's assessment. Men's reputations and women's respectability were uncomfortably enmeshed. Male status hinged on both the effective control of women in their own families, and on their personal exploits in seducing and bringing about the ruination of women in other men's families. This contradictory formula was bound to produce tension, a set of problematic conditions that favored the white and powerful.

Gender offers a lens through which to apprehend the intricate underpinnings of race and class in Cuba. Several scholars have tied gender in Cuba directly to racial boundary maintenance (Bengelsdorf 1997; Martínez-Alier 1974), reflecting a somewhat sociobiological interpretation of the rules of gender and kinship. "Control of access to women's sexuality [in Cuba] was seen by the white male oligarchy as the key to maintaining the 'purity' of the group and protecting it from unwanted outsiders" (Bengelsdorf 1997:244). Prevention of undesirable contact with "unwanted" males was accomplished by exerting iron control over women's lives. Women were denied personal freedom for the sake of upholding the "purity" of their lineage and class. The standard for female respectability was based on the untouchable virtue of elite white womanhood. The epitome of "unwantedness," the class whose intrusions were most guarded against, was the black male (Martínez-Alier 1974).

Colonial laws on adultery were extremely strict regarding the behavior of women and similarly lax regarding the conduct of men (Martínez-Alier 1974). Whereas white women were carefully sheltered from possible contact with Afro-Cuban males, the Afro-Cuban female, *la mulata*, served as the icon of sexual desire—the permissible object of the restless predatory virility of white men. "The archetypical mulatta continues to effect and epitomize a dangerous sexuality, which both challenges and sustains the sexual structures of society; that is, the mulatta is (and was) imaged as everything white women were traditionally not: sexually aggressive, immoral, and a threat to the established 'rules of the game'" (Bengelsdorf 1997:245.) In the "rules of the game," Afro-Cuban males posed a different kind of danger, both in potential for impregnating white females and in resorting to violence in defense of black women. This specifically sexual danger grafted neatly onto the more general specter of *el peligro negro* (Duharte Jimenez 1993; Moore 1986). The "black threat" was an Afro-Cuban man.

These sexual preoccupations of the dominant society caused race to be highly gendered. The positions of both Afro-Cuban males and females were fraught with irreconcilable conflicts and contradictions that inevitably affected relations between them. Afro-Cuban males lacked power to assert manhood within a system where male roles were strongly defined. Afro-Cuban females were, almost by definition, incapable of possessing the virtues that defined white womanhood (Bengelsdorf 1997; Kutzinski 1993). Based on social roles that cast them as concubines, black women could have freer access to resources and comfort (Dixon 1988a). Obtaining these prizes, however, rested on rejection or betrayal of Afro-Cuban men.

Afro-Cubans of both sexes who wished to assert respectability, to contest these stereotypically sexualized and debased images, had little choice but to follow the dominant paradigm of masculine authority, the cloistering of women under the stern discipline of men. Set within the dangerous and unfamiliar racial terrain of Florida, these issues became more complex. Afro-Cubans faced a multidimensional negotiation to maintain respectability and dignity within the Cuban colony in Tampa. Afro-Cuban males needed to demonstrate masculine control of their families to validate their status as Cuban men. Moreover, their women were more vulnerable, more in need of protection, than the wives and daughters of white Cubans and Spaniards. In Tampa, especially, where sex ratios among the immigrants greatly favored males, extra care was needed to guard against the sexual predations of both white and black cigarmakers. Finally, there was the danger of possible sexual liaisons with African American men.

This last concern was paramount in patterns of avoidance of African Americans. With the establishment of households and the birth of children, Afro-Cubans found added reasons to distance themselves. Their reasoning was described by an Afro-Cuban man who had grown up in an immigrant family.

> JORGÉ: And they tried to sort of isolate themselves from their black brothers, their black American brothers. Which in our day we see that they were wrong, but they did not know any better. I mean they thought they were doing the right thing by protecting their wives and their children from the liberal ideas that the Black American had. Like they had daughters of marriage age, they kept trying to keep them from marrying into black Americans. This is the thing they were trying; they were trying to protect their children, because they [black Americans] had different ideas of how a person should be raised, or how you should get married. And this was the thing that separated the black American from the Afro-Cuban. . . . The black Americans, like I say, they were a little more liberal minded.

Cubans, both black and white, perceived African Americans to be irresponsible parents and sexually immoral individuals. Their perceptions were variously distorted, and reflected little understanding of the dynamics of class and gender in the African American community. The Afro-American Civic League's campaign against prostitution was aimed at drawing similar distinctions of respectability, at vilifying low-class women within their community who survived by selling sex and shamed them all in the process. The upright women of the Baptist and Methodist Bible-study clubs were even more disdainful of their fallen sisters. The ribald music and dancing that went on in the jooks and bawdy houses were viewed as the work of Satan himself. These tensions between the sacred and profane, the contradictory dangers of sexuality, are resonant themes in discussions of gender, resistance, and power within African American communities (see Wolcott 1996; Mullings 1994a). "Respectable" African Americans, both men and women, struggled with the same problems that afflicted Afro-Cubans in Cuba. They were saddled with hypersexualized images that elicited dour performances of overcompensation.

My informant's parents were correct, however, about African Americans' "different ideas about how a person should be raised"—reflections of a more general contrast in the structure of social and economic relations between men and women in the African American community. Women's wages were critical to the survival of most African American families (Howard and Howard 1994b; Jones 1995; Mays and Raper 1927). Working women needed to be able to travel freely, outside the house and beyond the Scrub, and were somewhat safer than men going into the white areas of Tampa. Cloistering women at home may have been economically feasible for families of Afro-Cuban cigarmakers in Ybor City and West Tampa, but not so for most African American families in the wider community. Moreover, women's work covered a broader spectrum. African American girls had greater access to education than boys and more parental support for remaining in school as long as possible. There were niches for educated black women, as teachers and nurses, whereas educated black men confronted few opportunities.

Women teachers played important roles in Tampa's African American community and were among the leaders in civic and political organizations. Women also were the backbone of churches, the workers who organized the fund-raisers and recruited new members. Women's roles in the African American community were too important structurally to exclude them from decision-making. That did not mean, however, that gender equality prevailed in the customs and institutions of the community. Churches and most organizations were led by men, who were glad to have the help women provided, but less welcoming of their opinions on policy and management. The wage contribution of black women was labor added to the burden of caring for home and children, the double shift. Underemployment of black men diminished their capacity to fulfill expected male roles or contribute to family income. Relations between men and women are inherently affected by such problems, the subject of much conversation in the literature on African American gender and sexuality (Zinn and Dill 1994).

Such nuances were not evident across the cultural divide between Cuban and U.S.-born blacks, nor did it really matter. For Afro-Cuban males, African Americans posed a direct threat to their daughters, sisters, and wives and to their own status within the immigrant community. They also provided a bad example of "liberal" treatment that might lead Afro-Cuban women to ponder alternatives to the conditions of their own repressed lives.

In all other realms of political culture, Afro-Cubans were the "liberal" ones, the revolutionists whose struggle for independence was wedded to beliefs in human equality. Just as racism among white Cuban patriots belied their commitment to the ideals of Martí, the sexism embraced by both black and white Cuban males conflicted with ideologies of equality and human dignity. Martí himself was not immune to this inconsistency. In her perceptive discussion of this issue, Hewitt offers the following observation: "Martí frequently posed the martyred mother and warrior son [Maceo and his mother, Mariana Grajales] as the pillars of a free Cuba. But while men were also assigned a range of other roles in Martí's rendition of the insurgent drama, women were relegated to one position only—to as the 'repository of inspiration and beauty.' . . . Confronted in this period by what he considered the looser sexual mores of North American women, Martí hardened his own definition of appropriate female behavior" (Hewitt 1995: 23–24).

Gendered Spaces

The distinction between *la casa* and *la calle,* between home and the street, defined orbits of existence that carefully divided the experiences of Afro-Cuban men and women and the socialization of Afro-Cuban boys and girls. Although this inside/outside dichotomy has been criticized as denying the efficacy of female resistance (Stoner 1991), spatial distinctions fairly described the separate domains of men and women in Tampa's Afro-Cuban community. Men ranged freely and spent much of their time in extradomestic locations; women were expected to remain at home and ventured into public spaces only under supervision. Afro-Cuban women did find ways to mitigate these limits through social and creative expression, and individual circumstances varied in intensity; but especially in comparison with the positioning of women in the African American community, the inside/outside distinction was very pronounced among Afro-Cubans in Tampa.

Others who have written about gender relations in Ybor City (Hewitt 1991a, 1991b; Mormino 1983b) confirm a strong tradition of patriarchy, although they emphasize mediating effects of Ybor City's distinctive history. Mormino has argued that the economic strategies of Italians in

Tampa called forth an unusual partnership between spouses, although women retained highly traditional roles within their families. Hewitt suggests that the political backdrop of Cuban independence and labor struggles in the cigar industry provided immigrant women opportunities for leadership and activism, opened channels of expression and modes of resistance.

Afro-Cubans were little affected by either of these apparent departures from tradition in Ybor City families. The narratives I collected from both men and women who grew up in first-generation households are highly consistent on this topic. Gender roles were rigidly defined, few wives had jobs, and there was very limited organizational participation by Afro-Cuban women.

Paulina Pedroso is a legend, one of Tampa's best-known icons of Cuban independence. She exemplifies the activism Hewitt describes, and her contribution to the family boardinghouse business accords with Mormino's thesis. In the years after the war, however, Paulina receded into the background of Tampa's Afro-Cuban community. She remained a well-known figure, but it was for what she had done in the past, not her ongoing political involvement. Paulina was not present when the Martí-Maceo Society was founded in her front parlor in 1900. Nor was Teofilo Domínguez's wife, María de Jesús Viernes, permitted to attend or participate, despite their prior comradeship in independence activities. Revolutionary women who had struggled alongside fathers, brothers, and lovers in raising funds and mobilizing support for *Cuba libre* had no comparable role to play in the aftermath. Ruperto, Teofilo, Bruno Roig, and other men whose part in the revolution had conferred leadership continued to exert influence on community affairs. Their wives were expected to return to homemaking and childbearing.

María de Jesús Viernes became pregnant eighteen times in her life; ten of her babies survived to be born, and nine grew to adulthood. She worked as a stripper in a cigar factory and operated a boardinghouse in which her large family lived. She no longer had time for politics, only stories to tell children. They heard about Martí and Rafael Serra and other important Cuban men who had been in her house, about the flag she sewed that was carried by troops of the Liberation Army, about the excitement that stirred them over making Cuba free. As a woman, however, she was less free. Her actions and conduct were more limited than her husband's, and she was subordinate to his authority.

Teofilo and María married in 1899 in a rare ceremony performed in the white Catholic church. The bride and groom rode to the church in a fine carriage, and the nave was filled with flowers and overflowing with well-wishers. Teofilo was more progressive than most Cuban husbands, and he adored his beautiful young wife. He also gave thought to the contradictions in how women were treated in Cuban families. Two years earlier, in 1897, he published an essay in *El Sport* entitled "Moral Hygiene" that criticized the custom of neglecting women's education. His argument, however, rested not on the inherent rights of women to cultivate their talents. Rather he couched his plea in the important role of women as the primary instructors of their children.

> We all know that women have a double mission by natural law, but we will demonstrate that the mission is not reduced to just giving birth, but also to educate their children. The future of a generation depends on mothers, since they exercise a sweet influence starting at an early stage in life, something that is not appealing to the other sex. Mothers must care for the development of physical, moral, and intellectual qualities in their children. If they (mothers) do not know this indispensable knowledge, they will think that by simply giving birth and feeding the children they would have fulfilled their duties as mothers. (reprinted in Domínguez 1899)

His challenge to gender inequities was based on rationalizing, not revising, traditional roles and images of women. Because women were entrusted with the job of raising children, it was only logical that they be educated to perform this role. This emphasis may have been a ploy to persuade resistant readers who could not have accepted such radical ideas without the cloak of motherhood and the well-being of children to justify them. Teofilo's ideas and writings were cut short by his death at age thirty, in 1902, only three years after his marriage.

In the period following Cuban independence, a period that visited enormous pressures on black Cubans both at home and in Florida, Afro-Cuban community life in Tampa lost its qualities of defiant political exile and assumed instead a highly guarded respectability. Control of women by Afro-Cuban men in Tampa was directly related to this quest for respectability. Cloistering of women and strict enforcement of virginity emblemized the dignity and uprightness of Afro-Cuban husbands and fathers, legitimized their position as being on a par with the other males in Ybor City and West Tampa. And these practices distinguished the black Cubans from black

Americans, provided arguments that could be used in contending their superiority.

Afro-Cuban men were not themselves required to be sexually virtuous; quite the opposite. Carousing and keeping a mistress validated the manhood of Afro-Cuban males. A woman recalled this double standard enacted by her father and the other men she knew from this era.

> ROSA: A lot of the old time Spanish [Afro-Cuban] men, they would go out and have a ball. They would have a fling. Practically all of them had a mistress on the side, you know. But their wives, they kept their wives behind doors.

This dual pattern—stern enforcement of family women's virtue and male exploits aimed at violating someone else's wife/daughter/sister—added to the tribulations of Afro-Cuban women. It was also a factor that promoted contact between Afro-Cuban men and African American women, deemed more accessible than Afro-Cuban women. These liaisons were a source of conflict within families and with African American men who did not welcome encroachment by the arrogant, and more affluent, Cubans.

Fox (1973:277) argues that the male role in Cuban society reflects "an elaborate game played among men for social status ..., [where] the prize is not the woman, but the esteem of other men." Bengelsdorf voices a similar interpretation, based in part on Fox's ideas: "Traditional male 'attitudes' were the result not of an immutable male-female face-off, but were the historical means by which men challenged, contested, and bonded with other men, essentially over the bodies of women. . . . social esteem and position among the male brotherhood was measured by the degree to which [one] could undermine another's honor" (Bengelsdorf 1997:242–43). Themes of rivalry, challenging, and male bonding are rife in my interview narratives and other sources that examine men's lives in Ybor City.

Men

Ybor City was a good place for men. Revolutionary élan, and the confident pugnacity of workers who knew their skill was vital to production, nurtured an encompassing camaraderie. The political culture of the cigarmakers, their socialist beliefs about labor activism and cooperative endeavor, reinforced a strong sense of collective identity. Men were involved together in a variety of cooperative ventures aimed at the betterment of all their lives. These ranged from purely recreational activities, like musical groups and sports teams, to charitable activities, such as the frequent collections organized in cigar factories to aid individuals who found themselves in distress. Several cooperatives were formed for wholesale purchase of produce and commodities.

An ambitious cooperative called Los Cien (The Hundred) organized a system of home buying, based on rotation of pooled capital among the subscribers and collective labor in constructing the houses. The goal was to build, sequentially, one hundred houses. Each of the hundred members contributed $10, enough to build one house that was raffled off when completed. The lucky owner would continue to pay rent into the fund, with the other subscribers making new donations to construct another house to be raffled among the remaining participants, and so on until all had houses of their own. This ingenious scheme, a variant of rotating credit, was designed as a noncommercial solution to the housing problem. Of the hundred members, however, only one was black.

> LUIS: They [Los Cien] didn't have but one black. Paulo Valdés. That was it. Most of them was Spanish and Cuban, white. They had the best jobs. The black Cubans wanted to go to Cuba, and they didn't have nothing much. They didn't buy houses much, but they couldn't have belonged to it if they wanted to.

The seamless solidarity described by Mormino, Pizzo, and other chroniclers was disturbed only by the unspoken color line that excluded black men from several important realms of community life.

Divisions between males and females had a partial parallel in the boundaries that separated Afro-Cubans from the other immigrant groups. In exile, the distance between black and white Cubans widened in response to status concerns of the latter. All the Cubans were regarded as not quite white; even those who may have appeared to be were sometimes called "Cuban niggers" by Anglo Tampans. Local conceptions of race and ethnicity included exaggerated beliefs about the extent of miscegenation in Cuba, a tendency to assign the whole national group to a kind of mongrelized status. To counter this perception, white Cubans avoided associating with black Cubans. The other immigrants also held black Cubans at a distance for similar reasons.

Color hierarchy in Ybor City was more subtle and less complete than gender hierarchy. It left wider room for negotiation and resistance, was more ambiguous, and more blatantly unnatural. The essential difference between males and females was easy to apprehend; the race of a very light-skinned Afro-Cuban was often difficult to perceive. The ideological context of the community challenged individuals to question the validity of racism, even if that challenge was not fulfilled. Tandem concerns about the oppression of women were not similarly articulated.

Class hierarchy overlapped color, in that the vast majority of Afro-Cubans were on the lower rungs. Most were cigar rollers, the mass producers of the workforce. Rollers' wages were lower than those of other skilled jobs in the factory, the ones predominantly occupied by white Spaniards. However, the class of cigar rollers was broad and deep, the vast majority of the workers. This group was also the core of labor and political activism. Within this class, wages were comparable between black and white workers, and in the workplace, relations were primarily egalitarian. There were tensions over union policies, and about whether white women should be working in the vicinity of black men, but the factories were by and large an integrated experience. Work consumed the largest part of a man's day and week.

The work culture of cigarmaking offered many satisfactions. There was considerable pride in the skills of the craft, and rivalries about individual abilities. Men who made cigars competed over the artfulness of their product. The best cigarmakers won economic success and personal fame. Highly independent, they worked at their own pace and left the bench whenever they pleased. The workday ended when they decided they had made enough. *Lectores* read to them while they worked, and they took enormous pride in their knowledge about literature, politics, and contemporary events. In spite of stifling heat inside the factories, they wore starched white shirts and Panama hats.

After work they walked from the factories in groups, conversing about the *lectores'* readings, or recent developments in Cuba, or sports, or women. In bars, coffee shops, and clubhouse cantinas, discussions were continued over domino games, cards, chess, and billiards. Home for dinner, then back to their clubs, most men spent their evenings as well as their days in the company of each other. The social spaces carved from the interstices between working, eating, and sleeping were highly gendered. They were also very segregated. Most male socializing occurred inside the halls of their clubs, where whites and blacks did not mingle.

Like the other ethnic clubs, the Martí-Maceo was a male bastion. Its purpose was outlined in the founding minutes as a place to "meet outside the home in a way acceptable to men of dignity."[2] In the beginning only males belonged. As the community grew and families expanded, and especially after the construction of the social hall, it transitioned from a men's club to a place where Afro-Cubans of both sexes and all ages congregated. Adult men remained in control, however. Only men were eligible to vote or hold office. A "Ladies Committee" was formed in 1907, when money was needed to erect the building. Members were the wives and older daughters, whose purpose was to organize parties and other fund-raising affairs, and to help recruit new members. They did not vote, and their participation was limited to formal occasions.

> LEONARDO: Martí-Maceo, when I was coming up, used to be nothing but men, no women. . . . I remember that a woman, the only time she go to Martí-Maceo was when they have an affair [dance, play, etc.], because everything was run by men.

Single women who earned their living in the same factories as the men were ineligible to participate fully in the benefits system, and they never went into the social hall after work like the men did.

For the men, Martí-Maceo was the center of their social lives, an institution that provided an arena of male interests and activities—a context for affirming their role in the immigrant community that was comparable to the other ethnic clubs. It was comparable, but not equal; illustrated in an incident in 1917, when the *lectura* organizers (*presidentes*) in several large factories refused to accept an announcement from Martí-Maceo to be read by the *lectores*. Although club announcements were routinely included in the daily readings, theirs was declined on the grounds that it would only be of interest to the minority of black workers. Anger about this refusal elicited a rare public complaint in the local CMIU newspaper.[3] Francisco Flores, president of Martí-Maceo, wrote a scathing letter invoking strong images of revolution and class struggle to condemn this action. The editor, in his response, conceded the validity of their argument and urged that they be henceforth included.

Among the other ethnic societies, there were mutual invitations and cross participation in formal activities; members attended each other's dances and ceremonies, played on each other's baseball teams, drank in each other's cantinas. These courtesies did not extend to members of Martí-Maceo. Cuban national holidays and other events related to the shared patriotism of black and white Cubans posed problems in this regard. The minutes of Martí-Maceo are laced with references to problems associated with joining together for these occasions—split votes and vigorous debate about whether to extend or accept an invitation, admonitions about maintaining dignity and avoiding conflict. Often the choice of who to send was based on color.

> LUIS: Every time they have something happen, a national festival, the twentieth of May or something like that, they would invite us to the Círculo Cubano. Many of them [Martí-Maceo members] didn't want to go. They'd say [to me], "You go 'cause you're the lightest one and you can go." The dark ones didn't want to go. They resented what had happened.

Afro-Cubans who attended formal ceremonies at Círculo Cubano could not bring their wives, and they had to leave as soon as the dancing and socializing began. In contrast, however, members of the white clubs came to Martí-Maceo whenever they felt like doing so. If a popular Afro-Cuban musical group was playing, or when Martí-Maceo hosted patriotic events, white Cubans and Spaniards were free to attend and left only when they wanted to.

> TOMÁS: Whenever we had white visitors come to the club back then, like the foremen from the cigar factories, they won't bring their wives, they come with the males, then they want to dance with your wife. . . . The wives that would dance with the foreman, well, she was afraid she was gonna lose her job, so her husband find himself in a position where he don't like it.

Situations like these underscored the differences and assailed the manhood of Afro-Cuban husbands, gave them more reasons to keep their women at home.

Baseball

On Sundays, most men played or watched baseball, nearly a year-round pastime in the warm climate of Florida. Baseball was, and still is, tremendously popular in Cuba. The first teams were formed in the 1870s (Wagner 1984), coinciding with the period of anticolonial rebellion. Pérez (1994) has made much of this connection in a very interesting discussion of the significance of baseball in Cuban national identity. "Baseball was both symbol and surrogate for opposition at a time when alternative symbols were scarce. In the final years of Spanish colonialism, social and political passions, denied normal outlets, expressed themselves freely in baseball.

The ball field was a stage on which select individuals played representative roles that were charged with social and political significance. Simply by not being Spanish, baseball embodied a critique of the colonial regime" (Pérez 1994:509).

Pérez explores the metaphor of baseball as an organizing symbol of Cuban liberation. The terms of play, in which the team vanquished on one day can regroup in the next game and emerge victorious, reinforced confidence that the shameful surrender at Zanjón in 1878 was only a temporary setback. The communal organization of the game and its appeal to the masses, the inherently democratic emphasis on merit, reflected emerging ideologies of a just and modern society. "Cubans constructed out of baseball a usable paradigm of modernity in which interests and classes coexisted within a social order where service to the community gave individuals a chance for mobility, and in which membership derived solely from ability" (Pérez 1994:508). Embedded in this symbol, however, was its origin in the United States. The simple quality of "not being Spanish" was complicated by the fact that baseball was invented in the United States, where it became "the national pastime." As a symbol of nationhood, baseball in Cuba was encoded with dependency on the United States. It foreshadowed cultural penetration and eventual political control. Pérez does not address the racial segregation of U.S. teams, nor does he consider how color might have affected assessments of merit and access to opportunities for Afro-Cuban ball players.

Cubans in the United States were as avid about baseball as those in Cuba. Pérez notes that some of the earliest Cuban teams were formed in Key West, where baseball was incorporated into the collective fund-raising strategy devised to support the revolution. In Tampa, as well, baseball was directly associated with independence. Afro-Cubans were much involved. Julian González's magazine, *El Pelota*, was the official organ of the Tampa league. Profits from the sales were donated to the PRC. Domínguez's magazine, *El Sport*, bore the same name as an earlier publication in Cuba that was largely dedicated to baseball (Pérez 1994:493).

The first action taken by the newly formed Martí-Maceo Society in 1900 was the creation of a baseball team, Los Gigantes Cubanos. This name was likely derived from a black U.S. team formed in 1896 called the Cuban X-Giants (Brock and Bayne 1998:178), in which the owner and nearly all the players were African Americans. This deliberate misnomer seems to have been adopted to connect with Cuban leagues, which were integrated, thus enabling African American ball players to perform in Cuba, as well as in the less generous Jim Crow circuit in the United States. During this period, Cuban teams that played in the United States were also required to follow that circuit (Brock and Bayne 1998); inclusion of some black players defined them as black teams. This restriction affected the development of baseball in Cuba, "since it was only white Cuban players who got access to the major leagues, it was they and not Afro-Cubans who acquired more fame and financial success" (de la Fuente 1996:270–71). In Ybor City, the process followed the same course.

Los Gigantes Cubanos did not last; there is no mention of it in subsequent minutes, and local accounts of the history of baseball in Tampa do not include it. Indeed, Martí-Maceo was never able to develop its own team. It was the only ethnic society that did not have one. They were the smallest, and scale may have reduced the pool of potentially good players, but a more likely explanation was that they would not have been allowed to compete against white teams in Ybor City. Their competitors would have been the African American teams.

Although baseball withered in the Martí-Maceo Society, it flourished elsewhere in the immigrant community. There were more than a dozen teams. All the other clubs had their own teams, as did the larger factories. Teams were sometimes sponsored by local businesses. The games drew huge crowds.

ENRIQUE: When they'd have baseball games here [in West Tampa] they'd have thirteen to fourteen streetcars come full from Ybor City. You could see them walking in line on Chestnut Street. It used to be beautiful.

Small admission fees bulked to large profits for the organizers. The white ethnic clubs organized serious, semiprofessional baseball teams that recruited players from Key West and Cuba. By 1915, an elaborate "intersocial" league had been developed among the four white clubs. The intersocial teams had connections to minor league teams and scouts for the majors, forming a significant training ground for young talent.

Afro-Cubans, however, were largely excluded from this arena. They did not play on teams sponsored by the other clubs, or on the ones organized by the factories. An Afro-Cuban man (Leonardo) who grew up in the late teens recalled that "every single factory had a team at one time, but no colored, just white. Now, if you was white and you was a good ball player, they would sign you up and give you a job in the cigar factory in order to play. But a Negro, no."

Baseball offered a dreamlike path of mobility for immigrant youth in many parts of the United States (Reiss 1976). Raw talent, hard work, and personal determination could transcend the barriers of class and ethnicity and bestow fame and prosperity. A rarefied achievement made real by hometown boys who got there, Ybor City produced a goodly share of baseball stars. The careers of two of these men—Al López and Hipólito Arenas—illustrate the different realities that color imposed on this dream.

They were the same age, born only a year apart, and they exhibited comparable levels of skill. Al López had a prosperous forty-five-year career as major league player and manager. Hipólito Arenas spent thirteen years playing in the Negro Leagues, after which he returned to a low-paid job with the Gas Company and a small house in West Tampa, not far from where he grew up.

López was born in 1908 in Ybor City. His parents were Spanish immigrants from Cuba. His father worked as a selector in a cigar factory. He began playing on a local team while he was in junior high school. At sixteen, he quit school and began a stellar career in baseball. "We played ball between us kids and competed," said López. "I moved up, and a barber from Ybor City formed a team, and his wife made the uniforms for us. And there was a barber from West Tampa who made a team, and we had rivalries. And they both married sisters so there was a rivalry, they both thought that they were great managers. This guy approached me to come over and play for him" (quoted in Brandmeyer 1981:51–52). The barber's team offered exposure that led to recruitment by the intersocial league, where he was scouted by the Tampa Smokers, a class-D professional minor league team. At sixteen, he signed a contract for $150 per month, more than he might expect to earn in the cigar factories. From the Smokers, he moved up to a class-B team in Jacksonville, and then to the Brooklyn Dodgers, where he became a star catcher. He retired as a player in 1948, but a few years later was hired to manage the Cleveland Indians. In the late 1960s, he retired again and was inducted into the Hall of Fame in 1977. He never lost contact with Tampa, and after he left baseball he made his permanent residence there, a reigning local hero, "Tampa's Mr. Baseball" (Lawson 1985:59).

López deserves the accolades he has received. His were no easy accomplishments. He also experienced discrimination as a Spanish-accented immigrant on teams made up mostly of Americans. "They used to call me a Cuban 'nigger.' I'm not even Cuban, but they called me a Cuban 'nigger'" (quoted in Lawson 1985:68).

Hipólito Arenas was a Cuban, an Afro-Cuban. The venom that had been directed at López by his teammates inevitably targeted a surrogate, because real black Cubans were barred from playing on those teams.

Arenas's parents came from Cuba in the late 1880s; Hipólito was born in 1907 in West Tampa. His father was involved with independence and later Cuban political activities that led to his mysterious death in 1924. Hipólito, the oldest son, became a cigarmaker at thirteen, just before the strike of 1920.

HIPÓLITO ARENAS: That's when I started [making cigars]. And I was savin' some money and there come the strike. For a nine-month stretch. I got disgusted and took my [bunch-making] machine and cutters and throw it away. I shouldn't never make another.

At that time, he played on a neighborhood baseball team in West Tampa made up mainly of Afro-Cubans who lived near each other. Afro-Cubans in West Tampa formed an especially tight-knit group. Many were relatives. Households formed by children and grandchildren of the Barrios family occupied adjoining and nearby houses on the same street. The many children of these households, siblings and cousins, were the nucleus of a cohesive group of second-generation Afro-Cubans. Arenas was part of that group, although not one of the cousins.

ESTEBAN: In the 1910s, West Tampa had the only local Afro-Cuban team, although originally it was mixed. We had a nice baseball club here . . . very powerful. Black Cubans, but we used to have whites in there too. A good catcher, white, and the shortstop and center field, white; the rest is black.

Their team played against all-white teams in the intersocial league, a contest charged with the unstated appeal of black against white.

ARENAS: The only way that we played a white team was on Sunday. They get together. . . . They going to play against black Cubans. . . . We had a few white boys too. . . . We had a mixed team, but they just had white. . . . We were fighters to win.

Integrated baseball teams and mixed competition in West Tampa soon drew the attention of city police, who broke up the games.

ESTEBAN: The law came and broke it up. No niggers play with no whites. . . . We don't want no niggers playing over here with no whites.

Although short-lived, Arenas's performance on the West Tampa team caught the attention of an Afro-Cuban baseball promoter named Alexander Pompey, who recruited black Cubans to play in the Negro Leagues in the United States.[4] Arenas joined a minor league black team in Florida called the Cuban Stars. The Cuban Stars played mainly against other black teams in the state. A pullman porter named Mitch Williams traveled to games in the region scouting for the Atlanta Black Crackers, a team in the Negro League. He saw Arenas play and offered him a chance to try out.

> ARENAS: Mitch Williams, his daddy was a pharmacist and they had a big drug store [in Atlanta]. That's where I was living at, up over the drug store. A friend of mine from Key West, they draft him too. So we was the only two Cubans on this team. And this was a black team.

The owner of the team was white, and he had two teams in Atlanta.

> ARENAS: There was two teams. One called the White Crackers. That was the white team. And the black team, they called them the Black Crackers. We played Monday, Tuesday, and Wednesday, and they played Friday, Saturday, and Sunday.

From Atlanta, he moved up to the Kansas City Monarchs, then to Indianapolis, and finally to the Schenectady Mohawks.

> ARENAS: Babe Ruth, the year before he resigned he have to barnstorm with us, with the Mohawks. He always told me, he say, "I wish they'd given the black a chance." He told me that two or three times—he said, "I wished they'd give you a chance in the major leagues."

It would be too many years before that chance was extended, too late for Hipólito Arenas and hundreds of other talented black ball players. In 1939, he left New York to return to his growing family in Tampa. Each of his first two sons had been born while he was on the road, and another was on the way. His wife issued an ultimatum.

> ARENAS: She said either you and me, or either you and baseball. I say, I'll stay home. I said well, me and you baby. That's when I started to work for the Gas Company.

The job at the Gas Company did not pay much, but neither did baseball if you were in the Negro Leagues. After thirteen years of successful profes-

sional play, he was earning exactly what Al López got from the contract he
signed to play class-D ball at age sixteen.

> ARENAS: Well I was doing pretty good. . . . I was makin' $150 a month
> with three meals and a room.

The income he earned was roughly equivalent to what he could have made
as a cigarmaker. It was a very dim reflection of what a white professional
baseball player could earn, even in that era. Arenas offered a bitter reflection:

> It's a shame all that talent went to waste. You know I sit back and I
> think and I say, how can you do something like that just because of
> color?

There is no way to gauge the potential of Arenas's career if baseball had
been integrated. The comparison between him and Al López is merely a
metaphor. However, in this most American, and also most Cuban, field of
endeavor, the color line deprived him of any chance at ultimate success. In
his old age, Hipólito Arenas was left to ponder the question, and to savor a
judgment rendered by Babe Ruth. Reflecting again on Ruth's barnstorm-
ing tour with the Mohawks:

> ARENAS: And Babe Ruth was sittin' down watching. He asked me, he
> say, "Can you hit that pitcher there?" I said, "You watch and see."
> And he come and give a fast one. And I hit it over the scoreboard in
> center field. Babe Ruth said, "Damn, you hit it harder than me."

Hipólito Arenas's experiences exemplify the vast disparity of opportunities in baseball. Unlike his white immigrant counterparts in Tampa and
other cities at this time, this path to fame and fortune was blocked. Addi-
tionally, segregation in the teams that played in Ybor City was a barrier to
interaction between black and white males in the cigarmaking neighborhoods. Limits on participation of Afro-Cuban men in the recreational life
of the immigrant community demarcated their identity and heightened
their reliance on each other.

Segregation also promoted association with black Americans. Hipólito
Arenas's pursuit of a baseball career thrust his life into black America. His
teammates were African American. His travels took him through the black
districts of cities throughout the United States. He married an African
American woman. After returning to Tampa, he joined with African Am-

ericans to organize a black little league. The only channels open to his aspirations had led him in the direction of assimilation, gave him firsthand knowledge of the complexities and problems of the African American community, engendered empathy and a sense of identification. In contrast, however, most of the Afro-Cuban cigarmakers in his era still had little contact with African Americans, both passively and by design. Their sons, for reasons similar to those confronting Hipólito Arenas, would find such contact unavoidable. Institutional segregation created affinities in spite of the cultural differences. The common emotional experience of rejection and scorn, and the familiarity that arises in contexts where individuals meet and get acquainted, eventually, although gradually, dissolved the shell that Afro-Cuban men had attempted to erect around themselves and their families.

Bolita

Baseball complemented another passion of males in Ybor City and West Tampa—gambling. Wagering on the games intensified the excitement and fueled interest in the rivalries among teams, factories, clubs, and ethnic groups. Al López recalled how this factor greatly increased interest in the game.

> They loved to bet. At that time gambling in Tampa was wide open. They had gambling houses, you could go in there, and they had roulette, dice, everything, just wide open. (quoted in Brandmeyer 1981:59)

Cockfighting and prizefighting were also popular pastimes associated with gambling in Ybor City. Círculo Cubano built a boxing ring, and this sport also provided an alternative to cigarmaking for immigrant males. Martí-Maceo did not sponsor boxing, and black youth were not recruited by the local boxing promoters. The restrictions affecting Afro-Cuban men who wanted to play baseball also prevented those who might have pursued a career in boxing.

Gambling was illegal in Tampa, as were sales of liquor during Prohibition. Both, however, were enormously profitable. In the beginning, Cubans and Spaniards controlled gambling in Ybor City and West Tampa, and Italians assumed control of the bootleg liquor trade after the passage of the Volstead Act in 1920, which outlawed sales of alcohol. Operation of these businesses was made possible by paying off police and politicians (Mormino and Pozzetta 1987:281–84). These payments engendered dangerous relationships with the underside of the Anglo power structure, conditions that would burst into gangland warfare in the late 1930s.

Bolita ("little ball") was the most popular game of chance. Imported from Cuba, this was a numbers game. Players made bets on numbers between 1 and 100. Every night, in each of dozens of gambling houses, winning numbers were "thrown." One hundred numbered balls were placed inside a bag that was tied, shaken, and thrown in the air. A randomly chosen customer caught the bag, fingers around a single ball. Still holding the ball, someone would cut the bag, freeing the winning number. A nickel returned $8 to those who bet the right number. It was small stakes and large volume. *Bolita* salesmen traveled around the neighborhoods, and numbers could be purchased in most grocery stores, coffee shops, and saloons. A relatively small risk held the promise of a handsome return, and the excitement of winning or hearing about others who had won were prime topics of conversation in factories, clubs, and neighborhoods.

> ROSA: You know what eight dollars did for you in those days? Can you imagine, you used to work the whole six days a week, and if you made twenty dollars you were doing good. So you can imagine if you had eight dollars in one day.

Bolita has been described as Ybor City's second industry. Virtually everybody played, and few regarded it as a vice. Winning provided small windfalls that enabled purchases that would not have been affordable otherwise, and there were other ways to earn extra money from *bolita*. In the 1920s, it is estimated that as many as a thousand men earned added income from selling *bolita* numbers (Mormino and Pozzetta 1987:282). Some Afro-Cubans were involved in this trade.

> JORGÉ: Now my uncle was a man who made good money. He was a cigarmaker and he was in the gambling business. My uncle could go out and sell [numbers]. That would bring him anywhere from fifteen to twenty dollars, which in those days was good money. He used to put his money inside this sideboard drawer. And this drawer would be loaded with money.

Theirs was the only household in the neighborhood that had a telephone, and one of the very few to own a car.

Segregation was not rigidly enforced in the gambling halls in Ybor City and West Tampa. These operations were already illegal, so the law was less of a pretext. There were differences, however, in the extent of integration, and some of the halls specifically catered to Afro-Cubans. Seraphin's and Rudolph's, both on Seventh Avenue near the Martí-Maceo, were the two main houses that Afro-Cubans patronized.

LEONARDO: Rudolph was a Cuban. He was a white Cuban, but he had a lot of black Cubans working at his place, selling bolita and running the tables, and things. He was closest, out of all those big bankers that they had, he was the closest one to the black Cubans.

Afro-Cubans were a small but significant market, and their business was welcome. As employees, they offered an added advantage. Afro-Cuban *bolita* sellers could more easily penetrate the African American market on the other side of Nebraska Street.

Ties between white gamblers in Ybor City and black nightclub owners on Central Avenue increased in the 1920s and '30s. Although this relationship was competitive, it was also a source of collaborative ventures. Charlie Moon, the major *bolita* seller on Central Avenue, formed numerous ties to Afro-Cubans who were also involved in the gambling business. The Farraguts and the Mirabal brothers were second-generation Afro-Cubans who initially worked for Charlie Moon and later were able to open their own establishments in the Central Avenue district. Their customers were mainly African Americans, and they became well-known businessmen in the African American community. Charlie Moon also bankrolled a gambling house in West Tampa that was run by Afro-Cubans. Older boys from that community could earn unimagined sums by working there.

LEONARDO: Charlie Moon was right here in West Tampa; [he owned] a little old place that was run by the Lópezes, where I used to hang around. I used to run the dice table and they pay me fifty dollars, and when you have a good night they pay me seventy-five dollars. Charlie and two of those guys they used to come here and play, they had a big back room, and we put up a big poker table, and them people sit down and play, six-thousand-dollar table stake. Used to be a Cuban bakery shop on Main and around three o'clock [in the morning], the bread is hot. They tell us get a hundred-dollar bill, and we go get the bread, and they tell us, "Keep the change." And they get that bread and spread the butter, you know, and eat it playing poker. They don't break up until around five o'clock. It must have been thousands and thousands of dollars. I seen this guy Ramón lose seven thousand dollars.

Afro-Cuban boys, who could speak both English and Spanish, served as interpreters for older men who sold *bolita* in the American section.

JORGÉ: I was the one that had to drive him around. . . . I was maybe eleven or twelve and I could already drive a car. And I used to bring him all around. . . . He didn't speak English. . . . He would ask me to drive him around, and he'd be collecting and all that. On Saturday nights, and during the week, I used to go up there.

Contact with the nightlife on Central Avenue provided Afro-Cuban males, both boys and men, with a view of African Americans that contributed to the negative images that were widely held about them in the cigarmaking community. Although men like Charlie Moon were familiar figures with counterparts in the Cuban community, the women they encountered in bars and gambling houses epitomized disreputability. African American prostitutes offered sexual outlets for men, and sexual initiation for boys. The experiences of males who ventured into the African American section confirmed perceptions that this was a dangerous zone, especially to be avoided by Afro-Cuban women. Male involvement in gambling and other vices reinforced their belief that women should be sheltered and protected.

Women

Cuban husbands were privileged to lead pleasurable lives, and they were also permitted, indeed expected, to keep their wives and daughters safe inside the domestic unit. According to one informant (Rosa), "The wives couldn't even put their head out the window, because if they go out, she's gonna do so and so and so." This recollection by an Afro-Cuban woman who grew up in Ybor City accords with more general analyses of Cuban gender relations. "Strict social codes determined when and in what capacity 'honorable' women were permitted to be seen on the street. The *casa/calle* (house or home/street) distinction often used to describe the dividing mark between male and female spaces in prerevolutionary [pre-1959] Cuba is much more than a figure of speech" (Bengelsdorf 1997:242–43). Wives were expected to acquiesce in this lopsided arrangement, because the behavior of women was the prime measure of family respectability

(Martínez-Alier 1974; Dixon 1998a). Sequestration also prevented un-wanted contact between wives and their husbands' mistresses. The previous narrator continues:

> ROSA: We [women] sort of gave respectability. This is the reason why I say, a lot of the Cubans here, they wouldn't let their wives attend dances and things like that, because they [men] were, you know, do-ing so many things on the outside that they didn't want to bring about a confrontation between either their wives and maybe their mistresses coming around. So they made sure that their wives stayed in the house. They [men] could go out and burn the town down and they would still have that respectability.

The obvious hypocrisy in this posture was rarely acknowledged but did not fail to register an effect.

Two Suicides

Pressures on women, caught in a trap and unable to negotiate, often led to despair and sometimes tragedy. Women who failed to conform to these straitjacketing standards, whose reputations validated the sexualized im-age of Afro-Cuban women, became objects of scorn. An early news account illustrates this dilemma: "Consuela Obert, a notorious woman of the town, of Cuban negro race, swallowed 45 grains of morphine at her house . . . last night. Then she went into the 'parlor' where the usually giddy group of frequenters had assembled, and said, smilingly, to them: 'I have taken 30 cents worth of morphine. Don't bother to send for a doctor. It will soon be over.'" Those gathered did call the doctor, who was unable to save her. "Before he [the doctor] reached the place the woman had fallen into con-vulsions, in the midst of a ribald song. . . . She had taken a dose of the drug large enough to kill three or four people. It was said among her associates that the woman's lover had deserted her. Thirty minutes before she took the fatal dose Consuela was arrested . . . on charges of disturbing the peace."[5]

This sordid rendition of Consuela Obert's unhappy death is all that is known. The Tribune's characterization of her as a prostitute is unreliable, although it may have been true. The Tribune's reporting on people of color was invariably disparaging, and black women frequently were represented as lascivious and immoral. Nonetheless, Consuela had caused a scene, had gotten herself arrested in an altercation with a faithless lover. Scandalous behavior by black women, emblazoned and embellished by the press, was the image against which customs of female sequestration were set. Consuela's tragic death marked the consequences of her transgressions.

Respectable Afro-Cuban women also confronted dilemmas from which death was sometimes the only escape. A man whose mother was unable to face these circumstances recalled painful memories.

> JORGÉ: My mother didn't want to live in Tampa. She did not like it here . . . for a young woman and all her family's in Cuba. You know a lot of these women, when they came here, they had to make a sacrifice. In the first place they did not know the language. They were not used to the customs that they had here. Then they found themselves in the segregation, which they were not used to. And there was no outlet for them. Nothing to do. Nowhere to go. A lot of women didn't want to stay here. They wanted to go back to Cuba where at least they had a place they knew they could go to a theater, or do something. They couldn't do nothing here.

Many of the cigarmakers in Tampa had wives and families in Cuba. In the case of the woman described above, she initially persuaded her husband to permit her to return to Cuba. Later, however, she came back to Tampa.

> JORGÉ: I guess he convinced my mother to come and stay in Tampa instead of him having to come down to Cuba. And she came over, but that part of the story is not clear to me. From my aunt, I understand she was very unhappy about having to stay here and she, I understand, got sick. I have never been able to get the true story. So one day, what she did, she just went and got a whole can of gasoline or kerosene and pour it over herself afire. That's while I was in school, and when I came back they found out that my mother had committed suicide.

These two stories mark extreme cases, deliberately chosen as such. Both, however, suggest the scarcity of options for relieving the unhappiness of women unable to adjust to the gender inequalities that prevailed in their community. As suggested by the narrator, the difficulties of black Cuban women were intensified by segregation, were more of a departure from the conditions they were accustomed to in Cuba.

Severity of treatment by husbands varied, as did opportunities for relief. Women who had paid jobs were able to spend time outside of their houses, enjoy the company of other women, and gain exposure to daily events and issues. For others, neighbors provided social contacts and points of information. Weekend shopping and strolling on Seventh Avenue in Ybor City, baseball games, family activities at the Martí-Maceo, church, *bolita*—all provided diversions and channels of communication.

Neighbors

It was among neighbors that women found most of their daily social contacts, especially those who stayed home. Housing in Ybor City and West Tampa was very uniform, with little class differentiation based on real estate. Afro-Cubans lived in most sections of both districts, and there were no neighborhoods where only Afro-Cubans lived. The fact that white immigrants did not prevent blacks from living near them was a subject of derision and scorn by white Anglo Tampa. Living close promoted interaction and transaction, affection and reliance that knitted Afro-Cuban families into the larger immigrant community. These circumstances were of most consequence to women who spent the greater part of their lives within their homes. Just as the work culture of cigarmaking nurtured solidarity among men, relations among neighbors in these clearly defined foreign patches of Tampa engendered a strong sense of common identity among women.

Intimacy of daily contact—the verisimilitude of friendship—obscured the distinctions of color, but did not erase them. Neighborly relations were pregnant with the possibility of misunderstanding, the error of mistaking cordiality for equality. These distinctions were explained to me by two people who grew up in Ybor City.

> LUZ: White Cubans, black Cubans, Italians, Puerto Ricans, and everybody lived next to each other. We participated in whatever little thing that we had in the neighborhood, sociable. Social life was completely different. That's why the Italians made their club, the Asturians made their club. . . . In Ybor City we could all live together, but we could not socialize.

The distinction between informal socializing among neighbors of different ethnicity and more formal activities that occurred in the clubs exemplified the subtle tensions of interethnic relations, the invisible but firm differences that set Afro-Cubans apart in spite of proximity. The behavior of whites at critical junctures in the cycle of neighborhood social life served to define the parameters of Afro-Cuban participation. My informant recalled the peculiar hypocrisy in this arrangement.

LUZ: A white Cuban friend of Christina's family used to go to the house and he would play dominoes and he would eat and he would drink coffee, and you would think he was a great friend. He was always there. But he would never take the black Cuban family to his home to meet his wife and daughters. When his daughters got married, these people were not invited to the wedding. So, there was always a line.

A white Cuban woman described her recollections of black neighbors and the attitudes of white families.

LAURA: We didn't talk about racism. As a young girl I don't remember that. We knew the blacks. They wouldn't come into our homes, I mean on a social basis, but I don't have that feeling [racism].

A white Spanish man described the same conditions.

MIGUEL: We've had several black families that were very kind to us when we were growing up. We [Ybor City] were the cradle of integration in the U.S. Because we were able to get along with them. It isn't that we had to associate with them, or be normally with them. We could be separate and still enjoy our life with them. I am not a bigot, but on the other hand, if God would have wanted us all to be equal, we would have all been the same color. But he didn't. . . . We were made separate.

The logic invoked by this avowed nonbigot greatly resembles the biblical/natural explanations that bigots offer to justify racism. The politesse surrounding interactions between black and white immigrants, the situated dependency on the kindness of neighbors, concealed highly essentialist views of group differences. Children were often less able to handle such confusing nuance.

ISABELA: One day we, my sister and I, we walked out of the house and around the corner. We were sitting out in front of the steps playing with [a white Cuban girl]. The mother came out and caused the little girl, told her to come inside. So she came back outside and she says, "You have to go home, because my mother says I can't play with niggers in front of my house."

In spite of such underlying tension, the neighborhood was a source of comfort and contacts. Neighbors gave assistance, watched each other's children, reported inappropriate conduct of children, and passed gossip and news. In the evenings, women congregated on front porches waiting for husbands to return from their clubs. Children played together in the yards and streets. On holidays, especially the Christmas feast of Noche Buena, they shared each other's celebrations. In death and other tragedy, they helped and consoled each other. Their lives were very similar, their concerns and interests overlapping. Virtually all the surrounding households were involved in the cigar industry, spoke Spanish, ate similar food, followed similar customs, were nominally Catholic yet cynical about the Church, and had comparable values about family and gender. They understood each other, and they shared a common distaste for the "Americans." Interview narratives are consistently positive and nostalgic about neighborhood relationships, even those that include stories like the ones just cited. The muted racism was understood and accepted, especially when Afro-Cubans compared their own experiences with whites to those of African Americans.

Integrated neighborhoods, however, meant that Afro-Cuban women had less contact with each other. With the exception of West Tampa, where more than a dozen Afro-Cuban families lived within two blocks of each other, few of the Afro-Cuban women had close neighbors who were also Afro-Cuban.

They also moved frequently, disrupting ties that had been formed with all their neighbors. The narratives and city directories both confirm a highly transient pattern within and between West Tampa and Ybor City. Nearly all the Afro-Cubans were renters, and they changed houses frequently based on changing family circumstances. Babies were born, incomes rose and fell, relatives arrived in town, adult children married and moved out, disputes arose with landlords or neighbors, workers changed factories. Answers to my questions about neighboring usually began with a listing of addresses of the different places where they had lived and the causes attached to moves.

JORGÉ: Every two years one [baby] would be born and then we would have to move. I think we must have lived in about [lists six different moves all over Ybor City]. We had to keep movin' because the family kept growin' and had to look for larger quarters.

Stories of neighborhoods are fractured, have less to do with specific places than with customs of life found throughout Ybor City and West Tampa.

Communal space for Afro-Cuban women, as with Afro-Cuban men, was the Martí-Maceo Society, although their presence was far less frequent. The Ladies Committee, in which the women were charged with organizing social events and helping with recruiting and fund-raising, did afford opportunities for involvement. Their activities were of central importance, and members of the committee took their responsibilities very seriously. Operating funds for the Ladies Committee did not come from the treasury, but from weekly donations of 5 cents from the women themselves. Added donations were made for special events, and the revenues were turned over to the treasurer. Although they did not exert financial control or make major decisions, the women did carve a niche in the club that allowed them to be there and to be with each other. The plays performed in the club offered outlets that were even more satisfying. Roles for women in these productions opened opportunities for creative expression, allowed them to develop theatrical and musical talents, and step into fantasies enacted on the stage. Women were also primarily involved in youth productions in the club, directing plays and giving music lessons.

Religion

Churches have been central institutions in many immigrant communities in the United States, especially those with origins in Catholic countries. Spain, Cuba, and Italy were heavily Catholic, but the immigrants in Tampa had strong anticlerical tendencies. The Church in Cuba had been aligned with Spain during independence; and in Italy and Spain, as well as in Cuba, Catholicism was perceived as serving the interests of the wealthy. Predominant political views among the cigarmakers alienated them from the Church. Besides, Sundays were very busy days that should not be wasted sitting through a mass. Fewer than 3 percent of the immigrants attended services or contributed to the parishes in Ybor City (Mormino and Pozzetta 1987:214). Virtually no adult males attended church.

> TOMÁS: The male, he don't believe in the Church that much. It's not that they didn't believe in God, it was religion and such they didn't believe. My father used to say the priests should be working, instead of sitting there and doing nothing. I used to hear my father say that. They all used to feel the same way.

Women were more likely to attend, because it was one of the few places they were allowed to go. However, fewer Afro-Cuban women went to church than their white immigrant counterparts, because of the added barrier of segregation. An elderly woman explained her disdain for the segregated masses in Tampa.

> ANGELINA: I never went to church. I was brought up in a convent, and I sent my children to [Catholic] school, but I never went. Once I went with a girlfriend of mine who had come over from Cuba. However, we had to go and sit all the way in the back of the church, because blacks were not allowed to sit anywhere else. In my Catholic religion I believe that if you have a seat you paid for it the same way I did whether I'm black and you are white. . . . I didn't say anything at first, but when we got outside . . . I waited for the lady that had told me to go and sit at the back, and I told her: "Listen lady, you thought we were American blacks and that we did not understand what you were saying, but in God's house there is no racial discrimination. It seems that you come to church just to be worried about who sits where." I have never gone back to church. . . . Yet every night I kneel down in front of my bed to confess before the Almighty.

This woman made a clear distinction between religiosity and an institutionalized religion that, in Florida, enshrined racial discrimination. Her reference to "American blacks" is scornful of their acceptance of segregated religion.

Religious differences were a major barrier between African Americans and Afro-Cubans. Black Cubans had little understanding of the multileveled significance of the African American church. Viewed from the disenchantment they felt towards the church in their own community, African Americans were regarded as practicing a sort of eager compliance with the racist hegemony of organized religion in the United States.

> TOMÁS: Only the black Americans. They used to go to church. We didn't bother going to church. I never recall going to church, 'cause my father didn't believe in it. . . . Because of the reading. I think that's what it was . . . the reading they used to hear in the cigar factories. . . . Antichurch, you know, a lot of the writers. He [father] always told us, "Do right and don't do no wrong and you get along in the world." Says that's the best religion.

These perceptions had direct implications for interpreting gender roles in the two communities. Black Cubans regarded black American male participation in churches as unmanly, a reflection of slave mentality. Whereas African American women found satisfying roles through involvement with their churches, the Catholic Church in Tampa did not offer comparable opportunities for Afro-Cuban women.

Afro-Cuban women did have a role to play in the subterranean practice of Santería. Santería, discussed earlier in connection with the *cabildos,* is a Yoruba-derived religion, the most numerous of several syncretic Afro-Catholic religions in Cuba. Divination, healing, and ancestor worship were the main components. A pantheon of deities designated as Catholic saints, or *santos,* provided supernatural allies.

Santería offered control over the unforeseen, a system that could heal ailments and sustain a relationship with dead ancestors. Underground networks of believers, disciples of particular *santeros,* provided various kinds of assistance to each other. Although Afro-Cuban in its origins, believers included many white Cubans, and its alleged power attracted Spaniards and Italians, and sometimes African Americans.

Santería was a significant part of Afro-Cuban community life in Tampa, although it was deeply submerged. Ruthlessly suppressed in Cuba and antithetical to the doctrinaire Protestantism of white Tampa (which barely tolerated Catholicism), Santería was a hazard to the low-profile respectability that Afro-Cubans sought. Nevertheless, it was also a source of power that was respected and feared. There was a certain pride attached to the dependence of many whites on the ministrations of *santeros* (and *santeras*), and there were economic benefits in these transactions. Santería connected to potent and dangerous aspects of community life—illness, magic, gambling, and sexuality. This was a dimension in which women could assert unusual power, could transcend the secular limits on their influence and establish autonomy and control.

Supernatural supplications were a quotidian practice in connection with *bolita.* Patrons sometimes consulted with *santeras* about likely winning numbers, although more accessible and less costly advice was available from the Dream Books that were sold widely in Ybor City. These books, which were Chinese in origin, associated animals and other images with particular numbers. To dream of one of these particular objects was a sign indicating the number to choose. In Santería, numbers associated with particular deities also played a role in divination—Shango is four, Oya is nine,

Oshun is five, and so forth—which also became incorporated into the numerology of Dream Books. Santería was particularly important as a source of help with personal problems, especially those involving romance, and physical ailments. Medicinal herbs and rituals of healing were connected to the overall medical system in the community.

María Luaou, a midwife and Santería healer, was very well known within Ybor City. Her skills at delivering babies and offering spiritual remedies earned her a wide reputation and an independent livelihood. One of her relatives who remembered her from when he was a child described her unique appearance.

> TOMÁS: She looked like a saint or something. Well she was tall and dark, with nice features, and she always used to dress in white with a collar, or something. No skin shows, and long sleeves and white stockings. I got a picture [in my mind]. She used to have a remedy for everybody. [And] she gave advice . . . among the Cuban people, you know, she would always tell you what to do. I guess it must have worked, because sometimes two or three in the morning, people would go knocking at her door looking for her.

She had been born in Africa and brought to Cuba sometime in the 1850s. She died in the 1930s, at or near a century old.

> TOMÁS: She was a slave, but she could read and write. She was proud of that. She said that she live in the house, and they taught her to read and write. She would tell me about the other slaves, that they did not have the opportunity that she had. . . . She used to be a midwife among the Italian people. She learned that in Cuba during her slavery. But, uh, she practiced it here among the Italians. She used to have money all the time. But she wouldn't trust her family. Instead of coming to her granddaughter, she would give it to these Italian people [to keep for her]. I used to go with her to the store [owned by the Italians] . . . and they used to tell her, well, María, any time you want something from the store, you come and get it. . . . She died and the money was gone.

An Italian informant remembered her from his neighborhood while he was growing up:

> DOM: Right behind our home, next to the alley, there was a black woman, they called her María Luaou. She was a "voodooist" . . . and she was a very stately-looking woman. All dressed in white . . . always

smoking a black cigarette, she rolled her own. She was nice to every-body and, you know, people would go to her, if you were having trouble with your wife or you wanted some potion to give [a hus-band] to, uh, straighten him up, keep him from running around, or whatever. She was a really colorful character. And she made her own living that way. . . . You know, giving little potions and all that sort of thing.

Perhaps the most powerful Afro-Cuban woman in Tampa, one of the few widows with economic independence, María Luaou lived on the margins of the Afro-Cuban community. Her clientele was predominantly Italians and white Cubans.

Cordíta, another well-known *santera* in Ybor City, combined spiritual advice with a specialized rooming house where assignations could occur.

JORGÉ: She had her place on Twelfth Street between Eighth and Ninth Avenues. And she was the biggest *santera* in Tampa. Her clients were all big shots. White. Most were Spanish men. I used to do things for her, go to the store. When I came back she give me a dime. A lot of times she would tell me to come inside. She got all this fruit and stuff that the people bring, you know, for the Santería. The way Cordíta used to run this thing, say so and so was having an affair. Cordíta had maybe three extra bedrooms. And they would come in there just like a motel. So she was a little bit more than a *santera*. She had this business on the side. Her husband didn't work. She didn't work. So, they used to live off that. They used to live well.

These two women had unusual access to prosperity and power, roles that permitted them to step outside the limits that gender imposed. They were also dangerous, a danger that associated with Africa and the specter of *brujería*. María Luaou, with her striking appearance and African surname, exemplified this connection. In Cordíta's case, these practices also con-nected to sexuality. Antithetical to conventional respectability, Santería offered a contradictory status that tended to marginalize its practitioners.

Women's Work

The labor of women grew increasingly important for Afro-Cuban immi-grant families. In 1900, only 13 percent of Afro-Cuban wives worked; by 1910 it was 25 percent. There were also increases in single and widowed women who migrated to Tampa in search of work.[6] As time passed, more women in households had paid labor, and more women were present in factories. Wages remained stagnant in the industry while costs rose, prompting the need for more earners in households. The effect of these changes was that more women left their houses daily and mingled with the world around them. Despite rising levels of female employment, there remained a strong preference for wives to stay out of the workforce. When possible, added incomes derived instead from older children (girls as well as boys), but this pattern only shifted the burden more onto young women, the American-born daughters.

In 1910, the census for Tampa listed 371 Afro-Cuban women above the age of sixteen; 249 (68 percent) were married, 2 were divorced, 58 were single, 62 were widowed. Occupations were listed for about 25 percent of the married women, compared with 74 percent of single women and 55 percent of widows (both divorcees worked as cigar strippers). Although norms discouraged women from having jobs outside their homes, most (55 percent) Afro-Cuban women in Ybor City did such work.

Cigar work was the most common, accounting for 66 percent of listed occupations (compared with 87 percent of Afro-Cuban men who worked in cigar factories—virtually the same proportion as for white Cuban men [U.S. Senate Immigration Commission 1911:200]). The majority of women cigarworkers were strippers, although married women were more likely to be cigar rollers. Adult males outnumbered women (524 to 371). About half of the males (52 percent) were single or living apart from their wives. Against this potentially predatory cohort, and broader risks from men in the other groups, strict rules governed their movements to and from the factories.

> TOMÁS: As a rule, the majority of the wives stay home, but the ones that work, they would get together like we have a carpool today, they would have to walk together to go to work, so they wouldn't be alone. ... They used to gossip. If someone would go alone, they say they saw so and so talking to some man, and all that gossip.

Most of the other working wives earned income in their homes, as laundresses (7 percent) and dressmakers (4 percent).[7] Work done at home avoided outside contact while still adding to family revenue.

Women's work paid little, boosting the calculus that favored staying out of the labor force. Indeed, the $1.50 daily stipend paid by Martí-Maceo to sick male cigarmakers exceeded the amount earned by laundresses and servants, and was only slightly less than the $2.00 a day earned by average

tobacco strippers.[8] One of the purposes of the stipend was to avoid problems in relying on a wife's wages.

For women who worked, however, their extra income provided the margin needed to run the household, which was the responsibility of women.
Wives' incomes offered possibilities for independence, or at least greater
security. Money earned from dressmaking and washing passed directly
into the hands of the women who did the work. However small, it provided
leverage in making ends meet in case a husband decided to withhold his
pay or had lost it gambling. A woman who worked in a cigar factory was
more likely to have to surrender her entire earnings to her husband, who
would be very aware of when and how much she was paid. Work in the
factories, however, paid better, especially to those who were cigar rollers. A
woman might leave an abusive husband and survive on the income she
could earn, although the negligible number of divorcees in the 1910 population suggests that this was rare.

Most women cigar workers were strippers. Stripping was low-paid
piecework that involved removing the central stems from tobacco leaves
that were used to make the finished cigar. It was a task that required skill,
dexterity, and speed. Virtually all stripping was done by women, who
earned between one-half and one-third the wages paid to cigar rollers. The
feminization of this task was directly related to its low pay. In the early
period, strippers were prominently involved in strikes and union activities.
La Resistencia included a separate *gremio* (union) for strippers. The CMIU,
however, was not interested in organizing strippers and voiced policies that
discouraged female work (Hewitt 1991b).

An elderly Afro-Cuban woman, born in 1904, who had begun stripping
tobacco when she was fourteen, spoke of her work, and briefly about the
union. After a lapse of more than sixty years, she could still perform the
motions on an imaginary tobacco leaf.

> SERAFINA: So you take it from the tip of the leaf and you do it like that
> on the wrong side [removes the stem from one half of the leaf], and
> now the other way, on the right side, and you do like that with your
> hand [curls stem around her hand], then when you finished with that
> one, then you turn it, and you wrap it up. Four makes a bunch, and
> you have to make one at a time. Ten cents for a full bunch.
>
> SG: Did you belong to the union?
>
> SERAFINA: No, no, I never joined the union. Only for cigarmakers, not
> for strippers.

sg: The strippers didn't have a union at all?

serafina: No, no, only the cigarmakers. No, it was something, you know, it was just *natural* like that. [*Without stopping, or commenting further about the union, she returned to the craft.*] Like you pull back the strips, it's a little bit of a thing like that, it's what you start making the cigar with. . . . You take a little piece, you don't take the whole, you leave a little bit at the bottom. . . . Then you take one hand, but the other is holding, and you just take care with them, and that is the feeling for the cigarmaker.

However devalued this labor may have been, it was a source of satisfaction to be able to do it well. The pride of cigarmakers was shared by strippers, and work in the factory knitted women into this larger confraternity.

serafina: You could talk [with the other strippers], drink some coffee. They used to have the coffee man who used to come in at ten o'clock with two big baskets. . . . With the strippers, we had a nice working relation.

Cigar work helped equalize the status of Afro-Cuban women in relation to other immigrant women. Black and white strippers earned comparable wages. The groups of women who journeyed together from neighborhood to factory each day socialized along the way, joining the neighborhood and workplace as sites of common experience.

The other main occupation of Afro-Cuban women who worked outside the home was as domestic servant, a job in which black women were disproportionately represented. If cigar work reinforced equality, the role of maid and servant underscored the background of slavery. This was also an arena that Afro-Cuban women shared with African American women, a common heritage of subordination. An Afro-Cuban woman recalled her service in the household of a wealthy factory owner.

juana: I used to work for people over here in Palmetto. . . . Big house. I had to cook, started to work at seven, cook breakfast, cook lunch, cook supper. All day ironing clothes on my feet, then clean all the house. Start at seven and come out at seven, six days a week, for four dollars. They were Spanish, the owner of a big factory over here on Second Avenue.

Afro-Cuban maids and servants struggled to maintain the distinctions between themselves and African American women, who predominated in this work. Most Afro-Cubans worked for Spaniards, families of foremen, bookkeepers, and owners of cigar factories. Women who cooked and cleaned, with their unavoidable knowledge of family matters and close attachment to the children, created a dangerous ambivalence in relations between servant and master. These inherent conditions, the contradictions of intimate exploitation, were worked out in American households by paternalism and distance. Although Spanish customs towards servants were similar to Anglo American customs, Afro-Cuban domestics resisted these measures and deliberately defined their own prerogatives in contrast to the conditions imposed on African Americans. Two issues illustrate this context: accepting food from employers and addressing them in formal terms.

> JUANA: I never eat at nobody's house, 'cause if I'm cleaning, if I eat I don't finish my work, so I didn't eat, I keep on working. I say, "I'm not hungry." She had a colored [African American] woman wash her clothes . . . [who ate food offered by the mistress]. Food looked like it was for a dog. She mix it all together, and when that woman came [and took the food], I got so mad. I say, "Listen here, I told you that I don't want to eat, don't fix nothing." She say, "Well I'm going to throw it away." I say, "Well you might as well throw away that old food." I didn't holler or nothing, just talk nice. I say, "You can fool a black woman [doing laundry] in the yard, but not me. I see what you're doing."

Her refusal of the food was at once an assertion of control over her own work time, not letting herself be delayed by stopping to eat what was offered, and of her own personhood. "I'm going home, and I got fresh food at my house." It also marked a defiant pride that intentionally distinguished her own condition from that of the more servile African American woman who worked in the same household.

Terms of address, whether one may address another by his or her first name or must use more formal terms (e.g., "*doña*" [miss]), were salient markers of status in Cuba, as well as in the United States. Nomenclature offered avenues of defiance.

> JUANA: Nobody could say I called them "miss." I called them by their names. One time I worked three months for a lady, and I never called her miss. She was a Cuban girl. I say no, I'm not in Cuba, I'm right here in Tampa, in the United States. She got mad because I didn't call her miss. She told me to call her miss, and I said no. One day she was

out in the palmetto, somebody came to the door and wanted to see her. I went to the back porch and I called, "María, María." She come back and say, "You embarrassed me, calling me like that." I said, "I ain't going to walk that whole block to get you. That's why I called you." She told me she going to put me out. I said "I'm going to put you out." Plenty of Spanish people used to treat the black women, they used to work hard like a dog, and I said not me.

Similarities in custom between Cuba and the United States were subtly manipulated to privilege the immigrant servant of an immigrant household. My informant claimed rights she would not have had in Cuba, and that her native-born counterparts did not exercise. The ambiguity of being in a foreign environment permitted opening a wider space, allowed redefinition.

Dependency on hired servants, the relative scarcity of Spanish-speaking help (Afro-Cubans were a much smaller minority in Tampa than in Cuba), and possibly the progressive politics of the cigarmaking enclave all influenced a more liberal posture towards Afro-Cuban women servants. Implicitly, white Spaniards and Cubans expected black Cubans to be more prideful and less slavish than African Americans and, hence, tolerated them for being so (see Behar 1997).

Work in white households held certain potential benefits. Intimacy of the arrangement sometimes led to the acquisition of powerful friends, especially boys who grew to be men under their care. Those who held positions of influence in factories could be helpful to the husbands or children of their maids. Other types of largess flowed from these relationships.

The woman quoted above was the winning candidate for the 1929 Queen of the Bando Roja/Bando Azul (Red Ribbon/Blue Ribbon) dance held by the Martí-Maceo. This annual event pitted the members from West Tampa (Bando Roja) against those in Ybor City (Bando Azul) in a contest to see who could sell the most tickets in the name of their respective queen candidates. The honor of winning, however, entailed an obligation to give a party for supporters. Her employer learned of her candidacy from talk at the factory that the husband owned.

JUANA: She said, "Juana, are you running for queen?" I said, "Yeah." She said, "You didn't tell me." "What the difference, María? You don't know [about these things]." You know, they got everything for the party for me. I didn't spend a nickel. Everything, everything, and I didn't even tell them. . . . She bought everything.

This gesture on the part of her employers was a significant reflection of the quality of closeness that existed in Ybor City, a common understanding and shared traditions, even between the family of a factory owner and their maid. Although only an anecdote, this narrative and others that I collected from Afro-Cuban women who worked as maids suggest that the differences in their lives compared with African American servants were significant and clearly understood. Kindness of employers towards their African American maids was not unheard of, but it is deemed to have been extremely rare (Jones 1995; Mays and Raper 1927). Mistreatment was common. It is barely conceivable that white American employers would have knowledge about a maid's activities in her own community, and even less likely that they would care.

Afro-Cuban and African American maids earned the same low wages, worked comparably long hours, and endured haughtiness and condescension on the part of their employers, but Afro-Cuban women were less likely to suffer or tolerate abuse and were better able to resist the inherently dehumanizing aspects of servitude. They understood the privileges they enjoyed in this regard. That understanding added value to their Cuban ethnicity, and cultivated distance from African Americans. When they met as servants in the same household, one of the only contexts in which Afro-Cuban and African American women had any contact at all, it was on terms that were both competitive and contrastive.

Comparisons between Afro-Cuban and African American servants suggest the same status discrepancies that were more generally characteristic of the two groups. However, women in the African American community had a wider range of options in the roles they played. There was an abundance of religious and secular organizations—missionary societies, Bible study groups, Sunday schools, charitable organizations, sewing circles, literary clubs, and lodges—in which women could work together and find means of individual expression (Hewitt 1990a, 1991b; Jones 1995). Several of the best-known leaders of the early African American community in Tampa were women. Clara Frye, founder of the first black hospital in Tampa, was mentioned in the preceding chapter. Blanche Armwood, daughter of a pioneer landowning black family, was the first director of Tampa's Urban League, formed in 1922. She and her first husband, Daniel Perkins, were among the founding members of the local NAACP in 1915, and she became well known for her many projects aimed at uplifting the poor and contesting discrimination (Burke 1989). Christina Meachum, a woman of Bahamian descent married into the family of the famous Reconstruction leader Robert Meachum, was a schoolteacher well known for her involvement in numerous social and political organizations (Brady 1997; Jones and McCarthy 1993).

Raising Children

The relatively greater freedom of African American women was not necessarily known to the adult Afro-Cuban women in Ybor City and West Tampa, but for the girls in these families who went to public schools, where they got to know African Americans, and where their teachers were mostly African American women, the contrast was more easily understood. Reproduction of gender roles in the child-rearing practices of Afro-Cubans strained against these contradictory examples.

Whereas African American mothers often deliberately nurtured qualities of independence in their daughters (Collins 1997), Afro-Cuban mothers in Tampa followed different precepts.

> SOFIA: Well, the Cuban girls were always protected, subdued, and they had to give in to their brothers. The girls in the family had to give in to their brothers. We were really programmed to think about the men, whether it was brothers, fathers. I guess they were really lining us up to be future wives. The girls, as I see it, didn't really have too much fun. The boys were able to go out and sow wild oats and have fun. They were a lot freer.

Boys and girls followed very different paths, set in the direction of their parents' adulthood.

At age fourteen, boys were initiated into the Martí-Maceo Society, and even earlier they were allowed to spend time after school in the club, where they learned to play dominoes and chess. They played baseball in open lots, caught fish and crabs in the bay, explored the woods that surrounded Ybor City and West Tampa. They played marbles, spun tops, and flew kites.

Each of these games was highly competitive and essentially belligerent. Masculinity was about conquest. Kite flying was more than a simple game of keeping constructions aloft. They made fighting kites with long tails to which pieces of glass or razor blades were attached. The goal of the game was to maneuver one's kite to use the sharp edges to puncture the frame or cut the tail and "kill" the kites flown by other boys. Tops were made with sharp nails attached to the tips, both for spinning and for breaking other tops on the field. Intense aggressive rivalry was wound into the rules and conduct of boys' games. Boys were also allowed to hang around gambling halls and learned at an early age about the brothels in the south section of Ybor City and in the Scrub.

Girls were expected to stay at home and help their mothers, to learn to cook and sew and take care of babies. They could go to dances and other activities at the Martí-Maceo, but only under close supervision. Contact between boys and girls, especially as they approached puberty, was strictly regulated. "In a Latin home in those days," one of my informants (Ramón) told me, "it would be unheard of for a young girl to have a young man to visit her and to sit in the front room. . . . She had to be chaperoned at all times." For many years, the only black movie theaters were located on Central Avenue, a place that Afro-Cuban girls were strictly forbidden to go. In the mid-1920s, an Italian named Scaglione opened a "colored" movie theater across the street from the Martí-Maceo, which enabled Afro-Cuban girls to attend, but still they needed a chaperone. They could go to church with their mothers, something their brothers and fathers rarely did. Subordinated to the will of both mother and father and expected to wait on their brothers, femininity was about surrender.

Martí-Maceo sponsored a youth club called Club Juvenil. It was both recreational and instructional. There were separate sections for boys and girls. An older man from West Tampa was the originator and sponsor of the club. It had several purposes, the most important of which was to provide organized recreation for children of the members—an outlet for girls, who had little else to do, and a containment for boys, who might otherwise be getting themselves into trouble. Adult leaders devised activities that were also intended to reinforce their identity as Cubans. The emphasis in these events was on national identity, not ethnic identity as Afro-Cubans. A costume pageant they sponsored called Los Jovenes Guajiros y Las Jovenes Guajiras (*guajiro* is translated as "peasant") exemplifies this theme. The children dressed as peasants, the Cuban equivalent of cowboys, the sector of the Cuban population that had been most enthusiastically involved in carrying out the race war of 1912. This genre was selected over the elaborate costumed imagery of *cabildos* and *carnival,* or the more belligerent personae of the *mambi* freedom fighters. Before they emigrated, the parents had not been peasants; most were urban industrial workers. The symbols and images of the club reinforced an artificial, but bucolic and wholesome, sense of Cuban identity disconnected from its African roots. The club sponsored other types of youth activities—plays, poetry readings, and parties—all intended to provide supervised activities that could help ensure insularity in the social ties of Afro-Cuban children and deflect their interest in joining youth activities in the African American community.

In raising children, parents followed the patterns of their own childhood, attempted to bring them up as Cubans with proper values and the skills needed to be successful adults. As immigrants, however, these goals were complicated and to some extent contradictory. Values were learned at home, but skills came partly from schools controlled by Americans—Jim Crow schools that were tangibly inferior and where Afro-Cuban children would be thrown together with African American youths.

Many Afro-Cuban children went to St. Peter Claver Catholic School, where more of their classmates were also Cuban, but nuns, curriculum, and segregation were American. Black American students were still in the majority at St. Peter Claver, which was located in the Scrub, although they tended to come from the more prosperous and respectable African American families, which could afford the tuition. Blanche Armwood, for example, graduated from St. Peter Claver in about 1904 (Burke 1989:39). The split between Catholic and public school, for both segments of the black population in Tampa, served to reinforce emergent class distinctions and also was involved in breaking down barriers between Afro-Cubans and African Americans. Afro-Cuban children whose parents could not afford tuition, or who opposed the Catholic Church, went to public school in the Scrub, where they were an even smaller minority.

So long as children were destined for the cigar industry, most dropped out of school as soon as they were old enough to work, usually around fourteen, but in many cases earlier. The legal age was sixteen, but it was a law the immigrants scoffed at and evaded. The 1910 census lists 169 Afro-Cuban children between the ages of ten and sixteen; 31 (18 percent) had occupations, most in cigar work.[9] This official enumeration must be regarded as an undercount. Immigrant families were well aware that underage employment was against the law, and would not have been averse to lying to a census taker. They devised various means to avoid detection. A notary in Ybor City did a brisk business in attesting to false documents about the age of young workers, as one of my narrators (Caridad) explains: "They taught me [to make cigars] when I was thirteen years old. Both my sisters, my brothers, all of us . . . cigar makers. [We] learned it in my uncle's buckeye. In that day, they had to have some papers signed by a notary public. . . . You're supposed to be sixteen years old." Others simply relied on complicity by coworkers in avoiding detection. One woman (Serafina), who began working as a stripper at twelve, explained that "My godfather [a Spaniard] had a very good job in that factory. He used to select [was a selector]. So he had a little pull in there, and he got me a job. When the [child labor] inspector used to come, the ladies they used to cover me with bags, until the inspector leave." Apprenticeships were long for strippers and more so for cigar rollers, thus it was better to start as early as possible. A few years in school to learn English and to read, write, and figure, then apprenticeship and work. It was not that Afro-Cuban parents did not value education, but rather that they attached little value to the formal education that Florida provided black children. Parental tutelage and the *lectores* were considered a better source of enculturation and intellectual development. This strategy of early employment accomplished two purposes. It captured the added earnings of children, and it kept them close to the fold.

Exposure to Americans, inevitable while they were in classrooms together, was limited by shortening the period of risk. There was overt hostility to American schooling, both because of the segregated and inferior education provided to black people, and because things American were associated with the betrayal of Cuban independence. This antipathy posed a dilemma that some families solved by having their children drop out early. Others, however, recognized the need to get as much education as possible.

RAMÓN: My father thought very little of my school, the American school. However, he felt that this was the best of all possible evils, because we had to go to school. But these were the worst schools in the world. He thought all of my teachers were very stupid, but they were the only teachers we had. We had to go to school.

To ensure that children also knew about Cuba, a subject they did not learn in American schools, Martí-Maceo had classes in Spanish language arts and the history and culture of Cuba. In several of my interviews I was told of parents who spent time drilling their children in Spanish and reading to them from the writings of Maceo and other independence heroes.

JORGÉ: We were forced, actually, to speak Spanish. My father was very strict when it came to his language. He wanted to make sure that I spoke the language. And quite naturally he was under the impression, which he was right, that if he didn't set some kind of rule that eventually I would lose my identity, you know. And what he would do, he would give me different subjects or homework. And in the evening when he came home from work, after everybody ate and all that, I would have to sit down and tell him, you know. He had a little blackboard that he made, and he would write different words.

RAMÓN: [My father] would read from the writings of Maceo almost two and three times a week. He would drill us in the use of the language as often as he possibly could.

In addition to the classes at Martí-Maceo and less formal instruction by parents, there was a small private school operated in Ybor City by an Afro-Cuban woman named Antoníqua. Antoníqua's classes were mainly designed to teach children to speak English well enough to succeed in Tampa's schools, a kind of "bridge" program that alleviated the disadvantages they faced. It was also a way to obtain supplementary tutoring in a less threatening setting, and a further source of social bonding among the Afro-Cuban children in Ybor City. Antoníqua's classes were a concession to the obvious need for proficiency in English, but it was a mediated solution set alongside efforts to ensure Spanish proficiency as well. These measures, made necessary because they were immigrants, illustrate the varied pressures on Afro-Cuban children born in Tampa, pressures that affected cultural preferences as well as linguistic habits.

The second-generation Afro-Cubans were coming of age as the cigar industry was falling into its nadir. The popularity of cigarettes grew during the 1920s at the expense of cigars. Declining consumption led to layoffs in the Tampa factories. Pressures to increase production of cheap cigars coincided with development of machines that could replace skilled handwork (Campbell and McLendon 1939; Long 1968). The strike of 1920, which lasted ten months, was defeated by fierce repression and violence. This was the same strike that led Hipólito Arenas to forsake cigarmaking. These developments discouraged others who were younger than he was from learning the trade. Without the cigar industry, Afro-Cubans competed for the same jobs as African Americans. They entered a disadvantageous labor market carrying added burdens of little education and limited English. Some families recognized this problem early and forged a new strategy based on education.

RAMÓN: My father had one particular aim in life, and that was that none of his children ever set foot in a cigar factory. He had planned, even in the days when—conceptually this was unknown to most

Cubans—he had planned a high school and college education for all of us.

All the children in this family, including a daughter, did manage to obtain college degrees. However, they were, as the informant points out, unusual in this regard. For most of the Afro-Cuban families, where adult workers were experiencing diminished wages, threatened unemployment, and rising prices, there was little flexibility to alter their survival strategy. Most parents understood that education was the only way their children would be able to succeed outside of the cigar industry, but unaccustomed sacrifices were required at a time when resources already were diminished. Supporting prolonged education also risked alienating their children into the culture of African Americans. Many parents could not, or would not, undertake the costs.

> ESTEBAN: I went to work, because my parents couldn't buy no shoes for me, and so I had to work. . . . My father taught me how to make cigars, and I worked about a year. I didn't like it. I learned how to make them because I was under his rules, rules of my father. And in order for him to exploit me, and exploit the rest of them [siblings], he saw that I might have a trade. And when they get ready to get paid, he goes over to the window and he get the envelope. If I had made forty dollars in the week, why maybe he give me a dollar and a half, or two dollars, and he keep the rest.

Changing conditions surfaced contradictions and aggravated intergenerational tensions associated with patriarchy. Children of this era confronted pressures not faced by their parents. They had to devise new solutions. Many were unwilling to accept paternal domination at the expense of their own future well-being.

7

Afro-Cuban-Americans

We were always taught that, although we were black,
we weren't supposed to do the things the black Americans do,
because we were better than black Americans.

Ramón

Things came apart in the 1930s. Livelihoods disappeared. Neighborhoods thinned as jobless workers left town. Martí-Maceo's treasury plummeted. Businesses in Ybor City and West Tampa closed their doors. Destitute families squatted in empty cigar factories and warehouses. Beyond the crumbling bounds of the Latin community lay the merciless territory of the Jim Crow South.

Complex negotiations and novel alliances were played out in the process of becoming Afro-Cuban-Americans. This chapter is about that process, about how it unfolded in a particular historical moment, and what lessons might be derived for contemporary questions about the meanings of both black and Cuban ethnicity.

A large cohort of Afro-Cuban children born in Tampa during the early part of the century began reaching adulthood in the 1920s. They grew up in strange times. Congress passed a series of restrictive immigration laws, and the reach and power of the Ku Klux Klan attained new heights. In Florida and elsewhere the number of lynchings also rose, and there were large race "riots," like the 1923 destruction of the community of Rose-wood, located a hundred miles north of Tampa (d'Orso 1996), and the less well known massacre at Ocoee, seventy miles to the west, in which at least thirty-five people were killed in a 1920 conflict over black attempts to vote (McDonogh 1993:xx). An Afro-Cuban man recalled this era:

OSCAR: They had a sign just as you were going into Fort Kearney, just as you leave Plant City, on old 17. A great big billboard. Showed a hillbilly barefooted with a shotgun in his hand and a Negro with two watermelon under his arms runnin' like hell, and the hound dogs behind him. And the sign reads, "Nigger, read and run, or if you can't read, run anyhow." I played baseball as a boy, sixteen, seventeen, eighteen years of age. We'd go up to Dade City, and we was just playin' a game, just for the sport of it. Just for sport. It wasn't that we makin' a whole lot of money. If a black guy was managing a team up there at Dade City, he'd pass the hat around. The crackers just walk right on [past] and go to their cars. Niggers had to pay thirty-five cents to come in. Crackers just walk right in. Cracker come on a horse and have a bullwhip. And he sit there on that horse and pop that bullwhip. "Here, you black boys comin' this way. You hit that ball out of the park, you better not come down here 'cause I'm gonna cut you. Don't catch that ball, nigger." And all that. I've seen that happen in my lifetime. But, I had so much Cuban in me, that I didn't give a *sheshawshu*. Because I had made up my mind if one of them crackers hit me with a bullwhip, and he cut me with a bullwhip, and wrapped it around me, and I get my hand on it, and I'd snatch him off that horse and eat him up. See? But it never happened. That's just the type of boy I was. By bein' black and Cuban I wasn't gonna stand for it.

When the Depression began in the early 1930s, and work in the factories disappeared, a great many Afro-Cubans, especially those entering young adulthood, decided it was time to leave this inhospitable place. Oscar's tale continues.

OSCAR: I left here about 'thirty-five or 'thirty-six. I had to walk. The Depression was on. I left here walking. Got to Kentucky and I was going across a suspension bridge, there was a white bar there called the Silver Slipper. Covington, Kentucky, goin' across from Covington into Cincinnati. And I saw this white bar. I said, I'm goin' in there. I had about sixty-five cents in my pocket. I walked in there, and these three crackers sittin' at the bar drinkin' beer. The guy said to this cracker and the bartender, said, "Hey John, look at the darky over there. What he want? He's supposed to go around the back."

You know, I saw his sign up there. I read it.

I walked in, and I started speakin' Spanish to 'em. The cracker says, "Hey John, you better go get Tony out of the kitchen," said, "That nigger talk the same language Tony talk." When he said that, I just kept talkin' my Spanish. I talked my Spanish. So he called this Tally out of the back. And Tony happened to be Italian. And by he bein' an Italian, he said, "Habla Italiano?" I said, "Poco, poco." And he said [in either Spanish or Italian, or some combination], "What are you doin' coming in the front here?" I said, "I'm hungry, and I want to eat, and no black sign gonna tell me where to go." He told the guy and this Mr. John, "He's one of my homies. He just got off a ship down in Florida and walked all the way up here goin' to Cincinnati." He [John] said, "Take him in the back and give him anything he wants." And then he told me, "Come on, come on with him." Mr. John said to Tony, says, "Offer him the dishwasher's job and that room upstairs in the back over the garage. We could use a guy like [that], he look like he'll work. You say he don't speak no English?" I spoke more English than he did. Better than he did. So I went on back there. Tony fed me. Told me, "Get anything you want." Man, he had all kind of food back there.

It was a nightclub called the Silver Slipper. And Zack White and his Chocolate Beau Brummels played there every night. That was a hell of a good black band. Zack White and his Chocolate Beau Brummels. He had guy named Saturn that played trumpet in that band. Had a guy named Stumpy Woodcock. And Stumpy Woodcock played trumpet just like Louis Armstrong. And he even sing like Louis, because he played in Louis' band. The guy was a songbird. Puny. He was a little bit of a guy. And that's why we call him Stumpy. I doubt if the guy was four foot two but he could play that horn. He was a horn man. And every night, I'd sit up there and listen to him play that. 'Cause I stayed in the back of that place.

I stayed there for about nine months. And every Thursday night, the place would be closed. Me and this Tony would go over to Cincinnati, a place called Little Italy, and I found me a room over there on Lincoln Place, and I moved over there. And the very day I got ready to leave from over there [the Silver Slipper], I said, "Mr. John. Give me my money." "Oh, you done learned how to speak English, huh?" "Give me my money, because I am going to Cincinnati." He says, "You speak English better than me." I said, "I was born and raised right down in Florida. Give me my money." "Nigger, you been here all this time and you ain't been talkin' no English to me?" I said, "Give me my money or I'll shit on your face." And that's just the way I told that bastard. And got away from there too. Caught the suspension jitney. There's a little streetcar, only a jitney. Crossed the suspension [bridge]. It costs you a nickel to ride across. And I know if I once got to the middle of the bridge, he wasn't comin' over there foolin' with me, because I had all them Negroes on Sixth [in Cincinnati] and they were right there with me.

There on the margin between North and South, at a former crossing point of the Underground Railroad,[1] he escaped across the bridge into Cincinnati's black community. He knew them already, had met Stumpy, Saturn, and Zack—shared their humor, admired their talent, appreciated their music. His flight from the South led him into alliance with African Americans who earlier had made the same journey. They shared the same dark skin, the same legacy of a remote African past, and the same predicaments in this falling-apart time so filled with hatred and danger.

Second-generation Afro-Cubans grew up inside the Latin enclave, but they were well acquainted with many facets of African American life, especially the music. As a native-born Floridian, Oscar also knew about the "read and run" signs, and "No Colored" signs, and the hundred other brutal inconveniences that made many black people want to flee the South for places like Cincinnati. With his Italian friend Tony, he had reconnoitered the ethnic landscape of the city. When the moment came to unmask his identity to the crude and foolish Mr. John, he was ready to make his getaway.

His dual identity allowed him to be a con artist, to pass as Cuban and avoid being black. He could have slipped away unruffled, could have kept up the charade and maybe gotten the money he was owed. In a tamer version of a fantasized duel with a horse-sitting, whip-cracking, southern white thug, he acted out his defiance of the system that forced him into subterfuge.

Black Immigrants and Black Americans

Most discussions of black immigrant groups in the United States emphasize their resistance to assimilating into the African American community (Beck 1992; Bryce-Laporte 1972; Halter 1992; Portes 1995; Portes and Stepick 1987; Sánchez 1997; Waters 1996). Black immigrants avoid contact with African Americans, allegedly because it threatens their cultural solidarity and exerts negative influences on their children's values and behavior. It is also assumed that immigrants are naturally averse to joining a group that has such low status (Waters 1996).

When Oscar privileged his Cuban identity in order to get food and a job, it was a temporary ruse, a clever expedient. He played a trick that caught his opponent by the hairs of his own bigotry. In feigning foreignness he was not repudiating African Americans, but rather manipulating a common enemy. It is not hard to imagine that he shared the story of his play-acting with the musicians at the Silver Slipper. Interpretations of avoidance fail to reckon the ingenuity of social performance, or the empathy and attractions that complicate rationality.

This is only one story, of course, and ethnic identity is more than a mask that one puts on and takes off. But it hints at the shortcomings of analyses that hold African Americans to be harmful to black immigrant interests and suggest that the ones immigrants should want to please are "Mr. John" and his group.

A prominent trend in contemporary analyses of the cultural capital of immigrants, in contrast with native-born minorities, emphasizes their tendencies to value hard work, thrift, and what Ogbu (1990) has called "effort optimism"—they believe that opportunities exist, and they behave appropriately in pursuit of success. The danger to black immigrants is that their children will hear a different story from African Americans, who know the opportunity structure better, that they will lose the optimism that helps them succeed in spite of discrimination. "The acceptance of an American black identity also means the acceptance of the oppositional character of that identity. Oppositional identities, as Ogbu (1990) clearly argues, are self- and group-affirming identities for stigmatized groups—defining as good and worthy those traits and characteristics that are the opposite of those valued by the majority group. This tends to draw the aspirations of the [black immigrant] teens downward" (Waters 1996:196).

Portes (1995) makes a similar point, that taking on oppositional identities causes problems of "downward assimilation" by black immigrants. "An adversarial stance toward the white mainstream is common among inner city minority youth who, while attacking the newcomers' ways, instill in them an awareness of American-style discrimination" (Portes 1995:251). He goes on to say that bad attitudes about diminished opportunities in a racist society discourage children from doing well in school or adopting appropriate values towards work.

Second-generation Afro-Cubans in Tampa were raised on the politics of opposition. Their parents made war against Spain and the Cuban slavocracy. As late as 1931, immigrants in Ybor City taunted the Ku Klux Klan in massive May Day parades down Seventh Avenue. Afro-Cubans in

Tampa did not need African Americans to teach them about anger towards injustice. Oscar attributes his defiant attitude to the fact that he "had so much Cuban" in him. It is true that in their daily interactions and individual encounters, Afro-Cubans had learned to be respectable and get along, to "stay in their place." But they were not forced into the dehumanizing postures imposed on African Americans and only rarely confronted situations where dignity had to be sacrificed for safety. Afro-Cubans did not surrender conscious understanding of the iniquities of racism and the value of taking action against oppression. Indeed, many perceived African Americans as not oppositional enough. Another male informant, about Oscar's age, explained.

> JORGE: The Cubans, when they got here, they were already organized in Cuba. . . . When they came here, they brought that knowledge with them. Which is the reason why they considered themselves a grade above the black Americans. They could see the way that, you know, a black man in those days, if a white man came to him and say something, "Hey, boy." "Oh yassa sahh, yassa sahh." You know? Why I couldn't see myself telling nobody 'yassa sahh.' . . . I mean we didn't go for that kind of thing. . . . To us, we felt that a man is just another man.

Actually, a great many African Americans shared this same sentiment, "that a man is just another man." On Central Avenue and in the Scrub, and in the churches, lodges, and clubs of African Americans in Tampa, new movements were stirring. By the 1940s, younger Afro-Cubans were becoming increasingly involved with the local struggle for voting rights and desegregation. This common effort, and the admiration that both older and younger Afro-Cubans ultimately felt towards the Civil Rights movement, created a bond. In joint opposition to conditions that oppressed them both, Afro-Cubans fully discovered and embraced the commonalities that linked them with African Americans. And Afro-Cubans benefited from the victories they won together and the relationships they forged in this process.

Access to education was among the most significant benefits gained by Afro-Cubans through their association with African Americans. Although Portes, Ogbu, Waters, and others claim that African Americans exert a negative influence on the educational success of black immigrant children, this was certainly not the case for Afro-Cubans in Tampa at mid-century. Evelio Grillo, a retired school administrator and political activist in Oakland, California, has written his memoirs about growing up black and Cu-

ban in Tampa during the late 1920s and 1930s. His writing reflects two recurrent themes—how he learned to "love his blackness," and gratitude to
African Americans for their tutelage in this process. According to Grillo,
"It was from black Americans that we learned about black colleges. . . . We
learned we could attend them. I don't know of any black Cuban college
graduate of my generation who is not a graduate of a historically black
college" (Grillo 2000:11)."Not a single conversation about college was ever
held in my home. . . . Had it not been for Mr. Martin and our black American teachers it would have been very difficult for us to land places in black
American life. They shoe horned us into a place in Black America, the very
few lucky ones among us" (Grillo 2000:51).

Other African American institutions and allies helped support the adjustment of Afro-Cubans growing up in Tampa during the 1930s and
1940s—the Urban League, the "colored" recreation program, the Harlem
Library, black businesses that provided jobs and supported scholarships.
Charlie Moon, the kingpin gambler on Central Avenue, opened a soup
kitchen that fed hungry black families from both sides of Nebraska Avenue, and he loaned money for businesses started by black Cubans as well
as black Americans. It is difficult to imagine how Afro-Cuban families and
individuals would have survived without reaching out to African Americans during this period.

Ties to what remained of the Latin community were not diminished.
Afro-Cubans still drew benefits and preferred treatment from their ethnic
status, and they were still a part of the immigrant enclave. With the collapse of cigarmaking, there were fewer left from which to cobble a community, and there were new reasons to work together. Ties between black and
white families and friendships between former coworkers remained. Relationships between black and white Cubans, and especially between Martí-
Maceo and the Círculo Cubano, improved. Surviving Latin businesses provided opportunities for employment, especially for those individuals who
spoke little English.

Assimilation was a heterogeneous process, affecting mainly the young.
Although older Afro-Cubans became more accepting of African Americans, and of the realities of American in-laws, speaking English and accepting new cultural practices did not follow. The core of the older adult Afro-
Cuban community remained anchored in their memories and committed
to their habits. For all Afro-Cubans—young and old, progressive or conservative, assimilated or not—the overwhelming significance of color remained the dominant parameter of life. It limited their options and chan-

neled their associations. When it was no longer possible to maintain self-sufficient isolation, Afro-Cubans were still black. For those who remained in Tampa, that fact more than any other determined the new boundaries of their lives.

Exodus

A significant fraction of the second generation did not remain in Tampa. As with Oscar, many Afro-Cubans felt suddenly encouraged to leave Florida. Massive outmigration during the 1930s created a fork on the path to assimilation: one way led to the cosmopolitan neighborhoods of Spanish Harlem in New York; those who stayed behind were drawn further into Tampa's growing African American community.

Cigar factories closed, or mechanized, idling thousands of immigrant cigarmakers. A failed strike in 1931, a last violent clash with the power structure of Tampa, transformed the factories and ended a way of life. An elderly cigarmaker recalled these changes.

LUIS: The first factory that really put in a machine was Havatampa. We had a strike. They broke the strike, and they didn't want any Spanish-speaking people working there. They brought [in] ... almost all Americans. They pay 'em better. They make more money than we made. They give 'em more fringes we didn't have. But you couldn't belong to a union.[2]

Neither mechanization nor the defeat of the union could save the cigar industry in Tampa. By the mid-1930s, Ybor City and the rest of the nation were deep in crisis. From a peak production of 505 million cigars in 1929, Tampa's output dropped in 1935 to 311 million.[3] Workforce reduction was even greater than the drop in production, because machines could make twice as many cigars per worker. An estimated five thousand Tampa cigar workers were unemployed by 1935.[4] For those still working, or their native-born replacements, average annual wages had dropped from $850 in the mid-1920s to $550 in 1933.[5]

ISABELA: During the crash, the cigar factories were closed and everything. My father was out of work. . . . We were in the street begging for food. Completely out of work. We were begging. My father left [for New York]. My mother was left here with ten kids. And this lady took us in. I remember sleeping on the floor. She was Cuban, Afro-

Cuban, she never had any children, and she used to take everybody in.

Cigarmakers did what they always had when there were layoffs. They left town. This was different, however. The Depression engulfed the entire industry, the whole migratory circuit from Havana to Florida to New York. Few places were worse than Tampa, where the relief policy was stingy to all, more so to blacks, and where local bureaucrats freely discriminated against the defeated immigrant cigarmakers.

Out-of-work cigarmakers, most of whom spoke little or no English, fared poorly in competition with native workers for the few remaining jobs in Tampa. The strike of 1931, in which union leaders were jailed as Communists and workers were blamed for the collapse of Tampa's main industry, left bitter residues in a labor market that already had been un-friendly to foreigners. Narratives collected by the Federal Writers' Project in the late 1930s reflected this pressure. As one narrative put it, "We must all leave Ybor City as we are now a superfluous people. We are good for nothing now as we do not work, and cannot give life to commerce. In the bread-line formed at the Relief office there are at least eight Cubans for each Spaniard or Italian. We are the most destitute, and only by leaving this city, can we hope to live under better conditions."[6] Between 1930 and 1940, 35 percent of the Cuban-born population of Tampa departed. Black Cubans confronted the bleakest opportunities, and they left in the largest numbers. More than half (51 percent) of Tampa's Afro-Cubans emigrated during the 1930s.[7]

The community divided nearly in half. Departure of so many created a sudden void in community life and institutions, and marked a radical turn-ing point in the lives of the second generation. Several narratives I col-lected recalled this outmigration.

TOMÁS: They were mostly young people that went. Older people went too, but most of the ones that stayed didn't want to risk going to the big city. You know back then New York had a reputation for being so big and reckless, but the younger people went to try to make a living and get away from the conditions here.

ESTEBAN: I left Tampa, because I couldn't find no jobs here. Well, they pay the white man, they pay him three dollars, they're gonna pay me a dollar fifty or two dollars to do the same thing. I need some air. So the only place that I could get some air, go up north. I felt that I'd have more freedom there.

SERAFINA: My husband said, "I don't want my son to grow up in this place." We're happy because my son got a good education. He has a very nice job.

GUSTAVO: 'Cause all the colored people, colored girls, could be was a maid. They were washing clothes and ironing clothes for the white people. I say I wouldn't do that, but my sister did. Used to clean houses. I say, "I am not going to raise my daughter here." So that's why I left here. Now today, my daughter, she works for Metropolitan Life Insurance. It's a computer [job]. She pay all claims. She got a good job, she make good money, which I knew that she would never get a job here in the South.

Those who remained and those who left followed very different trajectories, although they did not lose contact with each other.

New York

Cubans had been living in New York for decades. It had been headquarters for the Cuban exile leadership and was a familiar destination of itinerant cigarmakers.

JORGÉ: When we moved north, my uncle went to New York first. He already had a few people that he knew that had already settled in New York. When he got there, right away they found an apartment for him, and they found him a little something to do, and told him, "Bring your family over and we'll put them in the, uh, what we call 'temporary welfare.'" All you had to do just go down to the Welfare Department, apply for temporary relief. Right away, they would pay your rent and give you money to buy food and stuff like that. And we left here in November of 'thirty-eight, all of us left in a big Cadillac. All packed up. This fella used to do that, those trips to New York. He would charge something like six or seven dollars per person. There were seven of us, and the driver was eight. We drove to New York.

Aid from friends who were already there eased the transition from Tampa to New York. Most were able to get help finding jobs and apartments; and valuable advice about how to circumvent New York's two-year residency requirement for public assistance. A writer for Tampa's Federal Writers' Project described this subterfuge.

> There are persons in New York who explain to the Tampa families just what they should do in order to obtain Home Relief immediately. Once it is explained it is comparatively easy to obtain relief. This consists in restamping old letters. The date printed by the Post Office Department is carefully erased by means of a lemon, then an old date is stamped in its place. This serves as proof that they have been living in New York the required length of time. They also arrange with the janitor of the building where they are living, and also with certain commercial houses so that they will declare them old residents of New York.[8]

In Tampa, the cash assistance for out-of-work families amounted to 50 cents a week per person, plus vouchers to exchange for unleavened flour, for butter and bacon (which were usually rancid), and for government-issue clothing. Evelio Grillo remembered these clothes: "The clothes were hot, black woolen knickers and shirts made out of thick blue denim material. Glad to get them, I wore them with no sense of undiminished pride, for many of the other boys wore them also" (Grillo 2000:49). A few dollars a week might be earned from federally subsidized work programs, but these jobs were hard to get and paid a lower rate to blacks. New York Relief paid families $28 a week in cash assistance, covered 90 percent of the cost of rent, and provided food commodities.

Stories about conditions in New York impelled more families to leave Tampa. A few instant entrepreneurs operated a brisk trade transporting migrants in trucks and large cars (like the Cadillac described above) that had been refitted to hold as many as eight or ten people, each of whom paid between $5 and $10 to be driven to New York. Representatives of the Tampa relief agency also traveled north in a mean-spirited, but largely ineffectual, attempt to help their counterparts in New York identify the Ybor City migrants and thwart their schemes to establish false residency.[9]

Both black and white Cubans settled predominantly in the area between Lennox and Lexington Avenues from 110th Street to 115th Street. This was about ten blocks below the main section of Harlem where native-born and Caribbean blacks were concentrated in this period. Many of the Afro-Cubans later moved into Harlem and the Bronx, but in the early periods of the exodus, Ybor City migrants formed a temporary cluster of their own, a community of Tampeños. In some ways, it was like the neighborhoods of Ybor City, polyglot and multiethnic.

ISABELA: We went to live on 113th Street between Fifth and Atlantic Avenues. Spanish Harlem. The Cubans were beginning to go up, from here, from Tampa. And they had some Puerto Ricans, and they had some blacks, Jews, Italians. It was really sort of a melting pot.

In many other ways, it was starkly different from life back in Florida. As was discovered by legions of other migrants out of the U.S. South and the Caribbean during that same period, New York was a challenging destination, especially in winter.

ISABELA: When we got to New York City, it had snowed. I had, naturally, never seen snow. I never had seen a tall building. When we got out of that car and I saw this, this thing [their new apartment building], the garbage cans in the street with all the snow on top. And they said we were gonna live there, I cried for about a month. I broke out completely, my whole body in a rash.

In the beginning, many of the refugee Tampeños yearned for what they had lost in Florida, hoped the cigar industry might be revived, and they could go back home. Federal Writers' Project narratives with Cubans in Tampa expressed these sentiments.

I know of many Cubans in New York who will return immediately when better times come to Tampa and there will be work. Since they have been accustomed to the tranquil life, they do not feel there as they do here [Ybor City], where they had their friends and their families and other bonds of closer union. It is true that in New York the Relief is more plentiful: it is a great city and there are more resources, but life is less friendly than in Tampa; life is more individual there; here it is more collective. The homes are different there, and each person leads his own life, while in Tampa they lead the life of all.[10]

Organizations were formed in New York to help fill that void and ease the difficulties of transition.

Club Tampa, established in the early 1930s on 112th Street near St. Nicholas Avenue, was mainly recreational, a social club where dances were held and former neighbors were able to get together. In the beginning, both black and white Cubans belonged and participated. A simple change of geography temporarily eliminated the barriers that had existed in Tampa preventing this type of socializing. This club lasted only a few years, however, and had become nearly all white by the time it disbanded. Another club, to which both black and white Cubans belonged, was the Julio Antonio Mella Society, located in the same area (at 115th Street and Fifth Avenue). This was also a social club, but its purposes were political. It was named for a martyred Cuban intellectual who was assassinated in 1929, reportedly at the behest of the Cuban dictator Gerardo Machado y Morales. Along with a former Tampa cigarmaker, Carlos Baliño, Mella had helped organized the Communist Party in Cuba in 1925. His vocal opposition to Machado led to arrest and murder in exile in Mexico (Liss 1987:91). The early 1930s marked a turbulent era in Cuba, and exiled Cubans in New York were again drawn into the politics of *patria,* although on a much smaller scale than during independence. An Afro-Cuban New Yorker explained.

> EUGENIA: There was a club which was a little leftist, the Julio Antonio Mella, and my family was affiliated with that. My mother and father were strong laborites. They were probably more politically involved than any of the people who stayed, you know, in Tampa. . . . Mella was social. They used to give little dramas. My mother used to act, just like she had in Martí-Maceo. And my Uncle Mariano was *el lector,* which is kind of a carryover from the traditions of the factory.

Uncle Mariano had been active in Martí-Maceo before he left, a memorable speaker who exhorted them to support the strike in 1931. He had been among the few Afro-Cubans who were prominently involved. When the strike collapsed, armed thugs swept through the neighborhood looking for him and the other leaders, promising a deadly confrontation that he narrowly missed. In New York, he was safe from these kinds of threats, and his politics found ample company.

Leftist labor organizations, like the Alianza Obrera (Workers' Alliance), provided help in resettling cigarmakers into new jobs in the city. Unions were stronger in New York, part of the New Deal progressive political alliance in the city, and they tended to be less discriminatory than union shops in the South. In New York there were more government work programs and subsidized training in skilled trades. As one informant (Esteban) explained, "The government had . . . the bureau of the blacks, and they sent a man to school if he want to learn a trade. . . . Gave me $115 a month. And I learn it [body and fender repair]. And I came out of there. I went to work,

eight dollars a day." Many of the migrants took advantage of such opportunities and trained themselves for new careers. Children of migrants
completed their education in the New York public schools, a system that
was dramatically better than the one they had left in Tampa. Opportunities
were more plentiful in New York. There was still discrimination, but of a
different character than in Tampa. The enormity of the city, the vastly
greater ethnic heterogeneity, and the skilled political activism of its various black and brown populations offered safer, more negotiable conditions.

When war chased away the depression, the New York migrants were
positioned to move into a variety of unionized trades and white-collar occupations. In the postwar period most moved away from their old neighborhoods in Spanish Harlem. Increasingly dispersed, Afro-Cubans in New
York kept contact with each other through a social club that was formed in
1945.

The Mella Club languished after the fall of Machado in 1933, when a
large number of the members returned to Cuba. Many who remained in
New York became less involved in radical politics, discouraged by the viru-
lent anticommunism that emerged in the postwar period.

EUGENIA: My parents came from that [radical] tradition and they
maintained it when they first went to New York City. But as things
changed, they too felt that it was no longer, um, intelligent to belong
to organizations that identified. . . . They stopped identifying with
anything leftist. They were involved in things that were social after
that rather than political. There was no longer a need for the struggle.
People became afraid. And when you know that you are on a list
because you signed a petition, people began to be a little wary of what
they did.

June 14, 1945, was the centennial of Antonio Maceo's birth. The mayor of
Havana contacted former members of the Mella Club to stage a centennial
observance in New York. The banquet they organized for this occasion
yielded an unexpected net profit of $200. In possession of a small collective
fund and newly convinced that they had sufficient numbers to support
social events, the organizers decided to form a new club.

It was named the Club Cubano Interamericano. It began in a rented hall
at 914 Prospect Avenue in the Bronx; later moved a few blocks down to 671
Prospect. The first president, Generoso Pedroso,[11] operated a barbershop
on Prospect Avenue that was a focal gathering spot for Afro-Cubans in the
Bronx. Some of the members lived within walking distance of the new club

building, but most came to meetings on the subway from all parts of the city. It was a social club that sponsored dances and banquets. They went on excursions to Cuba, and they entertained visiting Cuban dignitaries. Famous Cuban musicians, like Benny Moré, gave performances in their large social hall.

The club was not chartered to be Afro-Cuban; all Cubans were welcome to join. However, another organization was begun in New York somewhat earlier, by white Cubans, which was also named Círculo Cubano, open only to white Cubans.[12] Club Cubano Interamericano became black by default and "inter-American" by necessity. The New York migrants retained a strong sense of Cuban identity that membership in the club reinforced. Many of the children who grew up in these families, however, married non-Cubans. The club reflected those realities, as well. Spouses from other Spanish-speaking countries, especially Puerto Rico, broadened the national focus of the club and the community, but helped retain a distinctive Latin identity. Although there were some marriages with African Americans and English-speaking West Indians, the Afro-Cubans who moved to New York remained more closely identified with Spanish language and culture than those who stayed behind in Tampa.

Few thought about returning to Tampa, where Jim Crow still reigned, the schools were still terrible, and labor unions remained a dangerous enterprise. Many kept in touch with the Tampa families, though, and sometimes made visits for weddings, funerals, and vacations. They knew about the bad old things that had stayed the same, and about changes that they also felt were unfortunate.

ISABELA: We knew it was dying, that it had turned black, Afro-American. S——, she was the one had daughters all married black Americans, because she say that's all there were. You know they had black [African American] bands playing there [Martí-Maceo]. She said that the Cubans were all gone. There was nothing they could do, and then they used to rent the club to, uh, the blacks [African Americans], 'cause there was nothing else they can do. There were no more Cubans left. Everybody left for New York.

Tampa

Although exaggerated, the foregoing portrayal captured the essential changes that had been occurring in Tampa since the outmigration of the

1930s. Reduced numbers of Afro-Cubans led to increased contact with African Americans. There were not enough members left in Martí-Maceo to
maintain its social activities, and there were not enough Afro-Cubans in
town to ensure against intermarriage. A man whose family remained reflected on the implications:

> TOMÁS: It changed, because we find ourselves, that we were less than
> the American black, and they began to marry some of our women,
> and there was a closer relationship. Panic changes things. People un-
> derstand one another more as time goes by.

In the post–World War II period, the vast majority of marriages by Afro-
Cubans in Tampa were with African Americans. Of necessity, directors of
the Martí-Maceo Society rented their hall frequently to African Americans, and they started playing American music at their own dances. The
society was not dying, however, nor were all of the Afro-Cubans gone.

Those who stayed in Tampa had fewer employment options than their
New York counterparts. Some continued to make cigars, and some of the
younger Afro-Cubans got jobs operating cigarmaking machines. In the
early 1940s, production increased, sparking a modest revival of the industry. Although machines made the bulk of cigars that were manufactured
during this period, there was still a demand for the high-quality handmade
Havanas.

> TOMÁS: There were some that were left in the cigar factory, but they
> were real good cigarmakers. They were real good at it. Used to call
> them experts. They were real artists. So the cigar factories they kept
> them on. I imagine that if they would have found a white man who
> could have done it, they would have let him, but these people, they
> had that special skill, you know, to make those special cigars.

One Afro-Cuban cigarmaker, Laureano Díaz, was so renowned for the artistry of his product that he reportedly personally supplied Winston
Churchill, perhaps the most famous cigar smoker in the world at that time.
Several of my informants recalled that on Saturday afternoons during the
war, a special car would arrive at the factory to collect Laureano's weekly
production. From there it was reportedly sent straight to London.[13]

Most of the cigarmakers, however, were forced into other occupations
or into retirement. Jobs available to them were the same as those for African Americans. Primarily, this meant that the men could labor, and women

could be domestics—menial work that paid a pittance. Two Afro-Cuban men recalled starting their careers in Tampa during the 1930s.

JORGÉ: I went to work on the waterfront, and I was fourteen years old. I loaded banana boats at eight cents an hour. You work all day for eighty cents.

ESTEBAN: I was about eighteen years of age, and I went to work in Tampa washing dishes. And I worked a couple of days there. The majority of the time I was out of work. I worked for the City, makin' I think it was a dollar and a half a day.

Both of these men finally left Tampa and spent most of their lives in New York. Others who stayed, however, confronted this same restricted range of opportunities. Older Cuban-born workers who lost jobs in cigar factories and chose not to migrate found it especially difficult to adjust. Many spoke no English, nor were they accustomed to the deferential behavior expected of black workers in Tampa.

Bolita continued to provide a marginal living for some. At least two former cigarmakers found work in Charlie Moon's bars on Central Avenue. Two others owned their own establishments on Central, where both liquor and *bolita* numbers were sold. These and a handful of other Afro-Cuban businesses—a barber shop, a café, a broom factory, a cleaners, and a few others—provided a living for proprietors and employment for others. Other Ybor City businesses hired displaced Afro-Cuban cigarmakers, but as dishwashers, loaders, truck drivers, and other jobs that paid little. Others got work on the docks as stevedores, where wages were especially low for blacks. Older Afro-Cubans adapted as well as they could, and most experienced a reduced standard of living. Many younger Afro-Cubans focused on school as the best means to escape the economic dilemma confronting their parents.

Relations with African Americans

Segregated schools produced inevitable contact with African Americans. Afro-Cuban students, who could no longer count on jobs in the cigar factories, were encouraged to remain in school longer. Exposure was prolonged into puberty, which greatly enhanced the likelihood of interethnic romance and marriage. The changing ecology of relations between Afro-Cubans and African Americans, the nexus of which was shared experiences in school, was more than a simple overlap in space. School was the gateway to the transition from child to adult, initiation rites for the process of assimilation.

Schools were located at the center of African American community life, institutions designed deliberately to socialize the young, and covertly aimed at resisting and overcoming the particular problems they faced. The Harlem School in the Scrub had its origins in Reconstruction, paid for primarily by the families who needed it. In 1889 they pooled sufficient funds to erect a building. After white thugs burned it down a few days later, they regrouped and built another. Commentators who argue that African Americans value education less than other groups ignore a long history of efforts like this one, and persistent agitation for better facilities and more equitable instruction.

There were nine public schools for African Americans by the 1930s, including a high school that only opened in 1930 (Mays and Raper 1927). These schools were all measurably inferior to those provided whites. Most had unsafe ramshackle buildings with leaky roofs, little equipment, and no playgrounds. There were not enough teachers, and there were not enough books. Salaries paid to black teachers were about half those paid to white teachers. The only books available for black schools were those discarded by the white schools. The school year was much shorter for the black schools, a cost-saving measure that also ensured the availability of cheap labor for agriculture (Burke 1989).

These institutions were controlled by the white school board, but they were staffed by African American teachers. Within classrooms, many of these teachers carried out quietly seditious work. By exhorting students to achieve and making extra efforts to help them learn, the teachers were not only doing their jobs, but waging a war against discrimination. Schools became explicit sites of contest and mobilization, especially during the 1930s and '40s. Teachers agitated for better conditions. They succeeded in lengthening the school year for black children, and in the early 1940s filed a lawsuit over racial disparities in salaries.

Teachers were highly respected individuals, an important segment of the black middle class. The majority of black teachers were women. Blanche Armwood, mentioned previously, served as supervisor of Negro schools between 1922 and 1930. Many of the civic leaders and social activists—both men and women—were teachers, individuals who were also involved in churches, lodges, and charitable organizations. African American teachers often viewed their classrooms as fields of political or missionary endeavor, proselytizing correct behavior and encouraging students to challenge stereotypes by succeeding in school. Within these settings, Afro-Cubans were drawn into the culture and struggles of African American life.

Although Tampa's Afro-Cuban community had shrunk considerably during the 1930s (down to only 510 in 1940), the African American population continued to increase in size. Black population growth in the preceding decade had been dramatic (83 percent), from 11,531 to 21,172.[14] This had been a boom time in Tampa's economy. Real estate sales and tourism fueled the growth of jobs in construction and domestic service. Activity in the port increased the availability of dock work. Chances for employment in the city, combined with Klan terror in the countryside, drew thousands of black migrants from rural areas throughout the region.

The Central Avenue district expanded greatly. Black-owned business more than doubled in the first half of the 1920s (Mohlman 1995:122)—dozens of small establishments, like restaurants, funeral parlors, barbershops, and grocery stores. Doctors, dentists, and a lawyer opened offices on Central. A group of black business owners and professionals joined in establishing the Central Life Insurance Company in 1922. This enterprise was very successful and grew to be one of the largest black-owned businesses in the state, rivaling the Afro-American Insurance Company in Jacksonville, which also had a branch office in Tampa. Central Life investors also combined to purchase a hotel and office building, the Pyramid, on Central Avenue. By the 1930s there were two African American weekly newspapers, the *Bulletin* and the *Sentinel*.

The most numerous business establishments were bars and nightclubs that offered music, gambling, bootleg liquor, and assorted other vices, adding to the district's prosperity and heightening its reputation as a dangerous but tantalizing terrain. The social and economic order on Central Avenue reflected a tension between respectability—rectitude and industry that could win approval from whites—and scandalous, but lucrative, enterprises that flouted white values. Charlie Moon epitomized the latter. In Wilson's (1969) term, Charlie had "reputation."

Central Avenue and the Scrub, viewed from the outside as squalid and disorganized, was a complex territory on which African Americans established a full range of communal institutions. The 1920s also brought an increase in new churches, and the older congregations grew in size. Lodges and social clubs proliferated. Membership in these various organizations defined and refined the internal class structure, but also laid the framework for effective struggle in the years to come.

"Uplift" was a popular metaphor that joined competing ideological and organizational goals, an ambiguous concept signifying both patronizing largess and collective resistance (Meier 1963). During the 1920s, the lingering influence of Booker T. Washington's message of constructive accommodation, Du Bois's program of education and agitation, and Marcus Garvey's plan for galvanizing African solidarity competed and converged in the social organization of Tampa's African American community. There were two chapters of Garvey's Universal Negro Improvement Association in Tampa in the early 1920s (Howard and Howard 1994b).

Several of the civic clubs were explicitly dedicated to stamping out iniquity. Under the banner of uplifting the race, members hoped to tame the unruly behavior of the poor, who embarrassed and endangered the relatively better off. Temperance was a popular cause among the respectable club men and women (Mays and Raper 1927). Protecting ignorant young girls who had recently arrived from the country, rehabilitating fallen women, and instilling sober responsibility in defiant and careless young men were all viewed as proper civic goals.

But so was charity. A variety of women's clubs—sewing circles, drama clubs, service organizations—also engaged in fund-raising and support for social services, emergency relief, and scholarships. The City Federation of Colored Women's Clubs coordinated these efforts and launched ambitious projects, like building a community center (Mays and Raper 1927). Members of these clubs were an elite segment, comprising no more than 3 percent of the adult black women in the community (Mays and Raper 1927), those who could afford to set aside 25 cents a month for dues. Charitable activities combined with Christian outreach to assist impoverished families. It was a program of self-help designed to lift the poor and wayward among them. They also hoped to alter negative images, perceived as causing all blacks to suffer dangers and indignities. The respectable ladies of the City Federation of Colored Women's Clubs stood in sharp contrast to the loose women who frequented Charlie Moon's night spots on Central Avenue, but they were linked in blackness and needed each other.

Similarly, the virtuous men of the Negro Business League, who crusaded against vice in their community, could scarcely afford to ignore the financial power wielded by Charlie Moon. Charlie and other black *bolita* bankers in Florida were major shareholders in Central Life,[15] a presence that caused conflict when Mary McLeod Bethune, Florida's most famous black woman activist,[16] served a short stint as president of Central Life (Jones and McCarthy 1993). One of my narrators, an old *bolitero* who used to work for Charlie Moon, told me an interesting story about his relationship to Central Life. Charlie had a strange practice; he enlisted dock workers and other men who patronized his bars to take out life insurance policies with Central. He paid the premiums on all these policies, and he was also the beneficiary. When I asked why he did this, my informant claimed not to know. I asked if he was having these men killed, but he said confidently that that was not the scheme. Charlie was a gangster, but he wasn't a killer. My informant, who was still protecting the secrets of his own illegal past, who was evasive at many points in our interview, would say no more. Although I asked other informants about this, I could not verify his tale, nor could I get any further information on what these transactions were about. One theory, assuming the story is true, is that he was laundering illegal income through Central Life, collecting occasional payouts when his policy holders happened to die. Or he may have been investing in the likelihood that these rough, hard-living men would die at an early age. Whatever the reason, and whether or not the directors of the company were actually aware of what he was doing, there was clearly a symbiotic relationship between the notorious Charlie Moon and the respectable members of the African American civic elite. Their fates were also linked, and their combined resources were needed to respond to the crisis of the 1930s.

Charlie Moon's soup kitchens, which earned him considerable goodwill, were just one facet of this response. Tampa's Urban League, which had been formed in 1922 with Blanche Armwood as its first director, assumed a high-profile position in helping to orchestrate assistance during the Depression of the 1930s. The Urban League organized sewing rooms and work projects sponsored by the Works Progress Administration, and the Martí-Maceo Society collaborated with the Urban League in a WPA youth recreation program at the club. The National Council of Negro Women, which was founded by Eleanor Roosevelt and Mary McLeod Bethune, established a branch in Tampa in 1937. This organization, which initially grafted onto the City Federation of Colored Women's Clubs, experienced some class tensions at the outset. One of its early members recalled that "Our chapter [of the NCNW] was organized here in Tampa in 1937 by a group of prim ladies unaware of the meaning of Dr. Bethune's dream. They were finally dissolved. Later on another group was organized, and I was asked to become a member which I did" (Braukman 1992:67). The Urban League had undergone a similar transition, from the accommodationist leadership of Blanche Armwood, who skillfully courted the white establishment, to the more rebellious Benjamin Mays, who later won considerable renown for his national leadership in Civil Rights. Mays served in Tampa for only a short time, from 1926 to 1928, but he influenced its programs to pursue justice as well as charity. He provided legal assistance to black defendants in court and attempted to intervene in the problem of police brutality. He and Arthur Raper, a white sociologist who later was involved with the defense of the Scottsboro Boys,[17] undertook a major research project into the nature and scope of problems affecting black people in Tampa. When the study was released, only Raper was credited as author. Mays recalled this in his autobiography: "A quite exhaustive and comprehensive document, it revealed many things about Negro life in Tampa. Eager to know what the press had to say, I hurried to read the Tampa papers the next day, only to find that the (white) press had given Mr. Raper alone credit for having made the report.... If a white man gave the report, it was true; white Tampa would accept its authenticity only if it came from a white man" (Mays 1971:108).

Mays clashed often with his white benefactors/overseers. He refused to go along with a scheme to move all black people in Tampa onto a separate site on the edge of town, and he rankled whites he worked with by insisting they address his wife as "Mrs. Mays." The whites involved with the Urban League reflected a mixture of paternalism and control. In public, Mrs. Armwood's followers referred to them as "white angels," a designation that bothered Mays the moment he heard it (Mays 1971:107). They were supportive of the Urban League's attempt to tame the "dangerous classes," but they were wary of black leaders who might use this organization to challenge the injustices that produced the danger. Perhaps wisely, Mr. and Mrs. Mays left Tampa to carry out their work in more appreciative contexts.

Mays's departure was a loss to Tampa's black community, although some of the activism he brought to the work of the Urban League stayed behind. Shortly afterwards, the NAACP reemerged in Tampa. Unlike the Urban League, Tampa's NAACP had no white board of directors, and its objectives were very explicitly focused on challenging injustice. On March 19, 1929, a new local charter was issued (Howard and Howard 1994a). One of the board members was the wife of the Reverend Marcellus Potter, editor of the *Bulletin* and founder of the earlier NAACP branch in Tampa.

Potter was still alive and active; he took a leading role in securing legal help from the NAACP in preventing a lynching, defending a series of racially biased criminal court cases, and investigating a case of kidnapping and castration, all of which occurred during 1930 alone. Teachers were also centrally involved in the new NAACP; the first president was a male teacher named E. J. Wright (Howard and Howard 1994a:50). As well, teachers were heavily represented among the members of the National Council of Negro Women and the volunteers who supported the Urban League.

In the period of the 1930s through the Second World War, there was a quickening in the organizations and informal groups of the black community in Tampa (and in other U.S. cities), the gathering prelude of the Civil Rights movement. In this very same period, the Afro-Cuban community was loosening its grip on the younger generation, was shrinking and losing the capacity to provide for their own. The Afro-Cuban portion of Tampa's black population had steadily declined from 1900, when it was 18 percent, to 7 percent in 1930, and only 3 percent by 1940. The geographic separation between the two groups also began to diminish. As cigarmakers left Ybor City, their empty houses increasingly were occupied by African Americans, who were leaving congested and squalid conditions in the Scrub. Ybor City, especially in the southwestern section, where Martí-Maceo was located, was slowly transitioning into a black neighborhood.

Black Cubans from Ybor City attended school in the Scrub; both the public Harlem School and the Catholic St. Peter Claver were located there. The high school, named for Booker T. Washington, was also in this area. Afro-Cubans were a small minority at school, and relations with African American classmates were often hostile. Territory and ethnicity played familiar scenarios.

> JORGÉ: We had a lot of trouble coming to the theaters, the Central and the Maceo, they were both in the Scrub. We wanted to go to the movies, quite naturally, so we would take the chance of coming down into the Scrub, where we knew that if a gang caught us, they were going to whip the devil out of us, or run us away. A lot of these kids [black Americans] when they saw black Cubans, Afro-Cubans, they wanted to beat us up. They used to call us "black wops." And when we came into their neighborhood we were lucky if we didn't get beat up. But we didn't see it as any threat to us, because we knew it was a thing that was happening, because if those kids came into our section they would get the same from us.

Nevertheless, the intimacy of shared classrooms, the stirrings of sexuality among young adolescents, the two-way lure of lives different from one's own, created attractions. Friendships between classmates opened windows on the parallel existence of the African American community, a world of neighborhoods, families, customs, and pleasures that had remained previously hidden. Afro-Cuban parents told only about dangers and unpleasantness of associating with African Americans, but their children were getting a more textured view.

Afro-Cubans who were thrust into this situation, outsiders and outnumbered, struggled to negotiate. Evelio Grillo related his own ambivalence and discomfort over this experience.

> The significant events in Tampa's black life took place in the big Baptist church across the street from the [St. Peter Claver] school, and in the AME church on Harrison St, and in other venues about which I knew absolutely nothing. . . . I felt isolated [from] black American life that was commonplace for my black American friends, but that was new and different and, even, strange for me. Similarly, I would sometimes give expression to something peculiarly Cuban with which my black American friends were unfamiliar. The quizzical looks, and sometimes laughter, which followed would leave me feeling embarrassed, awkward, and very, very alone. (Grillo 2000:44)

Experiences in school began to undermine their identification as Cubans.

> JORGE: We would sit in class and they, when they would call my name, "Jorgé." That's why, after a while I wouldn't even let them call me Jorgé. I called myself George. To me, I thought that they would think that I was trying to be inferior, different, you know. I start calling myself George, instead of Jorgé.

A similar recollection from another Afro-Cuban man of about the same age:

> RAMÓN: We were ridiculed so much in public school because, you know, speech, dress, and the like, that we shied away from the idea of being Latin. And, as we got into the fifth, sixth . . . grades we always spoke English, except at home. And I, for a few years, I forgot that I was, almost forgot consciously, intentionally forgot that I was from Cuba.

The evident scorn of African Americans for the Cubans in their classes reflected envy, as well as the inverted power they enjoyed as the majority group. Language and speech were, as Ramón observed, critical factors in marking differences.

> PHIL: Because they would speak Spanish and we wouldn't. And sometime when we'd be around, they'd be speaking Spanish and [we] didn't know what they were talking about. Some [African] American people, well they felt . . . "Are they talking about me, are they cussing me out behind my back?"

More than the simple tensions that arise from an inability to understand foreign speech, the Cubans had a prideful reputation and were viewed as more cosmopolitan and successful by many young black Americans.

> EDDIE: The black Cubans really took advantage of the advantage that they had. That mental alertness, awareness that they had, that we locals did not have. We local blacks just didn't have that sense of, you know, vision; not as broad as theirs.

Although Eddie admired the sense of pride that black Cuban parents tried to instill in their children, he also believed that the parents were not serving their children's best interests.

> EDDIE: If they had given them, you know, that sense of self worth in a different, more positive vein . . . I think it was more negative, you know, something they were holding onto. It had no life giving.

Many young Afro-Cubans felt that their parents' attitudes were a problem for them. A desire to fit in, and erase the differences that created feelings of awkward inferiority, produced growing confusion in the lives of young Afro-Cubans and increased tensions in their family relations.

Many Afro-Cuban children were pleased with their ability to speak English, a capacity that conferred autonomy and a degree of power over their parents.

> LYDIA: When I went to school for the first time, about a week or so, I was more American than George Washington. Me and my brother were talking [in English] and she [mother] said no, "You talk that out there, but here you talk Spanish." She did not understand what we were saying. In fact, that time that she said that, me and my brother were saying something that we were not supposed to be saying.

Parents, and especially mothers, did not learn English as a rule, had little need and few opportunities to do so. Spanish was the household language, a matter of pride and identity as well as a practical necessity. Children needed to be bilingual, a condition that posed a threat to the established authority of the adults in the family.

Intermarriage

From the parents' perspective, the greatest danger was that a son or, worse, a daughter would fall in love with an American. In various combinations, however, sexual attractions across ethnic boundaries in these settings were enhanced by the manner in which gender differences were constructed on both sides. The contrasts were highly pronounced. African American women played very different roles in family and community life than their Afro-Cuban counterparts, exercised wider prerogatives, and were far less restricted in movement. Although relations between African American men and women were not unproblematic, they were economically and socially far more bilateral than between Afro-Cuban spouses. These differences in gender and family relations implicitly promoted sexual relationships and marriage between the two groups.

Between Afro-Cuban and African American adolescent males there was often rivalry and antagonism; between females there tended to be distance and avoidance. Jealousy and proprietary concerns about sexual encroachment played into, and out of, these negative sentiments. Cross-gender contacts, however, were more positively charged. Excited by romance spiked with alluring cultural differences, males and females of both groups also were able to perceive more practical advantages in crossing ethnic boundaries in quest of each other.

For Afro-Cuban boys, American girls were unhindered by Cuban traditions of chaperoning, were considered easy and available. An Afro-Cuban male described these advantages.

> JORGÉ: In those days you didn't go around socializing with a Spanish woman unless your intentions were honorable. You know what I mean? Like me, I never had no Spanish girlfriends. But I was a young fella. Because if you went to, if you try to, uh, date a Spanish girl, first you had to [be chaperoned]. If you want to take her to the movies, you had to bring her father, or her mother, or her brother, or somebody, with you. And I wasn't for that. Because I could just go to one

of my [American] girlfriends and say, "Hello there, I pick you up tonight." That's it.

Dalliances with African American girls were not actively discouraged, as long as they did not lead to marriage. This perspective was explained by an Afro-Cuban man reflecting on the attitudes of his immigrant parents.

> ESTEBAN: Our parents they used a psychological idea to separate [us] from the black [American] women, so not to marry them. And the psychology was to use them, but don't marry them. Well, we have a good time with them. Because they did not want the American people within their family. That's the old people. That's the way [we were raised].

Overtures from Afro-Cuban males—reputed to be more courtly than American males, and also more prosperous—often found reciprocation. An Afro-Cuban man explained what he believed were the attractions.

> TOMÁS: The black American girl, she liked the Cubans because they were different. They would make cigars, they had more money, and they had ways that were different from the black American males, and that made the black American male mad.

Transgressing the territorial boundaries between Ybor City and Central Avenue posed dangers from rival African American boys, who jeered at the Afro-Cubans and called them "black wops" and "Tally wops." Like the white patrons in the Silver Slipper, black Americans did not distinguish the sounds of Italian and Spanish, and they coined an ethnic slur that did not quite fit, but served its purpose. Afro-Cuban males who messed with African American girls were particular targets, especially if they happened to venture alone onto Central Avenue. Evelio Grillo recalled one of his encounters with this danger.

> They could have had it in for me, for I had captured the attention of Pauline, an absolutely ravishing black American beauty, whom they thought "belonged to them." I had the temerity to take Pauline to the movies twice and to walk her home the long way, where dark streets and trees provided wonderful settings for heavy petting. So the fear was real and I took no chances. I came downstairs from the dentist's office and waited at the entryway of the building until certain that none of the feared group remained within one block of the building. Dashing to an alley across the street in the middle of the block, I lost

myself quickly within it. Then, I threaded my way carefully, from alley to alley, until I reached safety on the other side of Nebraska Avenue, in my neighborhood. (Grillo 2000:13–14)

Danger can add excitement to lust and love, raising the stakes on conquest. But conquest could fall to either side. However rakish the intentions of some black Cuban males, and despite strong discouragement from their parents, liaisons with African American females not infrequently resulted in marriage.

The other combination in mixed marriages, Afro-Cuban females with African American males, was the most discouraged. An African American son-in-law was considered a dreadful prospect, whereas a daughter-in-law might be more controllable.

RAMÓN: If a male married an American female, it might have been tolerated and completely forgotten if the American female would align with the society and learn how to speak Spanish, and what not.

Some African American wives did "align" themselves.

ESPERANZA: Our next door neighbor, she's American, but she married a Cuban. She can speak Spanish and cook like any Spanish people, because her mother-in-law didn't speak English. She [neighbor] couldn't speak Spanish when she married the son. So her mother-in-law told her I'm gonna teach you Spanish, and I'm gonna teach you how to cook."

Many other new "American" wives of Afro-Cuban husbands bridled at those requirements. The narratives I collected are replete with stories of failed marriages, of African American wives who proved to be "bad."

TOMÁS: My uncle, his first wife was American, a black American, and she turned out to be bad, very bad woman. My mother told him not to marry this woman. See, goes to show you.

Many tell the same stories, a kind of collective lore about what happened to those who defied their parents and did not marry "one of their own kind." There are no reliable data to reveal whether divorce was any more frequent in these mixed marriages, or why some of them failed. The domineering tendencies of Afro-Cuban husbands cannot have been without consequence, however. For women who had grown up in families where females were encouraged to be strong and independent, the harsh expectations of Cuban husbands may have been difficult to accept.

Afro-Cuban girls sometimes envisioned marriage to a non-Cuban as an escape from those restrictions. An Afro-Cuban woman who married an American reflected on her own choice.

RAQUEL: Never, not me. I never wanted to marry a Cuban. I didn't want to bow down to a Cuban man. I didn't want to be bare feet and pregnant and underprivileged. This was the way that they thought. They think the man is the king, and that's all right for a spell. But, hey, if I'm gonna treat you like a king, then you oughta treat me like a queen. Not like I'm one of the serfs, one of your great servants.

Another woman, whose failed marriage to an American was followed by a long and successful marriage to a Cuban, recalled her thoughts on why she married her first husband.

LUZ: My first husband was African American. My parents definitely didn't like him, and they were so right. But you can't see those things. What did I see in him? I loved to dance and he was a good dancer. Then, they [parents] were very strict on me. They had a whip, you know. So, they were very strict. And I think sometimes that hurts you, 'cause sometimes you want to get out and you want to go to dances, and they're thinking you're going to have sex, 'cause that's all people think about, you know. But there are so many things that you want to enjoy. They were too strict with me. That's why I say if they never had been that strict with me, I would have never married my first husband.

Forces operating in both directions heightened the attraction. African American males were also drawn to Afro-Cuban females, who were reputed to be submissive—to wait on their men and bow to their authority. They were also exotic, and many had light skin and "good" hair. Inaccessibility posed a challenge, either to persuade an Afro-Cuban girlfriend to slip out and defy her parents, or perhaps to accept the manly challenge of facing the gauntlet of paternal approval.

The latter was extremely difficult to obtain, an obstacle that would prove self-defeating to many Afro-Cuban parents who held firm. Afro-Cuban customs of chaperoning and seeking parental permission to visit a daughter were a deterrent to these relationships, but also encouraged subterfuge and rebellion.

LUZ: Now my cousin, the [American] fella she married, he was a nice fella, and she had a nice marriage. When he came to the house, to ask her father if he could come visit his daughter, he [father] said no. I think he should have let the fellow come, 'cause it was nice of him [to ask]. Because when they [parents] do those things, then it makes you want him more. You like the fella and you're infatuated, you're gonna see him anyway.

Parental resistance could backfire, producing the worst possible outcomes.

ROSA: The black Cubans, they couldn't see their daughters marrying a black American. In other words, you were an outcaste. I know of one family, I'm not going to call the name . . . he had five daughters and two sons. They were all beautiful kids. They all had that olive skin, looked like Indians. And one of the girls, she was pretty friendly with my family. She fell in love with an American black kid, and they went around, you know, and she became pregnant. Oh, they kick her out of the house, and she had nowhere to go. We had to take her in. Then this same person [the girl's father], his wife found out that he was, you know, running around with a black American. And then, she decided, "That's it." She went and started running around herself, and all her daughters got married to American fellas. All of them.

The barriers were crumbling. Demographic constraints and the agency of youth were stronger than parental resistance. The pool of potential mates who were Cuban had shrunk, making endogamy less feasible. The rigidity of Afro-Cuban gender relations made it more difficult to adjust and produced stresses that undermined their ethnic self-containment.

The Cuban Hall Patio

The Martí-Maceo Society, symbol of that insularity, also underwent changes; but it survived and, in many ways, grew stronger. The organization had suffered damaging blows from the exodus of the 1930s.

LYDIA: You know the majority of them left, and that is what made Martí-Maceo go down because a lot of them left. Like they had dances and things like that, a lot of people were not there.

Membership dropped from 128 in 1929 to 48 in 1939. After a few failed attempts, social events were discontinued, at least temporarily.

LUZ: They used to give dances, and then they couldn't give those affairs because they didn't have enough members. That's when I realized it. They didn't have, you know, enough members. And then they had a time trying to keep the club.

The remaining members tended to be older, including some of the original founders. Aging members placed a heavier demand on sick benefits, further straining the solvency of the organization. In 1929, 27 percent of members collected *dietas* at some time during the year (35/128); by 1939, the proportion had jumped to 58 percent (28/48). The duration of benefits increased as well. In 1929, only 6 individuals (5 percent) collected benefits for more than twenty weeks; in 1939, 14 (29 percent) received such extended benefits. Dues revenues had declined, benefit claims had escalated, alternative funds from social events had dried up. The actuarial prognosis was not good.

> LUIS: When the Depression came, I was president of the club. We owed Franco drugs three hundred dollars. We didn't have but thirty-six dollars. He knew me. He said, "I'm gonna go bankrupt. Y'all owe me three hundred dollars, but I'm gonna make out like you pay me. I'm gonna give you a receipt, and when I go bankrupt you don't owe me nothing if they come and try to collect from you. I know you ain't got nothin.'" Another guy, Dr. González. He worked for twenty dollars a month. He said, "I'm gonna work for you all for fifteen. If you have it pay it, and if you don't have it, you don't pay it."

With help from others who were struggling to keep Ybor City's institutions intact, or who were willing to falsify documents to shield them from creditors, and members who agreed to forgo benefits to enable more needy recipients, and other emergent aid and adjustments, they were able to keep the organization going. They had paid off the mortgage in 1929. They got some revenue from rental of their houses.

The hall itself was sometimes rented to African Americans, who used it for parties, benefits, and meetings. This source of financial support grew increasingly important and became the critical factor in rescuing the organization. Commercial ties between African Americans and the Martí-Maceo Society paved the way for increased social contact. Martí-Maceo also became an arena for cultural exchange along an axis of easy appreciation.

> LUIS: We rent the hall and then we build it up a little. They had big bands, Cab Calloway, Nat King Cole, Louie Armstrong, they used to go on tour. They'd charge a percentage, you know. When they make

their contracts, like they were gonna play in Tampa for the blacks, so they would get the Cuban Hall [Martí-Maceo]. Big bands used to come here.

The local vernacular name for Martí-Maceo became the "Cuban Hall." There was no need to call it the "black" Cuban hall, no reason to distinguish it from Círculo Cubano, which did not rent its facilities to blacks. Within the African American community, Martí-Maceo was the hall run by Cubans. Grillo remembered these contacts over music, this coming together in shared appreciation of black American culture: "Some of the young adult black Cubans, mostly males, attended dances held by black American organizations at our center [Martí-Maceo], where a large dance hall was a favored venue.... Our community fluttered for days in anticipation of the appearance of Cab Calloway" (Grillo 2000:15). The leadership of Martí-Maceo instituted a way to capitalize on the musical interests of young Afro-Cubans and their African American friends and, at the same time, subsidize social activities for the older members. They began holding what were called "Top and Bottom" dances. The hall had two ballrooms, one on each floor. On the top floor, African American bands played for the younger crowd, and on the ground floor, a Cuban band entertained parents and their older friends. Still chaperoned but on their own, mingling with the outside but tucked within the Martí-Maceo, the Afro-Cuban youth were afforded a kind of safety valve. Adults who ventured upstairs—and there were growing numbers who did so—went in order to take part rather than to supervise. The second-story ballroom would become so packed that the floor trembled through the ceiling below. These activities breathed new life into the organization, and the institution that had symbolized their separateness became an agent in their incorporation.

The Martí-Maceo Society survived the Depression by commercializing its property. Benefits were maintained only by subsidizing the costs with rental revenue. In 1941, on a vacant lot next to the hall, they decided to build an outdoor patio, similar to the one that Círculo Cubano members recently had added to their social hall. Although by that time Martí-Maceo was solvent again, the treasury did not have sufficient surpluses to pay for such an ambitious expansion. They financed it mainly through the cultivation of social capital. In carrying out this project they improvised a wide spectrum of resources, nearly all of which were from inside Ybor City. Al López, the baseball player, was one of the major benefactors in the enterprise. His help was one of a complex set of arrangements and donations that were mobilized in order to accomplish the task. The man who had been president at the time explained how they devised and implemented this plan.

> LUIS: The Círculo Cubano had made their patio. They're doing good. Pepito [a member of Círculo Cubano], he said, "Why don't you get that empty space they got there [next to Martí-Maceo] and make a patio?" He said, "I'll lend you the money." I went and I told a few guys, and they say okay. We spoke with a guy who is an architect, a white guy, member of Círculo Cubano, he made the plan and he didn't charge us nothin.' Went to a colored [African American] man, a colored, we knew he was going to do it cheap, a bricklayer. Bricks they cost eighteen cents a piece, but we got them for sixteen. But we need twenty-five hundred dollars to buy the rest of the stuff. Pepito went to his brother, Al López, the one that play ball. And López loaned us the money, every cent. They had a guy, a Cuban guy from Círculo Cubano that paint those murals. He said, "I'll paint it for nothing. You just put two signs that say Pepsi Cola. I'll paint it for nothing and they [Pepsi-Cola] will put up the paint." I went to Círculo Cubano, and they give me thirty-five dollars. I say, "I don't want no thirty-five dollars, I want you to give me something more, loan me some tables, that's where we gonna make the money." He called the committee, and they gave us their tables, a hundred tables. They're gonna buy new ones. That's good relations. Plumber, black Cuban [who] belonged to Martí-Maceo, he give us all the appliances, sink, toilets for men and ladies, four men done it in two days, didn't charge but two dollars an hour. We went to the Tampa Electric, to the Coca-Cola, and like that we got everything. Centro Español, they give us a hundred dollars. Centro Asturiano, they give us a hundred dollars. Beer was rationed because of the war, they give me a hundred dollars to buy the beer. Italian club gave us a benefit. Tony Pizzo [Italian American civic leader] told me about an abandoned dance floor in Cuscaden Park, and I went down there and got thirty pieces of wood, you put 'em together and make a beautiful platform.

In building the patio, Martí-Maceo members improved their own quarters, enhanced the rental value of the property, and erected tangible proof of the organization's vitality. It was not an easy project. Their strategy for accomplishing it relied heavily on the other groups in Ybor City, who provided an unusual amount of assistance. This support for Martí-Maceo's efforts contrasted with that in earlier periods, when relations with the other clubs had been more distant. It would also stand in contrast to circumstances two decades later, when no one intervened to help save them from Urban Renewal. During the Depression and war years, however, all the groups in Ybor City were struggling to hold on and hold together. And they were animated by the global struggle against fascism in Spain and Italy. In this liminal period of Depression and war, the white immigrants were perhaps more nostalgic and less discriminating.

The finished patio was a spacious and attractive outdoor venue, a broad, paved surface surrounded by stucco walls with a raised bandstand at one end. Tables and chairs were set up on the margins, with most of the space reserved for dancing. There were decorative features, landscaping, and lush tropical scenes of Cuba painted on the walls. On warm nights, it offered escape from the sweltering conditions indoors. Music from the bands that played there filled the night air of surrounding neighborhoods. The expanding presence of the Martí-Maceo reinforced the Cubanness of those neighborhoods and affirmed the ongoing existence of the Afro-Cuban community. But most of the music that wafted from Martí-Maceo's patio, the "Cuban Hall Patio," was not Cuban.

The patio opened on Easter Sunday, April 5, 1942, with a ribbon-cutting ceremony held in the afternoon. The printed program was in English. An appeal to "Buy defense bonds and stamps" appeared in large letters on the front cover. The program booklet contained ads from 34 local businesses, 19 from Ybor City and 15 from Central Avenue. The following night was the grand opening dance. Three bands played—one on the top floor, one on the bottom, and the third on the stage of the patio. Admission was 99 cents. Two bands were American, and only one was Cuban. One of the American bands, the Florida Collegiates, featured Nat and Cannonball Adderly. Frank Amaro, an Afro-Cuban, also played in this band (Turner 1998:23).

Music joined the souls of black Cubans and black Americans, supplied an idiom of understanding that laid bare the common root. If the Cuban "counterpoint" rhapsodized by Ortiz was the blended rhythms of Spain and Africa, the Afro-Cuban-American counterpoint was the polyrhythmic beat of blues, jazz, and bebop. Afro-Cuban music achieved huge popularity in Cuba during the 1920s and 1930s. The *son*, a rhythmic arrangement of African percussion and Spanish trumpet and guitar, formed the musical accompaniment of a cultural revolution in Cuba. Fernando Ortiz, who mixed ethnology and politics, and Nicolas Guillen, who added in poetry and the exaltation of African music, helped orchestrate a movement known as negrista (Ellis 1998). Part of a worldwide stirring of Africanity, negritude in Paris and the Harlem Renaissance in New York mingled with Cuban negrista and reached into the black neighborhoods of Tampa.

When it was first introduced, the *son* was considered scandalous music, nakedly sensual and unashamedly African. In October 1928, Martí-Maceo directors considered whether to allow it to be performed in the club. One of them had written a letter to the board formally complaining about the performance of the *son* in the last dance they had held. A debate ensued. Most argued that allowing it would jeopardize their respectability, but there was some dissent. The minutes briefly record this exchange.

> Mr. Pérez had attended a dance [at the club] and protested because the *son* had been allowed. Mr. Pérez said he had never been in agreement with allowing the *son*, since all the [Cuban] societies collaborating for the advancement of the black race did not allow this music. Mr. Gerbacio said that the *son* is regarded unfavorably in Havana. Mr. Puñales said that in Havana, the white societies are dancing the *son* and they are not degraded by it, and he sees no reason to believe that because we are black [that] we will be degraded for dancing the *son*. Mr. Villalon said that in Santiago de Cuba the *son* is not danced. Mr. Rodríguez spoke in favor of the *son*, since he believed it was harmless. Mr. R. Pérez spoke against the *son*. The president put the matter to a vote and the results were 4 against and 8 in favor. Having no other matters to discuss the meeting was adjourned.[18]

The motion to prohibit the *son* passed, but it was not enforced for very long. The two dissenters, Mariano Puñales and Francisco Rodríguez, were important figures in the club, the voice of the future. Puñales, who moved to New York after the strike of 1931 was briefly discussed earlier. Francisco Rodríguez, also a labor activist, left Tampa at the same time, but returned a few years later and lived the rest of his life in Tampa.

One of his sons, Francisco Jr., became a lawyer for the NAACP in the 1950s and '60s. Rodríguez's other son, Miguel, was a musician and would have a significant influence on music in Tampa's African American community, first as a performer, and later as music director for the city's black high schools. Miguel (a.k.a. "Mike") played with a very popular Tampa band named the Honeydrippers, formed out of the old Florida Collegiates in the late 1940s, in which he played with such notable musicians as Ray Charles, Nat and Cannonball Adderly, and Noble Watts (Kaster 1988:19). His Cuban background and early appreciation for musical trends like the *son* served him well. On the national level during this same period, Chano

Pozo and Mario Bauza joined with Dizzie Gillespie, fusing Afro-Cuban music with bebop (Jacques 1998). There were parallel creative relations between principals in the Harlem Renaissance and the Cuban Negrista movement, exemplified by the long-term intellectual comradeship between poets Langston Hughes and Nicolas Guillen (Ellis 1998). Powerful crosscurrents of Pan African expression, pregnant with themes of rebellion and diasporic kinship, were playing the stages of black Tampa. In the Martí-Maceo social hall, Top and Bottom, young and old, traditional and modern, belligerently Cuban and insistently American, were discovering common ground.

8

Revolution, Renewal, Revitalization

When I write that I do not remember VJ Day and VE Day, I do so with
complete candor. My amnesia is total. I did not feel Germany and Japan as
palpably as I felt the United States Army. The Army's oppression was direct,
immediate, constant. Only the irresistible forces of social and political
change have brought about the painfully slow, incremental changes that
have made conditions better in some ways, but more difficult in others.

Evelio Grillo

World War II was a watershed, a global upheaval that changed everything.
In Ybor City and other such neighborhoods throughout the United States,
young adults in immigrant families joined the military in disproportionate
numbers. For white immigrants, World War II opened new vistas of opportunity. The training that many were able to obtain during and after their
service, and the prosperity that came with victory, brought dramatic and
sudden changes. Jobs were plentiful, and a grateful government offered
veterans subsidies to pursue higher education and purchase new homes in
the suburbs. Throughout the United States, the offspring of barely literate
immigrant parents would parlay these advantages into an unprecedented
burst of intergenerational mobility.

For returning black soldiers, including those who grew up in immigrant
families in Ybor City, the scenario was different. Although no less involved
in the war and no less likely to die in the process, official gratitude and
generosity stopped at the color line. Higher education, especially in the
South, was still segregated and grossly unequal. Although many black veterans were able to use GI benefits to earn degrees and learn new skills,
their range of options in selecting schools, or finding employment afterwards, was severely limited. Blacks were also excluded from the expansive
new housing tracts, made affordable by VA mortgages for which they did
not qualify, and accessible via federally funded highways that destroyed
their old neighborhoods. Black soldiers returning to Tampa from the war

rode home in Jim Crow trains. They debarked in a segregated waiting room at Union Station and stepped back into a world where signs everywhere continued to denote their exclusion. Forbidden to enter most restaurants, forbidden to use most parks and beaches, forbidden even to drink from certain public water fountains, they were expected to pack their uniforms and resume their restricted lives. Yawning contradictions in this state of affairs deepened resentment and nurtured resistance. Returning black veterans of World War II parlayed their experiences and the marginal advantages they could wrest into a revolution.

For Afro-Cubans in Tampa, the experience of World War II and its aftermath served to define their blackness and distinguish them further from the white immigrants with whom they had grown up. The benefits that accrued to the white veterans from Ybor City families brought them accelerated advances in education and employment, and enabled many to move out of their old neighborhood and into new suburbs. Black Cuban veterans did not enjoy these same advantages. Growing disparities intensified distance based on color. Events in Cuba, more profound than any that had occurred in their lifetimes, would soon also transform relationships with their homeland.

Tampa's second-generation Afro-Cubans had maintained easy ties with Cuba and had remained ensconced in the Latin enclave. As their own children were growing up, however, forces were set in motion that effectively destroyed the Ybor City community and transformed the meaning of Cubanness in Tampa. The postwar departure of white families from Ybor City signaled the onset of an orchestrated decline leading in lockstep towards Urban Renewal. In Cuba a small band of guerillas was preparing for an insurrection, the success of which led to a tight U.S. embargo on contact with the island. The Cuban revolution also unleashed a huge exodus that would radically redefine the identity of Cuban Americans.

All of these factors pushed Afro-Cubans into a closer relationship with African Americans. There were also strong forces pulling the two groups together. Politics and marriage created an inseparable bond. Between 1946 and 1960, 84 percent of the recorded marriages of Afro-Cubans were with African Americans. These mixed marriages were fairly evenly divided between those where the wife was Afro-Cuban and husband African American (46 percent) and vice versa (54 percent).[1] The overwhelming majority of third-generation Afro-Cubans grew up in households where only one side of the family was Cuban. They had grandparents, aunts, uncles, and cousins who were tightly connected to the traditions and institutions of black Tampa. Many did not learn to speak Spanish, or did so only when conversing with Cuban grandparents. The Civil Rights movement embraced their adolescence and joined them in a struggle that had almost nothing to do with Cuba, and everything to do with being black.

By the end of the 1960s, the Afro-Cuban community in Tampa appeared to be poised on the edge of oblivion. The old Martí-Maceo hall was torn down by Urban Renewal in 1965. The members got another building, but far more modest than the one they had lost. Less attractive for rentals and less in demand because of desegregation, the hall was empty much of the time. Four elderly men, officers of the society, came each day to tend to its dwindling business and play dominoes with each other. And then there were three.

The story did not unfold as expected, however. A curious reversal was about to occur. Back in New York, Tampeño migrants of the 1930s were approaching the age of retirement. Troubled cities in the Northeast were shifting wealth and population south to the Sunbelt. Successes of the Civil Rights movement helped redefine the attractiveness of returning to Florida. These convergent forces propelled a chain of Afro-Cuban returnees—only a handful compared to the onslaught of new white Cubans, but more than sufficient numbers to revive Martí-Maceo. It was in these times of renewal and retrospective nostalgia that I first became acquainted with the Afro-Cubans in Tampa.

This chapter weaves together the effects of the foregoing events and circumstances, the changing nature of Afro-Cuban identity in the tumultuous period since the Second World War. It brings us to the edge of the present.

Civil Rights

The movement to overturn Jim Crow greatly intensified during the war, in what many African American newspapers termed the "double V" campaign—victory over fascism abroad and at home (Schnur 1993). The parallel drawn between Nazi racism and beliefs of the Ku Klux Klan was scarcely exaggerated, nor was military rhetoric inappropriate in referencing both struggles. In August 1944, the city of Tampa joined with other cities in Florida in developing a contingency plan for martial law in the event the "negroes" revolted. A "race riot" in Detroit the preceding year, in which thirty-four people died, was the inspiration for the Florida plan to contain urban unrest. The secret report described reasons for concern:

"There is an undercurrent of tension, activated by union organizers and the presence of Northern negro soldiers in the community. Increased earning power caused by war activities . . . result in idleness and disorderly conduct and a resentment on the part of the white population towards negroes' refusal to perform necessary work" (quoted in Mormino 1995). They were right about the tension, albeit disingenuous about the causes.

Tampa's wartime recovery was fueled in large part by the growth of MacDill Army Air Base, a major facility that opened in 1939. During the war, the base housed ten thousand military personnel, three thousand of whom were black (Mormino 1995). Like the Buffalo Soldiers who sojourned in Tampa before going to Cuba in 1898, black soldiers at MacDill were treated more like enemies than the foes they were preparing to fight. In the period between Pearl Harbor in 1941 and VJ Day in 1945, there were at least four major disturbances involving black soldiers in Tampa. Three of these occurred on Central Avenue, where the old Central Life Insurance building had been converted into a black USO. (Central Life had moved to a new building in West Tampa.) The USO and the nightclubs and restaurants on Central were the only places where African American soldiers were allowed to congregate off the base. Altercations between black soldiers and white Military Police periodically widened into general unrest with hundreds (and in one case thousands) of black civilians gathered in protest against police brutality. There were some injuries and numerous arrests. Military incursions into the Central Avenue district, which coincided with police crackdowns on black prostitutes and a vicious propaganda campaign that associated blackness with venereal disease, deepened resentments by black soldiers and civilians alike. Another violent incident, in 1943, occurred on the base and involved a cousin of one the members of Martí-Maceo—a New Yorker marooned in Florida, one of the feared "Northern negroes" who did not understand exactly where he was. When a black soldier was murdered by military police, the New Yorker reported it to the NAACP. Official response to their investigation was not arrest of the murderers, but rather the cousin was arrested, court-martialed for "inciting a riot," and sentenced to a ten-year prison term (Fere 1994:77).

The end of the war did not change much at MacDill. After the defeat of Germany, a group of German prisoners of war were incarcerated at the base and made to work in the hospital and dining room. The vanquished Aryans objected to the presence of black soldiers, refused to work around them in the hospital, and were offended that they ate in the same mess hall with whites (even though blacks were cordoned off in a separate section).

An obliging base commander responded to their complaints by establishing a separate mess hall for the black soldiers (Mormino 1995). This and other ongoing affronts led in October 1946 to an uprising among black soldiers at MacDill, more serious than any of the previous incidents and the largest ever to occur on any Air Force facility prior to the 1971 "riots" at Travis Air Force Base (Fere 1994:71). It began with attempts by black soldiers to gain admission to the NCO club. Violent clashes erupted with MPs called to the scene. Black soldiers broke from the fight and headed en masse towards an all white housing complex just outside the base. Reportedly they were throwing sticks and rocks and shouting "No more Jim Crow laws." This outbreak was quelled with the eager assistance of nine carloads of Tampa's white police. The incident was declared a "mutiny" that was probably instigated by Communists. Nine black soldiers got long prison terms (Fere 1994:79; Mormino 1995).

As all these events were unfolding at MacDill, local black civilians opened up two other fronts in the war against racism in Florida. They were part of a nationwide effort to challenge the legality of segregation and disenfranchisement. This movement was spearheaded by the NAACP and law faculty at Howard University, but success rested on the courage of people in local communities. Many were teachers, who jeopardized their jobs and their lives and offered stunning examples for the students they taught.

It was in the segregated public schools of Tampa that Afro-Cubans learned about, and were ultimately drawn into, a campaign against tyranny that paralleled the liberation movement their parents and grandparents had waged in Cuba. It marked the beginning of a new pantheon of heroes and, for many, a new definition of their own place in history. In his memoirs, Evelio Grillo paid frequent tribute to the influence of his teachers in Tampa's schools. "The characters and personalities," said Grillo, "of our great committed black teachers led us to develop a comfortableness with our identity as black Americans. Each of them a freedom fighter in his or her own way, their mission was ever before us: freedom and equality. In our daily contacts with them they made us feel as co-conspirators in the struggle to bring the walls of racial injustice and discrimination down" (Grillo 2000:46). He was not alone in this assessment. Another, younger, Afro-Cuban woman recalled her experiences with teachers in Tampa's segregated schools.

RAQUEL: We got the books after they had been squashed and the covers torn off, pages torn out, things like that. That's what we got. But one thing I can say about the black teachers, they were more concerned, and they worked with the kids, and they loved them.

Another man described how an incident with a highly respected teacher formed his inauguration into the nasty etiquette of southern racism.

RAMÓN: I think I was in junior high and I had a coach who, as far I was concerned, was just about the epitome of all manly virtues. And one day he took me downtown to the Office of Recreation. I don't know what for, maybe some supplies or something. And I was so shocked when I discovered that, here was this man who was my idol and the white people in the office would not speak to him.

Admiration for their black teachers and indignation at the way they were treated inspired empathy and identification with their struggles. It was also in school that young Afro-Cubans learned about the other role models of black liberation. Evelio Grillo revisited his own enculturation into the lore of African American ancestors and contemporary freedom fighters.

After my two years at Booker T. Washington High, the black American high school, my heart and mind belonged to Nat Turner, Frederick Douglass, Harriet Tubman, Sojourner Truth, Paul Lawrence Dunbar, John Brown, Paul Robeson, Langston Hughes, W. E. B. Du Bois, Allison Davis, and the two brothers, James Weldon Johnson and James Rosamond Johnson, who wrote the song very dear to my heart, "Lift Every Voice and Sing." (Grillo 2000:17)

"Lift Every Voice and Sing" is the unofficial African American anthem, widely performed in ceremonies where racial uplift and struggle form the keynote. James Weldon Johnson, the author, lived in Jacksonville at roughly the same time Grillo's father arrived in Florida. Johnson worked in cigar factories there and knew the Afro-Cubans who came and went from Tampa, could even have known Grillo's father, Antonio. The crosscurrents of their lives were deep already. The children of many of those early cigarmakers became firmly entwined in the culture of African America, and they became personally acquainted with young champions like Thurgood Marshall, Walter White, and Constance Baker Motley.

Marshall became well known to many in Tampa's African American community, in meetings and correspondence about voting rights and the salaries of teachers. In 1940, the president of Tampa's NAACP chapter sent a letter to Marshall seeking help in defeating the "white primary" system in Tampa that effectively disenfranchised black voters.[2] In 1941, he was also contacted for support in winning equal pay for Florida's black teachers, whose salary schedule was set at about 60 percent of that earned by white teachers.

Afro-Cubans played peripheral roles in the voting rights and teachers' pay equity campaigns. The Martí-Maceo Society held a benefit dance in 1943, the proceeds going to the legal fund for the teachers. When the suit was filed against the Hillsborough County School Board, there were only three Afro-Cuban teachers in Tampa's public schools, all members of the same family.[3] This was the Rodríguez family, cited in the last chapter, where all the children managed to go to college. Francisco Jr. became first a teacher, and later a lawyer for the NAACP. His brother, Miguel, and sister, Myrtle, also went into teaching. Myrtle was the first Afro-Cuban woman from Tampa to get a college degree, the example that other girls would use to argue with their parents for the right to do the same. During the early 1930s the Rodríguezes all attended Florida Agricultural and Mechanical University (FAMU), Florida's largest historically black college. There they became acquainted with a network of educated black Floridians who later would be instrumental in Civil Rights activities throughout the state.

The early cases over voting and teachers' salaries were successful in terms of judicial rulings, although much harder to bring into practice. The biracial pay scales were blatantly discriminatory, clearly in violation of the Fourteenth Amendment. When these arguments were finally brought to court, the dual pay system was defeated. The Hillsborough County School Board attempted to subvert this ruling by adopting new performance ratings for teachers that did not mention race, but were made purposely subjective to enable them to continue to pay black teachers less. The decision was only partly successful in redressing salary inequity, and black teachers still had dismal facilities and inferior instructional materials, but it was a critical landmark of the legal strategy to overturn Jim Crow. Nor was it an isolated victory.

The U.S. Supreme Court handed down the *Smith v. Allwright* decision in 1944, which made it illegal to prevent blacks from voting in Democratic primary elections. When a black minister in Jacksonville arrived at the courthouse to exercise his newly guaranteed franchise, he was told: "You won't go to jail [for voting], but you will get killed. This is Florida and . . . we don't allow niggers to vote here in Democratic primaries" (quoted in Schnur 1993:51). That promise was fulfilled in the case of Harry T. Moore, who founded the Progressive Voters' League in 1944. Moore had been a teacher in Mims, Florida (a small town on the east coast). He was fired in

1936 for instigating the campaign for salary equity. Undaunted, he proceeded to organize chapters of the NAACP and was appointed state secretary of the organization in Florida in 1946. He was highly effective in spite of persistent threats and harassment, increasing the number of local branches from nine to seventy-seven by 1951. His activities were abruptly terminated on Christmas day in 1951 when a bomb exploded in his house, killing both him and his wife (Green 1999; Saunders 1992).

In Tampa they used more finesse, although violence was not absent from their traditional arsenal against black rights. The Democratic political machine in Tampa determined that manipulation might be preferable to intimidation in managing the inevitable black franchise. Politics in Tampa differed from other Florida cities for the presence of a large bloc of white ethnic voters who, by the 1940s, were extremely active in local elections. The main thrust of this activism was inspired not by democratic ideology nor the patriotism engendered by war, but rather was an extension of the gambling business that dominated Ybor City's economy. The income from *bolita* topped $10 million per year, $1 million of which was used to pay off crooked politicians (Orrick and Crumpacker 1998:254). "*Bolita* galvanized Latin voters in the 1930s and in the process brought about a quarter century of machine politics. Gambling factions expended tremendous sums of energy and money to ensure the election of accommodating officeholders. . . . In addition to bribes, much of the monies were spent paying Latins to vote early and often" (Mormino and Pozzetta 1987:301–2).

During this period, Tampa had the reputation as one of the most corrupt cities in the United States. Gangland killings, police on the payrolls of gamblers, and rigged elections earned it the label of "Hellhole of the Gulf Coast" (Alduino 1991). The killings, which occurred regularly during the 1930s and 1940s, reflected a struggle over control of this lucrative business.

Gambling was an enterprise that wove together a volatile cast of characters. *Bolita* originated with the Cubans, but the need for protection against law enforcement brought them into early collaboration with the forces who ruled Tampa. Charlie Wall, black sheep of one of Tampa's most distinguished families, cousin of D. B. McKay, who was still mayor, was the kingpin of Ybor City's gambling industry, the indispensable partner who arranged to pay off police and other nosy officials. Charlie Wall and the Cuban *boliteros* were challenged for control of this lucrative operation by Italian mobsters, Santo Trafficante and his rival "Big Joe" Italiano. Also involved in this network of competing underworld figures were Charlie

Moon and his associates on Central Avenue and in other Florida cities. This multilateral struggle resulted in more than a dozen assassinations in Ybor City and the Scrub. Charlie Wall eluded several attempts on his life, but many of his Cuban colleagues were not so lucky. Italiano was also murdered, reportedly by Trafficante's faction, which emerged victorious at the end of this bloody war.

Ultimately among the victims was Charlie Moon, who was murdered in 1944 by a bad black policeman named Pearl McAdams. Pearl was as notorious as Charlie, but his reputation was far more sinister. He had killed many people. Often, these killings were at the behest of the corrupt police and gangsters who employed him, but he also had the reputation of attacking anyone who displeased him. It is not clear who ordered the murder of Charlie Moon, but it was believed to have been Trafficante. Pearl came to his house and shot him, although he initially did not die. Pearl insisted on getting in the ambulance that took him to Clara Frye Hospital, where Pearl threatened the nurses at gunpoint to refrain from saving his life. One of my narrators, who was a child when this happened, remembered going after school to the funeral parlor where Charlie was laid out. As they were peeking into the room where he lay in his casket, they suddenly saw a movement in the curtain behind the casket. Fearing it might be Charlie's ghost, or worse, Pearl in the flesh still lurking about, they shot out of the building and ran all the way home.

Gang warfare and disclosures of widespread bribery and extortion eventually led the Kefauver Crime Commission to schedule hearings in Tampa in 1950. Its report condemned both gangsters and public officials.

> The situation uncovered there was a repellent combination of sordidness and violence. . . . In nineteen years there have been fourteen murders and six attempted assassinations in the Tampa underworld—and only one conviction. The explosive element that keeps Tampa in a ferment of violence is the long-standing rivalry between two equally hot-blooded gang factions. One is the Mafia-backed clique composed of criminals of Sicilian or Italian extraction. The other is the numerically larger Cuban faction. Mixed in with these, of course, is a leavening of racketeers native to the section. The situation is not helped by the seeming willingness of some law enforcement officials—and the apathy of others—to go along with the underworld. (Kefauver 1951:69)

Pressures to reform the political system, in which the Ybor City district played a disproportionate role, included a drive to annex large suburban tracts to dilute the strength of ethnic voters. Reformers also instituted at-large elections to defeat the inner-city ward healers (Newton 1961). Likely in response to these threats to the Ybor City electoral strategy, selected groups of new black voters were recruited and quietly registered in the late 1940s. In this way, the establishment was able to capitalize on the voting-rights efforts of African Americans, in a cynical arrangement that invoked ties between black Cubans and immigrant politicians.

Vincente Valdés, one of the younger men who was active in Martí-Maceo in the mid-1940s, was drawn into this ploy. Valdés worked at the local Coca-Cola plant where he was very popular among the other black workers. He was also a member of a club named the Frogs, an African American social club that initially met in the Martí-Maceo hall and included several other Afro-Cuban members. Valdés was contacted by a fore-man in the plant and asked to organize blacks from the Coca-Cola plant, the Frogs, and Martí-Maceo. They were instructed to appear at City Hall at a certain day and time. One of the men he enlisted recalled these events.

TOMÁS: Fred Kelsey [white foreman at Coca-Cola] told Vincente to get some blacks and go to City Hall. Somehow he knew that there was going to be a time when we could vote. At City Hall, there was a small table set up underneath the stairs. This white lady she started registering us as Democrats. It was something out of this world. We were some of the first. I was proud that I was able to vote.

SG: Who was Kelsey working for? Was he a supporter of Civil Rights?

TOMÁS: I don't know who he was working for, but he was never a supporter of civil rights. He was a very prejudiced guy, but he was the one who got us together and sent us down there to register. The Frogs were just a social club to start. It was later that they got political, when Vincente brought them into Martí-Maceo. Politicians used to come and make donations to Martí-Maceo. They would give it [dona-tions] to Vincente, and he in turn would get them to Martí-Maceo. It was mostly the young ones who voted. The older ones were not citi-zens. They did not disagree with it, except to protect the by-laws.

The bylaws forbade political discussions in Martí-Maceo, restricted the organization from endorsing candidates or taking a public stand on politi-cal issues. Valdés's activities challenged this clause, but the problem was evaded through the creation in 1951 of a separate *"club politico"* where candidates could come and meet with the members to explain their positions and help them decide whom to vote for (and funnel gratuities to the organization). Objections to this proposal were resolved by permitting political activity as long as it did not involve politics in Cuba.[4] This latter restriction would be severely tested in the years that followed.

The Cuban Revolution

Tampa's participation in Fidel Castro's rise to power in 1959 was different from the earlier mobilization of support for Cuban independence. The former exiles had become immigrants, whose children were becoming Americans. Prior forums of revolutionary activity—factories and clubs—had been transformed. But Castro invoked symbols that still fired the souls of Tampa's Cubans, and many were involved in supportive activities. All were keenly interested in what was going on, but there was less energy and more ambivalence.

Afro-Cubans in Tampa had reasons to be wary of Fidel, and they had reasons to be grateful to Fulgencio Batista, the dictator he ousted. During the insurrection, opinion among Martí-Maceo members was sharply divided. The minutes during the mid-to-late 1950s contain frequent notations invoking the by-law against political discussion. During this period, there are also several references to correspondence from the Cuban government, and two sizable gifts made possible by Batista that provided wherewithal to repair their aging building. There is no recorded mention of the visit of Fidel Castro in 1955, or about the disagreement that occurred between him and Juan Casellas, president of Martí-Maceo.

Batista's initial rise to power as part of the coup that ousted Machado in 1933 increased the influence of Afro-Cubans in the military. Through connections with a naval officer who visited Martí-Maceo in the late 1940s, they secured a promise of a substantial gift from the Cuban government that would be funded from lottery revenues. One of the members at the time recalled:

TOMÁS: We'd been trying to get the Cuban government to send us some money. They would send money to Círculo Cubano, but they won't send money to Martí-Maceo. So 'round Gasparilla [annual pre-lenten parade in Tampa] time—I remember that's around that time—there was an officer in, uh, the ship [from Cuba], and there was an officer in that ship that had good connections with Batista. So he visited Martí-Maceo, and he said, "I give you my word, Martí-

Maceo is going to get some money from the Cuban government so you can fix your building."

It took several years to materialize, but the officer made good on his promise. In 1948, the president of Martí-Maceo traveled to Cuba to receive the money. An article in the Cuban newspaper *Havana Lunes*[5] announced his arrival, explaining the history of the club and the gratitude owed to the members for preserving their heritage, as well as their need for help in repairing the building. The amount of the gift is not disclosed. According to another former president of the club it was supposed to have been between $20,000 and $30,000. Actual transfer of the money was delayed for more than two years, and then the final amount was only $5,000.[6] Although the original estimate may have been wildly optimistic, the discrepancy between what they were promised and what they got also reflected the corrupt state of affairs in Cuba.

> LUIS: What I think happened was that they assigned so many thousand dollars, but you know politics in Cuba. Everybody had to get. Every time the money moved from one channel to another, somebody dip in a little bit, get a little piece of bribe. "Everybody get[s] wet." That's what the Cuban people say.

Corruption had been endemic in Cuban politics for a long time, but conditions got even worse after Batista seized power again in a military coup in March 1952. He cultivated ties to Tampa on several levels, most profitably with the organized-crime syndicate headed by Santo Trafficante. Trafficante was the son of the victor in the *bolita* wars. He inherited a large illegal enterprise in Ybor City—gambling, vice, extortion, and murder for hire. Trafficante invested heavily in hotels and casinos in Havana. He and his rival, Meyer Lansky, collaborated with Batista in making Cuba a decadent playground for U.S. gangsters (Ragano and Raab 1994).

Fidel Castro's political debut occurred on July 26, 1953, when he and a small band of revolutionaries staged a hapless assault on the Moncada Army Barracks in Santiago de Cuba. Following his release from prison in 1955, he traveled to Tampa.[7] Tracing Martí's steps to the site of the Pedroso house, he began a relatively quiet campaign to build local support for a renewed effort to overthrow Batista. One of my narrators recalled his presence.

> TOMÁS: He would go around the street; he would stand on the corners and talk, and people would listen to him. Stayed about a month. . . . I

used to see him on Thirteenth Street and Seventh Avenue. He used to hang around there all the time. He wore civilian clothes.

An Afro-Cuban woman, who was fifteen at the time, was briefly involved romantically with one of the young guerrillas who was with Fidel.

RAQUEL: I don't exactly remember Castro, but I know the very exact place where he was, where that little park is, there was a house, the Pedroso house. I used to go there with my grandmother all the time, and that was the place where all of the revolutionists would come. As a matter of fact, I dated a revolutionist, a guy that was here from Cuba in exile because Batista was going to kill him. And he knew about all the revolutionary activities and what have you, but my father kinda kept me away from that, even though the guy I was seeing [was part of it]. He left. Castro came in at twelve o'clock [one night], and at six or eight o'clock the next day they were gone. Haven't heard from 'em anymore. But the meetings they would go to, I think my father would go with them and what have you, but I never got involved in that. My father wouldn't, well, you know that they kept the women, "This is not for you women." Women didn't get involved in all that. You cooked and you entertained, but you didn't get too much involved in the revolution. But I do remember them talking about Castro, and he came and he would be at meetings. That's what my friend was doing. They had a group of exiles that were here and they would have meetings with the black and white Cubans here.

Sometime during his visit, Castro asked permission to give a speech in the ballroom of the Martí-Maceo Society. One of the officers at the time recalled the encounter.

TOMÁS: When he visited Tampa, we still had our club. Martí-Maceo, the old building was still there. So he was looking for a place to talk against Batista. By the by-laws of the club, we recognized the government of Cuba, whatever government it was. That was the legal government, so we had to recognize it by the by-laws. And Castro was a rebel. He wanted to overthrow them. So we couldn't let him use the club to talk against the government. So, Juan Casellas, he was the president, told him, "No. You can't do that." So he [Castro] said, "Do you mean to tell me that a government like that"—and this and that—"and you're not going to let me talk?" And we told him, "No.

I mean we are not going to let you talk." He called us stupid and [we] didn't know what he was doing for Cuba, and this and that.

Círculo Cubano, whose by-laws contained a similar provision, reportedly also refused the use of their hall, but Castro was able to find an alternative location. A union hall on Seventh Avenue in Ybor City, the building that is presently occupied by the Martí-Maceo Society, furnished the venue for this speech. But he also needed a Cuban flag, so he returned to the president of Martí-Maceo and asked to borrow theirs.

> CASIMIRO: So then he asked Casellas [president] for the flag. Casellas denied him the flag too. He told him no, that Martí-Maceo recognized the government of Cuba and couldn't do that. So he got mad. He got hot about it. He went over to Casellas's house and argued with him on the porch. He called him all kinds of names and everything.

This early confrontation between Castro and the directors of the Martí-Maceo left uneasy feelings on the part of many. To berate and call them names, when they were only following the rules of the club, was considered rude and thuggish. Although Castro's behavior in this moment is telling, the games entailed in this transaction were somewhat more complex.

The legality of Batista's government, which came to power forcefully after preventing scheduled elections, could have been disputed (as Castro, in fact, pointed out to them). Their insistence on scrupulous adherence to the club's by-laws also could have been questioned, had Castro been aware of the "*club politico*," or of the fact that Juan Casellas was born in Puerto Rico, not Cuba, which was a violation of the by-laws' eligibility criteria for the office of president. Had there been consensus among the members that Castro should be allowed to speak, he might have prevailed in his requests. As it was, however, his presence involved unacceptable risks and trade-offs, for what at first seemed to many to be an unlikely, not to mention unmannerly, candidate for power.

> TOMÁS: He was an unknown. Even though in Cuba they had this dictator, Batista, but who was Castro? When Martí came to Tampa, he was known, but nobody knew who Castro was. Maybe somebody else better known would find some rally behind him, but he didn't have nobody. We didn't care for him. But look at him now. He's running the country.

The assertion that Castro had "nobody" is exaggerated. There were Afro-Cubans who supported him, and some did so actively. The father of the woman whose boyfriend was a Castroite exile was personally acquainted with Fidel and was an ardent supporter. There were other Afro-Cubans in Tampa who joined July 26th clubs, cells in the anti-Batista network that Castro was fashioning in the United States.

At the time all this occurred, Batista was running Cuba. Legitimacy was perhaps less important than power in weighing the costs of opposing him. Few admired him. They all knew he was a dictator, ruthless and crooked, but those were not unusual characteristics in Cuban politics. There was some genuine gratitude for the assistance they had received a few years earlier, a gift that was attributed to Batista's largess in spite of the fact that he was temporarily out of power when it arrived. Never before in all their supplications to the Cuban government had any aid actually been delivered. Moreover, Batista sought to cultivate further goodwill among the Afro-Cubans in Tampa by presenting them with a second, this time more generous, donation. In September 1956 the club received $9,600 from the Cuban government, a godsend in their fund-raising campaign to finish repairs on the building.[8] Batista, like Castro, looked to Tampa in search of political support, sought to cultivate the symbols of Martí and the insurrection of 1895. His gift to the Martí-Maceo Society coincided almost exactly with his announced plans to create a museum in Ruperto and Paulina Pedroso's old house in Ybor City. It was to be a monument to Martí, sited in honor of the Afro-Cuban friends who sheltered him (Scheinbaum 1976:3). This was also a site of major significance for the Afro-Cuban community.

In the nearly fifty years since the Pedrosos sold the property and returned to Cuba, the house had continued to serve as a boardinghouse, mostly inhabited by Afro-Cubans. Within the Afro-Cuban community it was a well-known historical location and was home to a number of the members of Martí-Maceo over the years. Some of the Pedroso relatives continued to live there even after it was sold in 1905.[9] By the late 1940s, however, it had fallen into disrepair.

A Cuban businessman visiting Tampa in 1951, on a tour sponsored by the Ybor City Rotary Club, saw the house and decided to buy it for its historic importance (Pizzo 1985; Westfall 1973). On September 10, 1956, he deeded the property to the Cuban government, and Batista announced his intention to establish a museum. Some months later, he sent $18,235 via the Cuban consul, Guillermo Bolívar, to pay for costs of restoring the house.[10] The house had since been damaged in a fire. The cause of the fire is unknown. Arson was a popular political weapon in Tampa, and it could have been the object of anti-Batista or antiblack action. More likely, however, it was set afire accidentally by an old Afro-Cuban everyone called Bigote because of his huge moustache. He was the last one to live there, served as a kind of caretaker for the owners. He was a colorful figure who drank too much. One of my informants speculated that he had probably knocked over a lantern and started a fire.

Although not completely destroyed, the building was considered beyond repair. Instead, the funds were used to level the structure and create a park on the site. The plan also included a life-sized statue of José Martí. Groundbreaking for the park occurred in April 1957, but several years would pass before it was completed. The statue was installed on February 28, 1960. By that time, Batista had fallen and Bolívar, the former consul, reportedly was reduced to working as a dishwasher in a Spanish restaurant in Ybor City. Bolívar had been well known to Martí-Maceo members. His unpleasant persona was one of the reasons many in the club opposed Batista.

> LUIS: The consul during Batista, named Guillermo Bolívar. He had something to do with killing of a lot of black Cubans. They say he was a real killer. He came from a rich family, from the Bacardi family. He told me, "If they had done what I told 'em to do, them bastards wouldn't have gotten in power." After Castro took over, well he didn't have a job. So the Columbia Restaurant, they give him a job as a dishwasher. He lost everything. He died poor.

The revolution in Cuba had a profound effect on Cubans in Tampa. The embargo and the influx of refugees brought many changes. The cutoff in shipments of Cuban tobacco resulted in large layoffs in Tampa's remaining cigar factories, a deathblow to the industry. Santo Trafficante, who had been confident he could control the new government in the same fashion he had worked with Batista, soon discovered he was wrong (Ragano and Raab 1994). Mobs of Cubans descended on the casinos, smashing and destroying hated symbols of corrupt U.S. influence. Trafficante was living in Cuba when the takeover occurred. Arrested and deported, he left behind all his lucrative holdings in Cuba.

Others from Tampa were sojourning in Cuba when the revolutionaries seized power. One Afro-Cuban man had gone to Havana for Christmas.

> TOMÁS: I went there on the twenty-fifth [of December]. Nineteen fifty-eight. I took my daughter. So we went on vacation and we got

caught in the revolution over there, that changeover. Drinking rum and having a good time, that New Year, I went to bed and in the middle of the night I could hear shooting and people in the street. In the morning I'm waiting and I look and [saw] people on the street running, and rifles, people with rifles. A big, big Russian flag. They got a Russian flag up as wide as the street. I called the United States embassy. They told me they had a convoy, leaving the National Hotel on the third, going to Key West.

When they arrived at the hotel, his young daughter was afraid to board the ship. Unable to calm her, they watched the boatload of refugee Americans leave without them.

TOMÁS: And then I couldn't leave. Couldn't leave, 'cause everything was closed. I went to the airport twice. The soldiers wouldn't let you leave. Couldn't get out of the country. While I was [waiting] at the airport, they used to bring in planes from the interior of the island, with prisoners, and they treat them like cattle. I never saw anything like it. He was already executing people, and he was bringing them from inside the island. And I was in the airport, sitting there watching all that going on. Then some old man, he say, he pointed at me, told the soldier there that I was, uh, the chauffeur for some man they were looking for. And this man was supposed to be bad, during Batista. So they say, "Yeah, that's him. That's him." The soldier came and arrested me. I told him I was an American. I went to get my passport, but he pointed the rifle. I was shaking. I say, "These people gonna shoot me."

His daughter recalled what happened next.

LARA: He was gonna shoot him [her father], and I started crying. I remember Daddy had his hands up and he said, "Well, let me show you my papers." And the guy said, "No." But I started crying and, you know, diverted his attention to me. And then Daddy was able to go into his pocket and show him his, uh, the paper that he was an American citizen. But they were gonna shoot him right there and then. No questions asked.

I asked him what effects the revolution had had on Cubans back in Tampa, what had been the reaction to Castro's victory and the arrival of the exiles.

TOMÁS: They had a little revolution here in Tampa. I mean, because then there was some that liked Cuba—I mean, Castro, and another part, they didn't like him. Then they started throwing stuff at the Círculo Cubano, they got bombarded with these light bulbs, big light bulbs they would put red paint on them. You heard about this?

I had heard about it, stories about red paint, and name-calling, and raucous assemblies at Círculo Cubano. According to a Círculo Cubano member who witnessed the disturbance and who was quoted at a later time, "They [recent exiles] wanted to take over the club."[11] The incumbents nevertheless maintained control of Círculo Cubano. The new exiles built their own club, which was called Club Cívico and was styled more as a country club than as an immigrant mutual aid society, out in the suburbs near the MacDill Air Base. An Afro-Cuban informant described the new club.

TOMÁS: They had a lot of professionals that came right after Castro, but instead of going to Círculo Cubano, they started Club Cívico, which was an exclusive club. I think the initial fee was five hundred dollars and so much a month. The majority of other Cubans couldn't afford it. I guess that's why they had to stay so high, so they form their own club over there, and be separated. You see the difference was, the other Cubans [cigarmakers], they united and became all Cubans. There was no classes. Doctors belonged to the same community. The Cubans that came now had class, were professionals, so they won't belong to a club with cigarmakers.

An estimated ten thousand Cuban exiles settled in Tampa in the immediate aftermath of Castro's victory.[12] Although most were not wealthy professionals, virtually all were white, and they were highly unified in their opposition to the new government in Cuba. Suddenly outnumbered by newcomers with radically different views, many Tampa Cubans were initially drawn into an intense struggle. One of the exiles who arrived in 1961 recalled the conflict: "The tobacco workers were very active, very liberal, very strong-willed people. And when we arrived in Tampa, there was still a July 26 office (representing Castro's revolutionary movement) in the El Pasaje Hotel in Ybor City. They had an image of the revolutionaries as Robin Hoods who had romantic ideals. . . . When we arrived here we were (considered) the dregs of society, the *Batistianos*."[13]

Even Tampeños who had not actively supported the revolution were inclined to sympathize with its goals. In March 1959, Martí-Maceo voted to send a $25 donation to the new government.[14] It was noted in the minutes that other organizations from Tampa were also sending funds. Perhaps more significantly, in the following year a member offered a resolution supporting agrarian reform.[15] As Castro consolidated and articulated his position, as he became legitimized as the leader of Cuba, many Cubans in Tampa embraced the promises of the revolution. At the same time, the growing hostility of the U.S. government, the enduring anti-Communist sentiments of the local Anglo establishment, and the growing swell of outspoken anti-Castro exiles created a volatile climate within Ybor City. A later article in the *Tampa Tribune* described this period.

> As Castro's revolution swung left, some Tampa Cubans renounced their citizenship and went to live in the new Cuba. Others muted their support for Castro's revolution. But it was not quick enough for the new arrivals. There were some scuffles, some rocks thrown, some paint splattered, even some shots fired. The opposing camps took to removing each other's floral tributes at the Ybor City statue of Jose Marti, the 19th century liberator of Cuba. It became known as the "war of the roses" with the anti-Castro exiles vying to keep the traditional bouquets of white roses on display and the pro-Castro faction trying to replace them with red roses of revolution.[16]

Nowhere was the struggle between factions more overt than between the exiles and the group that called itself the July 26th Movement. Then, as now, pro- and anti-Castro Cubans ardently contested ownership of the celestial persona of José Martí. The statue in the park, however, was also the context for the first falling out between Tampa Cubans who supported Castro and his new revolutionary government.

The July 26th Movement in Tampa was part of a network of groups that Fidel had organized in the United States during his trip in 1955 (Paterson 1994:15; Pérez 1997:217). The leader in Tampa was Victoriano Mantiega, prominent editor of *La Gaceta*, Ybor City's leading immigrant newspaper (still in publication in 2001). During the revolution, they had mobilized various kinds of assistance. In the aftermath of victory, they raised funds to erect the stalled monument to José Martí. The park that had been planned for the site of the Pedroso house was finally completed in early 1960. Its dedication in late February turned into a microdrama of unfolding opinion about the new government in Cuba, which was still the legal owner of the property.

White roses were planted at the base of the statue, inspired by a passage from one of Martí's poems. The July 26th group planned an official unveiling on February 24, 1960, marking the anniversary of Martí's declaration of war against Spain in 1895—a war launched by orders concealed in a cigar that had been made in Tampa. Castro's newly appointed consul in Tampa, however, was unmoved by the symbolism and found that particular day to be inconvenient. The president of Tampa's July 26th group described the exchange that ensued in a newspaper article that appeared a few days later.

> The Cuban consul came to us and asked for the keys. So, because the park is Cuban property, we gave him the keys. So, the Cuban consul moves the dedication date up to the 28th. That day means nothing to us and means nothing to Cuba. The Cuban consul went ahead and held the dedication on Sunday [the 28th], but did he talk about José Martí? No, he talked about himself and his family. The Cuban consul told us that the 26th of July movement means nothing in Cuba and that he intends to abolish the movement here in Tampa. We have complained to the Cuban government but this is a little matter and they have bigger problems in Cuba. The Cuban consul doesn't like us and we don't like him. When Martí was here years ago, he told us how he loved white roses. The white roses we planted here [in the park] are gone. So, on the 24th of February [1960] members of our movement held a little ceremony on the sidewalk outside the park because we did not want to break the chain [around the gate]. Our ceremony was held with the white roses Martí loved. But in the park you do not find white roses—only the statue of Martí.[17]

Also missing from the invocation of symbols surrounding the park was the significance of Ruperto and Paulina, and the Martí-Maceo Society, whose origins traced to the site. Issues of race played strangely in the local rhetoric of revolution and counterrevolution, created a nettle of problems for Afro-Cuban inclusion that made them wary of all sides. Batistianos and Fidelistas were both perceived as having used race as a lever to advance their positions and were little trusted because of it.

> TOMÁS: Ones that left [exiles of 1959] were white. And they would talk about race. That was one of the issues. They would go out in the open and say that, uh, this man, Castro, liked the black people, "Negro this and Negro that." But then, the Castro supporters, I remember one time, a bunch of Cubans talking about Castro, and [they said], "He's a Negro," you know, Batista, the "Negro Batista." So they were using, uh, color as one of the propaganda [weapons] against Batista.

These contending vilifications, countercharges of excessive sympathy for Afro-Cubans, helped estrange black Cubans from the conflict. And they were pretty much ignored by both sides. None of the exiles had sought to take over Martí-Maceo, nor were Afro-Cubans welcome to join the new Club Cívico even if they had been able to afford it. The revolution in Cuba marginalized Afro-Cubans in Tampa even further, blocked contact with friends and relatives on the island, and resulted in an embargo on Cuban tobacco that killed the cigar industry in Ybor City.

Revolution at Home

Further complicating the role of Afro-Cubans in post-Castro Tampa was the escalating confrontation being waged in lunch counters and other public facilities, where organized groups of black teenagers sat down in forbidden places. These events were engaging the attention of Afro-Cubans as much as the developments in Cuba. Indeed, these maneuvers were of arguably greater consequence and represented actions in which they were more central participants.

On February 29, 1960, the day after the Cuban consul hijacked the dedication of Martí Park, the first Tampa sit-in occurred at the lunch counter of the downtown Woolworth store (Lawson 1982). Afro-Cubans accounted for at least two of the fifty-seven students who joined this gathering and seated themselves amid curses and threats. One was the young woman quoted earlier whose father, himself a participant in the July 26th Movement, was of the opinion that women should not "get too much involved in the revolution."

Many Afro-Cubans her age, and some who were older, followed their parents' example rather than their advice. She was also influenced by her classmates and teachers, and by the ubiquitous media coverage of incidents in Alabama, Mississippi, North Carolina, and Arkansas.

> RAQUEL: I remember there was a buzz in the school. You know, Martin Luther King and all this, Selma, Alabama, and everything was on television. . . . This was unheard of. The Student Nonviolent Coordinating Committee [gave instructions before the sit-in]. Everybody said, "Whenever you go, don't say anything. Just stay very organized, very quietly organized. We're walking in a line and everybody is meeting downtown. And they want as many people as possible to go down [there]." I thought, "Oh, God, what would happen if we go to jail?" I said, "My mother'll kill me." She didn't find out about it

until the next day—no, I think she found out about it that night, 'cause I was on television. Once we got downtown, we were right on the corner of Franklin and Cass, where you go through from Cass Street bridge, on through there. We all gathered there, and then this herd of people, walking silently and very orderly, conducted themselves very gentlemanly and ladylike, and we just walked, and then we went and we sat down. . . .

They were calling you all kinds of niggers, "Nigger this" and "Nigger that." And the whites were all mobbed. They had like the counters and some were sitting in the booths. All these white people were just lined up behind us, but there was an aisle. But then we just looked [forward] and we didn't say anything. . . . And then the [white] man that was sitting behind me, he had this blackjack. I do remember this blackjack. I had never seen anything [like that] before in my life. And it was shaped like, a thin thing to hold it here, kinda fat here and then coming down like that and his hand was here, and this heavy thing. You could just hear it slapping in his hand. But that was it. Then it was orderly, there was no fighting, no tussling, other than this incident that I had my hands like at the counter, and this lady comes and brings this [Closed] sign, she came and put one right in my face. Then I said, "You're not gonna put this in front of my face." She said, "Well, this counter is closed." I said, "Well, we're sitting here and we're not going anywhere."

The sit-in was part of a strategy coordinated in Tampa by the NAACP. The local leadership included Francisco Rodríguez, son of an activist cigarmaker, Marine veteran of World War II, former teacher in Tampa's black schools, and graduate of Howard Law School. He provided legal advice on avoiding arrest in direct action protests, arranged bail when arrests were made anyway, and traveled throughout the state defending blacks accused in criminal cases with racial implications. For Afro-Cubans in Tampa, he came to symbolize the transition from the politics of patria to the politics of black liberation. Within his family, and within the Afro-Cuban community, this change was not without controversy.

Francisco Rodríguez Sr. was a proud man, highly respected for his eloquence and intelligence. His visibility during the cigarmakers' strike of 1931 caused the whole family to have to leave town in the aftermath. His children, who were then entering college, were well exposed to rebellion and its consequences. As teachers during the 1942 lawsuit for better pay, they had not been directly involved, but were benefited by the outcome. Francisco Jr.'s first teaching assignment had been in Fort Pierce, Florida, a small town on the east coast not far from where Harry T. Moore lived and died. His unhappy experiences in Fort Pierce, followed by a sojourn in Asia during World War II, left him unsatisfied with the teaching profession and the limitations he confronted as a black man in the South. When he returned from the war, he determined to play a more active role in changing those conditions.

> FRANCISCO RODRÍGUEZ: After I was discharged, I came back [to Tampa]. I was so disappointed at finding things had not changed one iota that I just resigned my teaching job and went back to school. I left the profession completely and went over to Washington to school. I spent three years at Howard University and I got a law degree there.

At Howard, he gained direct exposure to the legal campaign to overturn Jim Crow that was being orchestrated by Charles Hamilton Houston and his young protégé Thurgood Marshall (Tushnet 1987).

When Rodríguez returned to Tampa in 1950, he was part of that movement. His own family was very disapproving. They were worried about the dangers and convinced that he could not succeed against such heavy opposition. His father was a rebel, known for his impassioned oratory and uncompromising views on social justice. But his father's passion was for Cuba; he had little interest in trying to change the United States. His older sister Myrtle, an unusually outspoken woman, had been the one who introduced young Francisco to the history of black struggle in the United States. He recalled the moment.

> F. RODRÍGUEZ: I think I was in the fourth grade and we had something called "Legal History Week." And my sister prepared a paper for me to present. I could almost [recite] it [from] memory, and in it she showed where there were black people who had achieved certain things, and she listed the people and what have you. And that, that was one of the turning points in my life.

Nevertheless, she, her father, and the other members of his family viewed his decision as reckless and frightening.

Others in the Afro-Cuban community were also skeptical about his activities and were concerned that he might bring problems to all of them. African Americans worried about the same thing, about this upstart Cuban who was stirring up trouble. His African American mother-in-law asked her daughter to try and make him stop. Mrs. Rodríguez recalled her husband's reaction.

BEATRICE RODRÍGUEZ: My mother, she would just say to me, "What's he doing? Because it's going to be dangerous for him. Why is he causing trouble?" I'd say [to him], "My mother says that you are causing trouble." He said, "Well, I hate to hurt your feelings, and your mother is the same as my mother. And your mother, my mother, nobody's mother will change my attitude." I would say to him, "I'm very scared." He said, "Well, isn't it better to die for something you believe in, than to sit back and do nothing?"

Being unafraid to die was the key to defeating Jim Crow. Black life was cheap in Florida at that time, although no less dear to black people and those who loved them. As the white citizen at the Jacksonville courthouse had explained to the would-be black voter, these were matters that could get you easily killed. Rodríguez, and Harry T. Moore, and Robert Saunders, the West Tampa native who succeeded Moore after his assassination, and countless others who challenged the system in court and in the streets, waged a high-stakes battle in which bravery was one of their only weapons. Although there were many, in both the Afro-Cuban and African American communities, who criticized Civil Rights movement leaders for endangering them and their children, a growing number admired their courage and took hope from their determination. For many older Afro-Cubans, Rodríguez exhibited a manly defiance worthy of Maceo. For those who were younger he was their link to a national movement, and to a global upheaval that included the rebellion in Cuba. An Afro-Cuban in the middle of this spectrum, a man who had been in his forties at the time, described his own feelings about Rodríguez's contributions.

TOMÁS: Oh, we loved him. We admired him for what he did. He's a man that we owe a lot. The blacks and the black Cubans owe him a lot. He's a very intelligent man, and I don't think he got the recognition of this city. When the rest of the blacks were afraid to speak and face the KKK and them people, he used to get in his car by himself, and he would drive off to North Florida, Georgia, all them places, fighting for the right of the black in the court. While he was in the court he was protected, but when he got in the car coming back there was no telling what could happen to him. He always was in front fighting for the right of the black. Every time I see him, I respect him for what he's done.

In Cuba, a dictator was toppled, and in Florida Jim Crow was over-turned. The revolution in Cuba and the defeat of segregation and disen-franchisement in Florida were both deceptively easy to achieve and dog-gedly difficult to effect. But in the glow of the 1960s the Afro-Cubans in Tampa stood at the intersection of remarkable circumstances.

The sit-ins that Rodríguez helped to organize, and Afro-Cuban stu-dents helped to conduct, resulted in sweeping changes in public accommo-dations. The Tampa business establishment sought to avoid the bad public-ity being visited on St. Augustine and Jacksonville, where white resistance had turned violent. Even in Tampa, shots were fired into the home of the Reverend Mr. A. Leon Lowry of the St. Paul AME Church. Lowry was another organizer of the Tampa sit-ins. His church hosted some of the meetings where the students received their instructions. The attack on his home inspired a compromise known as the "Tampa Technique" (Lawson 1982:267). National chain stores, under pressure from home offices, agreed to an orchestrated plan worked out by the Civil Rights movement leader-ship and the city's "biracial committee." In September 1960, some six months after the assault on Lowry's house, selected blacks entered lunch counters, sat down, ordered food, and were served. Thereafter, these facili-ties were no longer segregated. Other establishments slowly followed suit, collectively resolving their dilemma of choosing between black and white customers, expanding their own market without losing anything.

This easy victory did not solve all the problems. Some facilities, such as movie theaters, held off for a few more years and were the sites of addi-tional picketing before they were finally integrated (Lawson 1979). Al-though beaches and parks were nominally integrated, they remained dan-gerous to blacks who tried to use them. A woman recalled one such perilous encounter.

> MARÍA: The beach had been integrated for some time, maybe two or three years. So this time we were out there swimming and all of a sudden we saw all these crackers with black glasses on surrounding us, you know. We did not know what was going on. And when they got up right close, and they said, "Get out of here. We are talking to you. Get out of here, you get on the other side of the bridge, you do not belong down here." [A Spanish friend went and got the police.] The cops came right away and they wanted to know what was wrong, and these crackers were standing all around. They [the police] said, "Listen, this is their beach as much as it is your beach and you are not going to bother them. If you do, you go to jail, we will see that you go

to jail." [The police left.] So we went back in there and they [the white men with the black glasses] started again. It was just R—— and I. Those son of a guns would have drowned the two of us. I told R——, I said, "Honey let's get out of here." I said, "We have worked too hard for what little bit we have to let these son of a guns come in here and drown us, and that is what they will do." So we got out. I hate black glasses today. I cannot stand them.

He was very dark, and she was very light, which is possibly the reason they were targeted for harassment. Both held full-time jobs during the day and worked nights as musicians in the Floridano Sexteto, a well-known Afro-Cuban band. With their savings they had managed to buy a small hotel in Ybor City that catered to Afro-Cuban musicians traveling through Tampa. They survived the threat of the villains in black glasses, but soon after their hotel was destroyed by another, more insidious foe.

Urban Removal

A truism of urban economics is that neighborhoods like Ybor City cannot last; like life itself, they are born to die (Downs 1982). Like most truisms, this one is manifestly pernicious, designed to cover up and naturalize a constructed history of power and greed.

June 16, 1965: it was sunny and hot. By mid-morning a handful of people had gathered on the sidewalk across the street from Martí-Maceo. Looking south from where they stood, the landscape was bare and littered with rubble. They waited on the curb, not saying much to each other. There was little left to say. For nearly five years they had been expecting this day, had been debating and worrying, and trying to find another place to go.

Alongside the turbulent aftermath of the Cuban Revolution and the Civil Rights demonstrations, members of the Martí-Maceo Society had confronted the growing certainty that they were going to lose the building. The man from Urban Renewal had first visited them on May 11, 1960, less than three months after the Martí Park dedication and the sit-in at Woolworth's, and only a few short years since Batista's money seemingly had rescued the sagging structure. In spite of these recent repairs, city building inspectors began showing up and discovering various code violations, which mandated repairs they could not afford. These citations were designed to soften them up, to create financial burdens and cheapen the value of their property. In October 1962, Urban Renewal made them an offer, a very low offer that they refused. The following month, the alcohol inspector stopped in to inform them that their license had been suspended. And there were more inspectors, and finally the ultimatum of eminent domain. Francisco Rodríguez Jr. was their lawyer, but he could not help them. An Ybor City insider might have won them some concessions, although probably not, but Francisco was especially unpopular with the local power structure. In addition, the benefit system was collapsing. They could no longer pay all the costs of sick pay or operations, and their bill to Dr. Gonzalez's clinic had fallen hopelessly in arrears. In late 1963, they tried to mortgage the building in order to pay debts and make repairs. Their application was turned down. Early the next year, they gave up and formed a committee to look for another location. The banks, the city, and Urban Renewal were in collusion to force them to move and Martí-Maceo was powerless to prevent it.

> TOMÁS: So, they didn't have to negotiate with you, because they could close you down anyway. . . . No negotiation. They told us don't try to negotiate because you might get less. So that's what they told us, take it or leave it. If you didn't take it, they would condemn the building. So we decided there was nothing else we could do.

On the day the old building was torn down, most were reconciled to its loss. It was a weekday, and only a few came to watch.

The wrecking crew arrived around ten o'clock and began removing the iron work and other salvageable materials. The wreckers did not say much either; just doing their jobs, not really happy about it, but what could anyone do? Then they brought in the bulldozer to demolish in a few hours the edifice that had been "the center of our home" for three generations of Afro-Cubans in Tampa. The walls of the patio buckled, the dance floor splintered apart, sunny scenes of Cuba collapsed into rubble and dust. All they could do was watch.

> TOMÁS: I went there with my father. We had this man in the club, Luis Oxamendi, he cried. You know, when the wrecking came, he knelt down on the sidewalk and started praying and crying. Because they were tearing down Martí-Maceo. We loved that place, the only thing we had. That's all we had.

Oxamendi was one of the old-timers. He had joined Martí-Maceo in 1910, when he was nineteen. Too young to have fought for independence, but old enough to remember it, he represented the generation who built the club. Tall and straight, with an air of rectitude that people associated with the

"real Cubans," he had cut a handsome figure on the dance floor, perform-
ing the *danzon* with studied elegance, a white kerchief in his arched left
hand. On this sad occasion, his composure wilted as emotions overcame
him.

Martí-Maceo was demolished along with hundreds of other buildings
in Ybor City. The African American neighborhoods to the south were also
flattened. Interstate 75 (later 275) came through in the same period, sliced
Ybor City in half and dropped a spur that cleared a wide path adjacent to
the Central Avenue district. A few years later, in 1974, Central Avenue
itself was demolished and cleared.

This massive destruction was the final unraveling of a scheme that began in the years immediately following World War II—a local episode in a
complex process that was unfolding in cities throughout the United States.
In Tampa this process began in the Scrub. Tampa's oldest, largest, most
congested, and most squalid black neighborhood was a logical target for
federally subsidized slum clearance that got under way in the late 1940s.
Even earlier, white elites had nurtured a plan to move black people off of
this site. When Benjamin Mays first arrived in 1926, Tampa business leaders (including a familiar actor, the editor–mayor–vigilante kidnapper D. B.
McKay) sought his help in doing this. They offered an unctuous proposi-
tion Mays recalled in his memoirs.

> With my appointment to the office as the executive secretary of the
> Tampa Urban League, I automatically assumed the role of spokesper-
> son for my community. It was taken for granted that I would follow
> in the footsteps of my predecessor, Mrs. Blanche Armwood Beatty, an
> able woman, whose leadership was accepted by both Negroes and
> whites. Mrs. Beatty had endorsed a subdivision for Negroes so de-
> signed that in time all Negroes would live within its confines, with
> none in the other seven sections of Tampa. Lots were to be sold,
> houses built, streets paved, lights provided, sewerage put in, police
> protection given, and transportation installed. Soon after Sadie and I
> assumed our duties at the League, a delegation of white men called to
> get my approval for the subdivision. They extolled all the advantages
> of the new site for Negroes; reminded me that not only my predeces-
> sor but also the leading white people so thoroughly approved of it
> that they had promised to provide all facilities to make it a most
> desirable subdivision; and, finally, *told me that I was to have, free,
> two spacious lots of my own choosing* [emphasis added]. A meeting
> was set up for me, city officials, the executive secretary of the Tampa

Welfare League and Community Chest, and owners of the subdivision—a dozen or more white persons and one lone Negro.

Rightly skeptical, he put them off and went to confer with leaders of the black community.

> At the next meeting, I was accompanied by a dozen Negroes—all property owners, all property tax payers. One Negro, Doctor M. J. Anderson was paying $2000 a year in taxes, which represented a considerable sum in 1926. These men made it clear that the idea of the subdivision was highly undesirable, impracticable, unwise and unsafe for Negroes; that the facilities would be too long being provided; that in case of racial conflict Negroes could be located and abused too easily for comfort. Happily, the "ideal" relocation plan for Negroes was abandoned. (Mays 1971:111–12)

Well, not exactly abandoned, only deferred.

Urban Renewal provided, at last, an efficient and lucrative mechanism for accomplishing "Negro removal." The Scrub was not the only neighborhood targeted for this treatment. Ybor City, with its growing number of black residents, was also included. Whereas demolition in the Scrub and Central Avenue was designed for total clearance, the plan for Ybor City was more surgical. The business district and other valued structures would be saved, and a large swath of empty land would be created by demolishing the neighborhoods that ringed the district. The goal was not to destroy Ybor City, but rather to control and transform it. The old days were gone. Change was inevitable.

Tony Pizzo, an Italian American civic leader—the same man who had arranged the sale of the Pedroso house to the Cuban businessman and who had helped locate the dance flooring for the Martí-Maceo patio—recalled in a published interview the beliefs and circumstances that motivated his own involvement in this process.

> After the war the economy began to prosper, and the younger Latins, better educated and prepared for life, began to look towards new horizons. Then something happened in the early 1950s that started the downfall of Ybor City as we knew it, the colorful colony of Spaniards, Cubans, and Italians. Near the downtown area there existed a small area known as the "Scrub." That area is the site of today's Central Park Village, a housing project occupied by blacks. The "Scrub" was a world of its own. No one ventured into that quarter. Only the people

who lived there frequented the place. There were no paved streets. The houses were placed at random—thrown together in an incomprehensible maze. The frame houses dated back to the 1880s; they were weather beaten, shabby, and literally uninhabitable. It was probably the worst slum area in the state . . . a frightful place forgotten by time. . . . When a movement was starting for the clearing of the "Scrub," I remember Curtis Hixon, then mayor, telling me while [we were] flying to Havana, "we must do something to better the living conditions of our black people." (Pizzo 1985:144)

Although professing charitable motives, Mayor Hixon had much to gain from this effort, both directly and under the table. The Housing Act of 1949 provided cities with unprecedented levels of funding for slum clearance, money that flowed into his jurisdiction providing jobs, tangible evidence of progress under his leadership, and large sums that could be bundled in contracts to grateful friends. The act was far less generous in providing for replacement housing, and the problem of relocating displaced residents was sorely neglected (Anderson 1964; Pagano and Bowman 1995). Pizzo continues:

So when these people were displaced, where were they to go? Ybor City was the logical area. Many of the Latins were beginning to build new homes in other areas. Real estate agents grasped a golden opportunity and began selling Ybor City houses to the blacks who had nowhere to go. These agents gouged the black man, selling houses for more than double their worth. Many of the Ybor City houses were very old and in dire need of repair. The Latin section was classified as a blighted area. Many of the younger Latins had become Americanized—had been to war and were educated. They began to leave—it wasn't that they didn't like Ybor City—it was a question of economy. . . . And this is what was happening. The real estate people went to the blacks who were selling their houses [in the Scrub] to the federal government, and induced them to buy old houses in Ybor City. The old Ybor City dwellings were selling for $7,000 to $10,000—houses that weren't worth $1500. (Pizzo 1985:145)

Secondary profits accrued to real estate brokers who capitalized handsomely on the restricted choices of displaced black families. Mayor Hixon's contention that he wanted to "better the living conditions of *our* black people" was disingenuous as well as patronizing. Even in retrospect, in an interview conducted more than thirty years later, Pizzo appears to have been oblivious to these inconsistencies.

Tony Pizzo was no idle observer of these events, but rather an astute player whose special talents were in marketing heritage. A brief bio that accompanied his published interview (Pizzo 1985) relates that: "To promote and popularize the past, he became founder and first president of the Tampa Historical Society, the Ybor City Rotary Club, and the Pan American commission. A grateful city named him Outstanding Citizen in 1956" (Pizzo 1985:142). Pizzo had launched this career in early efforts to capture the large tourism business that then flowed from Cuba to Miami. He and his associates had reasoned that Tampa's historic connection to Cuban independence should offer sentimental advantages in attracting wealthy Cubans to Tampa instead. His interest in history was sparked by the initial research he did for a series of historical markers to be placed in various locations around Ybor City. He became an avid local historian and quintessential booster, venerated in life and memorialized in death, with a bronze statue in Ybor City and an elementary school named for him on the campus of the University of South Florida.

Pizzo was born into a Sicilian immigrant family in Ybor City. His parents operated a grocery store. He served in the army in World War II and was among the first Latin veterans to move into the exclusive Davis Island subdivision south of downtown Tampa. The story about the second generation departing but never losing affection for Ybor City was his story. It was a description that fit a great many white Latins of his era, individuals whose continuing interests in Ybor City combined nostalgia with real estate, commerce, and politics. These threads converged in the plans that were formulated to bring Urban Renewal to Tampa. In what is a little-appreciated irony, the man who would become most associated with historic preservation in Ybor City was the prime author of the rationale to destroy it. His account of this process continues:

> Well, actually to go in sequence, after the blacks moved to Ybor City the Federal Urban Renewal Act was passed. Florida could not take advantage of this legislation because a state court decision declared the act unconstitutional. Daytona Beach had instituted a test case, but the lower court ruled against her. The City of Tampa decided to test the constitutionality of the act before the State Supreme Court. . . . The main thrust of the petition was to show the importance in preserving and redeveloping the historic aspect of the area. Milo Smith [city planner] asked me if I could prepare an historical map showing

the historic sites, events, and buildings in Ybor City. I still have this "historic" map.[18] Because of the dynamic history of Ybor City the Supreme Court decided in [our] favor. . . . Ybor City made it possible for cities in Florida to participate in the use of Urban Renewal funds. (Pizzo 1985:146)

History provided a fig leaf, an argument that defeated the legal objections and enabled Florida cities to carry out this project, the main effect of which was the destruction of history.

Unimagined sums, $10 million or more in Urban Renewal funds alone, were available to acquire properties in Ybor City and what was left of the residential sections surrounding Central Avenue. Pizzo and his associates in the Ybor City Rotary Club discovered that they could not control the process once it got under way.

They tore down buildings because it was to their advantage. The more buildings they tore down, I imagine, the more money they were able to get. They wanted to prolong the project. On the local level a lot of people had no feeling for our city. They were actually, in my book, unconcerned about the community's welfare. They conducted the business of the bureaucracy, without feeling for the history or the future of our community. (1985:148)

The "they" is meant to refer to faceless bureaucrats, but many who profited from Urban Renewal were home guys, Latin politicians from Ybor City and some of the larger business owners in the area. Pizzo and others in this group were genuinely dismayed at the ugly destruction that transpired, the vast empty tracts and the broken hearts of those who lost their homes.

Even more tragic from their perspective, the big plans to restore the commercial vitality of Ybor City and transform it into a profitable "Latin Quarter," to remove the blighted black-occupied housing that handicapped their efforts, came to naught. They had lost their potential Cuban tourists to Fidel's revolution. And they failed to remove all the black people from Ybor City. Banks and insurance companies—the critical investors and underwriters of the new development that would be needed—red-lined the whole area and reneged on their earlier promises (Greenbaum 1990; Kerstein 1997).

Although some of the structures on Pizzo's "historic map" were demolished, the central core of commercial buildings on Seventh and Eighth Avenues were left intact. With the exception of Martí-Maceo, all the mutual aid societies were preserved. Houses and the people who lived in them were the main casualties of Urban Renewal in Ybor City. Elderly Latins and African Americans were displaced, including many Afro-Cubans. These dislocations produced hardships and stress, widespread afflictions that were documented in most cities where neighborhoods were destroyed by Urban Renewal (Hartman 1967).

Displaced residents had been promised that new houses would be built in the neighborhood, so they could move back and restore their lives. Such promises were official mendacity. Instead, the city conveyed a large, fifty-one-acre tract of vacant land to the newly constructed Hillsborough Community College, against the advice of consultants who correctly predicted that the school would not draw sufficient enrollment (Kerstein 1997). The consultants failed to understand the real purpose, which was to bank the land in order to prevent construction of housing. Then (and present) Mayor Dick Greco, born and raised in Ybor City, explained this in a later interview: "We just didn't want it [Ybor City] filled up with low cost housing. HCC serves as a catalyst in preserving a bit of our history that probably wouldn't be there if it weren't for that campus."[19] The apparent goal was to establish a sterile zone around what was left of the Ybor City commercial district. Under this plan, preserving Ybor City rested on preventing black occupancy, even if it meant that no one would live there. They would discover, however, that they were steering an unruly and ultimately unmanageable project.

In the process that came to be known as "Negro removal," implementers of the plan failed to account for the relocation of such large numbers of people. The Urban Renewal program did not really reckon this crucial part of the process, and the local planners did not worry about it either. They had a vague notion, heir to an earlier plan, that they could move most of the African Americans who had lived in the Scrub and Ybor City out to some distant location. Progress Village, a complex that had been built in eastern Hillsborough County, was the intended destination.[20] Completed in 1959, a joint effort of some of the African American leadership and local white businessmen and politicians, this project failed to absorb more than a small fraction of the displaced families. The cautionary warnings of earlier black leaders who advised Benjamin Mays were borne out in the experiences of Progress Village. Construction delays, failed promises about transportation and infrastructure, and hostile neighbors (this section of the county was dense in Klan members) contributed to the unattractiveness of the new neighborhood. It was also sited next to a phosphate mine, whose stack of mildly radioactive slag grew by degree into a mountain that looms over the playground of the Progress Village school—unsightly and a threat to the health of children.[21]

Strong opposition by the NAACP was another reason that Progress Village did not attract large interest. In addition to reasoned skepticism about how the project would be carried out, the NAACP opposed segregated housing on principle, and the organization refused to support the project.[22] The NAACP was also justly wary about Urban Renewal. Bob Saunders, the local field director, wrote a series of letters to both local and federal officials attempting to ensure that African Americans and their interests were represented in the process. The decision-making bodies for Urban Renewal in Tampa were composed entirely of whites, but the people affected by the program were overwhelmingly black. Local officials ignored NAACP complaints until federal pressure made them take notice. Forced to be inclusive, they resorted to co-optation.

Reminiscent of the promises made to Mays, the select African Americans who were appointed to the new "biracial advisory committee" were offered land in exchange for cooperation. The land was not in the outlying areas, however; it was in the Urban Renewal zone. A large, sixty-one-acre tract south of Seventh Avenue, including the site of the Martí-Maceo Society, was designated for development by a group of African Americans, including members of the biracial committee. At the same moment that distraught members were watching the demolition of Martí-Maceo's building and patio, a handful of their black neighbors from Central Avenue were contemplating profits they hoped to earn by its absence from the landscape.

This group included the president of the Longshoremen's Union and the owner and editor of the *Sentinel Bulletin*, the only black newspaper in Tampa. The more militant *Bulletin* had been taken over by the *Sentinel* not long after the death of the Reverend Marcellus Potter and his wife (Shofner 1983). Potter's will divided the paper and printing business he owned evenly among the NAACP, the Urban League, and the employees, who were charged with running it collectively. It was an idealistic legacy that failed in part because of the fragmented management. The newly created *Sentinel Bulletin* was linked to a burial society, known as the Lily White Security and Benefit, a family business started in the 1920s by the new owner's father. It was a breakaway from the larger older Grand Pallbearers Union (Ergood 1971). Subscribers were encouraged to join the society, and policyholders were encouraged to buy the paper. Although termed a lodge, it was actually a capitalist enterprise that competed with the Grand Pallbearers Union. The GPU, which was both nonprofit and involved with Civil Rights activism, had also been aligned with the *Bulletin*. By 1965, when the Urban Renewal deals were under way, Lily White was the largest black benefit society in Florida, with twenty-five thousand members statewide (Ergood 1971:26). It offered burial policies for premiums of $20 per year, payable at death in a lump sum amount of $350. Pure profit accrued after seventeen years, but even more profitable were policyholders who allowed payments to lapse and forfeited all they had contributed.

The contrast between the Lily White organization and the Martí-Maceo Society, the irony of assigning their dispossessed property to such an avowedly capitalist outfit, is noteworthy. I could not determine the origin of the unusual name "Lily White," although it seems to have been chosen to signify honesty and stainless virtue, perhaps intended to counteract the negative attention such burial plans attracted from race leaders like W. E. B. Du Bois (Weare 1993:17).

The Lily White investment group built 370 units of subsidized low-income housing on the site.[23] The residents were all black. This very large subdivision, situated between Ybor City and downtown, posed an obstacle to joining the two areas into a redevelopment zone. In the fringe neighborhoods just beyond the boundaries of the Urban Renewal zone, parts of old Ybor City where housing had been spared, occupancy soon became nearly all black. The Ybor City commercial district emerged from this process as an isolated island, ringed with empty lots and surrounded on all sides by black neighborhoods.

A group of Latin business owners in 1967 proposed making Ybor into a walled city, literally shielding the remaining commercial district from its nearby neighbors.[24] This idea was never carried out. It was too draconian and not really feasible. Civil Rights laws made such racial gatekeeping illegal. But for the next three decades (and continuing still) white Latins who own property or businesses, or who are involved with the social clubs, have struggled to project a mythologized image of Ybor City as it used to be, as a predominantly white immigrant neighborhood, part of the saga of the melting pot.

The Afro-Cubans, despite their long history of involvement in the neighborhood, were uncongenial for this image-making. The other Latin clubs in Ybor City had rallied in support of the Martí-Maceo patio project in the early 1940s, but when Urban Renewal arrived, the Afro-Cubans were friendless. The racist economics of urban real estate sorted black and white immigrants from each other even more effectively than Jim Crow.

Revival

For members of the Martí-Maceo Society, the loss of the building was the nadir, but it was not the end. By the time the structure was demolished, they had found a new location. This had not been an easy process. Imminent loss of the building had forced the members to confront the obvious realities of their situation. Pessimists argued that they would never again be able to maintain a building. Instead they favored banking the settlement funds and renting only a small office where the records could be maintained and necessary business transacted. The club would continue, but in name only. Their arguments were not without logic. There were not enough members to host social events, and renting the hall, an arrangement no longer protected by Jim Crow, could not be expected to produce sufficient revenue to pay the bills. The medical benefits had shrunk to token payments, meager supplements to the members' private insurance or public assistance. The old *independistas*, who constituted the spirit of the club, had nearly all died. Alejandro Acosta passed in 1956, Juan Franco having died the preceding year. By the 1960s, almost no one was left.

At a meeting in February 1964, when the special committee gave its report on available properties, the members voted to hold on, to overrule the pessimist/realists. They purchased the building on Seventh Avenue that was discussed that evening. It cost them $15,000, leaving a balance of $30,000 from the settlement. Part of the remainder was used to buy two small houses to replace their previous rental properties, which were also taken by Urban Renewal. Their new home was homely indeed, but the location was excellent—on Seventh Avenue at Thirteenth Street, within visual distance of the Martí Park. It was a small, one-story warehouse, with a narrow second-floor office carved from the attic, constructed of cinderblock faced in stucco. The inside walls were wainscoted, the floors linoleum—a dark windowless chamber. Built as a warehouse in 1950, the structure had served as a meeting hall for a variety of CIO union locals (the occupants at the time that Castro spoke there in 1955). At the time Martí-Maceo purchased the property, it was vacant, having most recently housed a storefront church.[25] Although somewhat adapted to their purposes, it needed further additions. One of the members was a carpenter, who built a raised platform along the back wall, for bands and speakers, and a bar on the side wall. They all worked to get it fixed up and add some decoration; but even after all their effort, it was far short of what they had lost. They were able to pay their bills, but the drain of members continued. Maybe the pessimists had been right.

In 1970, one of the officers died, an elderly ex-cigarmaker who had first arrived in 1910. His son, who had been involved in the club his whole life, took a trip to New York. He visited there somewhat regularly, went to see his relatives and old friends from Ybor City and West Tampa. On this particular occasion, however, his trip was animated by grief and nostalgia. His old friends who had migrated out of Tampa during the 1930s, who, like himself, were now approaching the age of retirement, listened with sympathetic interest as he described the current plight of Martí-Maceo. He also talked to them about Tampa, reminded them of its gentle winter and sunny beaches, and about the changes that occurred out of the Civil Rights movement. He was quietly trying to orchestrate a return migration that could revive the dwindling community and rescue the club. One of my informants recalled these conversations.

JORGÉ: Every time he would come to New York, he would stop by, and he kept telling me, "Why don't you come to Tampa? You can see that Tampa has changed." I used to say, "Tampa, I never want to see nothin' that look like Tampa," because I had a memory of Tampa.

At that juncture, he told a long story about a confrontation with a white policeman in Ybor City just before he left for New York. He and some friends were congregated in a yard late in the evening when two officers approached and told them to disband. Not swift enough in his departure, one cop drew his gun and threatened to shoot him right there, but his partner restrained him. Instead he slugged our narrator in the jaw and promised to kill him next time.

JORGÉ: Since then, my teeth . . . my jaw . . . every time I used to open my mouth to yawn, my jaw goes "clack, clack" . . . I say, "I don't want no part of the South." [But] I got tired of the cold weather, shoveling snow and fighting muggers. I was mugged twice. After you had twenty years of service [on his job] and you were over fifty, you could retire at half pay. And I said, "That's it." I had enough now of New York. I loved New York, because of everything you had. I just got tired of having four locks on the door.

They did move back to Tampa, and so did literally dozens of their other friends who were born in Tampa but grew up in New York. By the 1980s, forty-one members out of a total of ninety-seven were from New York. The newcomers helped revitalize Martí-Maceo. It offered a replacement for the Club Interamericano Cubano, which many had belonged to in New York—the club that originated as a replacement for the Martí-Maceo that they had left behind so long ago.

They came in a chain, inspired initially by the exhortations of their friend from Tampa. Attributing this whole movement to the actions of a single man would oversimplify the causes. Many forces converged to prompt this migration—age of the cohort, the rise of the Sunbelt, and, perhaps most important, elimination of the most obvious trappings of Jim Crow. One of the returnees remembered how this latter factor played in their own decision to move back.

> ESPERANZA: We came [for a vacation]. My mother, my sister and brother, came driving. And J—— [her husband] was shocked, the change through all the South, that any place that he'd go he was accepted and treated so well. So one day he told me, "Let's move to Tampa." And a friend [who moved earlier], my neighbor, she told me, "Why don't you buy this lot next to me?"

It was hard leaving the attractions of New York for Tampa, which in the 1970s (and even now) had little to offer in the way of entertainment. They created their own entertainment, and in the process brought the Martí-Maceo Society back to life. They were together again, reconnecting with the families who never left, retired in Florida with time on their hands. Among the returnees was a man who had been president during the Depression, who was still president when they built the patio. By the 1970s, he was in his eighties, older than most and too old to resume leadership. The current president was also in his eighties. They conferred with the other two remaining officers of Martí-Maceo, who were only slightly younger, and they decided to recruit one of the New Yorkers to serve as president. They chose the occasion of the treasurer's fiftieth wedding anniversary to stage a big party in the club. The organizer of the event, whom they had asked to become the new president, described the results.

> EMILIO: I talk to the people and the people give me money, somebody gives five dollars, some two dollars, you know. And we got two hundred dollars and some, to celebrate. Then I invite the women, because I say "Without women the club is nothing." I say to the women, "Do

something in here." Every woman started to working in there and we got a big party. We go house to house, invite the people to come over here.

The dance was a big success, followed by others featuring live music, and all-night parties that ended with breakfast. Daily domino games at the social hall offered added diversion. These events eased the transition for the newcomers and galvanized interest in the club. A woman, one of the first New Yorkers to return, described the social satisfaction that the club offered.

ROSA: Since we've come back, I have to say I am having a better time, a ball, as compared to the last years that we were in New York. A lot of our friends that had migrated to New York, they've come back. And we've been having a grand reunion almost every week, and we've been having a good time. I'm really glad that I came back. I'm enjoying the weather too, away from all that cold.

The newcomers generated a lot of activity that also served to attract some of their age-mates and relatives, who had not left Tampa, back into the club. A critical mass of numbers, interest, and energy had been established.

JORGÉ: And we decided, let's see if we can get the club up again. They had something like twenty-five members. So, we decided to give a chicken dinner and charge two dollars. We pooled the money, we put up I think fifty dollars a piece [to buy chicken]. Guy charged us $149, enough for a hundred people. We invited all these people, and since there was nothing doing here, the people were anxious for something to happen. The place got so packed that we ran out of chicken. And we started handing out the applications [membership] and maybe forty or fifty people joined that day.

This emergent awakening was not without friction. The New Yorkers were different, tended to hang together because they knew each other better. Many of them had married Puerto Ricans in New York, and some had married other Cubans, but very few married African Americans. Most of the Afro-Cubans who stayed in Tampa had married African Americans.

The new mixture of spouses and in-laws, whose ethnic differences aligned with the old-timer/newcomer split, also a black/Hispanic split, was another subtle distinction and a factor that unsettled the Cubanness of the club. A New Yorker's early attempt to redefine Martí-Maceo as a "Latin

American" club, in much the same manner that nomenclature was struck for the Club Interamericano Cubano, met angry resistance from the old Tampeño Cubans and drew no support from younger Tampeños who considered themselves African Americans. Some of my narrators who had stayed in Tampa criticized what they perceived as an air of superiority in the New Yorkers, based on these various differences, and the greater educational and employment advantages in New York. Their childhood friends, who moved away and avoided many of the problems that they had to face growing up in the South, did not seem to appreciate the battles they had fought. They felt that the New Yorkers viewed Tampeños as more provincial and less successful, and some of my New York narrators confirmed this belief.

There were other tensions, even within the New York group, over how the club should be managed. Leadership was contested at the outset by two men, both from New York, who were radically different in philosophy and style. The first new president, whose ties to Tampa were actually through his wife, sought to re-create the urban elegance of Club Interamericano Cubano, in which he had been very active, and to instill a more business-like, and less sentimental, approach to running Martí-Maceo. He actually had a somewhat negative disposition towards the old Martí-Maceo. Back in the twenties, when he was a young man, he had come to Tampa and was invited to join Martí-Maceo. He was one of a large number of Cubans who arrived at the same time, cigar workers who were fleeing a strike in Havana. Martí-Maceo held a dance to recruit them as members, offering promises that there would be young women there to dance with. Although willing to use their women as a lure, they were not willing to let them dance with strangers. When he arrived, there were no young women to be found, only a few "old maids in their forties." The ploy backfired in his case, and he decided not to stay in Tampa. He moved on to New York and did not return until the 1970s. He viewed the club, especially the condition it was in when he came back, as backward and parochial and in need of stern direction. He was heedless of the advice the older officers tried to give him. His presumption that the president gives orders, can simply say "Women, do something in here" when their help is needed with cooking and organizing, was another reason that he lost the contest for re-election as president of Martí-Maceo.

The old officers had quietly recruited another candidate. The man they chose had grown up in Tampa and left as a young adult. His father had been president of the club in the late 1920s. He was better known to the members, both from New York and Tampa, and his vision of the club was closer to the old ideas about cooperation and mutual aid. Compared with the incumbent, he was less formal, less concerned with either profits or pretensions, and explicitly interested in using the club's resources to provide maximum benefit for the members. He also had some new ideas about gender roles in the club. His administration included the first woman director in the club's history, his wife, who served as secretary. This inclusion was pragmatic as much as it was ideological. They needed all the help they could get, and the secretary's role was relatively subordinate. But this was nonetheless a significant departure from past tradition. For the first time, women members gained full voting rights and took part in debates and meetings along with the men.

His administration was not without conflict, and he eventually resigned in anger, but his leadership was effective and long. The whole of Martí-Maceo's organizational history was filled with acrimonious debate, argument, and rhetorical challenge. Contesting decisions, criticizing leaders, offering alternative opinions, speaking up with passion and fury, were part of the scenario in performance of Cuban manly rivalry. The course of the new leadership was, to that extent, continuous with past traditions. As well, his reputation for generosity, both with his own time and with the resources of the club, was consistent with traditional notions of the president's role. He devoted a tremendous amount of time to the job, and he assumed responsibility for helping individual members with problems. He also instituted practices designed to allocate benefits as broadly as possible and democratize governance and decision-making. The values that he held, the ideas he learned in Tampa while growing up and practiced in New York as a man, were the old values. He effectively bridged the divide between New Yorkers and Tampeños, and remained in office for more than a decade. He was still president when I first got involved with Martí-Maceo.

Through the 1970s and into the 1980s, Martí-Maceo grew and stabilized. New fund-raising and more members allowed them to pay off a $1,000 mortgage and settle an egregiously overdue bill at the González clinic. Medical benefits were deemed no longer viable, although prior benefits were retained for a handful of elderly members. Improvements were made in the structure, and air conditioning was added, making the hall once again attractive for rentals. Monthly meetings were well attended, and periodic dances and picnics drew large crowds. In the space of a few years, the Martí-Maceo Society had taken a dramatic new turn.

Things were changing in Ybor City as well, or at least a lot of well-heeled individuals were working very hard to make something happen. In the late 1970s, a local developer renovated the old Ybor factory, a handsome, three-story brick structure, into a mini-mall with spaces for offices, boutiques, and restaurants. It was hoped that this renovation would spark a commercial revitalization of the whole area, transform it into a charming Latin Quarter, and capitalize on the growing interest in ethnic heritage that swirled about the nation's bicentennial.

These aspirations foundered, however. Ybor City was not considered safe. It was too close to blighted black neighborhoods to be regarded as a comfortable place to shop or find recreation. Bankers were wary about investing, and insurers were reluctant to write policies. The area was still "red-lined." Ybor City had an image problem, a problem that connected directly to blackness. Development strategies increasingly focused on reimaging Ybor City by emphasizing the whiteness of its history.

Historicizing served the development process in more direct ways. By establishing an official historic district developers hoped also to capture subsidies and other advantages for properties inside the designated area. The architecture of the area was neither very distinctive nor impressive, in itself not sufficient to make the case for protected status—especially in view of all the destruction that had occurred already. Ybor City's claim to historical importance rested mainly on its unique ethnic heritage and its role in Cuban independence. The Martí-Maceo Society provided a living example of the Cuban culture and history in the district. Their continued existence should have been counted as an asset in authenticating the significance of Ybor City's Cuban heritage. Because the Martí-Maceo members were black, however, their value was deeply discounted. Because they no longer had a historic building—the original structure having been demolished—it was easy to ignore them. In efforts to protect their interests and get involved in the process, leaders of Martí-Maceo began butting against this contradiction.

It was at that point that I became involved with the club and began researching its history. Members of Martí-Maceo decided to challenge their invisible status by bringing forth tangible evidence of their right to be considered a significant historical resource. I became an accomplice in a strategy for packaging and promoting their cultural capital, and in optimizing certain features of their predicament. Cuban customs of ignoring race and professing to be color blind, customs that have continued to influence social relations in Ybor City, had reinforced Afro-Cuban invisibility, but also were implicitly inclusive. Afro-Cubans invoked cigarmaking and

Cuban independence, were wrapped in the hallowed symbols of Martí and Maceo, and stood on firm moral ground. When the issue was broached, there were few Cubans in Tampa who could openly deny their legitimacy. The politics of civil rights and multiculturalism offered other avenues of entry. Federal rules for historic districts do not permit racial discrimination, although securing justice under these auspices is not a simple matter. The next, and final, chapter examines the politics of historic preservation, exemplified and enacted within the context of Martí-Maceo's contemporary struggle to remain in existence.

9

Out of Time

I sat in a pew in St. Peter Claver Church gazing at the face of my old friend, smiling back from the brochure that had been printed for this dreary occasion. This was a memorial service, not a funeral. He had chosen cremation, so there was no waxy corpse in a casket to contradict and disturb last images—still handsome at eighty, an open generous face filled with mirth. His passing had unfolded over the course of two years. During that time, as I struggled to write this book, I watched the growing evidence of impending death. In my mind, his illness became a metaphor for time running out.

The Martí-Maceo Society, of which he had been president for many years, was growing thin also. The spark of life that occurred in the 1970s, when he and many others returned from New York, was sputtering. Membership was dwindling and aging; those who remained were becoming too frail to lead. The club had suffered a huge setback in 1997, when they elected as president a relatively recent Cuban immigrant whom they did not know well, who proceeded to plunder the treasury and besmirch their collective reputation. Juan had been part of the cabal that finally got her out of office, a last contribution for which he mustered a final burst of energy.

On the morning of his memorial service, as I looked around the nave of the church with its many empty pews, conjuring images of the many other funerals and services I had attended for those now missing from this one, I wondered how the Martí-Maceo Society would fare without him. The priest conducting the service, an amiable white man who obligingly interlaced his comments with Spanish, spoke of him warmly although he did not know him. He said, "The best way we can remember Juan, and give him eternal life, is to tell his story." His words, perhaps a stock phrase he used often on such occasions, stabbed with special meaning. Juan would never read the book I was writing, that was taking so long to finish, that he had helped to shape.

In large measure, this book is Juan's story. Not solely his, although he was one of my main collaborators, but essentially his, because he was part of a tight-knit group—a generation whose experiences and outlook were forged by convergent circumstances of growing up black and Cuban during the heyday of Tampa's cigar industry. This cohort, now elderly, is passing from the scene.

Is history a continuous stream, or a fragmented set of cycles that trace individual lifetimes, reaching back for memories of childhood, and then fading into oblivion? Is Afro-Cuban ethnicity in Tampa a mere epiphenomenon of the historical moment that once propelled Cuban cigar workers to this place? Will it too fade into obscurity as the city's power brokers and flood of new residents redraw the landscape and redefine the heritage of Ybor City? This is a crucial question. It speaks directly to whether ethnicity is ephemera constructed out of shifting contingencies, or something more palpable and enduring.

The usual term of ethnographic research is about a year, an annual cycle, long enough to learn one's way around and figure out what is going on. Then comes the ritual separation, pondering at a distance and making larger sense of what was found in this snapshot of life in another world (Clifford 1997). The research for this book lasted fifteen years. I never left the field, because I live and work there, a fifteen-minute drive from my office at the university to the Martí-Maceo hall, where I regularly attend meetings and dances, and work on projects with the members. This long term of involvement has provided a window on historical processes that could be observed directly rather than simply inferred. I could see the outcome of my own predictions, was forced periodically to reformulate my ideas when projections failed to materialize. There were several junctures at which it seemed that the club would surely die. Part of the urgency I felt, as I tried to bring my rendition of this story to a conclusion, was a reluctance to end it pessimistically, to close with an analysis of its unfortunate demise. But one of the forces that dragged it out was a desire to see and tell about what was going to happen. This work continues, but closure is necessary. I owe it to Juan; and to Sylvia, Laureano, Francisco, Hipólito, Manuel, and too many others who now have passed, and I also have a responsibility to those who are still here and have helped me all these years.

To the extent that Afro-Cuban identity rests on the continued existence of the Martí-Maceo Society—and I would argue that this connection is crucial—external forces easily could sweep it away. It is only the members' determination to remain—their agency—that has prevented its eradication.

My initial involvement with Martí-Maceo was a product of that determination. This chapter examines our work together over the past fifteen years. Embedded in the discussion is a small case study in applied anthropology, the practice of heritage conservation and its connections to larger theoretical issues of ethnogenesis and cultural capital. Saving the Martí-Maceo Society has always been the main purpose that has mobilized Afro-Cuban ethnicity in this place. It symbolized their national heritage, embodied homage to their ancestors, and its institutional resources nurtured their material, social, and spiritual wants.

Martí-Maceo was never secure; its maintenance always demanded a struggle. Outcomes of these various crises—Bruno's theft, the 1930s Depression, the Cuban Revolution, Urban Renewal, desegregation—were not determined in advance. Any one of these events might have shut its doors forever. Nor was the fact that this did not happen attributable to the desires and actions of the members alone. Each unfolded in its own moment. Actors involved made use of resources they could muster, and they formed alliances with those who could and would help them. They drew heavily on the store of history; not just the history of Cuban independence, but also larger legacies of shared oppression. In Adam Katz, refugee of Romanian pogroms, they found a biblical link in ancient diasporas and more proximal tyrannies of the late nineteenth century. In Bob Saunders and the Reverend Mr. A. Leon Lowry, allies in the Civil Rights movement, they connected to inheritors of Florida's black project during Reconstruction. In me, they constructed a modest counterpart of Fernando Ortiz, activist ethnologist and sympathetic scribe.

Preserving History

My first meeting with the board of directors occurred one fall afternoon in 1984. We met at the club on Seventh Avenue. I never noticed this building in my earlier excursions into Ybor City, because it is easy to overlook. Sitting by itself on an otherwise vacant lot at the west end of the district, it was a squat stucco structure with tiny grilled windows along the top of a stunted second story topped by a row of orange roof tiles, faux Spanish themes that did little to relieve its essential homeliness. A hand-painted sign on the front door defined its existence. When I arrived, I greeted

Sylvia Griñán, the teacher who had come to my class on urban anthropology. She introduced me to Juan Mallea, the president, and Ricardo Menendez, the vice-president. We sat at a table near the door and discussed their current dilemma.

Ybor City was going to be nominated as a National Historic District. They were both worried and hopeful about this new development. The publicity surrounding the campaign emphasized the importance of preserving the history of the cigarmakers and marketing the crucial role that Tampa had played in Cuban independence—the colorful culture of the Latin immigrants and their many contributions to the growth of the city. There was little left of Ybor City to save. Acres of cottages had been destroyed by Urban Renewal. Most of the stores that still stood on Seventh Avenue were empty. The social clubs were rapidly fading. El Centro Español already had closed its doors.[1] Círculo Cubano, L'Unione Italiano, and Centro Asturiano were struggling to avoid that same fate. Urgent action was needed to save these treasures. In the news story about Centro Español's closing the similarly declining condition of these other three was examined; no mention was made of the Sociedad la Unión Martí-Maceo, a journalistic practice I encountered repeatedly. They were missing from the inventory of Ybor City's cultural resources, even though they, among all the other clubs in the early 1980s, were actually growing in size and bustling with activity. They needed to find a way to remedy their obscurity, to benefit from the changes, and to avoid being swept away once again by the redevelopment that elected officials hoped would come from new federal programs.

The city of Tampa was growing—too rapidly, some said. Its modest skyline was reconfiguring itself with new glass-and-steel towers that were so popular in the 1980s. Thousands of new residents arrived each month. Ill defined and dwarfed by the growing international reputation of Miami, Tampa sought a coherent image, and its leaders also hoped to take advantage of tourism opportunities based on the city's only claim to distinctive status—cigars and the Spanish-American War. This was an old idea smothered in the late 1950s by Castro's revolution, and then revived in the 1970s, only to falter in the recession of the late years of the decade, and persistent reluctance to invest in an area that had become too black. This new effort would be different, they claimed. Little wonder that they did not open their arms to embrace the black Cubans. But the exact intentions towards this property, the building in which members of the Martí-Maceo had salvaged their existence after Urban Renewal, were not clear.

Were they quietly being targeted for yet another demolition, or were they being ignored because no one knew that they existed? It easily could have been the latter. None of the historic markers that went up in the 1950s mentioned them at all. None of the smarmy news articles about the wonderful system of medical care, the cooperative medicine that was so viciously attacked at the time by the Hillsborough County Medical Association, ever included Martí-Maceo. Accounts of the "Latin" immigrants neglected to mention that some of the Cubans were black. From the records that existed, the documentary evidence of Ybor City's historic significance, it was nearly impossible to glean the existence of Afro-Cubans or the Martí-Maceo Society. The first task, we agreed, was to shed their invisibility and put forth a case for inclusion.

It would not be easy. With so little in the way of secondary sources, we would have to construct the record ourselves, would have to piece together memories and search for documents that could enlarge and corroborate personal recollections. This project guided my research, joined us in a collaboration to find information and tell the story. Ybor City's centennial was coming in 1986, a nostalgic occasion that had been targeted for intense promotion. We decided to develop a pictorial monograph timed to coincide with the planned celebration. It would have to be rigorous, but written for the public—promoting awareness and offering a new bona fide entry in the documentation of Ybor City's history. My collaborators began identifying elderly informants for oral history and urging members to bring in family photographs. We moved the old record books and files to the library at the University of South Florida, where they could be curated properly and would be more accessible for research.[2]

I interviewed about forty people, men and women representing both the group that remained through the Depression and those who had moved away. I also interviewed white Cubans, Spaniards, Italians, and African Americans. One of my main Afro-Cuban informants, a man in his nineties, could reconstruct images that stretched nearly to the time of Martí. He had a saying that he voiced several times about the quality of his own understanding:

LUIS: They say the devil knows more for being old than for being the devil. That's what a Cuban says. You know more from being old than from being wise. Because you see things, so you know.

His father was an *independista*, an associate of Carlos Baliño and Guillermo Sorondo, who later were founders of the Cuban Communist Party.

When he was a young child living in Port Tampa, Martín Morúa Delgado, the famous Afro-Cuban journalist and politician, was his next-door neighbor. He knew Bruno Roig and the Pedrosos, had visited Paulina in Havana, and attended her funeral there in 1913. He himself had been a central figure in the Martí-Maceo Society, was president through the Depression and led the effort to build the patio. His accounts (I interviewed him on five different occasions), and those of the others I taped, yielded more than facts and interpretations, more than images and anecdotes.

Among the members of his generation and those who were slightly younger, there was a remarkable redundancy in political values and beliefs. Legacies of Martí's oratory, Maceo's defiance, and the cigarmakers' activism seemed palpable in the expressions and attitudes disclosed during the interviews. Theirs was not a doctrinaire socialism, but rather an everyday variety—mutualism and fairness, the inherent right of workers to resist and citizens to rebel.

My nonagenarian friend railed against Ronald Reagan with the same vituperative scorn he heaped on long-dead thugs in what he derisively called the "Ku Ku" Klan; and on his white Spanish uncles in Cuba, who had put his grandmother and her children out of the house after his white grandfather died. He had seen a lot in his long lifetime, remembered when the Jim Crow laws went into effect, was full grown when the Bolsheviks seized power in Russia, was still alive when their empire came apart. He did know a lot simply for being old, but his knowledge was ciphered through the ideology of the Cuban revolutionaries who raised him and the *lectores* who tutored his ideas.

This kind of research has a unique intimacy, an inescapably social dimension. It generates relationships. The more so in this case, because subject and object were joined in collaboration. Reciprocity is a crucial element of applied anthropology, and we all clearly understood that this was an exchange. My research did not simply belong to me, but rather had a purpose in which my own understanding was a necessary by-product. My collaborators were not simply willing to tell me what I needed to know, did more than comply in answering my questions: they actively attempted to make me understand. Their interest in the outcome encouraged cooperation and enriched my data. The line between theory and practice blurred, and the distance between researcher and informant closed. My own values were reflected and reinforced by the beliefs and observations they recounted in interviews, and I was touched by an affection that infiltrated my own life. One might question whether such an arrangement is conducive to "objectivity." In the conclusions, I will briefly explore the philosophical crannies of that well-worn question, but my response at this juncture is that fifteen years is a long time in which to contemplate validity. In the comfort of familiarity, pretenses evaporate and contradictions unfold in disclosure. There is no such thing as an objective ethnography, so this one is not either. To a greater extent than is usual, however, it is an authorized representation—an extended excursion into the lives of those whose story is told.

A small grant from the University of South Florida supported the collection of data and the production of a handsome twenty-five-page sepia booklet that described the history and current status of the club and the Afro-Cuban community (Greenbaum 1986). A wealth of photographs of individuals, families, and activities at Martí-Maceo were provided to illustrate the text. We printed a thousand copies and distributed them to schools, libraries, historic preservation agencies, public officials, and other potentially useful targets. It arrived on time in 1986, in the blush of the Ybor City Centennial. The weekly history column in the *Tampa Tribune* featured a two-page layout on the booklet and its contents.[3]

The news story brought forth requests for copies of the booklet and invitations to speak at various functions. There seemed to be widespread interest in this unique Tampa story, touching on themes of race, ethnicity, and local nostalgia. But there was more to it than that. My narrative also played well in the politics of invidious comparison and the myth of Cuban racial democracy. Also important was the fact that Tampa's Afro-Cubans were a small group, mostly elderly it appeared, not especially threatening.

In writing about their ancestors' accomplishments, I had emphasized (without exaggeration) their industry and tenacity, had attempted to demonstrate that they were little different in beliefs and behavior from white Cubans. The effects of racism were also part of my narrative, and I wanted readers to understand the thick vein of African traditions that informed Afro-Cuban religion and music, traditions that remain a significant component of Cuban national culture. Although not intentionally celebratory, my goal was to humanize, as it also would have been if I had been writing about African Americans. This effort was perhaps too nuanced, or there was nothing to balance it in the existing public images of African Americans.[4] The net interpretation, the public take on what I had written, seemed to be that the cultural background of Afro-Cubans distinguished them favorably from African Americans. This rendition also shed positive light on Ybor City and West Tampa, as sites that historically nurtured racial harmony.

Many white people who spoke to me about the booklet were quick to draw contrasts between Afro-Cubans and African Americans, whose large impoverished community they blamed for many of Tampa's ills. The Afro-Cubans provided a trope for sorting racism from disdain, a device for expressing bigoted ideas without having to acknowledge the bigotry in them. Not all black people were lazy and querulous, it could be said. Scorn for single black women and their dangerous teenaged sons, living in the projects at public expense, was not racism. Industrious law-abiding immigrants and their descendants, who also happened to be black, seemed to prove that there was something essentially inferior about African American culture.

One of the ironies of genetic proof that race is not biologically valid has been to refocus the analysis on misconstrued arguments about culture (Harrison 1998; Smedley 1998). Thomas Sowell, a widely circulated conservative black commentator, has written numerous essays about the alleged cultural superiority of black immigrants in comparison with native-born blacks (e.g., Sowell 1994; 1978). This line of thinking has been extended and made respectable in a large body of published sociological and economic research (Fernández-Kelly 1995; Fernández-Kelly and Schauffler 1996; Light and Rosenstein 1995; Portes 1995; Portes and Zhou 1993; Waters 1996), work that in turn has been challenged in an equally distinguished body of published research (Butcher 1994; Cotton 1993; James 1999; Model 1991; Watkins-Owens 1996). However, these jousts among intellectuals have little influence on most people who live in places like Tampa. Thomas Sowell, on the other hand, has a regular column in the *Tampa Tribune*. In the mundane discursive realities of racial politics in Tampa, the alleged virtues of Afro-Cubans became fodder for demagogic pronouncements about African Americans, condemnations that failed to distinguish between race and class, a pernicious alternative explanation for why so many poor people in Tampa are black. Observing this process in action, as people formulated anew their attitude about Afro-Cubans and fit them into their racial cosmologies, was a singular revelation in my experiences with the promotion of our historical monograph.

Folk Festivals

Many of the white people who expressed such views—who explained to me in hushed tones that Afro-Cubans always were a little better than black Americans—were Cubans, Spaniards, or Italians. In what became my next revelation, I learned about the subtleties of Cuban racism and the way these traditions filtered into the belief system of Ybor City.

In late summer of 1986, shortly after the booklet was released, I was asked to serve as a consultant for a folk festival. The Ybor City Museum Society and the Ybor City Chamber of Commerce planned to apply for a grant from the National Endowment for the Arts to stage a celebration of ethnic folk arts and crafts in honor of the centennial. Eligibility for the NEA funds rested on the involvement of qualified academics, and anthropology was deemed an appropriate discipline for a folk festival. I gladly accepted, viewing this as a good opportunity to promote the existence of the Martí-Maceo Society, not to mention the fact that they were willing to pay me. My involvement in the folk festival brought me into contact with the preservation establishment of Tampa and public officials who were orchestrating revitalization. As well, I became acquainted with leaders in the Spanish, Italian, and white Cuban mutual aid societies, and a variety of local business owners whose ethnic roots and real estate holdings provided double incentive to participate in promoting Ybor City.

The museum was a quaint yellow brick building a few blocks north of Seventh Avenue that originally had been an Italian bakery. The structure had been rescued during Urban Renewal and remodeled to serve as an exhibit gallery. On the lot adjoining the building, a shady outdoor courtyard was created with a bandstand, fountain, landscaped walks, and a bronze bust of Don Vincente Martínez Ybor. During the late 1970s five shotgun cottages were moved onto the site on the other side of the courtyard and restored as vernacular workers' housing. One of the cottages was furnished to show visitors an example of the domestic life of immigrant families; the others were refitted as offices and meeting space. The museum complex occupied an entire block. Across the street the city had constructed a large outdoor patio and pavilion in a failed attempt to develop a farmers' market. The entire site was slated for the festival.

Inside the museum a series of exhibits portrayed the history of Ybor City, Cuban independence and Teddy Roosevelt, and the various immigrant groups. In one section there was a demonstration space equipped with a cigar rollers' bench. The wall behind the bench was hung with a huge photo mural depicting cigarmakers in the gallery of a factory, with the *lector* reading to them from an elevated platform. A number of the workers in the photo are recognizably black. There also was a small section of one display case in which photos and a brief caption acknowledged the existence of the Afro-Cubans. The caption emphasized the harmony of race relations in Ybor City, and told the story of Paulina Pedroso and José Martí. Included was a mounted photocopy of the first minutes of the Martí-Maceo Society.

Pending the outcome of the NEA grant, an advisory committee was formed to plan the festival. The committee was composed of local preservationists, both amateur and professional, two anthropologists (myself and a folklorist who had worked on the cottages project), representatives of the ethnic clubs, and several businesspeople from Ybor City. I was asked to help identify a member of Martí-Maceo to serve on the committee, the first time the club had been included in such a body.

At our first meeting, we discussed representation in the festival. When I mentioned Afro-Cubans and the Martí-Maceo Society, one of the businesspeople who had grown up in Ybor City responded quickly and flatly that there had not been any black Cubans there. I was amazed at the denial, and worried about how to correct it without creating unpleasantness at the meeting. My intervention was not needed, however. In nearly the same moment, the Martí-Maceo representative arrived late to the meeting. Entering the room, he spied a familiar face, the same person who just had denied that he existed. The two briefly exchanged greetings, and the new arrival took his seat. Nothing further was said, and the discussion about representation was interrupted by introductions around the table. At the close of the meeting, the chair of the committee (a non-Latin preservationist) summarized, casually but carefully including Afro-Cubans on the list of ethnic communities to be represented in the festival. Afterwards, I told my friend from Martí-Maceo about the discussion that preceded his entry. He laughed and shook his head. His father used to work as a dishwasher in the woman's family-owned restaurant, a job he was forced to take when the cigar factory closed. She could have forgotten about the black Cubans she knew who worked there, or perhaps she assumed that no one would contest her assertion—that this would be like other committees on which she served, where blacks were not present, nor anyone else who might advocate their inclusion.

NEA did fund the festival, but their award letter cautioned that the agency had concerns about minority representation. Folk festivals in the South often provoked such concerns, about local uses of federal dollars to promote one-sided heritage representations. The Afro-Cubans suddenly took on new value in enabling the project organizers to satisfy diversity criteria. There was no further resistance to including them in the program, although negotiations were not over. Suggestions that African Americans also be included, perhaps the gospel choir from a church located not far from the museum, drew strong resistance. I could show that African Americans had lived in Ybor City almost from the beginning; the church in question was very old. However, the committee finally voted that, since this was a centennial event, only the original founding groups could be included. A further motion, also voted for approval, restricted Afro-Cuban representation in the festival to a level consistent with their relative numbers in the early population (about 15 percent). This formula was not invoked for any of the other groups (Italians in the 1880s were even less numerous). It seemed to me that this was a badly disguised device to limit blackness.

The limits on Afro-Cuban participation were not enforced, for several reasons. My folklorist colleague and I were principally responsible for identifying and recruiting performers and demonstrators. Our selections were based on professional judgment, familiarity with individuals who could serve, and an interest in subverting racist intentions. In the end, scarcity of available affordable talent, combined with the Martí-Maceo members' greater willingness to get involved in the festival, resulted in a large showing of Afro-Cubans in the food and crafts demonstrations. One of the cigarmakers was Hipólito Arenas, the retired baseball player. Then in his late seventies, he was one of a few old hand-rollers who were still working every day in a cigar factory in Ybor City. His display was set up inside the museum, against the backdrop of the photo mural showing one of the old factories. In a front row of the gallery, a young black man looked eagerly at the camera as the shot was taken. His smiling face is very noticeable in the photo. This young man was Hipólito Arenas, captured on film in the factory where he worked briefly prior to launching his baseball career. As interpreter for the exhibit, I was able to call attention to this coincidence, to invite the audience to focus on the faces in the photo and consider the multiracial composition of the factory workforce. The juxtaposition of the elderly man and his youthful photograph projected continuity and the essential authenticity of the demonstrator.

The first folk festival was considered a success. Crowds were large and disproportionately white. Although there are dense black neighborhoods literally within walking distance of the site, very few of these residents came. I believe that their absence from the event was what some of the festival organizers had hoped would occur. Discouraging black attendance could have been the motive for wanting to limit black participants, or not featuring any dimension of African American folk culture. When plans were made to have a second festival the following year, however, they were less able to pursue such a strategy.

The centennial was over, and a new theme was needed. This time they chose the 1940s, what they decided was Ybor City's "heyday." It was a curious choice, a time period when major transformations already had occurred, but also a remembered time of youth and prosperity for many on the planning committee. It had been *their* "heyday." This move forward in time removed all cover from arguments to exclude African Americans. By the 1940s, there was significant black residence in Ybor City, a presence that could not be denied or dismissed. NEA was willing to fund it again, but only if black participation was increased. Compliance with this pressure was grudging, but the funds were needed to stage the event. African American performers and demonstrators were added, and their recipes were gathered for inclusion in the catalog/brochure. However, no African Americans were added to the planning committee. The second festival also went smoothly, in spite of fears to the contrary. More black people attended, but only slightly more. It had remained primarily a white, middle-class, weekend tourist attraction.

There was one more Ybor City folk festival, held in 1989, after a gap of two years. The theme for this one focused on contemporary folk cultures of Ybor City. Under this formula, the solicitation broadened to include Caribbeans and Central Americans, the new immigrants in the neighborhood. The last festival was in many ways the best. It drew the largest crowds of any to date, more diversity in audiences, more dancing to the music. Steel drums, Jamaican dub poetry, wood carvers and flute makers, bright fabrics and spicy odors, Italian concertina, Spanish bagpipes, salsa rhythms, the throaty sounds of the Cuban *punto guaijiro*, the shouting hand clapping gospel choir—a gorgeous cacophony of Ybor City's cultural evolution. It was much too much for some of the older members of the committee. I was told that in the next meeting afterwards, they voted not to continue the event in the following year, ostensibly because the festival had not earned a profit. Profitability was never the intention, and most festival supporters believed it was defeated for other reasons.

Much has been written about festivals and cultural representation (Gable 1996; Gillis 1994; Karp, Mullen, Kreamer and Lavine 1992; Lavenda

1992; Lowenthal 1994; Macdonald and Fyfe 1996; Moore 1997; Rhea 1997). The short career of the Ybor City Folk Festival exemplifies the contestation theorized in this work. Making the Afro-Cubans visible was not a simple matter, and trying to do so illuminated the limits of tolerance and boundaries of power. The moderate success we had in staging the event three times, however, also revealed strategies of counter-contestation. The process generated alliances, sympathies, and shared indignation among others involved who disagreed with the conservative views of some committee members. Preservation activists in Ybor City reflect a plurality of interests, and many endorse federal rules about diversity. Participation in the festival brought Martí-Maceo members into contact with these individuals. Their help would be valuable in subsequent struggles over inclusion, like determining boundaries of the proposed historic district.

Historic Status

Ybor City was nominated as a Federal Historic District in 1986. The accompanying documentation described the rationale, identified important sites and structures, and delineated boundaries.[5] The area included was a small portion of the original neighborhood. On the west, it stopped at Thirteenth Street, only about fifteen feet from the lot line of Martí-Maceo. It would have been far more logical to have extended the boundary another block to where a major artery transected the area. The only standing structure affected by this choice was the Martí-Maceo building. The Centro Asturiano building, located even further west on Palm and Nebraska, posed a dilemma that had been resolved by an abrupt narrow spur that projected far enough west to include the structure (see Map 3). This awkward addition seemed to confirm the impression that the boundaries were deliberately gerrymandered to exclude black Cubans and enclose white Spaniards. In 1989, the National Park Service, whose responsibility includes designating Federal Historic District status, prepared to rule on Ybor City's application. It sent a historian to Tampa for a site visit. As one of the scholars involved in heritage research, I was contacted. We arranged a meeting with him, myself, and several Martí-Maceo board members. He listened with interest to our story and had already read the centennial booklet I wrote.

Like the folklorist sent by the NEA to evaluate the festival, the Park Service historian represented a set of values and rules different from the local boosters who were promoting Ybor City heritage. He was unwilling

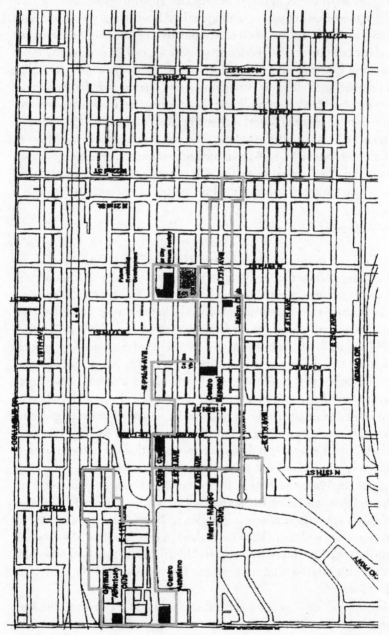

Map 3. Ybor City Historic District boundaries, 1985

to endorse boundaries that had no natural integrity, and excluded black interests that were historically legitimate. He related to us that he had come in with concerns about the way the boundaries were drawn. In initial meetings with the planners and officials who compiled the application, his queries about this had been met with candor. A white man with a very English-sounding last name, it seems that the historian had been mistaken for a race ally. They had explained openly their fear of the black neighborhoods that ringed Ybor City, the desire to narrow the boundaries in order to widen the separation between the district and that contamination. Unsympathetic to these arguments, the historian wrote his report to propose boundary changes in several locations, including the block on which Martí-Maceo was located. He inserted their history in the narrative justification for why the district is important, and designated the building as a "supporting structure," which meant it was culturally important, but not historic and of no architectural value.

Revisions to the historic district, the vindication of Afro-Cuban legitimacy by federal authority, made a comforting victory. The qualified inclusion as a "supporting structure" meant little, however. If redevelopment plans were to include the parcel on which it stood, there would be no effective restraints against its demolition. In terms of siting, the club would appear to be quite vulnerable. It is the only structure on an entire block, situated on the main drag at the western entry to Ybor City's commercial district. The Ybor Square complex (the boutiques and restaurants in the old Ybor factory building) is a short distance away. Part of the empty lot to the east of the Martí-Maceo building belongs to the developer who created Ybor Square, and the remaining lots belonged to the Hillsborough Community College (later transferred to the city), a public entity that could partner easily with private developers interested in the site.[6]

These various factors heightened the danger of dislocation. Pressure was relieved to some extent by the fact that the development process remained stalled, especially in the western portion of the district. Ybor Square had not achieved the success that was envisioned. Many of the commercial spaces were vacant and/or turned over frequently. There was greater activity in the eastern portion of Seventh Avenue, where the Columbia, a renowned Spanish restaurant, anchored a modest amount of revitalization of storefronts in its vicinity. This area was located directly off the expressway exit, a siting that presumably increased the comfort of outsiders coming into Ybor City. But throughout the 1980s, much the same as the 1970s, rebirth of the district faltered. Historic status helped market it as something separate and different from the larger distressed region in which it was located. Frequent news stories about crime in Ybor City tended to undermine those efforts. The failure of the developers to achieve their goals, a condition partly attributable to the racist calculus of real estate investment, ironically lent security to Martí-Maceo. There was no immediate danger of losing the building, because no one wanted it. We knew, however, that this could change at any time. So we sought preemption.

The regulations that excluded Martí-Maceo from historic status contain no provisions for remedying effects of past wrongs, such as the heedless destruction of Martí-Maceo's original, "historic," structure. This unfair loss mattered not at all in the legal protections available to the present structure, which were essentially none. A common paradox of racism, further victimization was made possible by prior misdeeds. However, the argument that Martí-Maceo deserved to be protected from any future molestation was not lacking in political force. James Hargrett, then a state representative from the district that included Ybor City, agreed to sponsor a bill in the Florida legislature that would confer special status on the Martí-Maceo building and help make its destruction unlawful. Representative Elvin Martínez, from West Tampa, joined him in sponsoring this effort. Hargrett is African American, direct descendant of Amos Hargrett, who served as county commissioner and justice of the peace in Wakulla County, Florida, during the 1870s (Brown 1998:182). Martínez descends from Cuban cigarmakers and grew up with many of the Afro-Cubans in the Martí-Maceo Society. Both were Democrats, the party that controlled the state legislature at the time. Martínez was able to marshal support from the Dade County (Miami) delegation of mostly Republican Cuban American representatives. Hargrett was able to mobilize the legislative black caucus, heavily Democratic and drawn from throughout the state, in support of the bill. The bill (HB 889) passed the legislature in April 1989. It was relatively uncontroversial, especially since it entailed no appropriation. The bill was entitled "An Act Relating to Historical Preservation; Formally Recognizing the Cultural Role of Certain Latin Societies in the Historical Development of Ybor City and Specifically Recognizing the Accomplishments of La Unión Martí-Maceo." The "whereas" sections emphasize the unfortunate effects of Urban Renewal and the need to avoid further unjust removals; the "therefore" clause reads as follows:

In recognition of the historical contributions made by La Union Martí-Maceo to the community of Ybor City and in recognition of the great historical loss to the community of the original building which housed La Unión Martí-Maceo, founded in 1904, the Legislature hereby recognizes the present headquarters of La Unión Martí-Maceo as a building of historical significance which should not be affected by urban renewal. The City of Tampa and Ybor City are requested to take any and all steps necessary to preserve the headquarters of La Union Martí-Maceo and protect it from the consequences of the urban renewal process.[7]

The passage of this bill, the enforceability of which remains unclear, represented a rare event in Florida politics, when African Americans and Cuban Americans joined in support of redefining the state's historical and cultural resources. This was also a rare occasion in which the dual identity of Afro-Cubans multiplied their value as a constituency.

Local preservationists, including some who were sympathetic to Martí-Maceo, were very unhappy with the new law. They regarded it as rank political intrusion into the process of determining historic significance. After reading the bill, one of these individuals called me to vent his dissatisfaction. The structure had neither the aesthetics nor antiquity required to preserve it, but they were being directed to treat it as if it did. If the legislature could act in this way on behalf of Martí-Maceo, they could get involved in other future decisions, jeopardizing the integrity of the whole process. I had to concede his point, although I responded that I thought politics had intruded into this process a long time ago, and that it was basically politics that explained the destruction of the original Martí-Maceo building. In the abstract, I could sympathize with his reluctance to compromise professional standards, but in reality I was elated at this small reversal in the direction of political influence.

Heritage Consortium

At about the same time that the legislation was passed on behalf of Martí-Maceo, Círculo Cubano was undergoing the biggest ordeal of its existence to date. By the mid-1980s, membership had dropped to seven hundred,[8] down from several thousand in the 1960s. This decline was alarming, although the club remained sufficiently large that it still had a doctor on contract, who came to the hall once a month to see to the ailments of its mostly elderly members. Their structure was also ailing. Built in 1918, a magnificent four-story stucco building with a leaking roof, no elevator, and a lot of deterioration in the interior, it needed repairs that far surpassed its dwindling treasury. Historic status offered a reprieve. With the aid of local preservationists, Círculo Cubano was able to secure grants from the state in excess of $300,000 to repair and shore up the structure. Despite the highly publicized revitalization efforts, and in spite of a large amount of publicity focusing on the historic importance of the club, membership continued to decline. By 1989, it had dropped to five hundred, down nearly 30 percent in just three years.[9] The Martí-Maceo Society had about 140 members at that point and was becoming increasingly visible. Martí-Maceo was growing, and Círculo Cubano appeared to be falling apart.

Publicity about Círculo Cubano's plight, and its newly acquired preservation wealth, apparently attracted the attention of an eloquent con artist named Ramón Hernández. Posing as a doctor who had been forced to flee Castro's regime in 1979, Hernández became involved with the club with offers to organize a membership recruitment drive. His overtures were welcome, and he was elected treasurer. One of Hernández's efforts to bolster membership was an invitation to the board of Martí-Maceo, asking them to merge with Círculo Cubano. After nearly a century of separation, a welcome was extended. There were attractive features in the offer—use of a much better facility, the monthly doctor's visits, the symbolic overturning of segregation. But there were risks and objectionable aspects also. They would have to sell their own building and turn the proceeds and their other assets over to Círculo Cubano. Who knew what kind of influence they might have in operating the merged organization? And it was galling to be invited at a juncture when they were so badly needed; they worried that they were just being used. The meeting at which this proposal was discussed was long and occasionally contentious. It was debated seriously, with a delicious gravity, and in the end the members voted unanimously to reject the offer—a doubly wise decision in view of what later happened.

Ramón Hernández was on probation when he was elected treasurer of Círculo Cubano, the result of pleading no contest to a charge of trying to cash a stolen U.S. Treasury check for $34,911. The arrest and plea bargain had occurred less than two months before he took office, although apparently no one in the club knew about it. He represented himself as an émigré physician-entrepreneur who owned a Spanish-language cable TV station. Hernández remained in office for about one year, until August 1989 when he was expelled for his troublesome behavior. At that juncture, the board was unaware that he was also embezzling from the club on a grand scale. Only a few weeks prior to his ouster, he had arranged a

$70,000 loan that was secured with the title to Círculo Cubano's building. By the time the note was foreclosed in April 1991, Hernández had disappeared along with most of the money he had borrowed. Interest, late charges, court costs, and attorneys' fees had ballooned the amount owed to over $100,000. Membership in Círculo Cubano had sunk to 165.[10] For the first time since the split in 1899, Martí-Maceo had nearly as many members as Círculo Cubano.

The crisis at the Círculo Cubano produced an outpouring of sympathy, along with privately expressed scorn at the foolishness that allowed it to happen. Lack of confidence in management of the member-run organization hindered efforts to raise funds and resolve the problem. Benefit events and other fund drives produced too little to save them. A group of mostly Latin entrepreneurs and politicians intervened to prevent foreclosure, but only on condition that a new management structure be installed, one that the members would not control. The building was too valuable to be trusted to amateur managers, especially given large recent investments of public monies to fix the roof.

Círculo Cubano had passed into the public domain, had become a monument. It no longer belonged to the members, although they were still allowed to use it. Two members died during the short time they were struggling with the debt, dropping the total from 165 to 163. Some of those now in control perhaps looked forward to a time when they would all be gone. A new bipartite entity was established, joining a nonprofit organization for member operations (Círculo Cubano) and a foundation (The Cuban Club Foundation) that assumed responsibility for developing and safeguarding the real estate value of the structure. All decisions regarding the building were left to a board of trustees that represented most major actors in Ybor City redevelopment.[11]

Only a few months after Círculo Cubano narrowly avoided sale at public auction, an organization was created to coordinate stewardship of all the remaining ethnic clubs and other threatened historic properties. Many of the same people who established the Cuban Club Foundation were also involved in this new entity, but it represented a very broad base of groups and individuals. The purpose was eminently sensible—to form a coalition among individual organizations to do joint fund-raising, negotiate building code problems, and otherwise work together to avoid dislocation by redevelopment. Representatives of all the ethnic clubs, including Martí-Maceo, were invited to join. City and county officials, Ybor City Chamber

of Commerce members, planners involved with Ybor City, real estate developers, preservation advocates, and university professors (including myself) also were invited to join.

In the beginning it was called the Historic Cultural Club Consortium,
but after about a year it was renamed the Heritage Structures Consortium
of Ybor City, Inc. (incorporation occurred in 1995). The size of the group
also shrank considerably during this period. The name change signifies the
unstated conflict between real estate and culture as objects worthy of preservation. Discussions in the early meetings, including a day-long retreat
aimed at finding a shared vision, revealed differences in this regard. Members of the clubs and some of the preservation advocates emphasized the
importance of supporting the ongoing existence of these organizations.
How else could Ybor City maintain its historic character? What better way
to ensure authenticity and avoid destroying the very things that give it
value? Countering these sentimental and intellectualized appeals was a
line of thinking that stressed the inevitability of change—a whispered reference to the advanced age of most of the members, a hint regarding the
calamity at Círculo Cubano, an appeal to practical reason. Developing a
historic district is serious business, and the fate of valuable properties cannot be left to the whim of amateurs. For Martí-Maceo, which was not such
a valuable property, the challenge in this conflict was even more difficult.

Martí-Maceo's inclusion in the consortium was in many ways a courtesy. Because its building was not technically historic, regardless of what a
state law might say, it remained ineligible for the kind of large historic
preservation grants that had gone to Círculo Cubano. A major goal of the
consortium was to locate grants to repair the structures and coordinate
applications to avoid competing with each other. Martí-Maceo was left out
of that discussion, and this status differential became a metaphor for
broader patterns of ignoring their presence. As the focus of the consortium
continued to shift from saving the clubs to finding adaptive reuses for the
buildings, this marginalization by architectural inferiority intensified.

The initial draft bylaws for the consortium, drawn up to enable incorporation, had left Martí-Maceo off the list of voting members. The banker
who drew up the bylaws argued that since their building had no value,
they did not have a stake in the decision-making of the group. A county
official, who was also active in the Italian club, intervened in the discussion
and succeeded in having them restored to the list of directors. Although
Martí-Maceo still had allies in the consortium, there was in fact little in the
consortium's activities that benefited Martí-Maceo. The discursive flow of

meetings was frequently diverted around them, and the club's representatives often found it difficult to get the floor. Meetings were usually held at Centro Asturiano, a forbidding site for most Afro-Cubans. In the late 1980s Sandy Amaros, a retired black Cuban catcher for the Brooklyn Dodgers, reportedly had been refused entry in the cantina to play dominoes, suggesting that little had changed in the racial attitudes of that club. One Martí-Maceo member remarked to me as we approached the building that the only other times he had been allowed in was when he shined shoes there as a kid.

A very telling example of how race continued to influence relationships in these settings occurred on a trip to Tallahassee, the annual bus ride to the state capitol for "Ybor City Day." Members of the different clubs travel together to meet with legislators and lobbyists to try and persuade them to help preserve the state's historic resources, or at least those located in Ybor City. On one such occasion, a group of about six Martí-Maceo members joined the delegation. Arrangements had been made to host a reception for their legislative friends and well-wishers. The Ybor City organizers thought that serving staff would be provided by the Dade County delegation, but apparently this was a misunderstanding. The food and drinks arrived for the reception, but no one showed up to serve it. This dilemma was resolved when one of the organizers from Ybor City asked the president of Martí-Maceo to recruit the other members present to act as servers. Rather than conscript volunteers from among the whole group, the instigator of this idea relied on a racial formula for defining who should fill this role. The president was shocked at this request, but she betrayed none of this emotion in response. Rather, she went and explained it to the other members who, annoyed but amused, proceeded to serve the guests who had begun to arrive. No one else seemed to notice or find it strange, and it is likely that the person who asked them to do it never gave it another thought. It was, however, a lively topic of conversation among Martí-Maceo members for weeks thereafter.

Involvement in the Heritage Structures Consortium yielded relatively few resources for Martí-Maceo, especially compared to the large restoration grants that the other clubs obtained. Participation exposed them occasionally to the sort of treatment described above, but it also led to some valuable acquaintances and genuine allies among the other groups. Inclusion heightened visibility, multiplied connections, and gave access to information about development plans that might affect them. By the mid-1990s, development in Ybor City had heated up considerably. The place finally had caught on as a nightspot, and a string of new bars and restaurants opened on Seventh Avenue. This activity enlivened and transformed the empty storefronts, but included some techno-pop retrofitting that drastically altered the original character of historic buildings. Escalating tax rates squeezed old ethnic businesses, such as Agliano's Fish Market, out of existence. The ethnic social clubs are tax exempt, thus avoiding this particular problem. The consortium managed to orchestrate a special bill in the state legislature entitling the Ybor City social clubs, including Martí-Maceo, to sell liquor to the public. This privilege offered an important device for raising funds from Ybor's large partying crowds, a strategy intended to capitalize on changing circumstances that were also threatening.

Conversion of these properties into commercialized entertainment venues offered a use that was compatible with current trends in Ybor's development, but also entailed new requirements for modernizing the structures. More stringent fire and building codes, and handicap access regulations, imposed new conditions for renting and staging public events in these sites. The bathrooms at Martí-Maceo were not in compliance with the Americans with Disabilities Act, which jeopardized their ability to rent the hall. With the aid of the consortium and the Ybor City Round Table (another collaboration of groups in the area), Martí-Maceo received a special donation of about $6,000 to make the necessary repairs. Although small in comparison with the huge state grants gotten by Círculo Cubano, Centro Asturiano, and L'Unione Italiana, it was a sizable contribution and an important gesture of support. Unfortunately, it arrived at precisely the wrong moment.

Leadership Crisis

In an eerie replay of the problem that afflicted Círculo Cubano nearly a decade earlier, Martí-Maceo fell prey to embezzlement. No one has been charged in the events I am about to describe, although the details are well documented. Efforts to involve law enforcement were unavailing, due mainly to the relatively small size of the embezzlement. The losses in this case were much less, although proportionally they were nearly as devastating. So, unlike Ramón Hernández of Circulo Cubano, who was indicted for his crimes and became a public figure, the individual involved in these events will be identified by a pseudonym.

Not since Bruno Roig misappropriated the treasury in 1915 had there been even a hint of scandal attached to Martí-Maceo's leadership. But never before had there been so few members who were willing or able to take the position as president. The job pays nothing, and it is far more than an honorary title. The most onerous part involves managing rentals of the building, which requires the president to come to the hall at the close of the evening, usually around two A.M., to check out its condition and lock the door. Elderly members with failing health and fading eyesight could not undertake this responsibility. By the mid-1990s, two decades after the reverse exodus of New Yorkers, too few members were young enough. The size of the membership had begun to dwindle, attrition caused by death. Funerals became the major communal rites, more frequent than dances and better attended. When the time came to elect a new president, no one from the ranks of the Ybor City descendants was willing to serve. The new president, "Rosalía," was very polished and correct in her speech and knowledgeable about Cuban history. There were many misgivings about her election. She had served as secretary a few years earlier and had not done a very good job. And she had a haughty demeanor that put many people off. Nonetheless, she seemed to be capable and well connected to the larger Cuban community and claimed that she could bring in many new members.

The installation occurred, as always, in January. The ceremony was well attended, and the new president was gracious in her praise for the organization and grateful for the honor of leading it. By the end of the next month, however, all that had changed. February is an important month in Ybor City, the time of the Knight Parade. This event parallels the annual Gasparilla Festival in Tampa, a pre-Lenten celebration of Tampa's mythical pirate founder, José Gaspar (d'Ans 1980). The main show of the festival involves a mock invasion by corporate moguls dressed as pirates, members of an elite all-male and all-white secret society named Ye Mystic Krewe. The spectacle of modern buccaneer capitalists seizing control of the city flaunts the ruthlessness of their literal power in this domain, an interpretation that has fascinated many commentators on this festival (d'Ans 1980; Schneider 1994; Yelvington, Goslin, and Arriaga n.d.). An added nuance is that they dress as swarthy Spanish pirates, an invasion of dangerous aliens, much like the one that launched Ybor City.[12] The Krewe's arrival, in a crude facsimile galleon, is followed by daylong festivities and a big parade through the downtown area. A week later, on Saturday evening, a second parade, called the Knight Parade, is held in Ybor City down Seventh Avenue.[13]

Martí-Maceo is located directly on the parade route, and this choice vantage point makes the Knight Parade a festive and lucrative event for the club. Chairs from inside are crowded onto the sidewalk in front of the hall; those not taken by members are sold to the public. Parking spaces next to the building are also sold. Drinks and food are sold in the cantina, and the hall is filled with members, parade goers, the odor of cigars and garlicky pork, and the sounds of salsa. In this particular year, however, the event was a series of disasters.

Problems began in the afternoon, when one of the other officers, a hold-over from the previous administration, arrived. Rosalía had been spreading rumors that she (the other officer) had stolen money from the club, a smear campaign that seemingly was designed to drive away this other officer and provide cover for her own planned malfeasance. When the rival walked through the door of the hall, Rosalía said in a loud voice from some distance away, "You are not allowed in here. We do not allow thieves in this hall." Such stunning behavior in such a public situation cast an instant pall on the festivities. Several people left in support of the other officer, but most remained. At that juncture, many were unsure about these rumors, which later proved false, in spite of long-standing relationships with the accused. By the end of the night, however, there would be few in the club who still believed or supported Rosalía.

The next incident occurred as the parade vehicles were assembling. Cars were provided for presidents of all the ethnic clubs, and Rosalía arrived to take her place. She spied what she thought was her car and stepped inside. At about the same moment, Representative Elvin Martínez (one of the club's legislative benefactors) also arrived, only to discover that Rosalía was sitting in his car. When he attempted to explain, she became angry and refused to exit. A high-ranking city official (and also a figure sympathetic to Martí-Maceo) attempted to intercede. She redirected her anger towards him, claiming that Martí-Maceo was being discriminated against and treated shabbily. Ultimately, she was persuaded to ride in another car, but this incident was the subject of much amusement in Ybor City meetings and coffee houses in the following weeks. I heard the story in three different places. When one of the Heritage Structures Consortium members mentioned the mishap to her at the next monthly meeting, she exploded in rage and told him he was never allowed to come to Martí-Maceo again. In that same meeting, she was also rude to the president of the Ybor City Round Table, who had provided part of the money for the bathrooms and help with the liquor license.

More disturbing and potentially more damaging was the final episode of the evening, a shooting inside the hall. The Knight Parade had become increasingly unruly with Ybor City's transformation into a massive wet zone. Drinking in the bars prior to and after the parade, as well as the actions of muggers and rapists drawn to the huge nighttime crowd, produced new levels of danger. For these reasons, and because they staged their own party, Martí-Maceo had a policy of not renting the hall on the night of the parade. Rosalía departed from that policy by renting it to another group, recent immigrants from Honduras, who started their party after the members left. The second party broke up around three A.M. While the band was packing up afterwards, a drunk wandered in from the sidewalk and tried to engage one of the band members in a conversation. Unsatisfactorily, it seems, because an argument ensued. When another band member intervened, the drunk drew a gun and shot him in the arm. According to the arrest report cited in a news article the next day, the perpetrator explained that the victim "had disrespected him." This dreadful publicity was contained in a larger story about violence after the Knight Parade, headlined "Rapists Target Ybor City's Party District."[14] These are exactly the kind of stories that discourage investment in Ybor City, and Martí-Maceo's association with this violence was damaging to its reputation.

It was only February. The president serves a twelve-month term ending in December. Members I spoke with about these events were extremely upset. In a matter of weeks she had fomented internal divisiveness, alienated important allies, and permitted the club to become the site of scandalous violence. This was only what appeared on the surface, and there was much more to come. She removed the safe from the building, placed some of the contents in a safe-deposit box under her name, and discarded the rest along with the old safe. Someone at the salvage yard where it landed discovered tax records and other documents still inside and contacted a former president whose name was on some of the papers. She sold an old refrigerator that had been donated by one of the members, and she threw out furniture, equipment, and an unknown number of other articles belonging to the club. She sent me a letter demanding an inventory of the Martí-Maceo records archived at the University of South Florida Library, in preparation for securing their return to her custody. Rumors about these activities excited alarm, but she refused to make any accounting or respond to the complaints. She also refused to hold monthly meetings, as required in the by-laws.

In March, she claimed that it was impossible to meet because the bathrooms were being remodeled. In April, it was because the floors had just been waxed. By May, when there was still no meeting, an opposition group coalesced in an effort to remove her. They did not succeed in doing so until July, when they demanded that she call a meeting, which she finally agreed to do. At the appointed hour, she failed to show up, having heard that she was going to be put out of office. The dissident members cut the lock off the front door. Two elderly men, hammering and struggling under a blazing sun, finally managed to pry it open. Those gathered entered and had the meeting without her, voting unanimously to oust her. By August, they had regained full control, blocking her from access to the building, bank account, and postal box. Negotiations assisted by one of the directors of Centro Asturiano brought the return of most of the records. What was missing was most of the money in the bank account. Small amounts had been bled out in checks made out to herself, but the main cause of the decline was an absence of deposits. She had been diverting the revenue from rentals. Only part of the money earmarked for the bathrooms actually went into this work, which was shoddy and unattractive.

It was impossible to tally the losses accurately. The records from the prior administration were very disorderly, making it hard to determine the exact size of the balance when she took office. These ambiguities made prosecution more difficult, and the small size of the alleged theft greatly reduced the likelihood of a criminal investigation. It was viewed by authorities as a petty complaint, a white-collar crime of an essentially private nature. Civil remedies were also unpromising, given that she possessed little that might be recovered. Beyond recriminations about the loss, however, it was clear that the present balance was much too small to cover upcoming bills. Martí-Maceo's crisis galvanized energy in the members who had snatched it back.

At the August meeting, the evidence was all laid out, complete with bank documents and witnesses who testified about Rosalía's rental practices. An extremely emotional occasion, members took turns expounding on their love for Martí-Maceo and what it had meant to their parents. Checkbooks opened. It was a small group, about thirty members, most dependent on Social Security and small pensions. In a matter of minutes, they assembled enough donations to more than double the balance and ensure that immediate bills could be paid. The vice-president agreed to step into the role of president, and a fund-raiser was planned to help regain solvency and recruit new members.

A public notice was drafted announcing that Rosalía had no further connection with Martí-Maceo, and explaining why. Ads with this copy were purchased in the local weekly papers, and notices were sent to all the committees and groups in which Martí-Maceo was involved. The new board of directors attended the next meeting of the Ybor City Round Table to express their shame at Rosalía's treatment of the president and her misuse of the funds for the bathrooms. It was a difficult moment, in which each speaker enunciated personal ties to Ybor City and its values and heritage. Embarrassing, but redemptive, a public proclamation of the return of the old leadership; they invoked shared traditions reaching across generations, and the cumulative reputation and achievements of their *sociedad*.

They had rescued the club from the brink, and they were repairing the damage caused to vital relationships, but this experience only reinforced a wariness of strangers. It convinced many that only the real Tampeños, whose ancestors had invested them with the necessary reverence, were suited for leadership. But that conviction only underscored the dilemma that gave rise to the problem initially. Everyone knew that this was only a temporary fix.

Second-Century Project

Standing at the edge of a century of existence, La Sociedad La Unión Martí y Maceo still held on. After Rosalía's ouster a new, younger, president came forward. Raised in New York, great-grandson of Cuban independence activists, he brought energy and education, although he also had a demanding job and a young family. During his presidency, and at his request, I decided to become actively involved in helping to shore up the club's future. I always had been involved, in the sense that I attended meetings and performed various tasks involving writing, research, or contacts with officials. In keeping with anthropological tenets of noninterference, however, I rarely offered suggestions or initiated ideas. In the aftermath of the crisis, I stepped beyond advocacy into a role of active participant. In so doing, I discovered the invisible line alluded to in the wisdom of noninterference. I also witnessed the excruciating difficulty of passing institutions across generations, and the inherent vulnerabilities of grassroots organizations against the power of corporations and the state.

In fall 1998 I was scheduled to teach a graduate seminar in social organization. It was a course designed to link theory and practice, to understand notions about social structure by examining how real groups organize to solve their problems. In an earlier meeting of Martí-Maceo, when those present were deliberating their own organizational problems, I volunteered to enlist the students in my upcoming class to help find short- and long-term solutions. The offer was accepted, and students in the class engaged in various projects—research on funding sources and steps needed to gain access, an inventory of local agencies and actors involved in Ybor development, and a focus group at Martí-Maceo that included most of the active members. The focus group session generated a set of goals, and a planning committee was formed. Recruiting new younger members was the primary goal. Students interviewed younger relatives of members, drawn from a fairly large cohort who lived in Tampa but did not participate in Martí-Maceo. This group was the primary target of recruitment; interviews were aimed at gauging interest, as well as collecting data on this cohort of Afro-Cuban-Americans.

The activities of the seminar led to the formation of a planning committee, known as the "Breakfast Club," because we met on Saturday mornings at a local Cuban restaurant. This group of seven members, two students, and myself focused on articulating the purposes of the club, revising the bylaws, and planning a recruitment drive. Students in the second year of the seminar (fall 1999) helped implement the committee's work and provided other kinds of support, such as the creation of a website and fundraising bake sales at the university. One of the younger descendants we had interviewed, an active and popular woman with scores of relatives still living in Tampa, volunteered to organize a reunion happy hour on a Friday afternoon to help revive their interest in belonging to Martí-Maceo. Fall 1999 also marked the centennial of the October 10 Club, the first Cuban mutual aid society, which had given birth to Círculo Cubano and Martí-Maceo. The new president of Círculo Cubano, a history professor at the University of South Florida who had grown up in Tampa, got a grant from the Florida Humanities Council to stage a series of programs, commemorating the two clubs and examining their divided histories. Martí-Maceo was a partner in the grant, and I became codirector with the history professor. The Ybor City Museum Society was the formal sponsor.

The celebration of Cuban mutual aid in Tampa anointed a history that began with a few months of unity, followed by a century of separation. It reunited black and white descendants who barely knew each other in discussions about why that was so. This was an ambitious project, animated in some part by the chance discovery by the president of Círculo Cubano that he was a cousin to a large family cohort of Martí-Maceo members. His desire to probe this unexplored dimension of his own family history, combined with practical concerns about the financial status of Círculo Cubano, were motives to reach out for a stronger alliance. Both clubs were in a shaky condition, and both were facing formidable pressures as the pace of Ybor development got closer to their doorsteps. Círculo Cubano earned large revenues from renting the hall and patio, but debt service on recent repair costs was extremely heavy, and the building still needed extensive renovations. Although the membership had increased in recent years, it still remained below two hundred. Martí-Maceo had problems of a lesser magnitude, but still very threatening. Monthly costs of operation were relatively low, because the building has no mortgage. Rental revenues, however, had dropped off considerably, and dues from the fewer than one hundred members were not enough to cover expenses. The treasury never had recovered from the losses during Rosalía's term in office, and costs were mounting. The roof had a leak, as did the plumbing, and the city had issued a code violation ordering them to paint the exterior of the building. Both presidents hoped that the festivities would attract sympathetic attention of potential members and benefactors, and there were allusions to the possibility of an ultimate merger. This latter suggestion aroused wariness on both sides.

The yearlong celebration involved five programs at intervals beginning in October 1999 and ending in November 2000. The first commemorated the split, but also served as the official birthday of Círculo Cubano, an awkward combination that seemed to betoken the continuity of the white Cubans in the original club, whereas black members who were expelled had to form one of their own. The next two focused on Cuban independence and the ideologies of Martí and Maceo. These two programs were celebratory and didactic, intended to inform the members of both clubs and the wider community about the unique legacies of local Cuban history. The fourth event was designed to discuss racial issues dividing black and white Cubans in Tampa, to bring into the open topics that long had been repressed. This panel discussion, which was not well attended by members of either club, brought forth bitter complaints by one Afro-Cuban in the audience, who in turn elicited strong condemnation inside Martí-Maceo. The final program was the hundredth anniversary of the founding of Martí-Maceo, an event that had to be postponed several weeks beyond its originally scheduled occurrence, because the club was falling apart.

Problems arose early in the year, when Martí-Maceo's president got a new job that consumed all of his time. Forced to step down, he was replaced by a new president who was far less committed to collaborating with white Cubans. Various problems beset the organization, and each succeeding Humanities event produced new tensions. The drive to recruit new members initially had been quite successful, attracting about a dozen young descendants and their friends. Several were from the family related to the president of Círculo Cubano. This influx met resistance—an unwelcoming attitude that caused them to lose interest—and reflected quiet rumors inside the club that the centennial was designed to engineer a takeover of Martí-Maceo. There was also gossip about the grant that funded the programs, suggestions that Martí-Maceo was not getting a fair share, or that academics were profiting at their expense. Between the humanities project, for which I was the visible representative, and my applied anthropology students, there were a lot of academics on the scene.

Discord among the members, a vacuum in leadership, and the mounting financial problems of the club, reduced attendance at meetings and willingness to be involved in organizing programs. There was a growing gap between my students' efforts and the members' response. The students' energy, which was supposed to help spark action by the members, came to be viewed as a substitute. The balance of collaboration too easily shifted in the wrong direction. Tensions associated with these activities brought to the surface underlying cliques and fractures in the social networks of the Afro-Cuban community, patterns of gossip, and lines of hostility. These developments revealed structural cleavages in the community related to class, distinctions between New Yorkers and Tampeños, family rivalries, and long-standing grievances—features I had not seen so clearly under conditions of greater cohesiveness. Meetings had become shrill and unpleasant, and decreasingly well attended. By late spring, when the fourth program was completed, it seemed likely that the organization would fold before reaching its centennial.

There was a long hiatus before the final event, scheduled for late October. During those months, as I despaired about my own role in causing this dissension, circumstances turned once again. On several prior occasions, when internal crises appeared to threaten the club's continued existence, rump caucuses had formed to challenge or animate the leadership. In late summer, when it came time to plan the club's centennial celebration, the current leadership failed to respond. Members of the "Breakfast Club" group and several new members who had remained at the periphery joined in an effort to resuscitate the membership and install new leaders. They managed to wrest control only a few weeks prior to the scheduled event. A burst of energy and a brief postponement resulted in a highly successful program—a two-day event with a banquet on Saturday night and a celebratory program the next afternoon. Both were well attended, by members of Círculo Cubano as well as Martí-Maceo. As the corner turned on the second century of Martí-Maceo's existence, all appeared to be well. The club had gained a new slate of officers, renewed interest among those who had been disaffected, new ideas about how to refashion the purpose of the organization, a large amount of good publicity, and a sizable profit from the banquet.

The struggle has only begun, however. A few days after the centennial program, the president was called to a meeting with the Ybor City Redevelopment Corporation, where plans were revealed to alter the entire block on which the building stands. Extensive and disruptive work will commence immediately, and by 2003 they plan to demolish the building. Martí-Maceo has been invited to negotiate, and the organization is not without assets or allies, but this is a perilous field of engagement. The entire eastern section of urban Tampa, the portion that has been traditionally black or incipiently so, is now the object of a massive redevelopment project orchestrated by the city (which also calls for the demolition of St. Peter Claver Church and School). Literally billions of dollars are at stake, and the players at the top are reflexively unsentimental. It remains to be seen how Martí-Maceo will fare in these negotiations, but this was coming anyway. The present state of the organization at least offers room for optimism.

My narrative ends inconclusively as the tale wends on. There is no way to forecast the outcome of impending displacement, or internal changes in leadership and membership that yet may occur in Martí-Maceo. The possibilities for surviving another hundred years, the future course of Afro-Cuban ethnicity in Tampa, are matters for pure speculation. Tenacity over the past sixty years since the collapse of the cigar industry that initially sustained this group contradicts conventional wisdom about the forces that pull communities apart. The factions that emerged around the centennial were not new, nor were they ultimately divisive. The same channels that served to fuel gossip and criticism were also used as conduits for messages of alarm and calls for consensus. These networks of mainly kin ties reflect the structure of the community, the underlying connections that continue to exist among descendants of the Afro-Cuban cigarmakers. The shape and constituency of these networks have been transformed greatly, incorporating diverse elements and interacting under very different circumstances, yet maintaining a collective sense of Afro-Cuban/Tampeño identity. So long as Martí-Maceo and St. Peter Claver continue to exist, this distinctive sense of identity is likely to endure. Both institutions, however, are currently in jeopardy.

Conclusions

The long history of this small community has relevance for theories of how race and ethnicity are constructed. The way Tampa's Afro-Cubans interacted with the structure in which their experiences were embedded also discloses much about how agency is fashioned and resistance is mobilized. Five generations have occupied this landscape during more than a century of radical change in cities throughout the United States. Millions of immigrants from all parts of the world have participated in the process, have confronted similar challenges, and have been beset by similar forces. African Americans have undergone a parallel process, even more destructive and difficult. Experiences of Afro-Cubans in Tampa, an obscure group in a little-known place, gather the threads of both of these American sagas.

So what can we learn from examining this unique set of circumstances? What larger lessons can be drawn from this tale of race, ethnicity, power, and endurance? The chapters in this book have touched on many themes. Organizing and making sense of this complexity is not a simple task. In attempting to do so, I return to the ideas of Pierre Bourdieu, especially those of habitus and cultural capital.

> The habitus, which is constituted in the course of an individual history, imposing its particular logic on incorporation, and through which agents partake of the history objectified in institutions, is what makes it possible to inhabit institutions, to appropriate them practically, and so to keep them in activity, continuously pulling them from the state of dead letters, reviving the sense deposited in them, but at the same time imposing the revisions and transformations that reactivation entails. (Bourdieu 1990a:57)

This passage fairly describes the process I have outlined in the foregoing chapters—the durability of the Martí-Maceo Society, the objectification of traditions brought forth from the *cabildos, sociedades,* and the *tabaqueros'* revolutionary organizations that provisioned war against the tyranny of Spain. Also evident are the revisions and transformations, adaptations to the loss of cigar work and dissolution of the cigar workers' community, shared participation in assaulting the Jim Crow regime. Change and the changeless find tangible expression in an organization that has outlived its founders and their children, a corporate institution that is both the symbolic and concrete representation of Afro-Cuban ethnicity in this location.

The institutions that Bourdieu refers to, however, are those of the "king, the banker or the priest . . . hereditary monarchy, financial capitalism or the Church made flesh" (57). He does not entertain the possibility that little institutions, like mutual aid societies, can also play a significant role in this process, that the "sense deposited in them" can be a tutored sensibility that enables autonomous action by those who are otherwise slated for exploitation. In writing this position, I believe he loses perspective on how habitus embodies agency that is productive, not simply reproductive. He similarly adopts a needlessly narrow frame in his concept of "cultural capital."

Cultural capital, according to Bourdieu, exists in two dimensions. First, it refers to formal education that confers skill and *savoir faire*[15]—fungible intellectual goods that permit the possessor to earn access to resources and economic wealth. Second, culture has to do with aesthetics and taste—unconscious values and preferences that mark distinctions and betoken subtle credentials that anoint privilege. These cultural commodities are hierarchical, a system of capital that reinforces inequality and helps promote reproduction of class relations. There is "legitimate" cultural knowledge, that of the elite, and "popular" cultural knowledge that reflects the cultivated habits of the masses. Bourdieu's analysis precludes the efficacy of popular cultural knowledge; its capital is discounted, and the practices it engenders are handicapped. Inconvertibility of this nonelite know-how is a crucial element in the maintenance of oppression. "Culture," as this term is used in North American anthropology, however, is a broader, more flexible concept, properties that permit us to see around the corners of Bourdieu's box. Indigenous culture has unappreciated wisdom, and oppressive circumstances may elicit novel solutions as well as slavish accommodation.

Cigar workers in Tampa had their own intellectual traditions, a system of tutelage that schooled them in the beliefs and ideas of the major counter-hegemonic thinkers of the Western world. From the *lectores*, they learned about Marx, Bakunin, and Kropotkin, and these theories reinforced their own convictions about labor, solidarity, and mutual aid. In addition, they and their children knew the classics of European literature, were equipped to think about global themes and large ideas in a critical frame. It was an educational system that they devised and controlled by investing a part of their wages to buy the services of *lectores,* and it was a system that they fought to maintain. The fact that removing the *lectores* was a major goal of the manufacturers in the lockout/strike of 1931 illustrates the importance their adversaries attached to defeating this institution.

As well, the practical knowledge needed to operate Martí-Maceo's benefit system represented inherited cultural capital, know-how that was invested profitably to create a protective structure in the threatening environment of Jim Crow Florida. The advantages Afro-Cubans were able to wrest—in health, recreation, education, and status—were measurable and large, and attributable mainly to their own collective action. They created an institution in which they stored capital and reaped dividends; part of a larger system of immigrant mutual aid in Ybor City, that enabled cigar workers to defy elite conceptions of their proper place in Tampa's hierarchy.

Similarly indigenous institutions in the African American community formed the basis of self-help, mutual aid, and organized resistance. Churches that were founded during the politics of Reconstruction, and political organizations brought forth in its aftermath (especially the NAACP), provided communal structures that later nurtured the Civil Rights movement. Political legacies of Afro-Cuban history, the rebellious traditions of the cigar workers, and shared experiences as black people, all helped promote Afro-Cubans' affiliation with the Civil Rights struggle in Tampa, and Martí-Maceo became a resource in the larger black community as well.

If the notion of cultural capital is to have any useful explanatory value, it needs to include these obviously cultural assets. Otherwise, it is simply nomenclature; a synecdoche for elite status, leading to the sterile conclusion that privilege begets privilege. If capital can only be construed as an instrument of domination, and exchanges are always asymmetrical, then how to explain the results of my investigation of the financial operation of Martí-Maceo? This analysis challenged the derived assumption that profitless cooperation—for example, pooling wages to provide collective benefits—cannot survive the internal tensions of individual greed or the external forces that destabilize face-to-face community. This case demonstrated that greed can be domesticated within institutions, that altruism can be engendered and reproduced, and that the actuarial principles that underlay the balance between costs and benefits were both complicated

and counterintuitive. The mobility of the cigarmakers, the presumed disadvantages of their transnational positioning, was shown to have un-
counted advantages in the calculus of mutual aid. Human nature also
proved to be more complicated than rational choice determinism. The selfish greed of Bruno's crime is counterbalanced by the unlikely generosity
of Adam Katz. Both offered lessons in survival that served the Afro-Cubans well in contending with future threats.

Mutual aid societies were fairly successful institutions in Ybor City.
Labor unions were not. Cigar workers in Tampa staged numerous strikes,
some long and bloody, virtually none victorious. Cubans in Tampa were
able to exert significant control over their own habitus in Ybor City, but in
more challenging arenas of wages and working conditions, their efforts
were effectively thwarted. This larger view of the agency of the Cubans,
one that tempers success with failure, is more in accord with Bourdieu's
pessimism. Assessing the agency of African Americans yields similar conclusions. The Civil Rights movement did win legal victories, reinstating
voting rights and overturning formal segregation. But desegregating the
schools has been a punishing process that destroyed black neighborhood
institutions and inflicted long bus rides on mostly black children. And desegregating public accommodations strained the viability of black businesses that once served a Jim Crow market.

That neither the Afro-Cubans, nor the African Americans, nor even the
white Cubans of Tampa were able to muster profound changes in their
conditions out of their sociocultural combinations suggests the limits of
agency, and lends support for Bourdieu's conclusions about social reproduction. The *lectores* were defeated after all. Of all the strikes the workers
staged, only the Weight Strike of 1899 succeeded in its demands. Martí's
program for social justice was subverted handily by U.S. influence in Cuba.
His pleas for racial unity were undermined easily in Cuba, and even more
so in Jim Crow Florida, where deadly violence backed up the more diffuse
messages (the "symbolic violence") of racial doctrines and patterns of social segregation.

Racial divisions within Ybor City fractured the solidarity of the cigar
workers' socialist posture and created structural disadvantages that were
visited on succeeding generations of Afro-Cubans. Against their accomplishments in operating the Martí-Maceo Society at all, were pitted the
obstacles they confronted that weakened their position, diminished their
status, and reduced their capacity to enlarge and protect what they had.
The intermediate status they occupied, just above African Americans,

nonetheless placed them squarely at the bottom of the immigrant hierarchy. Efforts to improve and secure that position, to cultivate distinctions between themselves and African Americans, led them into a conundrum of respectability based in oppression.

The gender contradictions that seemed to be entwined with the pursuit of respectability, the need to establish and maintain status, and demonstrate distinctions between one group of black people and another, are also consistent with Bourdieu's analysis of class reproduction. Divisions of gender, built on divisions of ethnicity, did not alleviate divisions based on race. What was created instead was simply divisiveness, the disabling inability of the powerless to act in concert or identify common enemies who benefit at their expense.

But gender contradictions also divided generations, and in the process created their own logic played out in a period of irresistible change. The propensity to marry across ethnic lines, to violate the rules in order to be free of them, reinforced and hastened the very outcome that the seclusion of women was explicitly intended to avoid. The second generation formed a cohort whose spouses were mostly African Americans, and whose children were only part Cuban, growing up in an era when women's liberation was cast in the idiom of black liberation. The elusive connection between gender oppression and other kinds of discrimination emerged in the rhetoric of this period and framed understanding of stories told by Cuban grandmothers. When self-isolation yielded to incorporation by intermarriage, it was not a case of "downward mobility," was not surrender to a loss of status. Rather, this process was alliance building and an act of survival, mutual fortification in which legacies are not lost, and pantheons of heroic figures are expanded rather than substituted. Antipathy towards African Americans was a false consciousness, unmasked more easily in the observable contradictions of Cuban gender relations. These processes of transculturation, as Ortiz (1947) might label them, did not lead to simple reproduction, or to the erasure of Cuban identity in black Tampa, but rather to a new definition of Martí-Maceo that includes all its family legacies. Afro-Cuban ethnicity in Tampa has undergone broad transformations, is a way of life far removed from that of early cigar workers. At the same time, Cuban visitors frequently remark about how unexpectedly Cuban these third- and fourth-generation exiles seem to be. Historical threads weave generations together, place the lives of the elderly within reach of the very young, and transfer stories and messages crafted from the values of a long-gone community.

The unusually long life of the Martí-Maceo Society reflects agency at work, the creation and maintenance of alternative structures that are only rational at the group level, and that respond to contingencies far more complex than self-interest alone. Legacies of mutual aid, and passion for Cuba that was a conscious metaphor for freedom and justice, were woven into the charter of the organization. The significance of Martí-Maceo, the major purpose it continues to play, lies in its symbolic expression of those ideals, and in the example it sets for how real people, one's own ancestors, can mobilize to achieve them.

Notes

Introduction

1. The term *enclave* is used with some frequency in this book. My usage is generic, referring to a definable community, in this case composed of immigrants connected to cigarmaking in Tampa, and somewhat interchangeable in meaning with "district" or "area." The early-twentieth-century Cubans in Tampa do reflect interesting parallels with work done by Portes (1987) on the enclave economy of Cubans in contemporary Miami. These issues are beyond the scope of the present endeavor, and I have not attempted any systematic comparisons, nor do I employ the word *enclave* within his specialized use of the term.

2. My work merged history and ethnography, raising conflicting issues of documenting sources versus protecting confidentiality. In conventional ethnographies, names of places and people are fictionalized to give cover against harming or embarrassing the individuals discussed. Such poetic license would scarcely serve in my particular study. Historical details and supporting evidence are inherently necessary. At the same time, individuals who helped me are entitled to privacy. My solution to this problem involved drawing a distinction between public and private figures. Individuals whose activities are part of the public record—public officials, officers in the Martí-Maceo, spokespersons for various purposes—are identified by name in this text. Information supplied by these individuals, which is directly relevant to public activities under discussion, will be attributed accurately. Pseudonyms will be used in all other cases. I have invented a list of alternative first names for the people I interviewed whose narratives are laced throughout the text. I wanted to personalize, but not to expose.

3. I do not capitalize the word *black* when used either as a noun or an adjective. This practice avoids need for parallel capitalization of "white," and the more ambiguous case where the operative descriptor might be "brown." Capitalizing tends to reify and nominalize, creating categories based solely on race. One of the purposes of this book is to challenge such simple devices. Lower-casing this concept helps to disarm its pretentiousness.

4. In 1990, I surveyed 53 members of Martí-Maceo, including a question about self-identification. Respondents were given a set of options, with a blank line for additions; 5 opted for Afro-Cuban, 5 for Afro-Cuban-American, 17 identified themselves as Cuban, 5 as African American, 6 as simply American (a write-in), 5 Puerto Rican (also a write-in), 3 refused to answer the question, and the remaining 9 were variant write-ins.

5. Although only a small number of the respondents in the survey selected "African American," the average age of the respondents was sixty-seven. Separate open-ended interviews with eight younger Afro-Cuban descendants, in their thirties and forties, confirmed their preference for identifying with African Americans and a belief that most in their age cohort would express the same opinion. This also accords with the perceptions of older Afro-Cubans I interviewed, when speaking of the younger descendants.

6. There is a growing population of recent black Cuban immigrants in Tampa, only a few of whom have joined Martí-Maceo. Only rough estimates can be made of the number of recent Afro-Cubans in the Tampa Bay region. There were 32,408 Cubans enumerated by the 1990 census for the Tampa Bay region (Greenbaum 1998:149). Even if black Cubans are only 5 percent, a conservative estimate, this amounts to more than 1,500 people. They do not have a separate organization, and are scantily represented in the organizations of the larger exile community in Tampa. During the 1980s, several Martí-Maceo members expressed wariness to me about the reputation of the Mariel exiles, and there are few family ties to this group. Most of the more recent Afro-Cuban immigrants in the club do have some kinship connection to Tampa.

José Martí and Jim Crow

1. Ada Ferrer's essay "The silence of patriots" (1998) provides an excellent analysis of the omission of Afro-Cuban contributions to the independence effort, a denial that is justified by reference to José Martí's admonitions against divisive discussions of race.

2. In 1997, the Tampa/Hillsborough County Preservation Board commissioned a historic marker to be placed on the sidewalk outside of the Martí-Maceo social hall. The text, which I wrote, does include a discussion of Afro-Cubans in the War for Independence.

3. The story about the flag was told to me by María Viernes's daughter, Fredesbinda Millet (now deceased). Her great-granddaughter, Sonia Menendez, also had been told of the flag by María before she died. A cousin visited Cuba in the 1980s and reportedly found the flag in a small exhibit in an old municipal building in the Marianao section of Havana. Subsequent visits by others have failed to rediscover the building, but directions were vague.

4. Teofilo Domínguez's will, in the possession of his great-granddaughter, Sonia Menendez, bears the signatures of Juan Gualberto Gómez and Gustavo Urrutia as witnesses.

5. The Bella Unión Habanera was one of the pan-Afro-Cuban mutual aid societies, with branches in several Cuban towns in addition to Havana, where education became a primary goal after the end of slavery.

6. Helg (1995:129) reports that a census conducted by the United States in Cuba in 1899 found that only 24 percent of Afro-Cubans over the age of ten could read and write, compared with 44 percent of white Cubans. The 1900 U.S. Census for Tampa, microfilm schedules, reveals that 72 percent of Afro-Cubans over the age of ten there could read and write. There are no separate data on white Cuban literacy, but Afro-Cuban cigarmakers who emigrated to Tampa were clearly more literate than average Cubans.

7. Microfilm of Twelfth U.S. Census for Hillsborough County. All the Pedrosos lived in Precinct 20 (Ybor City).

8. The 1901 *Shole's Directory for Tampa* lists 10 Afro-Cuban households in the three blocks surrounding the Pedroso house, along with 32 white Spanish and Cuban families, 5 Italians, 4 African Americans, 2 Jews, and 2 English-surnamed whites.

9. In May 1897, the Pedrosos repurchased the property and boardinghouse from Tampa Bay Real Estate, Inc., for $2,100. The selling price in 1895 had been $1,500, so the owners made a handsome profit from the transaction. There is no indication of how the Pedrosos managed to pay for the house. They sold it again in 1905, to Hanna Crenshaw (nothing known about her) for $4,500, more than twice what they had paid in 1897. Data are derived from Hillsborough County property records.

10. *Tampa Tribune* 10/29/1895, p. 1.

11. *Tampa Tribune* 10/19/1897, p. 1.

12. *Tampa Morning Tribune* 6/1/1898, p. 2, col. 3–5.

13. *Tampa Times* 5/16/1894.

14. Herman Monroe, "Centennial History of St. James Episcopal Church," 1991.

15. This article from the *Tampa Times* could not be retrieved from the microfilm, because holdings for both the University of South Florida and the Tampa Public Library are missing that date. The text was read by Sister Earlene, a teacher at St. Peter Claver School, and entered verbatim on tape during an interview conducted for the City of Tampa by Otis Anthony in 1978, transcript on file in Special Collections Dept. of the University of South Florida Library, Tampa, Fla.

16. *Tampa Tribune* 8/4/1895, p. 2, col. 2.

17. *Tampa Tribune* 4/13/1895, p. 1, col. 3.

18. *Tampa Tribune* 6/12/1895, p. 4, col. 2.

19. *Tampa Tribune* 6/12/1895, p. 1, col. 3.

20. *Tampa Tribune* 6/12/1895, p. 1, col. 3.

21. *Tampa Tribune* 6/14/1895, p. 1, col. 3.

22. *Tampa Tribune* 8/9/1895, p. 1, col. 4.

23. *Tampa Tribune* 9/29/1895, p. 1 col. 5.

24. *Tampa Tribune* 9/29/1895, p. 1 col. 5.

25. *Tampa Morning Tribune* 5/5/1898 p. 1, col. 4.

Exiles

1. There is no way to achieve an accurate estimate of the numbers of Tampa Cubans who returned home in 1898. No manuscript census exists for 1890, against which to compare listings in 1900. Even that source would be unreliable, covering too wide a period. For Afro-Cubans alone, I examined nineteen individuals listed in an 1893 city directory (a gross undercount of the Afro-Cubans reportedly in Tampa at that time) against the 1899 city directory; all but two from the earlier list were missing from the later one. *None* of the 366 Afro-Cubans listed in 1899 (an enumeration likely made in 1898) were included on the manuscript census forms for 1900, suggesting a very large proportion of the black (and most likely white) Cubans in Tampa returned to Cuba right after the war.

2. U.S. Senate Immigration Commission (hereinafter referred to as Immigration Commission), *Immigrants in Industries,* vol. 14: "Cigar and Tobacco Manufacturing" (Washington, D.C.: Government Printing Office, 1911), 187, 192.

3. "Narrative by Ramon Sanfeliz," Federal Writers' Project for Tampa, Dept. of Special Collections, University of South Florida Library.

4. Translation of minutes by Enrique Cordero.

5. The full list of founders included in minutes of October 26, 1900: T. Domínguez, D. Caballero, F. Frenzault, C. Gonzalez, Marcelino Castillo, A. Palacios, Y. Aguero, Y. C. Gonzalez, F. E. Mederos, F. Alvarez, M. Zarza, S. Alfonso, F. del Pino, R. Pedroso, G. del Pino, J. I. Ramos, A. Romero, G. Martinez, P. Ballan, P. Otero, E. Marrero, A. Acosta, Pablo Folas, Bruno Roig. Martí-Maceo Collection, Dept. of Special Collections, University of South Florida Library. Palacios's role in the Club Patria de Caballero is identified in the *Tampa Tribune* 10/19/1897, along with that of Emilio Alonso, who was the patriarch of a very large West Tampa family.

6. *Tampa Tribune* 6/13/1899, p. 1, col. 3.

7. Karl Marx, "The Eighteenth Brumaire of Louis Bonaparte," in *Selected Works* (New York: International Publishers, 1968), 97.

8. Personal communication from Raul Lavin, former president of Círculo Cubano.

9. *Tampa Morning Times,* 7/28/1899.

10. Immigration Commission, *Immigrants in Industries,* Table 147, p. 216. A slightly earlier study that compared cigar workers in various parts of the United States showed that Tampa paid the highest average wages—$630 per year, compared with $592 in New York, $517 in Ohio, and $400 in Pennsylvania (Jacobstein 1907:149).

11. Immigration Commission, *Immigrants in Industries,* 250.

12. Ibid., Table 133, p. 200.

13. Ibid., p. 191.

14. Ibid., p. 206.

15. Ibid., p. 207.

16. Ibid., p. 190.

17. Ibid., p. 208.

18. Ibid., p. 219.

19. Ibid., pp. 209–10.

20. *Tampa Tribune*, 8/3/1902.

21. *Tampa Tribune* 2/21/1904. Judge Robles, who owned a ranch in the section north and east of the city, was reportedly among those who blew up the power company's dam in 1899 according to Leland Hawes, author of the *Tampa Tribune's* history column.

22. Miguel Díaz appears on the Martí-Maceo membership list for 1902. Martí-Maceo Collection.

23. Twelfth and Thirteenth United States Censuses for Hillsborough County. The county, rather than the city, was used for this enumeration, because West Tampa was still a separate municipality.

24. Microfilm U.S. Census schedules for Hillsborough County, Twelfth Census, 1900.

25. *Tampa Daily Times* 1/28/1915.

26. Ibid.

27. *Tampa Tribune* 3/13/1993, Metro section, p. 1.

28. Mays and Raper (1927), whose study of black life in Tampa was conducted about a decade later than the period referenced here, after a considerable boom in black business development during the early 1920s, identified a total of 185 black-owned businesses in Tampa. Although somewhat numerous, these establishments had a combined workforce of only 400 people and a total gross value of stock and equipment of only $213,050 (see Business and Professions section of the report; available in the USF Library Special Collections Dept.).

29. *Tampa Tribune* 12/6/1903, p. 1, col. 3.

30. Martí-Maceo minutes, 8/22/1906.

31. Ibid., 4/2/1908.

32. Ibid., 3/24/1909, 6/9/1909.

33. Ibid., 10/5/1909.

34. *Tampa Tribune* 8/24/1906, p. 2.

35. By 1906 the Pedrosos no longer owned the boardinghouse. It was sold in 1905. There are no further records of Ruperto and Paulina living in Tampa after that date, although oral history accounts suggest they remained in Tampa until the cigar strike of 1910. Other oral histories by individuals who remembered them from childhood also confirm that they remained after the sale of the property. There is no precise information about when they went back to Cuba. Paulina died there in 1913 (funeral notice in Tony Pizzo Collection, Special Collections, USF Library). The coincidence of the sale of their property and renewed political unrest in Cuba suggests that they might have been involved in some way.

36. *Tampa Tribune* 8/25/1906, p. 2.

37. Ibid., 8/30/1906, p. 2.

38. Ibid., 5/23/1912, p. 2.

39. Ibid., 5/27/1912.

40. Ibid., 6/12/1912, p. 12; *La Lucha* 6/10/1912, p. 2; Martí-Maceo minutes, 6/12/1912.

Sociedad la Unión Martí-Maceo

1. The only source of data on relative incomes of Afro-Cubans and African Americans is a report compiled in 1927 (Mays and Raper 1927). At that time, cigarmaker wages are listed as $40–$50 per week, compared with $14 per week for male servants, $21 per week for black truck drivers, $16.50 per week for sanitation workers, $18 per week for construction workers. The only occupation listed that is close in wages to the cigarmakers was the head cook at the Tampa Bay Hotel, who earned $40 a week.

2. *Album-Exposicion de El Círculo Cubano y La Unión Martí-Maceo* 1918:14, Dept. of Special Collections, University of South Florida Library. This publication was compiled by both clubs in an effort to gain support from the Cuban government for the exile organizations in Tampa.

3. Martí-Maceo minutes, 2/3/1901.

4. Towards the end of the First World War, a massive outbreak of influenza infected populations throughout the world; 21 million people died as a result, more than 500,000 in the United States. In Tampa, an estimated 39 percent of the population contracted the flu, with 283 deaths (*Tampa Tribune* 9/25/1994, p. 16, special centennial edition for 1895–1918).

5. The calculations do not include revenues earned from other sources (such as fund-raising events), but also excluded are other costs associated with doctors and pharmacies, as well as other purchases and costs. These other elements, which cannot be individualized, are of a magnitude on both sides of the equation that effectively cancel each other. Dues revenues were the principal source of income, and *dieta* payments were the principal source of debits.

6. The gap in the records resulted from the loss of several minute and treasury books, and nearly all the correspondence files, at the time they moved in 1965, when the building was demolished by Urban Renewal.

7. This figure was derived by multiplying the total dues payments received from members over the entire period ($100,059) by the rate of return for those long-term members who never left Tampa ($n = 64$; rate = .406). This revision assumes that, if all the members had been stable, they would have been eligible to receive approximately $40,624, instead of the $22,686 that was paid under the actual rate of return for all members (.227).

8. Martí-Maceo minutes, 1/26/1910.

9. Benjamin S. Lidden, Thomas F. West, James C. B. Koonce, *Florida Compiled Laws, Annotated* (Tallahassee: West Publishing Co., 1915), section 731.

10. Martí-Maceo minutes, 10/17/1915.

11. *Tampa Daily Times* 1/8/1915. Later in that same month (1/20/1915), the

Tampa Daily Times also ran a story about proposed literacy restrictions that threatened to interfere with the entry of Spanish immigrants.

12. Immigration Commission, *Immigrants in Industries,* Table 185, p. 257. The naturalization rate, based on those who had been in Tampa for five years or more, was 9.8 percent for Cubans, 9.5 percent for Spaniards, and only 3.5 percent for Italians.

13. *Tampa Daily Times* 1/18/1915.

14. *Tampa Tribune* 1/28/1915.

15. *Tampa Tribune* 2/12/1995.

Divided Lives

1. Extracted from 1910 microfilm of U.S. Census schedules for Hillsborough County.

2. Martí-Maceo minutes, 10/26/1900.

3. *El Internacional* 10/5/1917, p. 10. This newspaper is available on microfilm at the University of South Florida Library.

4. Alexander Pompey, then a cigarmaker, briefly belonged to the Martí-Maceo Society in 1910, when he was eighteen (Membership Registry for 1910, Martí-Maceo Collection). He was one of many members who dropped out during the 1910 strike and, in his case, never returned. Pompey became famous, or notorious, as a numbers banker in New York during the 1920s and '30s. "Pompey was nationally known in black political and fraternal circles. Most sports-minded African Americans knew him as an influential member of the Negro National League (NNL), organized in 1920, and as the owner of the famous New York–based Cuban Stars baseball team, which he purchased with his numbers earnings" (Watkins-Owens 1996:140).

5. *Tampa Tribune* 5/11/1900.

6. Comparison extracted from microfilm U.S. Census schedules for Hillsborough County, 1900 and 1910. Occupations of women in this analysis included all types of paid work, not just the cigar workers, hence the proportion of working wives is larger here than the figure cited in Chapter 4.

7. All the statistics in this section were extracted from microfilm U.S. Census schedules for 1910.

8. Immigration Commission, *Immigrants in Industries,* 108, gives the wages earned by Cuban women in cigar factories in 1910 as averaging $1.20, which is actually less than daily *dieta* payments to male members of Martí-Maceo when they were too sick to work. Informants who did cigar stripping in the 1920s told me that they usually earned about $2.00 a day.

9. Extracted from microfilm U.S. Census schedules for 1910.

Afro-Cuban Americans

1. See Franklin (1980:189–94) for a discussion of the significance of passages across the Ohio River in the network of escape routes on the Underground Railroad.

2. The strike of 1931 reflected a combination of forces. Mechanization of cigarmaking had finally begun to take hold in the 1920s, threatening the security of the hand rollers. In addition, cigarettes were becoming increasingly more popular than cigars, reducing demand for the higher-quality products made in Tampa. Federal protections for union organizing encouraged the arrival of Communist organizers in 1931. Rallies and other public activities unleashed vigilante reactions and a new surge of violence against cigar labor activists. Tension built and on Thanksgiving Day (11/26/1931) the manufacturers removed the *lectore* platforms from factory floors and banned further reading on the grounds that the readers were inculcating radical ideas in the workers. A seventy-two-hour strike resulted in a lockout. When factories reopened in early December, about 30 percent of the strikers were not rehired and the union had been defeated (Ingalls 1988:152–57).

3. Cigar production in Tampa reached a peak in 1929, with an annual output of 505 million; by 1935, it had dropped to 311 million cigars. Average annual wages fell from about $850 a year in the mid-1920s to $550 in 1933, *Tampa Tribune* 9/25/1994 (centennial issue for years 1927–41), 13.

4. "Personal Observations of Emigration of Workers, as Translated from Spanish to English," p. 3, Federal Writers' Project for Tampa.

5. *Tampa Tribune* 9/25/1994 (centennial section), 13. In 1907 wages were $630 (Jacobstein 1907:149).

6. "Interviews Obtained by M. Marrero with Persons Leaving Tampa," p. 3, Federal Writers' Project for Tampa.

7. Sixteenth Census of the United States, 1940, "Report by Nativity and Sex for the City of Tampa, 1930 and 1940," Table C-36, p. 151.

8. "Interview with F. Valdes," p. 2, Federal Writers' Project for Tampa.

9. F. Valdes, "Interview with a Person Who Returned to Tampa from New York," pp. 2–3, Federal Writers' Project for Tampa.

10. "Interview Obtained by Mr. Marrero," p. 4, Federal Writers' Project for Tampa.

11. No known relationship to Paulina and Ruperto Pedroso.

12. "Interview with 'Mr. A.' of Ybor City, Fla., as Reported by Mr. F. Valdes, April 2, 1935," p. 2, Federal Writers' Project for Tampa.

13. I could find no documentary corroboration of this story, but it was told to me by several older cigarmakers.

14. Bureau of the Census, *Negroes in the United States, 1920–1932* (Washington, D.C.: Government Printing Office), 1932, Table 10, p. 55.

15. Huie (1956) writes about the murder trial of the wife of a black *bolita* banker in north Florida. In his book he describes the statewide network of black *bolita* sellers and bankers, including those in Tampa. He also discusses the connection between these entrepreneurs and the Central Life Insurance Company.

16. Mary McLeod Bethune began her career in Florida in 1904, when she established the Daytona Normal and Industrial Institute for Negro Girls. This institution grew into the Bethune-Cookman Institute, and Mrs. Bethune, by the 1920s, had

become nationally known for her work in education and human rights. She was a close friend of Eleanor Roosevelt and a member of FDR's "Black Cabinet" (Jones and McCarthy 1993:6–63).

17. After completing the work with Mays in Tampa, Raper collaborated with Morehouse College professor Walter Chivers in investigating lynchings; they coauthored an influential pamphlet in 1931 entitled *Lynchings and What They Mean.* Also in 1931, as an active member of the Commission for Interracial Cooperation, Raper was involved with the case of the Scottsboro Boys, nine young black men who were falsely accused of rape in rural Alabama (Goodman 1994:165).

18. Martí-Maceo minutes, 10/9/1928. Translated by Enrique Cordero.

Revolution, Renewal, Revitalization

1. The Hillsborough County marriage records curiously did not record the race of spouses until 1946. For the period between 1946 and 1960, I identified 73 marriages involving at least one Afro-Cuban spouse. Of these, 28 were between African American males and Afro-Cuban females; 33 between Afro-Cuban males and African American females; and 12 were between Afro-Cuban males and females. This only reflects marriages that occurred in Hillsborough County. I am aware of at least one marriage between Afro-Cubans that took place in Cuba, and there could have been others in the pre-embargo period.

2. A major mechanism of disenfranchisement was the system of primary elections in Florida and other southern states, in which the winner of the Democratic primary was the de facto winner of the general election. Blacks were excluded from membership in the Democratic Party and hence ineligible to vote in the Democratic primary elections. The legal argument held that political parties were private entities that could prescribe the terms of membership, and thus this practice was not in conflict with the Thirteenth and Fourteenth Amendments. In January 1944, the U.S. Supreme Court denied that argument in the *Smith v. Allwright* decision. Although it was no longer legal to deny registration in Democratic primaries, blacks were still discouraged from doing so by extralegal means (see Price 1957).

3. *Tampa Tribune* 5/29/1942, p. 20.

4. Martí-Maceo minutes, 6/3/1951.

5. *Havana Lunes* 9/6/1948.

6. Martí-Maceo minutes, 4/11/51.

7. *Tampa Tribune* 11/25/1955, p. 1.

8. Martí-Maceo minutes, 9/12/56.

9. The Pedroso house was sold in 1905 to an Anglo family named Crenshaw.

10. *Tampa Tribune* 12/12/1993.

11. *Tampa Tribune* 7/27/1984, p. 11A.

12. Ibid.

13. Ibid.

14. Martí-Maceo minutes, 3/11/1959.

15. Martí-Maceo minutes, 2/10/1960.

16. *Tampa Tribune* 7/27/1984, p. 11A.

17. *Tampa Times* 2/29/1960, p. 4.

18. Mr. Pizzo's extensive collection of documents, photos, and personal notes is housed in the Special Collections Department of the University of South Florida Library. The "historic map" he created for the Urban Renewal case is unfortunately not included in the collection.

19. *Tampa Tribune* 11/22/1988.

20. *Tampa Tribune* 10/10/1988, Northside, p. 2.

21. *Tampa Tribune* 7/18/1993, Metro, p. 1.

22. The issue of Progress Village divided the Afro-Cuban and African American leadership in Tampa. One of the main promoters of Progress Village was Aurelio Fernandez, a second-generation Afro-Cuban who was principal of a black elementary school and a civic activist (chair of the Clara Frye Hospital board; leader of the local United Negro College Fund). Francisco Rodriguez Jr., a close friend of Aurelio, also expressed support for Progress Village (reportedly out of loyalty to Aurelio), a position that the NAACP strongly opposed. Fernandez was killed in an auto accident in 1959, shortly before the subdivision was completed.

23. *Tampa Tribune* 5/16/1979, section D, p. 1.

24. *Tampa Tribune* 5/14/1979, section D, p. 2.

25. Tampa city directories for the period between 1955 and 1965 indicate that it served as a meeting hall for a variety of CIO union locals through 1958, was the Church of the Lord Jesus Christ of Apostolic Faith until 1963, and was vacant thereafter until the Martí-Maceo Society bought it in 1965.

Out of Time

1. *Tampa Tribune* 10/10/1983, p. 1A.

2. The historical records, correspondence, photographs, and library of the Martí-Maceo Society were transferred to the Department of Special Collections, University of South Florida Library, in 1984. These arrangements were made by Enrique Cordero, a master's degree student in anthropology. Mr. Cordero also wrote a very detailed and useful index to the holdings in this archive, as well as a literal transcription of all Afro-Cubans appearing in the 1900 and 1910 manuscript census schedules for Hillsborough County. References in the preceding text to individuals and computations of Afro-Cuban data from these two censuses are based on this valuable resource document created by Mr. Cordero.

3. *Tampa Tribune* 2/21/1987, Baylife, pp. 1–2.

4. Information about African Americans in Tampa was nearly as scant as that for Afro-Cubans when I began this work. To help remedy this problem, my colleague Cheryl Rodríguez (daughter of Francisco Rodríguez Jr.) and I wrote a proposal to the Florida Humanities Council to do a retrospective program on Central Avenue. This was conducted in 1994, the twentieth anniversary of the demolition of Tampa's black business district. Geoffrey Mohlman, then a master's degree student in anthropology, did a prodigious amount of archival research; Ericka Burroughs, another

master's degree student, assisted Robert Saunders in editing his memoirs about the NAACP in Florida; Jennifer Paul, also a master's degree student, developed exhibits; and Ginger Baber, a doctoral student, researched the effects of Urban Renewal and organized youth participation in the program; see *Practicing Anthropology* 20(1).

5. Proposed Ybor City Historic District, with commentary; draft nomination prepared by Robert M. Leary and Associates, Ltd., Raleigh, N.C., 3/28/1985.

6. In 1999 it was announced that the city would build a trolley barn directly across from the Martí-Maceo building. Early in 2000, a large ornamental iron arch was erected across Seventh Avenue just to the west of the building, and in that same period, the property was rezoned to permit a wider number of commercial uses. A trolley station is planned for the parcel just to the east of the building, and there are other major changes already planned for the area to the north.

7. Florida House of Representatives—1989, 158–64–1–9.

8. *Tampa Tribune-Times* 12/21/1986, p. 2B.

9. *Tampa Tribune* 4/21/1992, Metro, p. 1.

10. *St. Petersburg Times* 5/14/1992, p. 1B.

11. Additional news stories about the financial crisis of the Círculo Cubano include: *Tampa Tribune* 4/18/1992, Metro, p. 1; *Tampa Tribune* 4/20/1992, Metro, p. 1; 4/22/1992, Metro, p. 1; *Tampa Tribune* 4/23/1992, Metro, p. 1; *Tampa Tribune* 4/28/1992, Metro, p. 1.

12. D'Ans (1980:25) puts it nicely: "Nevertheless, it was not by chance that the myth makers adopted Latin characters. At the beginning of the century, Tampa was clearly divided into downtown and Ybor City, the respective headquarters of capital and labor. The American businessmen living downtown founded their prosperity on the labor of the Latin population of the city. Recognizing this ethnic and social division, one aspect of the Gasparilla celebration becomes clear. Disguised as Latin pirates, members of the Anglo establishment invaded the city, acting out violence that was as much a part of themselves as the pirates they played."

13. The Knights of Sant' Yago is a "krewe" that was begun in 1972, modeled on Ye Mystic Krewe of Gasparilla. Its members are predominantly descendants of Ybor City, although none is black; no women belong to Sant' Yago either. Despite these exclusions, they self-consciously define themselves as coming from humble backgrounds. Contrasting them with the elite Gasparilla Krewe, a commentator noted that "Gasparilla is old money, but the Krewe of Sant' Yago are real people." A member explained that "Our purpose is to perpetuate our Latin heritage. We do that by helping to revitalize Ybor City." The annual Knight Parade (also called the Illuminated Night Parade) is one of several events that Sant' Yago sponsors each year (*St. Petersburg Times*, 2/15/1992, p. 1D).

14. *Tampa Tribune* 2/17/1997, Metro, p. 1.

15. French phrase meaning "to know [what] to do," also connoting clever refinement.

Bibliography

Abel, Christopher. 1986. Martí, Latin America, and Spain. In C. Abel and N. Torrents (eds.), *José Martí: Revolutionary Democrat*. Durham: Duke University Press, 124–52.

Acheson, James (ed.). 1994. *Anthropology and Institutional Economics*. Monographs in Economic Anthropology, no. 12. New York: University Press of America.

———. 1989. Management of common property resources. In Stuart Plattner (ed.), *Economic Anthropology*. Stanford, Calif.: Stanford University Press, 351–78.

Adler, Jeffrey. 1995. Black violence in the New South: Patterns of conflict in late nineteenth century Tampa. In David R. Colburn and Jane Landers (eds.), *The African American Heritage of Florida*. Gainesville: University Press of Florida, 207–39.

Alduino, Frank. 1991. The smugglers' blues: Drug and alien traffic in Tampa during the 1920s. *Tampa Bay History* 13(2): 27–39.

Alexander, Tom. 1966. Those amazing Cuban emigres. *Fortune Magazine* (October): 144–49.

Anderson, Martin. 1964. *The Federal Bulldozer: A Critical Analysis of Urban Renewal, 1949–1962*. Cambridge: MIT Press.

Andrews, George Reid. 1992. Racial equality in Brazil and the United States: A statistical comparison. *Journal of Social History* 26(2): 229–63.

Ans, Andre-Marcel d.' 1980. The legend of Gasparilla: Myth and history on Florida's west coast. *Tampa Bay History* 2(2): 5–29.

Anthony, Otis. 1989. Black Tampa: The Roots of a People. Tampa: Office of the Mayor of Tampa.

✓ Appel, John. 1966. American Negro and immigrant experience: Similarities and differences. *American Quarterly* 18: 95–103.

Apte, Helen Jacobus. 1998. *Heart of a Wife: The Diary of a Southern Jewish Woman*. Edited and with essays by her grandson, Marcus D. Rosenbaum. Wilmington, Del.: SR Books.

Baker, Lee D. 1998. *From Savage to Negro: Anthropology and the Construction of Race, 1896–1954*. Berkeley: University of California Press.

Banks, Marcus. 1996. *Ethnicity: Anthropological Constructions*. London: Routledge.

Barcia, Luis 1957. Autobiography of Luis Barcia Quilabert. Unpublished manuscript, Dept. of Special Collections, University of South Florida Library, Tampa.

Barreda, Pedro. 1979. *The Black Protagonist in the Cuban Novel*. Amherst: University of Massachusetts Press.

Barth, Frederik 1969. *Ethnic Groups and Boundaries*. Boston: Little, Brown.

Basch, Linda, Nina G. Schiller, and Cristina S. Blanc. 1994. *Nations Unbound: Transnational Projects, Postcolonial Predicaments, and Deterritorialized Nation-States*. Langhorne, Pa.: Gordon and Breach.

Bascom, William R. 1950. The focus of Cuban Santeria. *Southwestern Journal of Anthropology* 6(1): 64–68.

Bates, Robert H. 1994. Social dilemmas and rational individuals: An essay on the New Institutionalism. In James M. Acheson (ed.), *Anthropology and Institutional Economics*. Monographs in Economic Anthropology, 12. New York: University Press of America, 43–65.

Bates, Thelma. 1928. The legal status of the Negro in Florida. *Florida Historical Quarterly* 6: 159–81.

Beck, Sam. 1992. *Manny Almeida's Ringside Lounge: The Cape Verdeans' Struggle for Their Neighborhood*. Providence, R.I.: Gavea-Brown Publications.

Behar, Ruth. 1997. Daughter of Caro. In Consuelo López Springfield (ed.), *Daughters of Caliban: Caribbean Women in the Twentieth Century*. Bloomington: Indiana University Press, 112–20.

Beito, David T. 1993. Mutual aid, state welfare, and organized charity: Fraternal societies and the "deserving" and "undeserving" poor, 1900–1930. *Journal of Policy History* 5(4): 419–34.

Belnap, Jeffrey, and Raul Fernández (eds.). 1998. *José Martí's "Our America": From National to Hemispheric Cultural Studies*. Durham: Duke University Press.

Bengelsdorf, Carollee. 1997. (Re)considering Cuban women in a time of troubles. In Consuelo López Springfield (ed.), *Daughters of Caliban: Caribbean Women in the Twentieth Century*. Bloomington: Indiana University Press, 229–55.

———. 1988. On the problem of studying women in Cuba. In Andrew Zimbalist (ed.), *Cuban Political Economy*. Boulder: Westview Press, 119–36.

Berkes, Fikret. 1989. Cooperation from the perspective of human ecology. In F. Berkes (ed.), *Common Property Resources: Ecology and Community-based Sustainable Development*. London: Belhaven Press, 70–88.

Besson, Jean. 1993. Reputation and respectability reconsidered: A new perspective on Afro-Caribbean peasant women. In Janet Momsen (ed.), *Women and Change in the Caribbean: A Pan-Caribbean Perspective*. Bloomington: Indiana University Press, 15–37.

Bodnar, John. 1981. Ethnic fraternal benefit associations: Their historical development, character, and significance. In Susan Shreve and Rudolf J. Vecoli (eds.), *Ethnic Fraternal Benefit Associations and Their Extant Records*. Pittsburgh: University of Pittsburgh Immigration History Research Center, 5–14.

Bodnar, John, Michael Weber, and Roger Simon. 1988. Migration, kinship, and urban adjustment: Blacks and Poles in Pittsburgh, 1900–1930. In Raymond Mohl (ed.), *The Making of Urban America.* Wilmington, Del.: SR Books, 170–88.

Bond, George C., and Angela Gilliam. 1994. *Social Construction of the Past: Representation as Power.* London: Routledge.

Bourdieu, Pierre. 1990a. *The Logic of Practice.* Stanford: Stanford University Press.

———. 1990b. *Reproduction in Education, Society, and Culture.* London: Sage.

———. 1984. *Distinction: A Social Critique of the Judgement of Taste.* Cambridge, Mass.: Harvard University Press.

———. 1977. *Outline of a Theory of Practice.* London: Cambridge University Press.

Brady, Rowena Ferrell. 1997. *Things Remembered: An Album of African Americans in Tampa.* Tampa: University of Tampa Press.

Brandmeyer, Gerald. 1981. Baseball and the American dream: A conversation with Al Lopez. *Tampa Bay History* 3(1): 48–73.

Brandon, George. 1997. *Santería from Africa to the New World: The Dead Sell Memories.* Bloomington: Indiana University Press.

———. 1991. The uses of plants in healing in an Afro-Cuban religion, Santería. *Journal of Black Studies* 22(1): 55–76.

Braukman, Stacy. 1992. Women and the Civil Rights movement in Tampa: An interview with Ellen H. Green. *Tampa Bay History* 14(2): 62–69.

Brock, Lisa, and Bijan Bayne. 1998. Not just black: African-Americans, Cubans, and baseball. In Lisa Brock and Digna Castaneda Fuertes (eds.), *Between Race and Empire: African-Americans and Cubans before the Cuban Revolution.* Philadelphia: Temple University Press, 168–204.

Bromley, Daniel (ed.). 1992. *Making the Commons Work: Theory, Practice, and Policy.* San Francisco: Institute for Contemporary Studies Press.

Brown, Canter Jr. 1999. *Jewish Pioneers of the Tampa Bay.* Reference Library Series, no. 7. Tampa: Tampa Bay History Center.

———. 1998. *Florida's Black Public Officials, 1867–1924.* Tuscaloosa: University of Alabama Press.

———. 1997a. African Americans on the Tampa Bay frontier. Reference Library Series, no. 3. Tampa: Tampa Bay History Center.

———. 1997b. *Ossian Bingley Hart: Florida's Loyalist Reconstruction Governor.* Baton Rouge: Louisiana State University Press.

———. 1997c. Prelude to the poll tax: Black Republicans and the Knights of Labor in 1880s Florida. In Mark Greenberg, William W. Rogers, and Canter Brown, Jr. (eds.), *Florida's Heritage of Diversity: Essays in Honor of Samuel Proctor.* Tallahassee: Sentry Press.

Browning, James B. 1937. The begininnings of insurance enterprise among Negroes. *Journal of Negro History* 22: 417–32.

Bryce-Laporte, Roy S. 1972. Black immigrants: The experience of invisibility. *Journal of Black Studies* 1: 29–56.

Burke, Mary. 1989. The success of Blanche Armwood (1890–1939). *Sunland Tribune* 15: 38–43.

Butcher, Kristin. 1994. Black immigrants in the United States: A comparison with native blacks and other immigrants. *Industrial and Labor Relations Review* 47(2): 265–84.

Butler, John Sibley. 1991. *Entrepreneurship and Self-Help among Black Americans: A Reconsideration of Race and Economics.* Albany: State University of New York Press.

Campbell, A., W. Stuart, and P. McLendon. 1939. *The Cigar Industry in Tampa, Florida.* Gainesville: University of Florida.

Canizares, Raul. 1993. *Walking with the Night: The Afro-Cuban World of Santería.* Rochester, N.Y.: Destiny Books.

———. 1990. Cuban racism and the myth of the racial paradise. *Ethnic Studies Report* 8(2): 27–32.

Carbonell, Walterio. 1993. Birth of a national culture. In *Afrocuba: An Anthology of Cuban Writing on Race, Politics, and Culture,* P. Perez Sarduy and Jean Stubbs (eds.). Melbourne, Australia: Ocean Press, 195–203.

Carson, Emmett D. 1993. *A Hand Up: Black Philanthropy and Self-Help in America.* Washington, D.C.: Joint Center for Political and Economic Studies Press.

Casals, Lourdes. 1979. Race relations in contemporary Cuba. *Minority Rights Group,* Report no. 7, London.

Chalmers, David. 1965. *Hooded Americanism: The History of the Ku Klux Klan,* 3rd ed. (1987). Durham: Duke University Press.

Chyz, Yaroslav J., and Read Lewis. 1949. Agencies organized by nationality groups in the United States. *Annals of American Academy of Political and Social Science* 26(March): 148–58.

Clifford, James. 1997. Spatial practices: Fieldwork, travel, and the disciplining of anthropology. In Akhil Gupta and James Ferguson (eds.), *Anthropological Locations: Boundaries and Grounds of a Field Science.* Berkeley: University of California Press, 185–222.

Coleman, James S., and Thomas J. Fararo. 1992. *Rational Choice Theory: Advocacy and Critique.* Newbury Park, Calif.: Sage.

Collins, Patricia H. 1997. The meaning of motherhood in black culture and black mother/daughter relationships. In Mary M. Gergen and Sara N. Davis (eds.), *Towards a New Psychology of Gender.* New York: Routledge, 325–40.

Cooper, Patricia. 1987. *Once a Cigar Maker: Men, Women, and Work Culture in American Cigar Factories, 1900–1919.* Urbana: University of Illinois Press.

———. 1983. The "traveling fraternity": Union cigar makers and geographic mobility, 1900–1919. *Journal of Social History* 17: 127–38.

Cotton, Jeremiah. 1993. Color or culture? Wage differences among non-Hispanic black males, Hispanic black males, and Hispanic white males. *Review of Black Political Economy* 21(4): 55–67.

Croucher, Sheila. 1997. *Imagining Miami: Ethnic Politics in a Postmodern World.* Charlottesville: University Press of Virginia.

Cummings, Scott. 1980. Collectivism: The unique legacy of immigrant economic development. In Scott Cummings (ed.). *Self Help in Urban America*. Port Washington, N.Y.: Kennikat Press, 5–29.

Day, Allen Willey. 1898. Cuban settlers in America. *Chautauquan* 27(July): 346–48.

Degler, Carl N. 1971. *Neither Black nor White: Slavery and Race Relations in Brazil and the United States*. New York: Macmillan.

Deschamps Chapeaux, Pedro. 1974a. *Rafael Serra y Montalvo: Obrero Incansable de Nuestra Independencia*. Habana: Union de Escritores y Artistas de Cuba.

———. 1974b. *Contribución a la Historia de la Gente sin Historia*. Habana: Editorial de Ciencias Sociales.

———. 1963. *El Negro en el Periodismo Cubano en el Siglo XIX: Ensayo Bibliografico*. Habana: Ediciones R.

Deulofeu, Manuel. 1904. *Heroes del Destierro: La Emigración*. Cienfuegos, Cuba: Imprente de M. Mestre.

Dixon, Heriberto. 1988a. The Cuban-American counterpoint: Black Cubans in the United States. *Dialectical Anthropology* 13: 227–39.

———. 1988b. Sombras que solo yo veo: The black Cuban odyssey to the United States. Paper presented at the 2nd Annual Hispanic Cultures and Literatures Conference, Slippery Rock University, Slippery Rock, Pa., November 3–4.

———. 1982. Who ever heard of a Black Cuban? *Afro-Hispanic Review* 1(3): 10.

Dodson, Jualynne E. 1998. Encounters in the African Atlantic world: The African Methodist Church in Cuba. In Lisa Brock and Digna Castaneda Fuertes (eds.), *Between Race and Empire: African-Americans and Cubans before the Cuban Revolution*. Philadelphia: Temple University Press, 85–103.

Domínguez, Teofilo. 1899. *Ensayos Biograficos: Figuras y Figuritas*. Tampa: Imprenta: Lafayette Street 105. [Manuscript in Schomburg Center for Research, New York]

Domínguez, Virginia. 1987. Sex, gender, and revolution: The problem of construction and the construction of a problem. *Cuban Studies/Estudios Cubanos* 17: 7–23.

d'Orso, Michael. 1996. *Like Judgment Day: The Ruin and Redemption of a Town Called Rosewood*. New York: G. P. Putnam's Sons.

Downs, Anthony. 1982. *Neighborhoods and Urban Development*. Washington, D.C.: Urban Institute.

D'Souza, Dinesh. 1995. *The End of Racism: Principles for a Multiracial Society*. New York: Free Press.

Duany, Jorge. 1982. Stones, trees, and blood: An analysis of a Cuban Santero ritual. *Cuban Studies/Estudios Cubanos* 12(2): 38–53.

Du Bois, W. E. B. 1907. *Economic Cooperation among Negro Americans*. Atlanta University Publications, no. 12. Atlanta: Atlanta University Press.

Duharte Jimenez, Rafael. 1993. The nineteenth century black fear. In Pedro Pérez Sarduy and Jean Stubbs (eds.), *Afrocuba: An Anthology of Cuban Writing on Race, Politics, and Culture*. Melbourne, Australia: Ocean Press, 37–46.

Dworkin, Kenya. 1998. What's black and white and read all over? Race, gender, and class in Cuban literary nation building, 1902–1934. *Cuban Studies/Estudios Cubanos* 27: 110–39.

Ellis, Keith. 1998. Nicolas Guillen and Langston Hughes: Convergences and divergences. In Lisa Brock and Digna Castaneda Fuertes (eds.), *Between Race and Empire: African-Americans and Cubans before the Cuban Revolution.* Philadelphia: Temple University Press, 129–67.

Ergood, Bruce. 1971. The Female Protection and the Sun Light: Two contemporary Negro mutual aid societies. *Florida Historical Quarterly* 50(1): 25–38.

Farkas, George. 1996. *Human Capital or Cultural Capital? Ethnicity and Poverty Groups in an Urban School District.* New York: Aldine de Gruyter.

Fere, Catherine. 1994. Challenges to Jim Crow: African American legal struggles in Tampa during World War II. Master's thesis, University of South Florida, Tampa.

Fermoselle, Rafael. 1974. *Politica y color en Cuba: La Guerrita de 1912.* Montevideo: Ediciones Géminis.

Fernández, Nadine. 1996. The color of love: Young interracial couples in Cuba. *Latin American Perspectives* 88(1): 99–117.

Fernández-Kelly, Patricia. 1995. Social and cultural capital in the urban ghetto: Implications for the economic sociology of immigration. In Alejandro Portes (ed.), *The Economic Sociology of Immigration.* New York: Russell Sage Foundation.

Fernández-Kelly, Patricia, and Richard Schauffler. 1996. Divided fates: Immigrant children and the new assimilation. In Alejandro Portes (ed.), *The New Second Generation.* New York: Russell Sage Foundation, 30–53.

Fernández Robaína, Tomás. 1993. The twentieth-century black question. In Pedro Pérez Sarduy and Jean Stubbs (eds.), *Afrocuba: An Anthology of Cuban Writing on Race, Politics, and Culture.* Melbourne, Australia: Ocean Press, 92–108.

———. 1998. Marcus Garvey in Cuba: Urrutia, Cubans, and Black nationalism. In Lisa Brock and Digna Fuentes (eds.), *Between Race and Empire: African Americans and Cubans before the Cuan Revolution.* Philadelphia: Temple University Press, 120–28.

Ferrer, Ada. 1999. *Insurgent Cuba: Race, Nation, and Revolution, 1868–1898.* Chapel Hill: University of North Carolina Press.

———. 1998. The silence of patriots: Race and nationalism in Martí's Cuba. In J. Belknap and R. Fernández (eds.), *José Martí's "Our America": From National to Hemispheric Cultural Studies.* Durham: Duke University Press, 228–49.

———. 1991. Social aspects of Cuban nationalism: Race, slavery, and the Guerra Chiquita, 1879–1880. *Cuban Studies/Estudios Cubanos* 21: 37–56.

Foner, Nancy. 1987. The Jamaicans: Race and ethnicity among migrants in New York City. In Nancy Foner (ed.), *New Immigrants in New York.* New York: Columbia University Press, p. 195–218.

Foner, Philip S. (ed.). 1989. *José Martí: Political Parties and Elections in the United States.* Trans. Elinor Randall. Philadelphia: Temple University Press.

Fox, Geoffrey E. 1973. Honor, shame, and women's liberation in Cuba: Views of working-class émigré men. In Ann Pescatello (ed.), *Male and Female in Latin America*. Pittsburgh: University of Pittsburgh Press, 273–90.

Franklin, John Hope. 1980. *From Slavery to Freedom*, 5th ed. New York: Alfred A. Knopf.

Fuente, Alejandro de la. 1999. Myths of racial democracy: Cuba, 1900–1912. *Latin American Research Review* 34(2): 39–72.

———. 1998. Race, national discourse, and politics in Cuba: An overview. *Latin American Perspectives* 25(3): 43–69.

———. 1997. Two dangers, one solution: Immigration, race, and labor in Cuba, 1900–1930. *International Labor and Working-Class History* 51(spring): 30–49.

———. 1996. "With all and for all": Race, inequality and politics in Cuba, 1900–1930. Ph.D. diss., University of Pittsburgh.

Gable, Eric. 1996. Maintaining boundaries or "mainstreaming" black history in a white museum. In S. Macdonald and G. Fyfe (eds.), *Theorizing Museums: Representing Identity and Diversity in a Changing World*. Cambridge, Mass.: Blackwell Publishers, 177–202.

Garvin, Russell. 1967. The free Negro in Florida before the Civil War. *Florida Historical Quarterly* 46(1): 1–17.

Gatewood, Williard B. 1990. *Aristocrats of Color: The Black Elite, 1880–1920*. Bloomington: Indiana University Press.

———. 1972. Black Americans and the quest for empire, 1898–1903. *Journal of Southern History* 38: 545–66.

———. 1970. Negro troops in Florida, 1898. *Florida Historical Quarterly* 49: 7–9.

Gillis, John R. 1994. Memory and identity: The history of a relationship. In John R. Gillis (ed.), *Commemorations: The Politics of National Identity*. Princeton: Princeton University Press, 3–26.

Gilroy, Paul. 1987. *There Ain't No Black in the Union Jack*. Chicago: University of Chicago Press.

Glazer, Nathan, and D. P. Moynihan. 1970. *Beyond the Melting Pot*. Cambridge, Mass.: MIT Press

Goings, Kenneth W., and Raymond Mohl. 1995. Toward a new African American urban history. *Journal of Urban History* 21(3): 283–95.

González, Reynaldo. 1993. A white problem: Reinterpreting Cecilia Valdés. In Pedro Pérez Sarduy and Jean Stubbs (eds.), *Afrocuba: An Anthology of Cuban Writing on Race, Politics, and Culture*. Melbourne, Australia: Ocean Press, 204–13.

Goodman, James. 1994. *Stories of Scottsboro*. New York: Random House.

Góveia, Elsa. 1966. Comment on "Anglicanism, Catholicism, and the Negro Slave." *Caribbean Studies in Society and History (CSSH)* 8(3): 328–30.

Granovetter, Mark. 1995. The economic sociology of firms and entrepreneurs. In Alejandro Portes (ed.), *The Economic Sociology of Immigration: Essays on Networks, Ethnicity, and Entrepreneurship*. New York: Russell Sage Foundation, 128–65.

Green, Ben. 1999. *Before His Time: The Untold Story of Harry T. Moore, America's First Civil Rights Martyr.* New York: Free Press.

Greenbaum, Susan. 1998. Urban immigrants in the South: Recent data and a historical case study. In Carole Hill and Pat Beaver (eds.), *Cultural Diversity in the U.S. South: Anthropological Contributions to a Region in Transition.* Athens: University of Georgia Press, 144–63.

————. 1993. Economic cooperation among urban industrial workers: Rationality and community in an Afro-Cuban mutual aid society, 1904–1927. *Social Science History* 17(2): 173–93.

————. 1991. A comparison of African American and Euro-American mutual aid societies in nineteenth century America. *Journal of Ethnic Studies* 19(3): 95–119.

————. 1990. Marketing Ybor City: Race, ethnicity, and historic preservation in the Sunbelt. *City and Society* 4(1): 58–76.

————. 1986. *Afro-Cubans in Ybor City: A Centennial History.* Tampa: La Unión Martí-Maceo.

Gregory, Steven. 1998. *Black Corona: Race and the Politics of Place in an Urban Community.* Princeton: Princeton University Press.

Grillo, Evelio. 2000. *Black Cuban/Black American: A Memoir.* Houston: Arte Público Press.

————. 1999. Remarks made during celebration of Black History Month [at the] Miami Dade Community College, February 24–25. Typescript in possession of the author.

Grismer, Karl. 1950. *A History of the City of Tampa and the Tampa Bay Region of Florida.* St. Petersburg: St. Petersburg Printing Co.

Guerra, Armando. 1947. *Martí y los Negros.* Habana:

Hall, Gwendolyn M. 1971. *Social Control in Slave Plantation Societies: A Comparison of St. Domingue and Cuba.* Baltimore: Johns Hopkins Press.

Halter, Marilyn. 1992. *Between Race and Ethnicity: Cape Verdean American Immigrants, 1880–1965.* Urbana: University of Illinois Press.

Handlin, Oscar. 1973. *The Uprooted.* Boston: Little, Brown.

Hardin, Garrett. 1968. The tragedy of the commons. *Science* 162: 1243–48.

Harker, Richard, Charleen Mahar, and Chris Wilkes. 1990. *An Introduction to the Work of Pierre Bourdieu: The Practice of Theory.* New York: St. Martin's Press.

Harris, Abram L. 1936. *The Negro as Capitalist: A Study of Banking and Business among American Negroes.* New York: Negro Universities Press.

Harris, Marvin. 1964. Racial identity in Brazil. *Luso-Brazilian Review* 1(6): 21–28.

Harris, Robert L., Jr. 1981. Charleston's free Afro-American elite: The Brown Fellowship Society and the Humane Brotherhood. *South Carolina Historical Magazine* 82(4): 289–310.

————. 1979. Early black benevolent societies, 1780–1830. *Massachusetts Review* 20(3): 603–25.

Harrison, Faye V. 1998. Expanding the discourse on race. *American Anthropologist* 100(3): 609–31.

———. 1995. The persistent power of "race" in the cultural and political economy of racism. *Annual Reviews of Anthropology* 24: 47–74.

———. 1988. An African diaspora perspective for urban anthropology. *Urban Anthropology* 17(2–3): 111–41.

Hartman, Chester. 1967. The housing of dislocated families. In J. Bellush and M. Hausknecht (eds.), *Urban Renewal: People, Politics, and Planning*. Garden City, N.Y.: Doubleday Anchor, 315–53.

Hawes, Leland. 1987. The "white-capping" of W. R. Crum. *Sunland Tribune* 13: 3–8, 12.

Hechter, Michael. 1987. *Principles of Group Solidarity*. Berkeley: University of California Press.

Hechter, Michael, Karl Dieter Opp, and Rheinhard Wippler (eds.). 1991. *Social Institutions: Their Emergence, Maintenance, and Effects*. New York: Aldine de Gruyter.

Helg, Aline. 1997. Race and black mobilization in colonial and early independent Cuba: A comparative perspective. *Ethnohistory* 44(1): 54–74.

———. 1995. *Our Rightful Share: The Afro-Cuban Struggle for Equality, 1886–1912*. Chapel Hill: University of North Carolina Press.

———. 1991. Afro-Cuban protest: The Partido Independiente de Color, 1908–1912. *Cuban Studies/Estudios Cubanos* 21: 101–21.

Helmreich, Stefan. 1992. Kinship, nation, and Paul Gilroy's concept of diaspora. *Diaspora* 2(2): 243–49.

Hewitt, Nancy. 1995. Engendering independence: Las Patriotas and the socialist vision of José Martí. In Louis A. Pérez (ed.), *José Martí in the United States: The Florida Experience*. Special Studies, no. 28. Tempe: Arizona State University Center for Latin American Studies, 23–31.

———. 1991a. Paulina Pedroso and Las Patriotas of Tampa. In Ann Henderson and Gary Mormino (eds.), *Spanish Pathways in Florida, 1492–1992*. Sarasota, Fla.: Pineapple Press, 258–79.

———. 1991b. Politicizing domesticity: Anglo, Black, and Latin women in Tampa's progressive movements. In Noralee Frankel and Nancy S. Dye (eds.), *Gender, Class, Race, and Reform in the Progressive Era*. Lexington: University of Kentucky Press, 24–41.

———. 1990a. Varieties of voluntarism: Class, ethnicity, and women's activism in Tampa, Florida. In Patricia Gurin and Louise Tilly (eds.), *Women, Politics, and Change*. New York: Russell Sage Foundation.

———. 1990b. Charity or mutual aid?: Two perspectives on Latin women's philanthropy in Tampa, Florida. In Kathleen D. McCarthy (ed.), *Lady Bountiful Revisited: Women, Philanthropy, and Power*. New Brunswick: Rutgers University Press, 55–69.

Hildebrand, Reginald F. 1995. *The Times Were Strange and Stirring*. Durham: Duke University Press.

Hirabayashi, Lane. 1993. *Cultural Capital: Mountain Zapotec Migrant Associations in Mexico City.* Tucson: University of Arizona Press.

Holcomb, Briavel. 1993. Revisioning place: De- and re-constructing the image of the industrial city. In Gerry Kearns and Chris Philo (eds.), *Selling Places: The City as Cultural Capital, Past and Present.* Oxford: Pergamon Press, 133–44.

Howard, Phillip A. 1998. *Changing History: Afro-Cuban Cabildos and Societies of Color in the Nineteenth Century.* Baton Rouge: Louisiana State University Press.

Howard, Walter T., and Virginia M. Howard. 1994a. The early years of the NAACP in Tampa, 1915–1930. *Tampa Bay History* 16(2): 41–56.

———. 1994b. Family, religion, and education: A profile of African-American life in Tampa, Florida, 1900–1930. *Journal of Negro History* 79(1): 1–17.

Hughes, Diane O. 1974. On voluntary associations in history: Medieval Europe. *American Anthropologist* 76(2): 333–34.

Huie, William Bradford. 1956. *Ruby McCollom: Woman in the Suwanee Jail.* New York: Dutton.

Hutter, Michael, and Ilde Rizzo (eds.). 1997. *Economic Perspectives on Cultural Heritage.* New York: St. Martin's Press.

Ingalls, Robert. 1988. *Urban Vigilantes in the New South: Tampa, 1882–1936.* Knoxville: University of Tennessee Press.

———. 1985. Strikes and vigilante violence in Tampa's cigar industry. *Tampa Bay History* 7(2): 117–34.

Jackson, Jesse J. 1960. The Negro and the law in Florida, 1821–1921: Legal patterns of segregation and control. Master's thesis, Florida State University.

Jacobstein, Meyer. 1907. *The Tobacco Industry in the United States.* Studies in History, Economy, and Public Law, Vol. 26, no. 3. New York: Columbia University Press.

Jacques, Geoffrey. 1998. CuBop! Afro-Cuban music and mid-twentieth century American culture. In Lisa Brock and Digna Castaneda Fuertes (eds.), *Between Race and Empire: African-Americans and Cubans before the Cuban Revolution.* Philadelphia: Temple University Press, 249–65.

James, Winston. 1999. New light on Afro-Caribbean social mobility in New York City: A critique of the Sowell thesis. Paper presented at the Institute on Black Life Research Conference, Tampa, Fla., March 24.

———. 1998. *Holding Aloft the Banner of Ethiopia: Caribbean Radicalism in Early Twentieth Century America.* New York: Verso.

Jenkins, Richard. 1992. *Pierre Bourdieu.* London: Routledge.

Johnson, James Weldon. 1965. *The Autobiography of an Ex-Colored Man.* In *Three Negro Classics.* New York: Avon Books.

Jones, Maxine D. 1995. No longer denied: Black women in Florida, 1920–1950. In David R. Colburn and Jane Landers (eds.), *The African American Heritage of Florida.* Gainesville: University Press of Florida, 240–74.

Jones, Maxine D., and Kevin M. McCarthy. 1993. *African Americans in Florida.* Sarasota, Fla.: Pineapple Press.

Karp, Ivan, C. Mullen, M. Kreamer, and S. D. Lavine (eds.). 1992. *Museums and Communities: The Politics of Public Culture.* Washington, D.C.: Smithsonian Institution Press.

Kaster, Kent. 1988. "I'm a stranger here": Blues music in Florida. *Tampa Bay History* 10(2): 5–23.

Kazal, Russell A. 1995. Revisiting assimilation: The rise, fall, and reappraisal of concept in American ethnic history. *American Historical Review* 100(April): 437–71.

Kearney, M. 1995. The local and the global: The anthropology of globalization and transnationalism. *Annual Reviews of Anthropology* 24: 547–65.

Kefauver, Estes. 1951. *Crime in America.* Garden City, N.Y.: Doubleday.

Kelley, Robin D. G. 1993. "We are not what we seem": Rethinking black working-class opposition in the Jim Crow South. *Journal of American History* 80 (June): 75–112.

Kennedy, Stetson. 1989. *Palmetto Country.* Original publication in 1942. Tallahassee: Florida A&M University Press.

Kerstein, Robert. 1997. From annexation to Urban Renewal: Urban development in Tampa during the 1950s and 1960s. *Tampa Bay History* 19(1): 69–92.

Kilson, Marion D. de B. 1976. Afro-American social structure, 1790–1970. In Martin L. Kilson and Robert Rotberg (eds.), *The African Diaspora: Interpretive Essays.* Cambridge, Mass.: Harvard University Press, 414–58.

Kirk, John M. 1985. Reflections on José Martí, radical and revolutionary. *Cuban Studies/Estudios Cubanos* 15(2): 83–86.

Klein, Herbert S. 1966. Anglicanism, Catholicism, and the Negro slave. *Comparative Studies in Society and History* 8: 295–330.

Klingman, Peter D. 1982. Race and faction in the public career of Josiah T. Walls. In H. Rabinowitz (ed.), *Southern Black Leaders of the Reconstruction Era.* Urbana: University of Illinois Press, 59–78.

Knight, Franklin. 1970. *Slave Society in Cuba during the Nineteenth Century.* Madison: University of Wisconsin Press.

Knoke, David. 1990. *Organizing for Collective Action: The Political Economy of Associations.* New York: Aldine de Gruyter.

Kusmer, Kenneth L. 1995. African Americans in the city since World War II: From the industrial to the post-industrial era. *Journal of Urban History* 21(4): 458–504.

Kutzinski, Vera M. 1993. *Sugar's Secrets: Race and the Erotics of Cuban Nationalism.* Charlottesville: University Press of Virginia.

Kuyk, Betty M. 1983. The African derivation of black fraternal orders in the United States. *Comparative Studies in Society and History* 25(4): 559–92.

Landa, Janet Tai. 1994. *Trust, Ethnicity, and Identity: Beyond the New Institutional*

Economics of Ethnic Trading Networks, Contract Law, and Gift-Exchange. Ann Arbor: University of Michigan Press.

Landers, Jane. 1995. Traditions of African American freedom and community in Spanish colonial Florida. In David R. Colburn and Jane Landers (eds.), *The African American Heritage of Florida.* Gainesville: University Press of Florida.

Lavenda, Robert H. 1992. Festivals and the creation of public culture: Whose voice(s)? In Ivan Karp, Christine M. Kreamer, and Steven D. Lavine (eds.), *The Politics of Culture.* Washington, D.C.: Smithsonian Institution Press, 76–104.

Lawson, Steven F. 1985. Ybor City and baseball: An interview with Al Lopez. *Tampa Bay History* 7(2): 59–76.

———. 1982. From sit-in to race riot: Businessmen, blacks, and the pursuit of moderation in Tampa, 1960–1967. In E. Jacoway and D. R. Colburn (eds.), *Southern Businessmen and Desegregation.* Baton Rouge: Louisiana State University Press, 257–81.

———. 1979. Civil Rights protests in Tampa: Oral memoirs of conflict and accommodation. *Tampa Bay History* 1: 37–54.

Lewis, David Levering. 1992. Introduction to *Black Reconstruction in America,* by W. E. B. Du Bois. New York: Atheneum.

Lewis, Earl. 1995. To turn as on a pivot: Writing African Americans into a history of overlapping diasporas. *American Historical Review* 100(June): 765–87.

Light, Ivan. 1972. *Ethnic Enterprise in America.* Berkeley: University of California Press.

Light, Ivan, and Carolyn Rosenstein. 1995. *Race, Ethnicity, and Entrepreneurship in Urban America.* New York: Aldine de Gruyter.

Lincoln, C. Eric, and Lawrence H. Mamiya. 1990. *The Black Church in the African American Experience.* Durham: Duke University Press.

Liss, Sheldon R. 1987. *Roots of Revolution: Radical Thought in Cuba.* Lincoln: University of Nebraska Press.

Lofgren, Charles A. 1987. *The Plessy Case: A Legal-Historical Interpretation.* New York: Oxford University Press.

Long, Durward. 1971a. The making of modern Tampa: A city of the New South, 1885–1911. *Florida Historical Quarterly* 49(4): 333–45.

———. 1971b. Labor relations in the Tampa cigar industry, 1885–1911. *Labor History* 8: 551–59.

———. 1968. The open-closed shop battle in Tampa's cigar industry, 1919–1921. *Florida Historical Quarterly* 47: 101–21.

———. 1965a. An immigrant co-operative medicine program in the South, 1887–1963. *Journal of Southern History* 31(4): 417–34.

———. 1965b. "La Resistencia": Tampa's immigrant labor union. *Labor History* 6: 193–213.

López Valdés, Rafael L. 1973. Discrimination in Cuba. *Cuba Resource Center Newsletter* 2: 6–14.

Lowenthal, David. 1994. Identity, heritage, and history. In John R. Gillis (ed.), *Com-*

memorations: The Politics of National Identity. Princeton: Princeton University Press, 41–60.

Macdonald, Sharon, and Gordon Fyfe (eds.). 1996. *Theorizing Museums: Representing Identity and Diversity in a Changing World.* Cambridge, Mass.: Blackwell Publishers.

MacGaffey, Wyatt. 1961. Social structure and mobility in Cuba. *Anthropological Quarterly* 34 (April): 94–109.

Mallon, Florencia E. 1994. The promise and dilemma of subaltern studies: Perspectives from Latin American history. *American Historical Review* 99(December): 1491–1515.

Manach, Jorge. 1950. *Martí: Apostle of Freedom.* Trans. Coley Taylor. New York: Devin-Adair.

Martí, José. 1959. "Mi raza." In *La Cuestion Racial.* Habana: Bibiloteca Popular Martiana, 25–29.

Martínez-Alier, Verena. 1974. *Marriage, Class, and Color in Nineteenth Century Cuba: A Study of Racial Attitudes and Sexual Values in a Slave Society.* London: Cambridge University Press.

Mays, Benjamin E. 1971. *Born to Rebel: An Autobiography.* New York: Charles Scribner's Sons.

Mays, Benjamin, and Arthur Raper. 1927. A study of Negro life in Tampa. Manuscript in Special Collections Dept., University of South Florida Library, Tampa, Fla.

McCay, Bonnie J., and Svein Jentoft. 1998. Market or community failure? Critical perspectives on common property research. *Human Organization* 57(1): 21–29.

McDonogh, Gary W. (ed.). 1993. *The Florida Negro: A Federal Writers' Project Legacy.* Jackson: University Press of Mississippi.

McGarrity, Gayle, and Osvaldo Cardenas. 1995. Cuba. In Minority Rights Group (eds.), *No Longer Invisible: Afro-Latin Americans Today.* London: Minority Rights Publications, 77–108.

McLaurin, Melton A. 1978. *The Knights of Labor in the South.* Westport, Conn.: Greenwood Press.

Meier, August. 1963. *Negro Thought in America, 1880–1915: Racial Ideologies in the Age of Booker T. Washington.* Ann Arbor: University of Michigan Press.

Mendez, Armando. 1994. *Ciudad de Cigars: West Tampa.* Tampa: Florida Historical Society.

Mintz, Sydney, and Richard Price. 1992. *The Birth of African American Culture: An Anthropological Approach.* Boston: Beacon Press.

Mirabal, Nancy R. 1995. "Mas que negro": José Martí and the politics of unity. In Louis A. Pérez (ed.), *José Martí in the United States: The Florida Experience.* Special Studies, no. 28. Tempe: Arizona State University Center for Latin American Studies, 57–69.

———. 1998. Telling silences and making community: Afro-Cubans and African Americans in Ybor City and Tampa, 1899–1915. In Lisa Brock and Digna Fuentes (eds.), *Between Race and Empire: African Americans and Cubans before the Cuban Revolution.* Philadelphia: Temple University Press, 49–69.

Model, Suzanne. 1991. Caribbean immigrants: A black success story? *International Migration Review* 25(2): 248–76.

Mohl, Raymond. 1997. Blacks and Hispanics in multicultural America: A Miami case study. In Raymond Mohl (ed.), *The Making of Urban America,* 2nd ed. Wilmington, Del.: Scholarly Resources, Inc.

Mohlman, Geoff. 1995. Bibliography of resources concerning the African American presence in Tampa: 1513–1995. Master's thesis, University of South Florida.

Mohlman, Geoffrey. 1999. "An insult and a blow": The Buffalo Soldiers at Tampa Bay. In Brent Weisman (ed.), *Soldiers and Patriots: Buffalo Soldiers and Afro-Cubans in Tampa, 1898.* USF Anthropology Studies in Historical Archaeology, no. 2. Tampa: University of South Florida.

Momsen, Janet. 1993. Introduction. In Janet Momsen (ed.), *Women and Change in the Caribbean: A Pan-Caribbean Perspective.* Bloomington: Indiana University Press, 1–12.

Montejo Arrecha, Carmen. 1998. *Minerva:* A magazine for women (and men) of color. In Lisa Brock and Digna Castaneda Fuertes (eds.), *Between Race and Empire: African-Americans and Cubans before the Cuban Revolution.* Philadelphia: Temple University Press, 33–48.

Moore, Carlos. 1986. Congo or Carabali? Race relations in socialist Cuba. *Caribbean Review* 15 (spring): 13–44.

Moore, Robin. 1997. *Nationalizing Blackness: Afrocubanismo and Artistic Revolution in Havana, 1920–1940.* Pittsburgh: University of Pittsburgh Press.

Moreno-Fraginals, Manuel. 1987. Plantations in the Caribbean: Cuba, Puerto Rico, and the Dominican Republic in the late nineteenth century. In M. Moreno Fraginals, F. Moya Pons, and Stanley Engerman (eds.), *Between Slavery and Free Labor: The Spanish-Speaking Caribbean in the Nineteenth Century.* Baltimore: Johns Hopkins University Press, 3–24.

Mormino, Gary. 1995. GI Joe meets Jim Crow: Racial violence and reform in World War II Florida. *Florida Historical Quarterly* 71: 194–228.

———. 1983a. Tampa: From hell hole to the good life. In Richard Bernard and B. R. Rice (eds.), *Sunbelt Cities.* Austin: University of Texas Press, 138–59.

———. 1983b. Immigrant women in Tampa: The Italian experience. *Florida Historical Quarterly* 61: 296–312.

———. 1982a. Tampa and the new urban South: The weight strike of 1899. *Florida Historical Quarterly* 60(3): 337–56.

———. 1982b. "We worked hard and took care of our own": Oral history and Italians in Tampa. *Labor History* 19: 395–415.

Mormino, Gary, and George Pozzetta. 1987. *The Immigrant World of Ybor City: Italians and Their Neighbors in Tampa, 1885–1985.* Urbana: University of Illinois Press.

Mullen, Edward J. 1987. *Los negros brujos:* A reexamination of the text. *Cuban Studies/Estudios Cubanos* 17: 111–29.

Mullings, Leith. 1994a. Images, ideology, and women of color. In Maxine Baca Zinn and Bonnie T. Dill (eds.), *Women of Color in U.S. Society.* Philadelphia: Temple University Press, 265–90.

———. 1994b. Ethnicity and representation. In George C. Bond and Angela Gilliam (eds.), *Social Construction of the Past: Representation as Power.* London: Routledge, 25–28.

Mulroy, Kevin. 1993. *Freedom on the Border: The Seminole Maroons in Florida, the Indian Territory, Coahuila, and Texas.* Lubbock: Texas Tech University Press.

Muñiz, José Rivero. 1976. *The Ybor City Story, 1885–1954.* Trans. Eustasio Fernández and Henry Beltran. Tampa, Fla.

———. 1963. Tampa at the close of the nineteenth century. *Florida Historical Quarterly* 41: 332–42.

———. 1962. Letter to the editor. *Florida Historical Quarterly* 40: 313–15.

Nagel, Joane. 1994. Constructing ethnicity: Creating and recreating ethnic identity and culture. *Social Problems* 41(1): 152–76.

Newton, Virgil. 1961. *Crusade for Democracy.* Ames: Iowa State University Press.

Ogbu, John. 1990. Minority education in comparative perspective. *Journal of Negro Education* 59(1): 45–57.

Olson, Mancur. 1965. *The Logic of Collective Action.* Cambridge, Mass.: Harvard University Press.

Orrick, Bentley, and Harry L. Crumpacker. 1998. *The Tampa Tribune: A Century of Florida Journalism.* Tampa: University of Tampa Press.

Ortiz, Fernando. 1993. For a Cuban integration of whites and blacks. In P. Perez Sarduy and Jean Stubbs (eds.), *Afrocuba: An Anthology of Cuban Writing on Race, Politics, and Culture.* Melbourne, Australia: Ocean Press, 27–36.

———. 1987. *Los Negroes Esclavos.* Havana: Editorial de Ciencias Sociales.

———. 1973. *Hampa afro-cubano: Los negros brujos.* Originally published in 1906. Miami: Ediciones Universal.

———. 1947. *Cuban Counterpoint: Tobacco and Sugar.* New York: Alfred A. Knopf.

———. 1943. Por la integracion cubana de blancos y negros. *Revista Bimestre Cubana* 51(March-April): 256–72.

———. 1942. Cuba, Marti, and the Race Problem. *Phylon* 3(3): 253–76.

———. 1921. Los cabildos afro-cubanos. *Revista Bimestre Cubana* 16(1): 5–39.

Orum, Thomas T. 1975. *The Politics of Color: The Racial Dimension of Cuban Politics during the Early Republican Years, 1900–1912.* Ann Arbor, Mich.: Xerox University Microfilms.

Ostrom, Elinor. 1992. The rudiments of a theory of the origins, survival, and performance of common property institutions. In Daniel W. Bromley (ed.), *Making the Commons Work: Theory, Practice, and Policy.* San Francisco: Institute for Contemporary Studies Press, 293–318.

Pacheco, Ferdie. 1994. *Ybor City Chronicles: A Memoir.* Gainesville: University Press of Florida.

Pagano, Michael A., and Ann O'M. Bowman. 1995. *Cityscapes and Capital: The Politics of Urban Development.* Baltimore: Johns Hopkins University Press.

Palmie, Stephan. 1994. Some notes on time, space, and units of analysis in the historiography of *ekpe/abakua*. Paper presented at the African Studies Center and Institute of Latin American Studies, University of London, November 3.

———. 1993. Ethnogenetic processes and cultural transfer in Afro-American slave populations. In Wolfgang Binder (ed.), *Slavery in the Americas.* Würzburg: Königshausen and Neumann, 337–63.

Paquette, Robert L. 1988. *Sugar Is Made with Blood: The Conspiracy of La Escalera and the Conflict between Empires over Slavery in Cuba.* Middleton, Conn.: Wesleyan University Press.

Paterson, Thomas G. 1994. *Contesting Castro: The United States and the Triumph of the Cuban Revolution.* New York: Oxford University Press.

Pérez, Lisandro. 1992. Cuban Miami. In G. Grenier and A. Stepick (eds.), *Miami Now.* Gainesville: University Press of Florida, 83–108.

Pérez, Louis A. Jr. 1997. *Cuba and the United States: Ties of Singular Intimacy.* Athens: University of Georgia Press.

———. 1994. Between baseball and bullfighting: The quest for nationality in Cuba, 1868–1898. *Journal of American History* 81: 493–517.

———. 1985. Cubans in Tampa: From exiles to immigrants, 1892–1901. *Tampa Bay History* 7(2): 22–35.

———. 1983. *Cuba between Empires: 1878–1902.* Pittsburgh: University of Pittsburgh Press.

———. 1975. Reminiscences of a *lector:* Cuban cigar workers in Tampa. *Florida Historical Quarterly* 54: 443–49.

Pizzo, Tony. 1985. Tony Pizzo's Ybor City: An interview with Tony Pizzo. *Tampa Bay History* 7: 142–60.

Pollard, Leslie. 1980. Black beneficial societies and the Home for Aged and Infirm Colored Persons: A research note. *Phylon* 41: 230–34.

Porter, Kenneth. 1996. *The Black Seminoles: History of a Freedom-Seeking People.* Gainesville: University of Florida Press.

———. 1943. Louis Pacheco: The man and the myth. *Journal of Negro History* 28: 65–72.

Portes, Alejandro. 1996. Introduction: Immigration and its aftermath. In A. Portes (ed.), *The New Second Generation.* New York: Russell Sage Foundation.

———. 1995. Children of immigrants: Segmented assimilation and its determinants. In Alejandro Portes (ed.), *The Economic Sociology of Immigration.* New York: Russell Sage Foundation, 248–80.

———. 1987. The social origins of the Cuban enclave economy of Miami. *Sociological Perspectives* 30(4): 340–72.

Portes, Alejandro, and Alex Stepick. 1987. Unwelcome immigrants: The labor market experiences of 1980 (Mariel) Cubans and Haitian refugees in south Florida. *American Sociological Review* 50: 493–514.

Portes, Alejandro, and M. Zhou. 1993. The new second generation: Segmented assimilation and its variants. *Annals of the American Academy of Political and Social Science* 530: 74–97.

Poyo, Gerald. 1991. The Cuban experience in the United States, 1865–1940: Migration, community, and identity. *Cuban Studies/Estudios Cubanos* 21: 19–36.

———. 1989. *"With All, and for the Good of All": The Emergence of Popular Nationalism in the Cuban Communities of the United States, 1848–1898*. Durham: Duke University Press.

———. 1986a. Evolution of Cuban separatist thought in the émigré communities of the United States, 1848–1895. *Hispanic American Historical Review* 66(3): 485–507.

———. 1986b. José Martí: Architect of social unity in the émigré communities of the United States. In C. Abel and N. Torrents (eds.), *José Martí: Revolutionary Democrat*. Durham: Duke University Press, 32–64.

———. 1985a. Tampa cigarworkers and the struggle for independence. *Tampa Bay History* 7: 94–105.

———. 1985b. The anarchist challenge to the Cuban Independence Movement, 1885–1890. *Cuban Studies/Estudios Cubanos* 15(1): 29–42.

———. 1984. Cuban communities in the United States: Toward an overview of the nineteenth century experience. Paper presented at Cuban-American Studies: Status and Future, seminar, Massachusetts Institute of Technology, Cambridge, Mass., May 26–28.

———. 1983. Cuban emigre communities in the United States and the independence of their homeland, 1852–1895. Ph.D. diss., University of Florida.

Pozzetta, George. 1981. ¡*Alerta tabaqueros!* Tampa's striking cigar workers. *Tampa Bay History* 3:19–29.

———. 1980. Italians and the Tampa general strike of 1910. In G. Pozzetta (ed.), *Pane e Lavoro: Proceedings of the Eleventh Annual Conference of the Italian American Historical Association*. Toronto: Multicultural History Society of Toronto, 29–46.

Price, H. D. 1957. *The Negro and Southern Politics: A Chapter of Florida History*. New York: New York University Press.

Rabinowitz, Howard N. 1994. *Race, Ethnicity, and Urbanization: Selected Essays*. Columbia: University of Missouri Press.

———. 1982. The changing image of Black Reconstructionists. In H. Rabinowitz (ed.), *Southern Black Leaders of the Reconstruction Era*. Urbana: University of Illinois Press, xi–xxiv.

Ragano, Frank, and Selwyn Raab. 1994. *Mob Lawyer*. New York: Charles Scribner's Sons.

Reiss, Steven A. 1976. Race and ethnicity in American baseball: 1900–1919. *Journal of Ethnic Studies* 4(4): 39–55.

Rhea, Joseph Tilden. 1997. *Race Pride and the American Identity*. Cambridge, Mass.: Harvard University Press.

Río, Emilio del. 1950. Yo Fui Uno de los Fundadores de Ybor City. Tony Pizzo Collection, Dept. of Special Collections, University of South Florida Library, Tampa, Fla.

Ripoll, Carlos. 1994. The falsification of José Martí in Cuba. *Cuban Studies/Estudios Cubanos* 24: 3–38.

Rivers, Larry, and Canter Brown. 2001. *Laborers in the Vineyard of the Lord: The Beginnings of the AME Church in Florida*. Gainesville: University Press of Florida.

Rodríguez de Cuesta, Vincentina Elsa. 1952. *Patriotas Cubanas*. Havana:

Rodríguez Sosa, Enrique. 1982. *Los Nañigos*. Havana: Casa de las Americas.

Rose, Harold M. 1989. Blacks and Cubans in Miami's changing economy. *Urban Geography* 10(5): 464–86.

Ruffins, Fath Davis. 1992. Mythos, memory, and history: African American preservation efforts, 1820–1990. In Ivan Karp, C. Mullen, and M. Kreamer, and Steven D. Lavine (eds.), *The Politics of Culture*. Washington, D.C.: Smithsonian Institution Press, 506–611.

Runge, C. Ford. 1992. Common property and collective action in economic development. In Daniel W. Bromley (ed.), *Making the Commons Work: Theory, Practice, and Policy*. San Francisco: Institute for Contemporary Studies Press, 17–39.

Rushing, Fannie Theresa. 1992. Cabildos de Nación, Sociedades de la raza de color: Afro-Cuban Participation in Slave Emancipation and Cuban Independence, 1865–1985. Ph.D. diss., University of Chicago.

Russell, Kathy, Midge Wilson, and Ronald Hall. 1992. *The Color Complex: The Politics of Skin Color among African Americans*. New York: Anchor Doubleday.

Sánchez, Gina. 1997. The politics of Cape Verdean identity. *Transforming Anthropology* 6(1): 54–71.

San Juan, E. Jr. 1992. *Racial Formations/Critical Transformations: Articulations of Power in Ethnic and Racial Studies in the United States*. Atlantic Highlands, N.J.: Humanities Press.

Saunders, Robert W. 1992. The profile of school desegregation in Hillsborough County. *Sunland Tribune* 18: 73–79.

Scheinbaum, Mark I. (ed.). 1976. José Martí Park: The story of Cuban property in Tampa. Special Collections Dept., University of South Florida Library, Tampa, Fla.

Schneider, Ray. 1994. Tampa: A tale of two cities. *Text and Performance Quarterly* 14: 334–41.

Schnur, James A. 1993. Persevering on the home front: Blacks in Florida during World War II. In Lewis N. Wynne (ed.), *Florida at War*. St. Leo, Fla.: St. Leo College Press, 49–70.

Schwartz, Rosalie. 1989. *Lawless Liberators: Political Banditry and Cuban Independence*. Durham: Duke University Press.

Scott, Rebecca J. 1985. *Slave Emancipation in Cuba: The Transition to Free Labor, 1860–1899.* Princeton: Princeton University Press.

Serviat, Pedro. 1993. Solutions to the black problem. In Pedro Pérez Sarduy and Jean Stubbs (eds.), *Afrocuba: An Anthology of Cuban Writing on Race, Politics, and Culture.* Melbourne, Australia: Ocean Press, 77–90.

Sheller, Mimi. 1999. The "Haytian Fear": Racial projects and competing reactions to the first black republic. *Research in Politics and Society* 6: 285–303.

Sheriff, Robin E. 2000. Exposing silence as cultural censorship: A Brazilian case. *American Anthropologist* 102(1): 114–32.

Shofner, Jerrell. 1983. Florida. In H. L. Suggs (ed.), *The Black Press in the South, 1865–1979.* Westport, Conn.: Greenwood Press, 91–118.

Simpson, George E. 1978. *Black Religions in the New World.* New York: Columbia University Press.

Skidmore, Thomas E. 1993. Bi-racial U.S.A. vs. multi-racial Brazil: Is the contrast still valid? *Journal of Latin American Studies* 25: 373–86.

Smedley, Audrey. 1999. *Race in North America: Origin and Evolution of a Worldview.* Boulder: Westview Press.

———. 1998. "Race" and the construction of human identity. *American Anthropologist* 100(3): 690–702.

Southall, Eugene P. 1934. Negroes in Florida prior to the Civil War. *Journal of Negro History* 19: 77–86.

Sowell, Thomas. 1994. *Race and Culture: A Worldview.* New York: Basic Books.

———. 1978. Three black histories. In T. Sowell (ed.), *American Ethnic Groups.* Washington, D.C.: Urban Institute, 7–63.

Soyer, Daniel. 1997. *Jewish Immigrant Associations and American Identity in New York, 1880–1939.* Cambridge, Mass.: Harvard University Press.

Squires, Gregory D. 1994. *Capital and Communities in Black and White: The Intersection of Race, Class, and Uneven Development.* Albany: State University of New York Press.

Stack, Carol. 1998. Holding hands: An American struggle for community. In Carole Hill and Pat Beaver (eds.), *Cultural Diversity in the U.S. South: Anthropological Contributions to a Region in Transition.* Athens: University of Georgia Press, 93–103.

Stafford, Susan B. 1987. The Haitians: The cultural meaning of race and ethnicity. In Nancy Foner (ed.), *New Immigrants in New York.* New York: Columbia University Press.

Steffy, Joan M. 1975. The Cuban Immigrants of Tampa, Florida: 1886–1898. Master's thesis, University of South Florida.

Stoner, K. Lynn. 1991. *From the House to the Streets: The Cuban Woman's Movement for Legal Reform, 1898–1940.* Durham: Duke University Press.

Stubbs, Jean. 1985. *Tobacco on the Periphery: A Case Study in Cuban Labour History, 1860–1958.* Cambridge: Cambridge University Press.

Suggs, Henry Lewis. 1983. *The Black Press in the South, 1865–1979.* Westport, Conn.: Greenwood Press.

Sutton, Constance R. 1974. Cultural duality in the Caribbean: Review of *Crab Antics. Caribbean Studies* 14(2): 96–101.

Taylor, Michael, and Sara Singleton. 1993. The communal resource: Transaction costs and the solution of collective action problems. *Politics and Society* 21(2): 195–214.

Thomas, Hugh. 1971. *Cuba: Pursuit of Freedom.* New York: Harper and Row.

Throsby, David. 1997. Seven questions in the economics of cultural heritage. In Michael Hutter and Ilde Rizzo (eds.), *Economic Perspectives on Cultural Heritage.* New York: St. Martin's Press, 3–12.

Trotter, Joe W. 1995. African Americans in the city: The industrial era, 1900–1950. *Journal of Urban History* 21(4): 438–57.

Turner, Diane. 1998. Black musical traditions of Central Avenue. *Practicing Anthropology* 20(1): 21–24.

Tushnet, Mark V. 1987. *The NAACP: Legal Strategy against Segregated Education, 1925–1950.* Chapel Hill: University of North Carolina Press.

Twine, France Winddance. 1998. *Racism in a Racial Democracy: The Maintenance of White Supremacy in Brazil.* New Brunswick: Rutgers University Press.

Urban, C. S. 1957. The Africanization of Cuba Scare, 1853–1855. *Hispanic American Historical Review* 38: 29–45.

U.S. Senate. Immigration Commission. 1911. Cigar and tobacco manufacturing. In *Immigrants in Industries*, vol. 14. Washington, D.C.: Government Printing Office.

Vélez-Ibañez, Carlos G. 1983. *Bonds of Mutual Trust: The Cultural Systems of Rotating Credit Associations among Urban Mexicans and Chicanos.* New Brunswick: Rutgers University Press.

Verrey, Robert, and Laura Henley. 1991. Creation myths and zoning boards: Local uses of historic preservation. In Brett Williams (ed.), *The Politics of Culture.* Washington, D.C.: Smithsonian Institution Press, 75–107.

Vondracek, Felix J. 1972. The rise of fraternal organizations in the United States, 1868–1900. *Social Science* 47(1): 26–33.

Wagner, Eric A. 1984. Baseball in Cuba. *Journal of Popular Culture* 18: 113–20.

Waters, Mary C. 1996. The intersection of gender, race, and ethnicity in identity development of Caribbean American teens. In B. J. Ross Leadbeater and Niobe Way (eds.), *Urban Girls: Resisting Stereotypes, Creating Identities.* New York: New York University Press, 65–84.

Watkins-Owens, Irma. 1996. *Blood Relations: Caribbean Immigrants and the Harlem Community, 1900–1930.* Bloomington: Indiana University Press.

Weare, Walter B. 1993. *Black Business in the New South: A Social History of the North Carolina Mutual Life Insurance Company.* Durham: Duke University Press.

Weisman, Brent. 1987. *Like Beads on a String: A Culture History of the Seminole Indians in North Peninsular Florida*. Gainesville: University Press of Florida.

Westfall, Glenn. 1995. Martí City: Cubans in Ocala. In Louis A. Pérez (ed.), *José Martí in the United States: The Florida Experience*. Special Studies, no. 28. Tempe: Arizona State University Center for Latin American Studies, 81–93.

———. 1985. Latin entrepreneurs and the birth of Ybor City. *Tampa Bay History* 7(2): 5–21.

———. 1973. History of the Ybor City Chamber of Commerce. Special Collections Dept., University of South Florida Library, Tampa, Fla.

Williams, Charles, and Hilda J. B. Williams. 1992. Mutual aid societies and economic development: Survival efforts. In Hans Baer and Yvonne Jones (eds.), *African Americans in the South: Issues of Race, Class, and Gender*. Athens: University of Georgia Press, 26–33.

Williams, Edwin L. 1949. Negro slavery in Florida. *Florida Historical Quarterly* 28: 93–110.

Williams, V. J. Jr. 1989. *From a Caste to a Minority*. New York: Greenwood Press.

Wilson, Peter J. 1973. *Crab Antics: The Social Anthropology of English-Speaking Negro Societies of the Caribbean*. New Haven: Yale University Press.

———. 1969. Reputation and respectability: A suggestion for Caribbean ethnology. *Man* 4(1): 70–84.

Wolcott, Victoria W. 1996. Mediums, messages, and lucky numbers: African-American female spiritualists and numbers runners in interwar Detroit. In Patricia Yeager (ed.), *The Geography of Identity*. Ann Arbor: University of Michigan Press, 273–306.

Woodson, Carter. 1929. Insurance business among Negroes. *Journal of Negro History* 14: 202–26.

Yelvington, Kevin. 1995. *Producing Power: Ethnicity, Gender, and Class in a Caribbean Workplace*. Philadelphia: Temple University Press.

Yelvington, Kevin, Neil Goslin, and Wendy Arriaga. n.d. Whose history? Museum-making and struggles over ethnicity and representation in the Sunbelt. Unpublished manuscript in possession of the author.

Yglesias, José. 1985. The radical *Latino* island in the Deep South. *Tampa Bay History* 7: 166–69.

Zinn, Maxine Baca, and Bonnie Thornton Dill (eds.). 1994. *Women of Color in U.S. Society*. Philadelphia: Temple University Press.

Index

Susan Greenbaum is professor of anthropology at the University of South Florida, Tampa. She has published numerous articles on African American and immigrant communities.